Lecture Notes in Computer Science 7108

Commenced Publication in 1973
Founding and Former Series Editors:
Gerhard Goos, Juris Hartmanis, and Jan van Leeuwen

W0246101

Shinji Kikuchi   Aastha Madaan
Shelly Sachdeva   Subhash Bhalla (Eds.)

Databases in Networked Information Systems

7th International Workshop, DNIS 2011
Aizu-Wakamatsu, Japan, December 12-14, 2011
Proceedings

 Springer

Volume Editors

Shinji Kikuchi
University of Aizu, Ikki Machi, Aizu-Wakamatsu
Fukushima 965-8580, Japan
E-mail: d8111106@u-aizu.ac.jp

Aastha Madaan
University of Aizu, Ikki Machi, Aizu-Wakamatsu
Fukushima 965-8580, Japan
E-mail: d8131102@u-aizu.ac.jp

Shelly Sachdeva
University of Aizu, Ikki Machi, Aizu-Wakamatsu
Fukushima 965-8580, Japan
E-mail: d8111107@u-aizu.ac.jp

Subhash Bhalla
University of Aizu, Ikki Machi, Aizu-Wakamatsu
Fukushima 965-8580, Japan
E-mail: bhalla@u-aizu.ac.jp

ISSN 0302-9743   e-ISSN 1611-3349
ISBN 978-3-642-25730-8   ISBN 978-3-642-25731-5 (eBook)
DOI 10.1007/978-3-642-25731-5
Springer Heidelberg Dordrecht London New York

Library of Congress Control Number: 2011941685

CR Subject Classification (1998): H.2, H.3, H.4, H.5, C.2, J.1

LNCS Sublibrary: SL 3 – Information Systems and Application, incl. Internet/Web
and HCI

Typesetting: Camera-ready by author, data conversion by Scientific Publishing Services, Chennai, India

Printed on acid-free paper

Springer is part of Springer Science+Business Media (www.springer.com)

Preface

Large-scale information systems in public utility services depend on computing infrastructure. Many research efforts are being made in related areas, such as cloud computing, sensor networks, mobile computing, high-level user interfaces and information accesses by Web users. Government agencies in many countries plan to launch facilities in education, health-care and information support as part of e-government initiatives. In this context, information interchange management has become an active research field. A number of new opportunities have evolved in design and modeling based on the new computing needs of the users. Database systems play a central role in supporting networked information systems for access and storage management aspects.

The 7th International Workshop on Databases in Networked Information Systems (DNIS) 2011 was held during December 12–14, 2011 at the University of Aizu in Japan. The workshop program included research contributions and invited contributions. A view of the research activity in information interchange management and related research issues was provided by the sessions on related topics. The keynote address was contributed by Divyakant Agrawal. The session on Accesses to Information Resources had an invited contribution from Susan B. Davidson. The following section on Information and Knowledge Management Systems had invited contributions from H.V. Jagadish and Tova Milo. The session on Information Extration from Data Resources included the invited contributions by P. Krishna Reddy. The section on Geospatial Decision Making had invited contributions by Cyrus Shahabi and Yoshiharu. We would like to thank the members of the Program Committee for their support and all authors who considered DNIS 2011 for their research contributions.

The sponsoring organizations and the Steering Committee deserve praise for the support they provided. A number of individuals contributed to the success of the workshop. We thank Umeshwar Dayal, J. Biskup, D. Agrawal, Cyrus Shahabi, Mark Sifer, and Malu Castellanos for providing continuous support and encouragement.

The workshop received invaluable support from the University of Aizu. In this context, we thank Shigeaki Tsunoyama, President of the University of Aizu. Many thanks are also due for the faculty members at the university for their cooperation and support.

December 2011

S. Kikuchi
A. Madaan
S. Sachdeva
S. Bhalla

Organization

The DNIS 2011 international workshop was organized by the Graduate Department of Information Technology and Project Management, University of Aizu, Aizu-Wakamatsu, Fukushima, Japan.

Steering Committee

Divy Agrawal	University of California, USA
Umeshwar Dayal	Hewlett-Packard Laboratories, USA
M. Kitsuregawa	University of Tokyo, Japan
Krithi Ramamritham	Indian Institute of Technology, Bombay, India
Cyrus Shahabi	University of Southern California, USA

Executive Chair

N. Bianchi-Berthouze	University College London, UK

Program Chair

S. Bhalla	University of Aizu, Japan

Publicity Committee Chair

Shinji Kikuchi	University of Aizu, Japan

Publications Committee Co-chairs

Aastha Madaan	University of Aizu, Japan
Shelly Sachdeva	University of Aizu, Japan

Program Committee

D. Agrawal	University of California, USA
S. Bhalla	University of Aizu, Japan
V. Bhatnagar	University of Delhi, India
Dr. P. Bottoni	University La Sapienza of Rome, Italy
L. Capretz	University of Western Ontario, Canada
Richard Chbeir	Bourgogne University, France
G. Cong	Nanyang Technological University, Singapore
U. Dayal	Hewlett-Packard Laboratories, USA
Pratul Dublish	Microsoft Research, USA
Arianna Dulizia	IRPPS - CNR, Rome, Italy
W.I. Grosky	University of Michigan-Dearborn, USA

J. Herder	University of Applied Sciences, Fachhochschule Düsseldorf, Germany
Chetan Gupta	Hewlett-Packard Laboratories, USA
Y. Ishikawa	Nagoya University, Japan
Sushil Jajodia	George Mason University, USA
Q. Jin	University of Aizu, Japan
A. Kumar	Pennsylvania State University, USA
A.Mondal	Indraprastha Institute of Information Technology, Delhi, India
K. Myszkowski	Max-Planck-Institut für Informatik, Germany
Alexander Pasko	Bournemouth University, UK
L. Pichl	International Christian University, Tokyo, Japan
P.K. Reddy	International Institute of Information Technology, Hyderabad, India
C. Shahabi	University of Southern California, USA
M. Sifer	University of Wollongong, Australia

Sponsoring Institution

Center for Strategy of International Programs, University of Aizu, Aizu-Wakamatsu City, Fukushima, Japan.

Table of Contents

Cloud Computing

Access to Information Resources

Information and Knowledge Management

Bio-medical Information Management

Information Extraction from Data Resources

Geo-spatial Decision Making

Networked Information Systems: Infrastructure

Secure Data Management in the Cloud

Divyakant Agrawal, Amr El Abbadi, and Shiyuan Wang

Department of Computer Science, University of California at Santa Barbara
{agrawal,amr,sywang}@cs.ucsb.edu

Abstract. As the cloud paradigm becomes prevalent for hosting various applications and services, the security of the data stored in the public cloud remains a big concern that blocks the widespread use of the cloud for relational data management. Data confidentiality, integrity and availability are the three main features that are desired while providing data management and query processing functionality in the cloud. We specifically discuss achieving data confidentiality while preserving practical query performance in this paper. Data confidentiality needs to be provided in both data storage and at query access. As a result, we need to consider practical query processing on confidential data and protecting data access privacy. This paper analyzes recent techniques towards a practical comprehensive framework for supporting processing of common database queries on confidential data while maintaining access privacy.

1 Introduction

Recent advances in computing technology have resulted in the proliferation of transformative architectural, infrastructural, and application trends which can potentially revolutionize the future of information technology. *Cloud Computing* is one such paradigm that is likely to radically change the deployment of computing and storage infrastructures of both large and small enterprises. Major enabling features of the cloud computing infrastructure include *pay per use* and hence *no up-front cost for deployment, perception of infinite scalability,* and *elasticity of resources.* As a result, cloud computing has been widely perceived to be the "dream come true" with the potential to transform and revolutionize the IT industry [1]. The Software as a Service (SaaS) paradigm, such as web-based emails and online financial management, has been popular for almost a decade. But the launch of Amazon Web Services (AWS) in the second half of 2006, followed by a plethora of similar offerings such as Google AppEngine, Microsoft Azure, etc., have popularized the model of "utility computing" for other levels of the computing substrates such as Infrastructure as a Service (IaaS) and Platform as a Service (PaaS) models. The widespread popularity of these models is evident from the tens of cloud based solution providers [2] and hundreds of corporations hosting their critical business infrastructure in the cloud [3]. Recent reports show that many startups leverage the cloud to quickly launch their businesses applications [4], and over quarter of small and medium-sized businesses (SMBs) today rely on or plan to adopt cloud computing services [5].

S. Kikuchi et al. (Eds.): DNIS 2011, LNCS 7108, pp. 1–15, 2011.

With all the benefits of storing and processing data in the cloud, the security of data in the public cloud is still a big concern [6] that blocks the wide adoption of the cloud for data rich applications and data management services. In most cases and especially with Platform-as-a-Service (PaaS) and Software-as-a-Service (SaaS), users cannot control and audit their own data stored in the cloud by themselves. As the cloud hosts vast amount of valuable data and large numbers of services, it is a popular target for attacks. At the network level, there are threats of IP reuse, DNS attacks, Denial-of-Service (DoS) and Distributed Denial-of-Service (DDoS) attacks, etc [7]. At the host level, vulnerabilities in the virtualization stack may be exploited for attack. Resource sharing through virtualization also gives rise to side channel attacks. For example, a recent vulnerability found in Amazon EC2 [8] makes it possible to cross virtual machine boundary and gain access to another tenant's data co-located on the same physical machine [9]. At application level, vulnerabilities in access control could let unauthorized users access sensitive data [7]. Even if the data is encrypted, partial information about the data may be inferred by monitoring clients' query access patterns and analyzing clients' accessed positions on the encrypted data. The above threats could compromise *data confidentiality*, *data integrity*, and *data availability*.

To protect the confidentiality of sensitive data stored in the cloud, encryption is the widely accepted technique [10]. To protect the confidentiality of the data being accessed by queries, *Private Information Retrieval* (PIR) [11] can completely hide the query intents. To protect data integrity, Message Authentication Codes (MAC) [12], unforgeable signatures [13] or Merkle hash trees can validate the data returned by the cloud. To protect data availability and data integrity in case of partial data corruption, both replication and error-correcting mechanisms [14, 15, 16] are the potential solutions. Replication, however, potentially offers attackers multiple entry points for unauthorized access to the entire data. In contrast, error-correcting mechanisms that split data into pieces and distribute them in different places [17, 18, 19, 15, 16] enhance data security in addition to data availability. These techniques have been implemented in a recently released commercial product of cloud storage [20] as well as in Google Apps Service for the City of Los Angeles [21].

Integrating the above techniques, however, cannot deliver a *practical* secure relational data management service in the cloud. For data confidentiality specifically, practical query processing on encrypted data remains a big challenge. Although a number of proposals have explored query processing on encrypted data, many of them are designed for processing one specific query (e.g. range query) and are not flexible to support another kind of query (e.g. data updates), yet some other approaches lose balance between query functionality and data confidentiality. In Section 2, we discuss the relevant techniques and present a framework based on secure index that targets to support multiple common database queries and strikes a good balance between functionality and confidentiality. As for data confidentiality at query access, PIR provides complete query privacy but is too expensive in terms of computation and communication.

As a result, alternative techniques for protecting query privacy are explored in Section 3. The ultimate goal of the proposed research is to push forward the frontier on designing practical and secure relational data management services in the cloud.

2   Processing Database Queries on Encrypted Data

Data confidentiality is one of the biggest challenges in designing a practical secure data management service in the cloud. Although encryption can provide confidentiality for sensitive data, it complicates query processing on the data. A big challenge to enable efficient query processing on encrypted data is to be able to *selectively retrieve data* instead of downloading the entire data, decoding and processing them on the client side. Adding to this challenge are the individual filtering needs of different queries and operations, and thus a lack of a consistent mechanism to support them. This section first reviews related work on query processing on encrypted data, and then presents a secure index based framework that can support efficient processing of multiple database queries.

2.1   Related Work

To support queries on encrypted relational data, one class of solutions proposed processing encrypted data directly, yet most of them cannot achieve strong data confidentiality and query efficiency simultaneously for supporting common relational database queries (i.e., range queries and aggregation queries) and database updates (i.e., data insertion and deletion). The study of encrypted data processing originally focused on keyword search on encrypted documents [22, 23]. Although recent work can efficiently process queries with equality conditions on relational data without compromising data confidentiality [24], they cannot offer the same levels of efficiency and confidentiality for processing other common database queries such as range queries and aggregation queries. Some proposals trade off partial data confidentiality to gain query efficiency. For example, the methods that attach range labels to bucketized encrypted data [25, 26] reveal the underlying data distributions. Methods relying on order preserving encryption [27, 28] reveal the data order. These methods cannot overcome attacks based on statistical analysis on encrypted data. Other proposals sacrifice query efficiency for strong data confidentiality. One example is homomorphic encryption, which enables secure calculation on encrypted data [29, 30], but requires expensive computation and thus is not yet practical [31]. Predicate encryption can solve polynomial equations on encrypted data [32], but it uses public key cryptographic system which is much more expensive than symmetric encryption used above.

Instead of processing encrypted data directly, an alternative is to use an encrypted index which allows the client to traverse the index and to locate the data of interest in a small number of rounds of retrieval and decryption [33, 34, 35, 36]. In that way, both confidentiality and functionality can be preserved. The other alternative approach that preserves both confidentiality and functionality is to use a secure co-processor on the cloud server side and to put a database engine and all sensitive data processing inside the secure co-processor [37]. That apparently requires all the clients to trust the secure co-processor with their sensitive data, and it is not clear that how the co-processor handles large numbers of clients and large amount of data. In contrast, a secure index based approach [33, 34, 35, 36] does not have to rely on any parties other than the clients, and thus we believe that it is promising to be a practical and secure framework. In the following, we discuss our recent work [36] on using secure index for processing various database queries.

2.2   Secure Index Based Framework

Let I be a B+-tree [38] index built on a relational data table T. Each tuple t has d attributes, $A_1, A_2, ..., A_d$. Assume each attribute value (and each index key) can be mapped to an integer value taken from a certain range $[1, ..., MAX]$. Each leaf node of I maintains the pointers to the tuple units where the tuples with the keys in this leaf node are stored. The data tuples of T and indexes I are encoded under different secrets C, which are then used for decoding the data tuples and indexes respectively. Each tree node of the index and a fixed number of tuples are single units of encoding. We require that these units have fixed sizes to ensure that the encoded pieces have fixed sizes. The encoded pieces are then distributed on servers hosted by external cloud storage providers such as Amazon EC2 [8]. Queries and operations on the index key attribute can be efficiently processed by locating the leaf nodes of I that store the requested keys and then processing the corresponding tuple units pointed by these leaf nodes.

Fig. 1 demonstrates the high-level idea of our proposed framework. The data table T is organized into a tuple matrix TD. The index I is organized into an index matrix ID. Each column of TD or ID is an encoding unit. ID is encoded into IE and TD is encoded into TE. Then IE and TE are distributed in the cloud.

Encoding Choices. Symmetric key encryption such as AES can be used for encoding [33, 34], as symmetric key encryption is much more efficient than asymmetric key encryption. Here we consider using Information Dispersal Algorithm (IDA) [17] for encoding, as IDA naturally provides data availability and some degrees of confidentiality.

Using IDA, we encode and split data into multiple uninterpretable pieces. IDA encodes an $m \times w$ data matrix D by multiplying an $n \times m$ ($m < n$) secret dispersal matrix C to D in Galois filed, i.e. $E = C \cdot D$. The resulting $n \times w$ encoded matrix E is distributed onto n servers by dispersing each row onto one server. To reconstruct D, only m correct rows are required. Let these m rows form an $m \times w$ sub-matrix E^* and the corresponding m rows of C form an $m \times m$ sub-matrix C^*, $D = C^{*-1} \cdot E^*$. In such a way, data is intermingled and dispersed, so that it is difficult for an attacker to gather the data and apply inference analysis. To validate the authenticity and correctness of a dispersed piece we apply the *Message Authentication Code* (MAC) [12] on each dispersed piece.

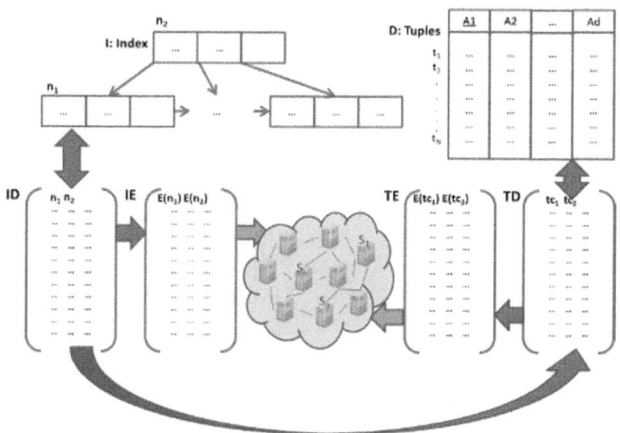

Fig. 1. Secure Cloud Data Access Framework

Since IDA is not proved to be theoretically secure [17], to prevent attackers' direct inference or statistical analysis on encoded data, we propose to add *salt* in the encoding process [39] so as to randomize the encoded data. In addition to the secret keys C for encoding and decoding, a client maintains a secret seed ss and a deterministic function fs for producing random factors based on ss and input data. Function fs can be based on pseudorandom number generator or secret hashing. The generated random values are added to the data values before encoding, and they can only be reconstructed and subtracted from the decoded values by the client.

Encoding Units of Index. Let the branching factor of the B+-tree index I be b. Then every internal node of I has $[\lceil b/2 \rceil, b]$ children, and every node of I has $[\lceil (b-1)/2 \rceil, b-1]$ keys. To accommodate the maximum number of children pointers and keys, we fix the size of a tree node to $2b+1$, and let the column size of the index matrix ID, m be $2b+1$ for simplicity. We assign each tree node an integer column address denoting its column in ID according to the order it is inserted into the tree. Similarly, we assign a data tuple column of TD an integer column address according to the order its tuples are added into TD.

A tree node of I, *node*, or the corresponding column in ID, $ID_{:,g}$, can be represented as

$$(isLeaf, col_0, col_1, key_1, col_2, key_2, ..., col_{b-1}, key_{b-1}, col_b) \tag{1}$$

where $isLeaf$ indicates if *node* is an internal node ($isLeaf = 0$), or a leaf node ($isLeaf = 1$). key_i is an index key, or 0 if *node* has less than i keys. For an internal node, $col_0 = 0$, col_i ($1 \leq i \leq b$) is the column address of the ith child node of *node* if key_{i-1} exists, otherwise $col_i = 0$. For existing keys and children, (a key in child column col_i) $< key_i \leq$ (a key in child column col_{i+1}) $< key_{i+1}$. For a leaf node, col_0 and col_b are the column addresses of the predecessor/successor leaf nodes respectively, and $col_i (1 \leq i \leq b-1)$ is the column address of the tuple with key_i.

We use an *Employee* table shown in Fig. 2 as an example. Fig. 3(a) gives an example of an index built on *Perm No* of the *Employee* table (the upper part) and the corresponding index matrix *ID* (the lower part). In the figure, the branching factor of the B+-tree $b = 4$, and the column size of the index matrix $m = 9$. The keys are inserted into the tree in ascending order 10001, 10002, ... 10007. The numbers shown on top of the tree nodes are the column addresses of these nodes. The numbers pointed to by arrows below the keys of the leaf nodes are the column addresses of the data tuples with those keys.

	Perm No	Salary	Age
t_1	10001	4000	25
t_2	10002	5000	28
t_3	10003	4000	25
t_4	10004	4000	26
t_5	10005	6000	30
t_6	10006	5500	28
t_7	10007	6000	31

Fig. 2. An Employee Table

Encoding Units of Data Tuples. Let the column size of the tuple matrix TD also be m. To organize the existing d-dimensional tuples of D into TD initially, we sort all the data tuples in ascending order of their keys, and then pack every p tuples in a column of TD such that $p \cdot d \leq m$ and $(p+1) \cdot d > m$. The columns of TD are assigned addresses of increasing integer values. The p tuples in the same column have the same column address, which are stored in the leaf nodes of the index that have their keys. Fig. 3(b) gives an example of organizing tuples in *Employee* table into a tuple matrix TD, in which two tuples are packed in each column.

Selective Data Access. To enable selective access to small amount of data, the cloud data service provides two primitive operations to clients, i.e. storing and retrieving fixed sizes of encoding units. Since each encoding unit or each column of ID or TD has an integer address, we denote these two operations as store_unit(D, i) and retrieve_unit(E, i), in which i is the address of the unit. store_unit(D, i) encodes data unit i, adds salt into it on the client side and then stores it in the cloud. retrieve_unit(E, i) retrieves the encoded data unit i from the cloud, and then decodes the data unit and subtracts salt on the client side.

2.3   Query Processing

We assume that the root node of the secure index is always cached on the client side. The above secure index based framework is able to support exact, range and aggregation queries involving index key attributes, as well as data updates, inserts and deletes efficiently. These common queries form the basis for general purpose relational data processing.

Exact Queries. Performing an exact query via the secure B+-tree index is similar to performing the same query on a plaintext B+-tree index. The query is processed by traversing the index downwards from the root, and locating the keys of interests in leaf nodes. However, each node retrieval calls retrieve_unit(IE, i)

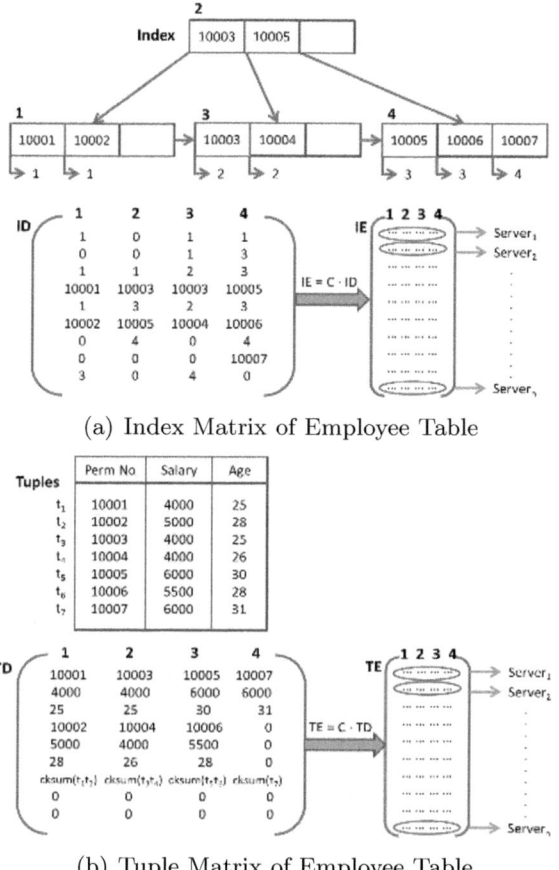

(a) Index Matrix of Employee Table

(b) Tuple Matrix of Employee Table

Fig. 3. Encoding of Index and Data Tuples of Employee Table

and the result tuple retrieval is through retrieve_unit(TE, i). Fig. 4 illustrates the recursive procedure for processing an exact query at a tree node. When an exact query for key x is issued, the exact query procedure on the root node, $ID_{:,\mathbf{root}}$, is called first. At each *node*, the client locates the position i with the smallest key that is equal to or larger than x (Line 1), or the rightmost non-empty position i if x is larger than all keys in *node* (Line 2-4).

Range Queries. To find the tuples whose index keys fall in a range $[x_l, x_r]$, we locate all qualified keys in the leaf nodes, get the addresses of the tuple matrix columns associated with these keys, and then retrieve the answer tuples from these tuple matrix columns. The qualified keys can be located by performing an exact query on either x_l or x_r, and then following the successor links or predecessor links at the leaf nodes. Note that since tuples can be dynamically inserted and deleted, the tuple matrix columns may not be ordered by index

---

Define: x, search key.
Define: t, the tuple with index key x.
Define: $nkeys(node)$, number of keys in $node$.
 1: Find the smallest i s.t. $x \leq node.key_i \land i \leq nkeys(node)$
 2: **if** not exist i **then**
 3:     $i \leftarrow nkeys(node) + 1$
 4: **if** $node.isLeaf = 0$ **then**
 5:     $ID_{i,node.col_{i+1}} \leftarrow$ retrieve_unit$(IE, node.col_{i+1})$
 6:     exact_query$(ID_{i,node.col_{i+1}}, x, process\_on\_not\_found)$
 7: **else**
 8:     **if** $i < nkeys(node) \land x = node.key_i$ **then**
 9:         $TD_{i,node.col_i} \leftarrow$ retrieve_unit$(TE, node.col_i)$
10:         Locate t with key x in $TD_{i,node.col_i}$
11:         Return $(t, node.col_i, node)$.
12:     **else**
13:         t does not exist

Fig. 4. Algorithm exact_query$(node, x)$

keys, thus we cannot directly retrieve the tuple matrix columns in between the tuple matrix columns corresponding to x_l and x_r.

Aggregation Queries. An aggregation query involving selection on index key attributes can be processed by first performing a range query on the index key attributes and then performing aggregation on the result tuples of the range query on the client side. Some aggregation queries on index key attributes can be directly done on the index on the server side, such as finding the tuples with MAX, MIN keys in a range $[x_l, x_r]$.

Data Updates, Insertion and Deletion. Data update without change on index keys can be easily done by an exact query to locate the unit that has the previous values of the tuple, a local change and a call of store_unit(TD, i) to store the updated unit. Data update with change on index keys is similar to data insertion, which is discussed below.

Data insertion is done in two steps: tuple insertion and index key insertion. Data deletion follows a similar process, with the exception that the tuple to delete is first located via an exact query of the tuple's key. Note that the order that the tuple unit is updated before the index unit is important, since the address of the tuple unit is the link between the two and needs to be recorded in the index node.

We allow flexible insertion and deletion of data tuples. An inserted tuple is appended to the last column or added to a new last column in TD regardless of the order of its key. A deleted tuple is removed from the corresponding column by leaving the d entries it occupied previously empty. Index key insertion and deletion are always done on the leaf nodes, but node splits (correspondingly adding an index unit for the new node and updating an index unit for the split node) or merges (correspondingly deleting a tuple unit for the deleted node and updating an index unit for the node to merge with) may happen to maintain a proper B+-tree.

Boosting Performance at Accesses by Caching Index Nodes on Client.
The above query processing relies heavily on index traversals, which means that
the index nodes are frequently retrieved from servers and then decoded on the
client, resulting in a lot of communication and computation overhead. Query
performance can be improved by caching some of the most frequently accessed
index nodes in clear on the client. Top level nodes in the index are more likely
to be cached.

3   Protecting Access Privacy

In a secure data management framework in the cloud, even if the data is encrypted, adversaries may still be able to infer partial information about the data
by monitoring clients' query access patterns and analyzing clients' accessed positions on the encrypted data. Protecting query access privacy to hide the real
query intents is therefore needed for ensuring data confidentiality in addition
to encryption. One of the biggest challenge in protecting access privacy is to
strike a good balance between privacy and practical functionality. Private Information Retrieval (PIR) [11] seems a right fit for protecting access privacy, but
the popular PIR protocols relying on expensive cryptographic operations are not
yet practical. On the other hand, some lightweight techniques such as routing
query accesses through trusted proxies [36] or mixing real queries with noisy
queries [40] have been proposed, but they cannot quantify and guarantee the
privacy levels that they provide. In this section, we first review relevant work
on protecting access privacy, and then discuss hybrid solutions that combine
expensive cryptographic protocols with lightweight techniques.

3.1   Related Work

The previous work on protecting access privacy can be categorized as Private
Information Retrieval and query anonymization or obfuscation using noisy data
or noisy queries.

Private Information Retrieval (PIR) models the private retrieval of public data
as a theoretical problem: Given a server which stores a binary string $x = x_1...x_n$
of length n, a client wants to retrieve x_i privately such that the server does
not learn i. Chor et al. [11] introduced the PIR problem and proposed solutions
for multiple servers. Kushilevitz and Ostrovsky followed by proposing a single
server, computational PIR solution [41] which is usually referred to as cPIR. Although it has been shown that multi-server PIR solutions are more efficient than
single-server PIR solutions [42], multi-server PIR does not allow communication
among all the servers, thus making it unsuitable to use in the cloud. On the
other hand, cPIR and its follow-up single-server PIR proposals [43], however,
are criticized as impractical because of their expensive computation costs [44].
Two alternatives were later proposed to make single-server PIR practical. One
uses oblivious RAM, and it only applies to a specific setting where a client retrieves its own data outsourced on the server [45, 46], which can be applied in the

cloud. The other bases the foundation of its PIR protocol based on linear algebra [47] instead of the number theory which previous single-server PIR solutions
base on. Unfortunately, the latter lattice based PIR scheme cannot guarantee
that its security is as strong as previous PIR solutions, and it incurs a lot more
communication costs.

Query anonymization is often used in privacy-preserving location based services [48], which is implemented by replacing a user's query point with an enclos-
ing region containing $k - 1$ noisy points of other users. A similar anonymization
technique which generates additional noisy queries is employed in a private web
search tool called TrackMeNot [40]. The privacy in TrackMeNot, however, is bro-
ken by query classification [49], which suggests that randomly extracted noise
alone does not protect a query from identification.

To generate meaningful and disguising noise words in private text search, a
technique called *Plausibly Deniable Search* (PDS) is proposed in [50, 51]. PDS
employs a topic model or an existing taxonomy to build a static clustering of
cover word sets. The words in each cluster belong to different topics but have
similar specificity to their respective topics, thus are used to cover each other in
a query.

3.2   Hybrid Query Obfuscation

It is hard to quantify privacy provided in a query anonymization approach. Since
the actual query data and noisy data are all in plaintext, the risk of identifying
the actual query data could still be high. k-Anonymity in particular has been
criticized as a weak privacy definition [52], because it does not consider the
data semantic. A group of k plaintext data items may be semantically close, or
could be semantically diverse. In contrast, traditional PIR solutions can provide
complete privacy and confidentiality. We hence consider hybrid solutions that
combine query anonymization and PIR/cryptographic solutions.

A hybrid query obfuscation solution can provide access privacy, data confidentiality and practical performance. PIR/cryptographic protocols ensure access
privacy and data confidentiality, while query anonymization upon these protocols reduce computation and communication overheads, thus achieving practical
performance. Such hybrid query obfuscation solutions have been used in preserving location privacy in location-based services [53, 54] and in our earlier work
on protecting access privacy in simple selection queries [55].

Bounding-Box PIR. Our work is built upon single-server cPIR protocol [41].
It is a generalized private retrieval approach called *Bounding-Box* PIR (*bb*PIR).
We describe how *bb*PIR works using a database / data table as illustration.
For protecting access privacy in the framework given in the last section, we can
consider an index nodes, an index / tuple column as a data item and treat the
collection of them as a virtual database for access.

cPIR works by privately retrieving an item from a data matrix for a given
matrix address [41]. So we consider a (key, address, value) data store, where each
value is a b-bit data item. The database of size n is organized in an $s \times t$ matrix

M ($s = t = \lceil \sqrt{n} \rceil$ by default). Each data item x has a numeric key KA that determines the two dimensional address of x in M. For example, the column address of an index / tuple column can be the key for identifying the index / tuple column.

A client can specify her privacy requirement and desired charge budget (ρ, μ), where ρ is a privacy breach limit (the upper bound probability that a requested item can be identified by the server), and μ is a server charge limit (the upper bound of the number of items that are exposed to the client for one requested tuple). The basic idea of bbPIR is to use a bounding box BB (an $r \times c$ rectangle corresponding to a sub-matrix of M) as an anonymized range around the address of item x requested by the client, and then apply cPIR on the bounding box. bbPIR finds an appropriately sized bounding box that satisfies the privacy request ρ, and achieves overall good performance in terms of communication and computation costs without exceeding the server charge limit μ for each retrieved item. The area of the bounding box determines the level of privacy that can be achieved, the larger the area, the higher the privacy, but with higher computation and communication costs.

The above scheme retrieves data by the exact address of the data. To enable natural retrieval by the key of data, we simply let the server publish a one-dimensional histogram, H, on the key field KA and the dimensions of the database matrix M, s and t. The histogram is only published to authorized clients. The publishing process, which occurs infrequently, is encrypted for security. When a client issues a query, she calculates an address range for the queried entry by searching the bin of H where the query data falls. In this way, she translates a retrieval by key to a limited number of retrievals by addresses, while the latter multiple retrievals can be actually implemented in one retrieval if they all request the same column addresses of the matrix.

Further Consideration on Selecting Anonymization Ranges. In current bbPIR, we only require that an anonymization range bounding box encloses the requested data, and although the dimensions of the bounding box are fixed, the position of the bounding box can be random around the requested data. In real applications, the position of the bounding box could also be important to protecting access privacy. Some positions may be more frequently accessed by other clients and less sensitive, while some positions may be rarely accessed by other clients and easier to be identified as unique access patterns. These information, if incorporated into the privacy quantification, should result in a bounding box that provides better privacy protection under the constraints of the requested data and the dimensions. One idea is to incorporate access frequency in privacy probability, but we should be cautious that a bounding box cannot include all frequent accessed data but the requested data, since in this case the requested data may be also easily filtered out.

4   Concluding Remarks

The security of the data stored in the public cloud is one of the biggest concerns that blocks the realization of data management services in the cloud, especially for sensitive enterprise data. Although numerous techniques have been proposed for providing data confidentiality, integrity and availability in the context and for processing queries on encrypted data, it is very challenging to integrate them into a practical secure data management service that works for most database queries. This paper has reviewed these relevant techniques, presented a framework based on secure index for practical secure data management and query processing, and also discussed how to enhance data confidentiality by providing practical access privacy for data in the cloud. We contend that the balance between security and practical functionality is crucial for the future realization of practical secure data management services in the cloud.

Acknowledgement. This work is partly funded by NSF grant CNS 1053594 and an Amazon Web Services research award. Any opinions, findings, and conclusions or recommendations expressed in this material are those of the authors and do not necessarily reflect the views of the sponsors.

References

[1] Armbrust, M., Fox, A., Griffith, R., Joseph, A.D., Katz, R., Konwinski, A., Lee, G., Patterson, D., Rabkin, A., Stoica, I., Zaharia, M.: Above the Clouds: A Berkeley View of Cloud Computing. Technical Report 2009-28, UC Berkeley (2009)

[2] Amazon: AWS Solution Providers (2009), http://aws.amazon.com/solutions/solution-providers/

[3] Amazon: AWS Case Studies (2009), http://aws.amazon.com/solutions/case-studies/

[4] Li, P.: Cloud computing is powering innovation in the silicon valley (2010), http://www.huffingtonpost.com/ping-li/cloud-computing-is-poweri_b_570422.html

[5] Business Review USA: Small, medium-sized companies adopt cloud computing (2010), http://www.businessreviewusa.com/news/cloud-computing/small-medium-sized-companies-adopt-cloud-computing

[6] InfoWorld: Gartner: Seven cloud-computing security risks (2008), http://www.infoworld.com/d/security-central/gartner-seven-cloud-computing-security-risks-853?page=0,1

[7] Mather, T., Kumaraswamy, S., Latif, S.: Cloud Security and Privacy. O'Reilly Media, Inc., Sebastopol (2009)

[8] Amazon: Amazon elastic compute cloud (amazon ec2), http://aws.amazon.com/ec2/

[9] Ristenpart, T., Tromer, E., Shacham, H., Savage, S.: Hey, you, get off of my cloud: exploring information leakage in third-party compute clouds. In: ACM Conference on Computer and Communications Security, pp. 199–212 (2009)

[10] NIST: Fips publications, http://csrc.nist.gov/publications/PubsFIPS.html

[11] Chor, B., Kushilevitz, E., Goldreich, O., Sudan, M.: Private information retrieval. J. ACM 45(6), 965–981 (1998)

[12] Bellare, M., Canetti, R., Krawczyk, H.: Keying Hash Functions for Message Authentication. In: Koblitz, N. (ed.) CRYPTO 1996. LNCS, vol. 1109, pp. 1–15. Springer, Heidelberg (1996)

[13] Agrawal, R., Haas, P.J., Kiernan, J.: A system for watermarking relational databases. In: Proc. of the 2003 ACM SIGMOD International Conference on Management of Data, pp. 674–674 (2003)

[14] Plank, J.S., Ding, Y.: Note: Correction to the 1997 tutorial on reed-solomon coding. Softw. Pract. Exper. 35(2), 189–194 (2005)

[15] Bowers, K.D., Juels, A., Oprea, A.: Hail: a high-availability and integrity layer for cloud storage. In: CCS 2009: Proceedings of the 16th ACM Conference on Computer and Communications Security, pp. 187–198 (2009)

[16] Abu-Libdeh, H., Princehouse, L., Weatherspoon, H.: Racs: a case for cloud storage diversity. In: SoCC 2010: Proceedings of the 1st ACM Symposium on Cloud Computing, pp. 229–240 (2010)

[17] Rabin, M.O.: Efficient dispersal of information for security, load balancing, and fault tolerance. J. ACM 36(2), 335–348 (1989)

[18] Shamir, A.: How to share a secret. Commun. ACM 22(11), 612–613 (1979)

[19] Agrawal, D., Abbadi, A.E.: Quorum consensus algorithms for secure and reliable data. In: Proceedings of the Sixth IEEE Symposium on Reliable Distributed Systems, pp. 44–53 (1988)

[20] CleverSafe: Cleversafe responds to cloud security challenges with cleversafe 2.0 software release (2010), http://www.cleversafe.com/news-reviews/press-releases/press-release-14

[21] InfoLawGroup: Cloud providers competing on data security & privacy contract terms (2010),
http://www.infolawgroup.com/2010/04/articles/cloud-computing-1/cloud-providers-competing-on-data-security-privacy-contract-terms

[22] Song, D.X., Wagner, D., Perrig, A.: Practical techniques for searches on encrypted data. In: SP 2000: Proceedings of the 2000 IEEE Symposium on Security and Privacy, pp. 44–55 (2000)

[23] Chang, Y.-C., Mitzenmacher, M.: Privacy Preserving Keyword Searches on Remote Encrypted Data. In: Ioannidis, J., Keromytis, A.D., Yung, M. (eds.) ACNS 2005. LNCS, vol. 3531, pp. 442–455. Springer, Heidelberg (2005)

[24] Yang, Z., Zhong, S., Wright, R.N.: Privacy-Preserving Queries on Encrypted Data. In: Gollmann, D., Meier, J., Sabelfeld, A. (eds.) ESORICS 2006. LNCS, vol. 4189, pp. 479–495. Springer, Heidelberg (2006)

[25] Hacigumus, H., Iyer, B.R., Li, C., Mehrotra, S.: Executing SQL over encrypted data in the database service provider model. In: SIGMOD Conference (2002)

[26] Hore, B., Mehrotra, S., Tsudik, G.: A privacy-preserving index for range queries. In: Proc. of the 30th Int'l Conference on Very Large Databases VLDB, pp. 720–731 (2004)

[27] Agrawal, R., Kiernan, J., Srikant, R., Xu, Y.: Order preserving encryption for numeric data. In: SIGMOD 2004: Proceedings of the 2004 ACM SIGMOD International Conference on Management of Data, pp. 563–574 (2004)

[28] Emekci, F., Agrawal, D., Abbadi, A.E., Gulbeden, A.: Privacy preserving query processing using third parties. In: ICDE (2006)

[29] Ge, T., Zdonik, S.B.: Answering aggregation queries in a secure system model. In: Proceedings of the 33rd International Conference on Very Large Data Bases, pp. 519–530 (2007)

[30] Gentry, C.: Fully homomorphic encryption using ideal lattices. In: STOC 2009: Proceedings of the 41st Annual ACM Symposium on Theory of Computing, pp. 169–178 (2009)

[31] Schneier, B.: Homomorphic encryption breakthrough (2009), `http://www.schneier.com/blog/archives/2009/07/homomorphic_enc.html`

[32] Katz, J., Sahai, A., Waters, B.: Predicate Encryption Supporting Disjunctions, Polynomial Equations, and Inner Products. In: Smart, N.P. (ed.) EUROCRYPT 2008. LNCS, vol. 4965, pp. 146–162. Springer, Heidelberg (2008)

[33] Damiani, E., di Vimercati, S.D.C., Jajodia, S., Paraboschi, S., Samarati, P.: Balancing confidentiality and efficiency in untrusted relational dbmss. In: ACM Conference on Computer and Communications Security, pp. 93–102 (2003)

[34] Shmueli, E., Waisenberg, R., Elovici, Y., Gudes, E.: Designing secure indexes for encrypted databases. In: Proceedings of the IFIP Conference on Database and Applications Security (2005)

[35] Ge, T., Zdonik, S.B.: Fast, secure encryption for indexing in a column-oriented dbms. In: ICDE, pp. 676–685 (2007)

[36] Wang, S., Agrawal, D., Abbadi, A.E.: A Comprehensive Framework for Secure Query Processing on Relational Data in the Cloud. In: Jonker, W., Petković, M. (eds.) SDM 2011. LNCS, vol. 6933, pp. 52–69. Springer, Heidelberg (2011)

[37] Bajaj, S., Sion, R.: Trusteddb: a trusted hardware based database with privacy and data confidentiality. In: Proceedings of the 2011 International Conference on Management of Data, SIGMOD 2011, pp. 205–216 (2011)

[38] Comer, D.: Ubiquitous b-tree. ACM Comput. Surv. 11(2), 121–137 (1979)

[39] Robling Denning, D.E.: Cryptography and data security. Addison-Wesley Longman Publishing Co., Inc., Boston (1982)

[40] Howe, D.C., Nissenbaum, H.: TrackMeNot: Resisting surveillance in web search. In: Lessons from the Identity Trail: Anonymity, Privacy, and Identity in a Networked Society, pp. 417–436. Oxford University Press (2009)

[41] Kushilevitz, E., Ostrovsky, R.: Replication is not needed: Single database, computationally-private information retrieval. In: FOCS, pp. 364–373 (1997)

[42] Olumofin, F.G., Goldberg, I.: Revisiting the computational practicality of private information retrieval. In: Financial Cryptography (2011)

[43] Gentry, C., Ramzan, Z.: Single-database private information retrieval with constant communication rate. In: Proceedings of the 32nd International Colloquium on Automata, Languages and Programming, pp. 803–815 (2005)

[44] Sion, R., Carbunar, B.: On the computational practicality of private information retrieval. In: Network and Distributed System Security Symposium (2007)

[45] Williams, P., Sion, R.: Usable private information retrieval. In: Network and Distributed System Security Symposium (2008)

[46] Williams, P., Sion, R., Carbunar, B.: Building castles out of mud: practical access pattern privacy and correctness on untrusted storage. In: ACM Conference on Computer and Communications Security, pp. 139–148 (2008)

[47] Melchor, C.A., Gaborit, P.: A fast private information retrieval protocol. In: IEEE Internal Symposium on Information Theory, pp. 1848–1852 (2008)

[48] Mokbel, M.F., Chow, C.Y., Aref, W.G.: The new casper: A privacy-aware location-based database server. In: ICDE, pp. 1499–1500 (2007)

[49] Peddinti, S.T., Saxena, N.: On the Privacy of Web Search Based on Query Obfuscation: A Case Study of Trackmenot. In: Atallah, M.J., Hopper, N.J. (eds.) PETS 2010. LNCS, vol. 6205, pp. 19–37. Springer, Heidelberg (2010)

[50] Murugesan, M., Clifton, C.: Providing privacy through plausibly deniable search. In: SDM, pp. 768–779 (2009)

[51] Pang, H., Ding, X., Xiao, X.: Embellishing text search queries to protect user privacy. PVLDB 3(1), 598–607 (2010)
[52] Dwork, C., McSherry, F., Nissim, K., Smith, A.: Calibrating Noise to Sensitivity in Private Data Analysis. In: Halevi, S., Rabin, T. (eds.) TCC 2006. LNCS, vol. 3876, pp. 265–284. Springer, Heidelberg (2006)
[53] Olumofin, F.G., Tysowski, P.K., Goldberg, I., Hengartner, U.: Achieving Efficient Query Privacy for Location Based Services. In: Atallah, M.J., Hopper, N.J. (eds.) PETS 2010. LNCS, vol. 6205, pp. 93–110. Springer, Heidelberg (2010)
[54] Ghinita, G., Kalnis, P., Kantarcioglu, M., Bertino, E.: A Hybrid Technique for Private Location-Based Queries with Database Protection. In: Mamoulis, N., Seidl, T., Pedersen, T.B., Torp, K., Assent, I. (eds.) SSTD 2009. LNCS, vol. 5644, pp. 98–116. Springer, Heidelberg (2009)
[55] Wang, S., Agrawal, D., El Abbadi, A.: Generalizing PIR for Practical Private Retrieval of Public Data. In: Foresti, S., Jajodia, S. (eds.) Data and Applications Security and Privacy XXIV. LNCS, vol. 6166, pp. 1–16. Springer, Heidelberg (2010)

Design and Implementation of the Workflow of an Academic Cloud

Abhishek Gupta, Jatin Kumar, Daniel J. Mathew, Sorav Bansal,
Subhashis Banerjee, and Huzur Saran

Indian Institute of Technology, Delhi
{cs1090174,cs5090243,mcs112576,sbansal,suban,saran}@cse.iitd.ernet.in

Abstract. In this work we discuss the design and implementation of
an academic cloud service christened Baadal. Tailored for academic and
research requirements, Baadal bridges the gap between a private cloud
and the requirements of an institution where request patterns and infrastructure are quite different from commercial settings. For example,
researchers typically run simulations requiring hundreds of Virtual Machines (VMs) all communicating through message-passing interfaces to
solve complex problems. We describe our experience with designing and
developing a cloud workflow to support such requirements. Our workflow
is quite different from that provided by other commercial cloud vendors
(which we found not suited to our requirements).

Another salient difference in academic computing infrastructure from
commercial infrastructure is the physical resource availability. Often, a
university has a small number of compute servers connected to shared
SAN or NAS based storage. This may often not be enough to service the
computation requirements of the whole university. Apart from this infrastructure, universities typically have a few hundred to a few thousand
"workstations" which are commodity desktops with local disk-attached-
storage. Most of these workstations remain grossly underutilized. Our
cloud infrastructure utilizes this idle compute capacity to provide higher
scalability for our cloud implementation.

Keywords: Virtualization, Hypervisors.

1   Introduction

Cloud Computing is becoming increasingly popular for its better usability, lower
cost, higher utilization, and better management. Apart from publicly available
cloud infrastructure such as Amazon EC2, Microsoft Azure, or Google App Engine, many enterprises are setting up "private clouds". Private clouds are internal to the organization and hence provide more security, privacy, and also
better control on usage, cost and pricing models. Private clouds are becoming
increasingly popular not just with large organizations but also with medium
sized organizations which run a few tens to a few hundreds of IT services.

An academic institution (university) can benefit significantly from private
cloud infrastructure to service its IT, research, and teaching requirements.

S. Kikuchi et al. (Eds.): DNIS 2011, LNCS 7108, pp. 16–25, 2011.

In this paper, we discuss our experience with setting up a private cloud infrastructure at the Indian Institute of Technology (IIT) Delhi, which has around 8000 students, 450 faculty members, more than 1000 workstations, and around a hundred server-grade machines to manage our IT infrastructure. With many different departments and research groups requiring compute infrastructure for their teaching and research work, and other IT services, IIT Delhi has many different "labs" and "server rooms" scattered across the campus. We aim to consolidate this compute infrastructure by setting up a private cloud and providing VMs to the campus community to run their workloads. This can significantly reduce hardware, power, and management costs, and also relieve individual research groups of management headaches.

We have developed a cloud infrastructure with around 30 servers, each with 24 cores, 10 TB shared SAN-based storage, all connected with 10Gbps Fibre Channel. We run virtual machines on this hardware infrastructure using KVM[1] and manage these hosts using our custom management layer developed using Python and libvirt[2].

1.1   Salient Design Features of Our Academic Cloud

While implementing our private cloud infrastructure, we came across several issues that have previously not been addressed by commercial cloud offerings. We describe some of the main challenges we faced below:

Workflow: In an academic environment we are especially concerned about simplicity and usability of the workflow for researchers (e.g., Ph.D. students, research staff, faculty members) and administrators (system administrators, policy makers and enforcers, approvers for resource usage).

For authentication, we integrate our cloud service with a campus-wide Kerberos server to leverage existing authentication mechanisms. We also integrate the service with our campus-wide mail and LDAP servers.

A researcher creates a request which should be approved by the concerned faculty member before it is approved by the cloud administrator. Both the faculty member and cloud administrator can change the request parameters (e.g., number of cores, memory size, disk size, etc.) which is followed by a one-click installation of the virtual machine. As soon as the virtual machine is installed, the faculty member and the students are informed about the same with a VNC console password that they can use to remotely access the virtual machine.

Cost and Freedom: In an academic setting, we are most concerned about both cost and freedom to tweak the software. For this reason, we choose to rely solely on free and open-source infrastructure. Enterprise solutions like those provided by VMware are both expensive and restrictive.

Our virtualization stack comprises of KVM[1], libvirt[2], and Web2py[3] which are open-source and available freely.

Workload Performance: Our researchers typically need large number of VMs executing complex simulations communicating with each other through message-passing interfaces like MPI[4]. Both compute and I/O performance is critical for such workloads. We have arranged our hardware and software to provide the maximum performance possible. For example, we ensure that the bandwidths between the physical hosts, storage arrays, and external network switches are the best possible with available hardware. Similarly, we use the best possible emulated devices in our virtual machine monitor. Whenever possible, we use para-virtual devices for maximum performance.

Maximizing Resource Usage: We currently use dedicated high-performance server-class hardware to host our cloud infrastructure. We use custom scheduling and admission-control policies to provide maximal resource usage. In future, we plan to use the idle capacity of our lab and server rooms to implement larger cloud infrastructure at minimal cost. We discuss some details of this below.

A typical lab contains tens to a few hundred commodity desktop machines, each having one or more CPUs, a few 100 GBs of storage, connected over 100Mbps or 1Gbps ethernet. Often these clusters of computers are also connected to a shared Network-Attached Storage (NAS) device. For example, there are around 150 commodity computers in the Computer Science department alone. Typical utilization of these desktop computers is very low (1-10%). We intend to use this "community" infrastructure for running our cloud services. The VMs will run in background, causing no interference to the applications and experience of the workstation user. This can significantly improve the resource utilization of our lab machines.

1.2   Challenges

Reliability: In lab environments, it is common for desktops to randomly get switched off or disconnected from network. These failures can be due to several reasons including manual reboot, network cable disconnection, power outage, or hardware failure. We are working on techniques to have redundant VM images to be able to recover from such failures.

Network and Storage Topology: Most cloud offerings use shared storage (SAN/NAS). Such shared storage can result in a single point of failure. Highly-reliable storage arrays tend to be expensive. We are investigating the use of disk-attached-storage in each computer to provide a high-performance shared storage pool with built-in redundancy. Similarly, redundancy in network topology is required to tolerate network failures.

Scheduling: Scheduling of VMs on server-class hardware has been well-studied and is implemented on current cloud offerings. We are developing scheduling algorithms for commodity hardware where network bandwidths are lower, storage is distributed, and redundancy is implemented. For example, our scheduling algorithm maintains redundant copies of a VM in separate physical environments.

Encouraging Responsible Behaviour: Public clouds charge their users for CPU, disk, and network usage on per CPU-hour, GB-month, and Gbps-month metrics. Instead of a strict pricing model, we use the following model which relies on good community behaviour:

- Gold: The mode is meant for virtual machines requiring proportionally more CPU resources than other categories and are well suited for compute-intensive applications. We follow a provisioning ratio of 1:1 that is we don't overprovision as it is expected that the user will be using all the resources that he/she has asked for.
- Silver: This mode is required for moderately heavy jobs. We typically follow a overprovisioning ratio of 2:1 which means that we typically allocate twice as much as resources as the server should ideally host.
- Bronze: The mode is meant for virtual machines with a small amount of consistent CPU resources typically required when we are working on some code and before the actual run of the code. We follow a 4:1 provisioning ratio which means that we typically allow the resources to be overprisioned by a factor of four.
- Shutdown: In this mode user simply shuts down the virtual machine and is charged minimally.

The simplicity and the effectiveness of the model lies in the fact that user can switch between the modes with the ease of a click without any reboot of the virtual machine.

The rest of this paper is structured as follows: in Section 2 we talk about our experiences with other Cloud Offerings. Section 3 describes key aspects of our design and implementation. Section 4 evaluates the performance of some relevant benchmarks on our virtualization stack over a range of VMs running over different hosts. Section 5 reviews related work, and Section 6 discusses future work and concludes.

2   Experiences with Other Cloud Offering

We tried some off-the-shelf cloud offerings before developing our own stack. We describe our experiences below.

2.1   Ubuntu Enterprise Cloud

Ubuntu Enterprise Cloud[5] is integrated with the open source Eucalyptus private cloud platform, making it possible to create a private cloud with much less configuration than installing Linux first, then Eucalyptus. Ubuntu/Eucalyptus internal cloud offering is designed to be compatible with Amazon's EC2 public cloud service which offers additional ease of use.

On the other side, there is a need to familiarize with both Ubuntu and Eucalyptus, as we were frequently required to search beyond Ubuntu documentation following the Ubuntu Enterprise Cloud's dependence on Eucalyptus. For example, we observed that Ubuntu had weak documentation for customizing images, which is an important step in deploying their cloud. Further even though the architecture is quite stable, it doesn't support the level of customization required for an academic/research environment like ours.

2.2   VMware vCloud

VMware vCloud[6] offers on demand cloud infrastructure such that end users can consume virtual resources with maximum agility. It offers consolidated datacenters and an option to deploy workloads on shared infrastructure with built-in security and role-based access control. Migration of workloads between different clouds and integration of existing management systems using customer extensions, APIs, and open cross-cloud standards serve as one of the most convincing arguments to use the same for a private cloud.

Despite these features and one of the most stable cloud platforms VMware vCloud might not be an ideal solution to be deployed by an academic institution owing to the high licensing costs attached to it, though it might prove ideal for an enterprise with sufficiently good budget.

3   Baadal: Our Workflow Management Tool for Academic Requirements

Currently Baadal is based on KVM as the hypervisor and the Libvirt API which serves as a toolkit to interact with the virtualization capabilities of a host. The choice of libvirt is guided by the fact that libvirt can work with a variety of hypervisors including KVM, Xen, and VMWare.[2] Thus, we can switch the underlying hypervisor technology at a later stage with minimal efforts.

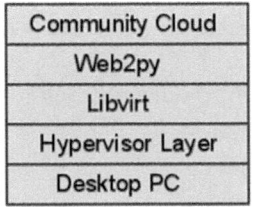

Stack of Technologies used

Fig. 1. Virtualization Stack

We export our management software in two layers - web-based and command-line interface (CLI). While our web based interface is built using web2py, a MVC based Python framework, we continue to use Python for the command line interface as well. The choice of the Python as the primary language for the entire project is supported by the excellent support and documentation by libvirt and Python community alike.

3.1 Deconstructing Baadal

Baadal consists of four components:

Web Server: The web server provides a web-based interface for management of the virtual machines. Our implementation is based on web2py.

All VMs

Name	Owner	Host	RAM	VNC Port	State	Commands
demovm1	cs1090174	10.16.71.2	512	6914	Running	❚❚ ■ ⏻ ✕ 🖥 ✉
demovm2	cs5090243	10.16.71.2	512	6915	Paused	▶ ■ ⏻ ✕ ✉
demovm3	cs1090174	10.16.71.2	512	6916	Off	⏻ ✕ ✉

Fig. 2. List of VMs in Baadal's database along with their current status and some quick actions

Hosts: Multiple hosts are configured and registered in the Baadal database using the web server interface. The hosts run virtual machines and a common storage based on NAS provides seamless storage to allow live migration of VMs.

Client: Any remote client which can access the virtual machine using Remote Desktop Protocol (Windows) or ssh.

VNC Server: This server receives requests from clients for VNC console access. Port forwarding has been set up so that the requests that come to the server are forwarded to the appropriate hosts, and consequently served from there. This server can be same or different from the web server based on the traffic that needs to be handled.

3.2 Workflow

Client requests a VM from Baadal using the web/command-line interface. The request, once approved by administrator leads to spawning of a VM on any of the hosts. The host selected for spawning is determined by the scheduling algorithm as described in the following section.

Once the VM has been setup it can be administered by the user which includes changing the runlevel of the VM apart from normal operations like shutting down and rebooting the VM.

Table 1. Some tests performed on different kinds of hardware infrastructure

Test[1]	KVM+Desktop[2]	KVM+Server[3]	VMware+Server[4]
Empty Loop(10000000)	21840μs	44321μs	44553μs
Fork(1000000)	29.72 s	6.88 s	3.97 s
Wget(685.29 MB)	54.09 s	20.36 s	9.5 s
cp(685.29 MB)	71.97 s	11.65 s	26.07 s
iscp(685.29 MB)	29.64 s	52.34 s	4.75 s
oscp(685.29 MB)	73.54 s	83.68 s	4.86 s
Ping Hypervisor	.2886 s	.3712 s	.1204 s

Note:
1. Each VMs is allocated 1GB RAM, 1 vCPU and 10 GB Harddisk.
2. Desktops used are lab machines with typical configuration as 4GB RAM, C2D, 500GB hard disk and on a 1Gbps Network
3. KVM+Server refers to KVM hypervisor running on HP Proliant BL460c G7 (16GB RAM, 24 CPU, 10Gbps Network)
4. VMware+Server refers to VMWare as hypervisor running on Dell PowerEdge R710 (24GB RAM, 16 CPU, 10Gbps Network)

4   Implementation

While designing Baadal the following have been implemented and taken care of:

4.1   Iptables Setup

For accessing the graphical console of the VM users can use VNC console. Due to migrations of VMs the host of a VM may change and it can be troublesome if we provide a fixed combination of host IP address and port for connecting to the VNC console. Baadal uses Iptables and thus setup port forwarding connections to the VNC server. Clients can connect to the VNC console with the IP address of the VNC Server and a dedicated port which will be forwarded to the appropriate host which is currently hosting the user's VM. In case of migration we change the port forwarding tables in background without causing any kind of inconvenience or delays to the user. So the user always connects to the VNC server with a fixed port number and the IP of the VNC server. The packets from user are forwarded by the VNC server to the appropriate host and thus all requests are served from there.

4.2   Cost Model

We have been observing that in an academic environment some people tend to reserve VMs with high resources which are never used in an optimal fashion. To reduce such number of occurrences we have implemented a cost model accounting for the usage case put up by the user (which can be dynamically changed by him) and the time the machine is running. We have defined three levels 1,2,3

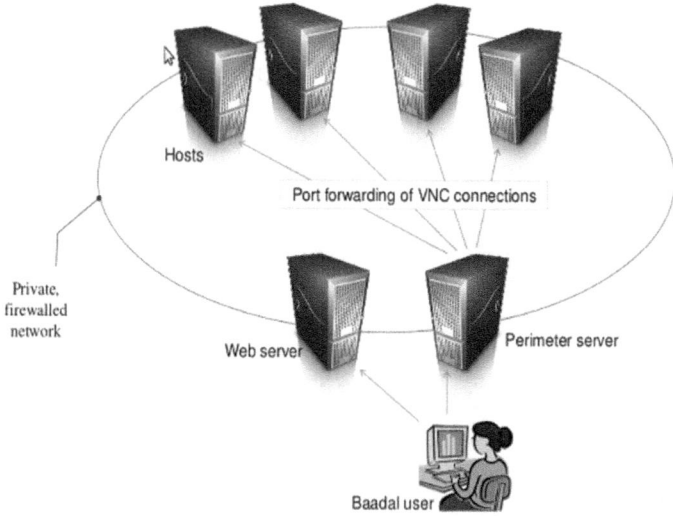

Fig. 3. Baadal workflow

with 1:1, 1:2, 1:4 as the over-provisioning ratios respectively and have associated a decreasing order of cost with each of them. The user is expected to switch between different runlevels according to his requirement. The overall process is defined in a way leading to better utilization without any need for policing. Since the runlevels are associated with cost factors users tend to follow the practice.

4.3   Scheduler

When the runlevel for any VM is switched by the user we need to schedule his VM into an appropriate host. So we use a scheduling algorithm which uses the greedy strategy for finding the host satisfying the given constraints (VM run-level and configuration of the hosts and the VM).

As a general observation it is hardly the case that all the VMs are optimally used. The usage is reduced further during the off-peak hours when we can probably save on our costs and energy by trying to condense the number of hosts actually running and switching off the others. While doing this proper care is taken so as to ensure that the VM doesn't see a degradation of the services during these hours.

5   Cost and Performance Comparisons

As both libvirt and KVM have undergone a rigorous testing phase before they are released as stable releases (which we are using), we need not do rigorous benchmark tests against the standard tests. We have subjected our scheduling algorithms to rigorous testing in an order to see if they are behaving as intended.

The testing has also lead us to further optimization of the algorithms as we are sometimes introduced to some cases that we didn't take proper care of.

A second part of testing/experimentation involved the identification of the constants responsible for overprovisioning of the resources. The constants may vary from institution to institution but generally tends to be in proximity with 1, 2 and 4 respectively for an academic/research environment like ours.

6 Future Work and Conclusions

6.1 Future Work

In a laboratory setup of any academic institution, resource utilization is generally observed to be as low as 1-10%. Thus quite a few of the resources go underutilized. If we can run a community based cloud model on these underutilized community infrastructure we would be able to over-provision resources (like providing each student with his own VM), thereby improving the overall utilization of the physical infrastructure without compromising on the user's experience with the desktop. A significant rise as high as from 1-10% to 40-50% is expected in the utilization of the resources in the mentioned scheme.

It is common in such environments for desktops to randomly be rebooted/ switched-off/disconnected. Also, hardware/disk failure rates are higher in these settings as compared to tightly-controlled blade server environments. Being able to support VMs with a high degree of reliability is a challenge. The solution we intend to investigate is to run redundant copies of VMs simultaneously to provide much higher reliability guarantees, than what the physical infrastructure can provide and seamlessly switching between them. We at IIT Delhi have implemented Record/Replay feature in Linux/KVM (an open source Virtual Machine Monitor) which allows efficient synchronization of virtual machine images at runtime. We intend to use this implementation to provide higher reliability guarantees to cloud users on community infrastructure.

Currently, we support VMs that run atop the KVM hypervisor, but plan to add support for Xen, VMware, and others in the near future. Also, we plan to optimize the software with storage specific plugins. For example, if one is using storage provided by Netapp he can take advantage of the highly optimized copy operation provided by Netapp rather than using the default copy operation.

Due to the diversity in hardware characteristics and network topologies, we expect new challenges in performance measurements and load balancing in this scenario.

6.2 Conclusions

Baadal, our solution for private cloud for academic institutions, will allow administrators and researchers to deploy an infrastructure where users can spawn multiple instances of VMs and control them using a web-based or command line interface atop existing resources. The system is highly modular, with each module represented by a well-defined API, enabling researchers to replace components for experimentation with new cloud-computing solutions.

To summarize, this work illustrates an important segment of cloud computing that has been filled by Baadal by providing a system that is easy to deploy atop existing resources, that lends itself to experimentation by the modularity that is inherent in the design of Baadal and the virtualization stack that is being used in the model.

Acknowledgments. Sorav Bansal would like to thank the NetApp Inc., Bangalore for their research grant which was used to partially support this work.

References

1. Laor, D., Kivity, A., Kamay, Y., Lublin, U., Liguori, A.: kvm: the linux virtual machine monitor. Virtualization Technology for Directed I/O. Intel Technology Journal 10, 225–230 (2007)
2. Libvirt, the virtualization api, http://www.libvirt.org
3. Di Pierro, M.: Web2py Enterprise Web Framework, 2nd edn. Wiley Publishing (2009)
4. Gabriel, E., Fagg, G.E., Bosilca, G., Angskun, T., Dongarra, J., Squyres, J.M., Sahay, V., Kambadur, P., Barrett, B.W., Lumsdaine, A., Castain, R.H., Daniel, D.J., Graham, R.L., Woodall, T.S.: Open MPI: Goals, Concept, and Design of a Next Generation MPI Implementation. In: Kranzlmüller, D., Kacsuk, P., Dongarra, J. (eds.) EuroPVM/MPI 2004. LNCS, vol. 3241, pp. 97–104. Springer, Heidelberg (2004)
5. Ubuntu enterprise cloud - overview,
   http://www.ubuntu.com/business/cloud/overview
6. Vmware vcloud director - deliver infrastructure as a service without compromise,
   http://www.vmware.com/products/vcloud-director/features.html

Identification of Potential Requirements of Master Data Management under Cloud Computing

Shinji Kikuchi

School of Computer Science and Engineering, University of Aizu,
Ikki-machi, Aizu-Wakamatsu City, Fukushima 965-8580, Japan
d8111106@u-aizu.ac.jp

Abstract. Master Data Management (MDM) has been evaluated under the contexts from Enterprise Architecture (EA), SemanticWeb, Service Oriented Architecture (SOA) and Business Process Intergration (BPI). However, there have been very few studies from the point of view of operations of MDM under a Cloud Computing environment. In this paper, the results of analysis of prospective new issues which arise in MDM under the complicated Cloud Computing envrionment such as integrating private Cloud and multi-SaaS have been explained. According to the analysis, there will be certain demand to develop a new protocol to realize a cooperative operation among them under strict security.

Keywords: Master Data, Meta-Data Management, Operational Constraints, Cloud Computing.

1   Introduction

The architecture of information systems for enterprises has changed since the era of open-downsizing from the mainframes. In particular, Enterprise Application Integration (EAI) for an enterprise, Business Process Integration (BPI) for integrating the autonomic business processes over multiple independent enterprises, and Service Oriented Architecture (SOA) which is generalized from the previous EAI and BPI, had arisen during this period. Currently, Cloud Computing which integrates the network aspects and the services is attracting the attention. Its various functional forms and usage patterns has usually been imagined as follows; the first is Software as a Service (SaaS)/Application Service Providing (ASP) in which administration and provided services are integrated for the operations by a single vendor. The second is Private Cloud for internal use of an enterprise. And the third is Platform as a Service (PaaS) and Infrastructure as a Service (IaaS). They provide the computing resources instead of value added applications [1].

Accordingly, the requirements for standardization of treated data have increasingly been extended. Since BPI has been implemented, it is mandatory to standardize the semantics of messages exchanged among business applications in order to realize the seamless operations for most of the enterprises. However, these efforts have remained

S. Kikuchi et al. (Eds.): DNIS 2011, LNCS 7108, pp. 26–40, 2011.
© Springer-Verlag Berlin Heidelberg 2011

in the syntax's level for a while, and the integration of semantics has relied on the individual mapping process of the practical projects, instead. Thus, it tends to be time consuming work and this is one of the potential causes that the adaptation speed of BPI and SOA in practical uses has been slow. Therefore, Master Data Management (MDM), which is the total solution for master data as one of the fundamental expressions of data semantics, has currently attracted a lot of interests.

As MDM is one of the solutions in meta data management, it has had relationships with various areas of information systems, so far. The notion of master data has been defined in the standard ISO/IEC-9594-7 OSI directory management as one of oldest instances [2]. The standard ISO/IEC10728 has been regarded as one of origins of the meta data management [3]. In recent years, there is the standardized effort of ISO/IEC19763 for a framework of interoperability, and exchanging meta data [4]. As an element and an extension, there are efforts for making the standards of Ontology from the point of view of Semantic Web, and Universal Business Language (UBL) [5], [6]. There is an actual instance of MDM applying Semantic Web such as [7]. Furthermore, the idea of MDM has also concerned Enterprise Architecture (EA) from the point of view of Data Architecture (DA) (E.g. [8]). This area has a long history, and one of the origins might be related to Enterprise Integration (E.g. [9]).

It is easily expectable that ideal figures of MDM and semantics management might be affected as the operational environment applying Cloud Computing has matured and has been adopted into practical uses more. The information systems under the complicated Cloud environment will soon be realized. For example, they might start their services by combining the multiple SaaS/ASPs which provides simple functions to mature the business processes, and by combining the applications on a Private Cloud with these of SaaS/ASPs. Under the current direction, research of MDM might rapidly become insufficient and out of date as far as remaining in the current position of existing studies. Most of the existing studies seem to aim at more generic matters instead of the specific cases, therefore the major points of research might remain around the traditional EA and semantic Web architecture. There might be quit few studies done which touch on the potential issues caused by adopting the new operation environments. If we would remain in the current position of research, it would sound impossible to improve on the difficult situations. In particular, due to the complicated Cloud environment, the distributed or failed control of the meta data management easily occurs. Therefore, we need a new analysis of the potential issues which might be caused in the operation of an enterprise information system under such complicated Cloud environments. In this paper, we mainly present the results of our analysis and considerations acquired through modeling these operations.

The remainder of this is organized as follows; in section 2, the definition, requirements and effects in regards to MDM are described through demonstrating the example of BPI in an enterprise. In section 3, the results of primitive analysis are mentioned. It is expectable that the effects described in section 2 might actually depend on the use cases. Therefore, it was analyzed what kinds of issues individually take place in these primitive cases which a typical complicated Cloud environment consists of. In particular, the relationship with Universal Description Discovery and Integration (UDDI) will be touched on. Based on the results in section 3, the potential issues occurring when MDM will be operated under such complicated Cloud environment will be analyzed in section 4. In section 5, the direction of the potential solutions will briefly be discussed after categorizing the issues. Each issue has its own complicated background and is also linked with other specific technical areas instead of having its isolated features. Thus, it might be difficult to propose potential solutions just with the simplified ideas. Mentioning the concrete solutions should be avoided here. In section 6, the related works will be introduced. The studies in regards to practical analysis, strategic matters and architectural aspects of MDM sound prominent as a general trend. This area deeply has the relationships with other research areas. So, picked works will be limited with the only studies focusing on MDM directly. Finally in section 7, conclusions and future's direction will be mentioned.

2   Motivation: Importance of MDM

2.1   MDM: Definition and General Requirements

According to A.Dreibelbis et al. a master data is defined as the following; 'Master data captures the key things that all parts of an organization must be agree on, both in meaning and usage' [10]. They also insist the importance of the master data management to realize more flexible business processes and balanced information systems. In particular, a single source of master data which has aspects of accuracy, consistency and maintainability in a coherent and secure manner is an ideal function. In order to realize this ideal function, the following capabilities are generally required. The first is an authoritative source of master data, which can be trusted to be a high-quality collection of data. The second is the ability to be used in a consistent way because of their various opportunities to be applied with normalized semantics. The third is flexibility that realizes the ability to evolve the master data and to manage them to accommodate changeable practical needs.

2.2   Issues in Business Process Integration Due to Lack of MDM

In this section, we explain the issues occurring in BPI due to lack of MDM. Fig.1 shows a typical model of the environment for BPI, in which a service provider and a service requester will execute an exchange process in peer to peer. This model also contains a function for design and building time, and shows the procedure using them.

On the other hand, Fig.2 shows a typical model of a runtime procedure by using the elements defined in Fig.1, and also shows the issues arising there.

The left side in Fig.1 corresponds to a service requester, whereas the right side corresponds to a service provider. The common message formats and interface definitions for exchanging between them might be managed at Centralized Repository during design and building time. At Procedure.B.1, the entities of the both roles will individually import these common message formats and interface definitions into their own Meta-data repositories which are respectively managed. There are several allowable variations for this phase. Centralized Repository should ideally be UDDI. But in some cases, these formats such as XML messages are decided as part of their contracts and localized rules for peer-to-peer uses. And they will somehow be shared along the localized rules without implementing any physical Centralized Repositories. In these cases, XML schema is usually adopted to express these formats. We do not here specify a particular architecture of Meta-data repositories. Respective Runtime builder as a software development tool will individually import the previous XML Schema instance at Procedure.B.2. Then, database internal schemas related to this building time are further imported at Procedure.B.3. After all, corresponding application runtime programs will be generated. At the service requester side, programs named Application Runtime-1 and Application Runtime-2, each of which generates an XML message by using data stored in their internal database management system, Business Database (in particular Database Meta-data), will be generated at Procedure.B.4, and B.5. In the same way, at the service provider side, programs named Application Runtime-3, Application Runtime-4, each of which decomposes an XML message and stores the fragments of data on the message into another Business Database, will be generated in parallel.

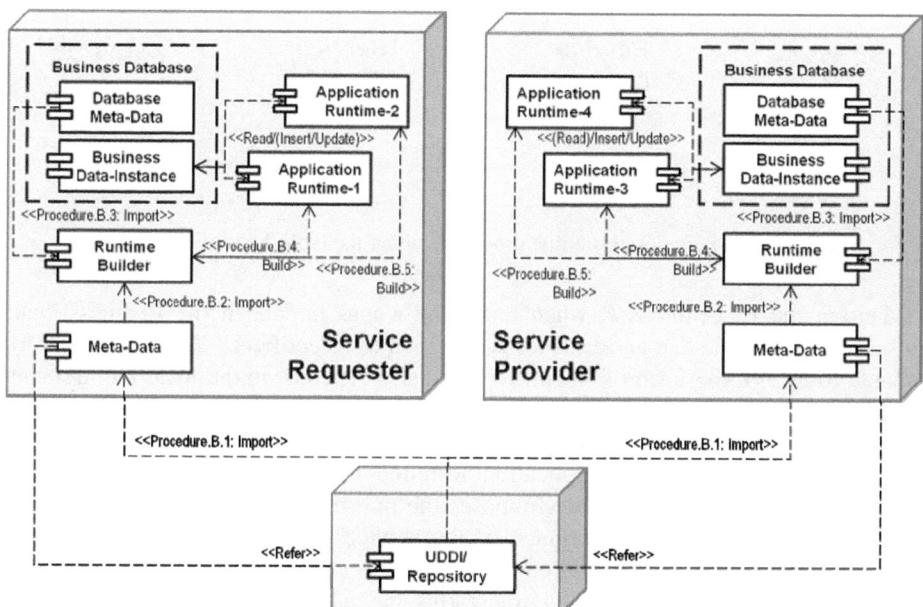

Fig. 1. A typical model of the environment for BPI. A service provider and a service requester execute an exchange process using peer to peer model.

In general, there are usually two categorized parts in a database management system. The first is Database Meta-Data part which contains catalogue data, type definition. The second is Business Data-Instance part which treats the real data related to business transactions and master instances. In the runtime, the procedure specified in Fig.2 will be executed. Firstly, programs Application Runtime-1, Application Runtime-2 of the service requester extract their corresponding data from their Business Data-instance at Procedure.R.1. During the Procedure.R.1, the retrieving Business Data-instance is the major process for yielding an XML massage instance, however there might partly be processes of updating and inserting data.

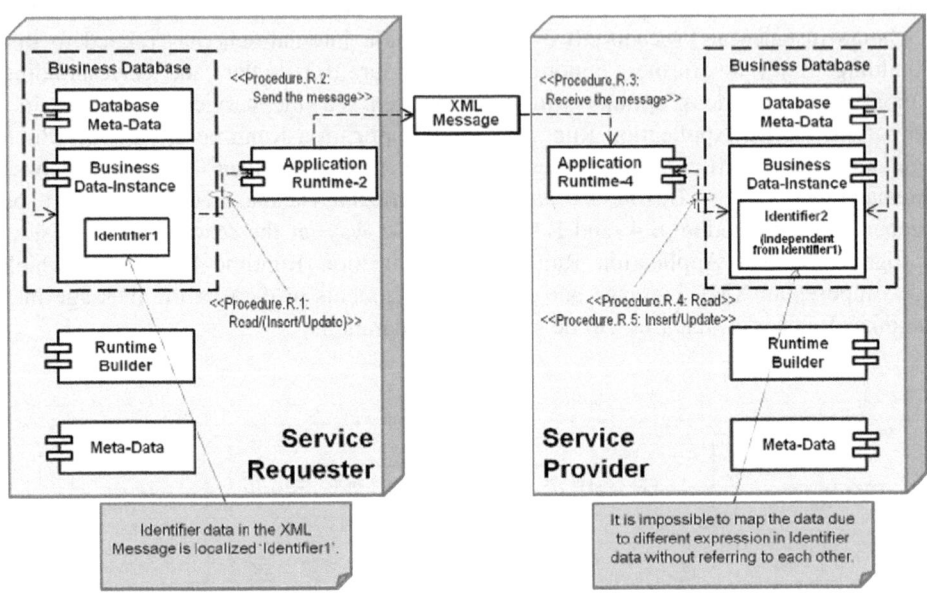

Fig. 2. A typical model of runtime procedure under the typical environment for BPI

During the Procedure.R.1, when retrieving a master data in the Business Data-Instance, we assume that an identifier is specified as 'Identifier1'. Without any efforts related to MDM, the form of 'Identifier1' usually depends on the local requirements of the service requester, and is autonomically decided. Once Application Runtime-2 generates an XML message, the message will be forwarded to the service provider at Procedure.R.2. Then, once Application Runtime-4 receives the XML message at Procedure.R.3, it continuously decomposes the message and stores the fragments of data into the Business Data-instance of the service provider at Procedure.R.4 and Procedure.R.5. During Procedure.R.4, Application Runtime-4 parses the XML message, then it manipulates and transforms the message fragments into suitable forms corresponding to the internal forms of Business Data-instance. If there is a gap between the identifiers, for example, the identifier of the corresponding master data inside Business Data-instance of the service provider would be 'Identifier2', Application Runtime-4 would have to somehow correspond by translating between both. After the translation, the program stores the fragments of message data into Business Data-instance at Procedure.R.5.

If the translation between 'Identifier1' and 'Identifier2' would be easy for example by using a simple and clear correspondence rule, there would be few issues. However, if there are no unified guidelines and principles in designing master data inside an organization, there would obviously be some risks which are difficult to translate in a reasonable business period. There is actually a report in regards to treating how much loss an organization will suffer by unregulated and non-uniformed data expressions and contents [11].

3   Analysis of MDM in Primitive Cases

3.1   Outline

In the previous section, we explained the issues caused by the poor quality of master data in BPI due to the lack of MDM. However, whether these issues occur or not actually, depends on the use cases. In general, as the cases of BPI can be categorized into several sub cases according to the operational conditions, it is required to analyze which operational cases in the macro level these issues depicted in Fig.2 actually occur. Therefore, the analysis of identifying potential issues and estimating their possibilities will firstly be carried out for individual primitive cases which the generic complicated Cloud environment consists of. The primitive cases are identified as follows;

(1) EAI inside an organization such as an enterprise.
(2) BPI between organizations such as enterprises.
(3) Master data management as a service.

The above (1) and (2) will be explained in the next section, and (3) will be done in section 3.3.

3.2   Use Cases of EAI Inside an Enterprise, BPI between Enterprises

When comparing between both internal case and mutual case of an enterprise for MDM, the requirements for the internal case inside the enterprise are obviously dominant. Therefore we might mention that different solutions should individually be adopted for each case, even if we would assume the seamless integration by BPI between an internal communication of an enterprise and an interconnection between enterprises.

Fig.3 depicts a model consisting of elements of information systems for enterprises integration. The information flow in this model is related to the life cycle of identification information from defining, managing to referring. Even before adopting MDM, the following matters have been general; firstly the multiple Applications-1,-2 in an enterprise individually have their master data in their independent forms. Secondly they deliver their master data to other applications between each other by batch programs. Then finally, they respectively modify the delivered data to adjust them to their own forms. Therefore, the cases where the issues depicted in Fig.2 explicitly appear might often be related to the structural changes inside enterprises such as rapid business integration like M&A.

Whereas, there is an element of doubt on the performance when applying the solutions having the same or equivalent contexts with internal enterprises to BPI with outside partners. There are several types of data corresponding to identification information to be exchanged between enterprises. However, product number, document number for a contract and a specification are usually generic. In usual cases, it is rare to disclose the definition of structure and their semantics of identification information to the outside of enterprises. Furthermore, as literal meaningless strings can function as an identifier, the potential needs for identifying persons, organizations by matching between different codes look a few excepted in the special cases. Even in the case of disclosing the definition of structure and their semantics of identification information to outside, it also empirically seems infrequent to update them during a short period except correcting errors. The situation is the same for defining the multiple identifiers to the same object. One of the typical instances of these cases is the specification of RosettaNet, Partner Interface Process (PIP) 2A1, 'Distribute Product Catalog Information'[17]. As the frequency of updating contents in a catalogue depends on the product life cycle, it is usually variable. However once every few months seems usual at best. If frequent updates occur, it seems more reasonable to adopt a private search system for information retrieval, or the model of UDDI instead of using BPI with exchanging messages.

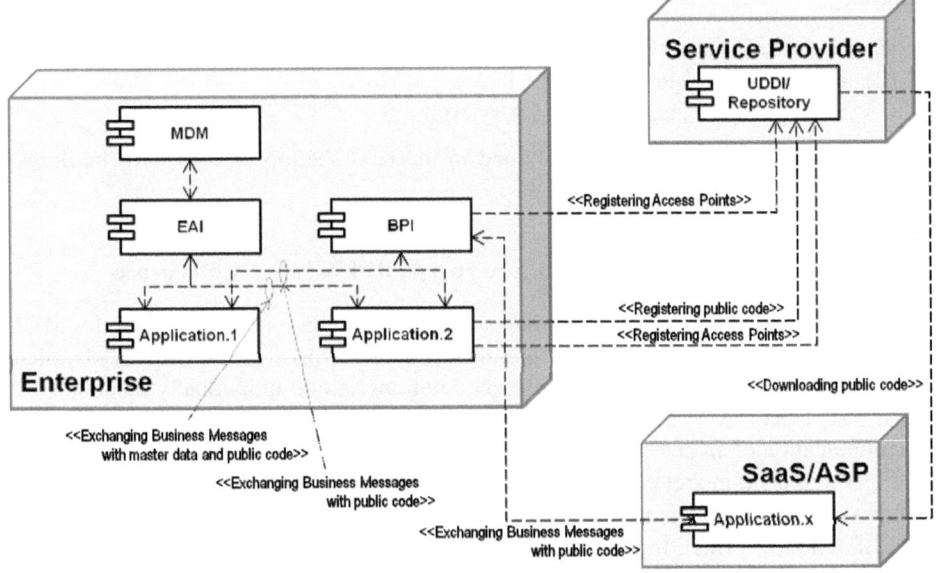

Fig. 3. A simplified model consisting of elements of enterprises information systems

Accordingly, we can conclude that most of cases where there are several synonyms in master data and needs to improve these situations for interoperability, remain in the internal uses in enterprises. If the same thing is required for interconnection between enterprises, another factor might potentially exist, for instance, poor quality of the information managed by UDDI, or hardness for practical operations.

3.3   Use Cases of MDM as a Service

We cannot disregard the possibility of MDM as a service. However, it is difficult to depict the definite model due to various existing factors which are hard to identify at this stage.

As the amount and size of the master data might loosely be correlative with the total amount of data in an enterprise, the needs for MDM might generally depend on the size of that enterprise. Additionally as MDM is a solution for the issues arising in the current information systems, the MDM is not sufficiently mature yet. Therefore, the approaches for a lot of small to medium size enterprises might be different from the larger ones, where the previous issues tend to arise prominently and the solution will be implemented by themselves. In the cases of the small to medium size enterprises, the total number of master data handled by an individual tenant might remain in the tens of thousands at most. Therefore the actual demands to manage them on a larger scale have remained ambiguous. However, it is absolutely impossible to deny the possibility of supplying functions of MDM as an outsourced service, because MDM is one of the applications and requires a huge amount of effort to realize an ideal figure.

Furthermore, not only the above possibility, there are also issues on the structural aspect of services as well. From the view point of saving the operational cost, the single site policy which promotes multiple users to share the functions, seems more effective when serving the functions to disclose the identification information of various objects to the public. In fact, this policy seems to be accepted in the practical operations such as UDDI. However, the MDM service for small and medium sized enterprises tends to treat the small scale of data for each and also requires strict security protection. Therefore, there are very few other positive reasons and motivation to adopt the single site policy or multi-tenancy oriented except effective operations. The hosting service is an alternative solution in this case.

Generally speaking, there are many points open to debate in defining MDM as an outsourced service when considering the requirements of its operations as mentioned. However, in the next section we assume the existence of this MDM as an outsourced service.

4   Workflows under Multiple Cloud Environments

4.1   Outline

When assuming a more complicated Cloud environment such as combining the multiple SaaS/ASPs, further important points would come up for MDM due to new operational requirements. Here, we will analyze the use cases of operations under complicated Cloud environments after modeling them. In section 4.2, after explaining a typical model of the environment, we will mention the procedure of exchanging master data among sites, and the potential issues arising under this environment. Then, in section 4.3, during exchanging business XML messages after exchanging the master data, the issues caused depending on the situation will be identified.

4.2   Model and Procedure for Exchanging Master Data: Definition

Under the assumed model, an enterprise will use various services and several platforms provided by multiple SaaS/ASPs, PaaS and IaaS providers, and these services and platforms will also be shared by multiple users. Fig.4 and Fig.5 show models as the typical environment. Here, we assume multiple users named as Enterprise.x (x:1,2,....,n) exist, and multiple providers named as SaaS/ASP.y (y:1,2,....,m) exist as well. Then, inside Enterprise.1 a MDM managed for local uses is implemented and named as 'Local MDM'. On the other hand, inside SaaS/ASP.1, another MDM managed for a commercial service and providing to others is also implemented. We can regard this as 'Global MDM', because this can handle the demands from multiple users as multi-tenancies. Global MDM can provide services to multiple Enterprise.x (x:1,2,....,n). Furthermore, we also assume UDDI and other repositories (UDDI/Repository) will be deployed inside SaaS/ASP.m.

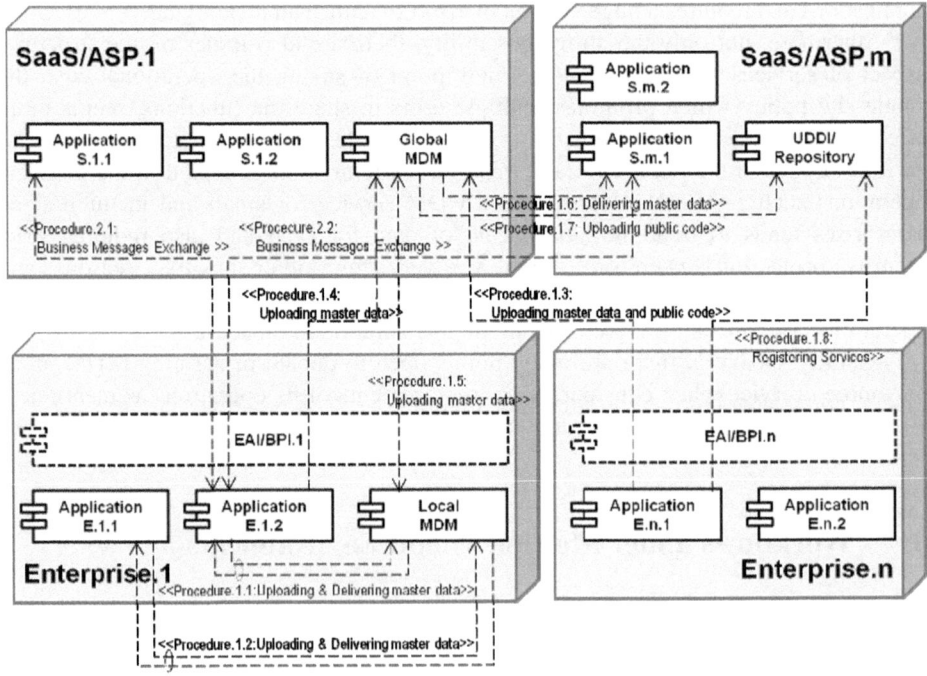

Fig. 4. A workflow inside an enterprise under complicated Cloud environment including MDM procedures

Fig.4 also depicts a workflow inside an enterprise including MDM procedures. In this figure, we assume Procedure.1.x corresponding to exchanging master data as a pre-process will be executed by using SOA. Whereas Fig.5 depicts a workflow for exchanging business XML messages between enterprises. However, this figure also includes the procedure for exchanging master data.

The procedures for exchanging master data will be executed as follows; Inside Enterprise.1, all of the application programs will update the master data which is managed by themselves locally by sending them to Local MDM. Procedure.1.1 and Procedure.1.2 will be activated in order to normalize these master data. Then data cleansing and normalizing these master data will be carried out. Delivering normalized master data coupled with the original master data to the original sender applications are continuously performed. Through these processes, semantics integration with uniformed expressions is realized among the master data. In the case of utilizing the Global MDM service at SaaS/ASP.1 by multiple Enterprise.x (x:1,2,....,n) , these Enterprise.x (x:1,2,....,n) must send their master data to Global MDM first. Enterprise.n for example, uploads all of its master data to Global MDM at Proccdure.1.3, then data cleansing will be started. In this case, the disclosed data to the outside by Enterprise.n such as identification information are also uploaded at that time. Enterprise.1 uploads all of its master data to Global MDM as well at Procedure.1.4 and 1.5, then data cleansing will be done. Procedure.1.4 corresponds to the procedure in the case of no existing Local MDM. So, the local Application.E.1.2 directly uploads its master data to Global MDM, and then data cleansing will be performed.

On the other hand, if a Local MDM exists, the alternative Procedure.1.5 will be carried out. In this case, an operational rule must be established, which Global MDM at SaaS/ASP.1 or Local MDM managed by Enterprise.1 should be prioritized. If Enterprise.1 prioritizes Global MDM at SaaS/ASP.1, Enterprise.1 must deliver the normalized master data from Global MDM to another SaaS/ASP.m at Procedure.1.6. As this procedure can be regarded as a proxy activity, it might cause an issue on the authentication mechanism. Furthermore, a suitable solution must be considered to avoid the situation where the service provider knows the contract of its client Enterprise.l to another service provider. In order to realize this solution, it is required to develop a method to make multiple service providers invisible to each other. If it is difficult to develop that method, this leads to a negative situation in prioritizing Global MDM. This means that this case will potentially be an operational constraint for MDM.

When Enterprise.n discloses data such as identification information to the outside, especially by registering them to UDDI deployed at SaaS/ASP.m, it must register the information at Procedure.1.7. Then, through the API of UDDI, the service must also be registered at Procedure.1.8. The procedure becomes complicated due to separated operations in this case.

As explained here, there are new issues related to the authentication mechanism and the operational rules. Accordingly we need to develop a suitable solution. As a conclusion, these issues are caused by commissioning the control of master data to outsourced services by multiple Enterprise.x (x:1,2,....,n).

36   S. Kikuchi

4.3   Issues in Execution of Workflows

After exchanging the master data along the procedures in the previous session, exchanging business XML messages will then be carried out. Exchanging these messages in Fig.4 can be regarded as follows; exchanging multiple business XML messages by Enterprise.1 are executed at Procedure.2.1 and Procedure.2.2. In spite of using multiple providers such as SaaS/ASP.1 and SaaS/ASP.m, actual workflow is substantially equivalent with EAI inside Enterprise.1. At that time, all of the master data have already been set with normalized data coupled with the original one. Therefore, there are very few possibilities required to exchange newer master data.

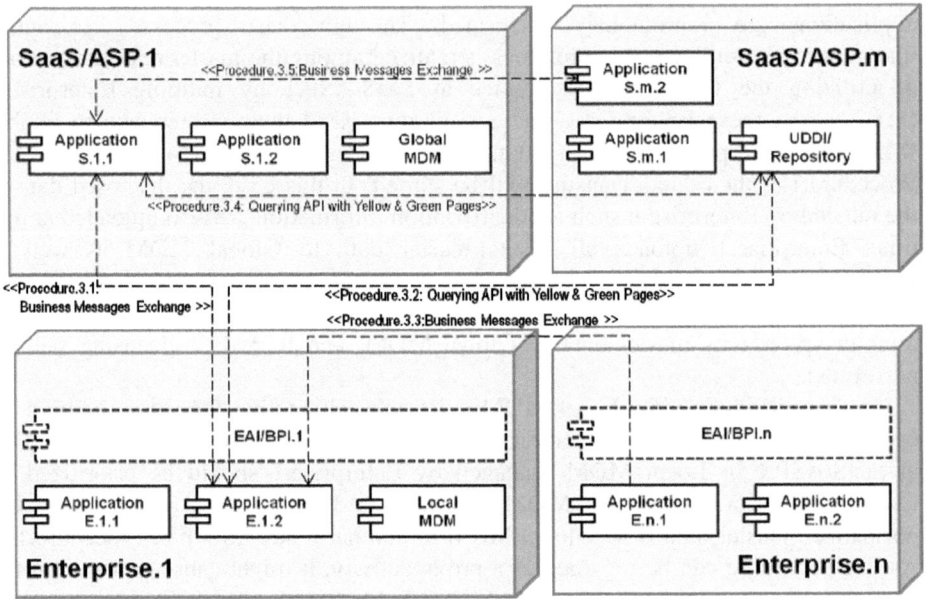

Fig. 5. A workflow for exchanging business XML messages between enterprises

On the other hand, in Fig.5 which depicts a workflow for exchanging business XML messages between Enterprise.1 and Enterprise.n, there are different aspects with respect to the two items listed below;

(1)   A constraint for exchanging business XML messages will be defined with dependency on the deployed location of process control function.
(2)   New elemental functions such as UDDI will be needed.

As for (1), firstly we will consider the case where the business process is controlled by Application.E.1.2 implemented in Enterprise.1. In this case, Application.E.1.2 will send an XML message to the provider SaaS/ASP.1 at Procedure.3.1. Then, before sending an XML message to Enterprise.n, Application.E.1.2 needs to access Yellow and Green Pages in UDDI deployed in SaaS/ASP.m to get API and the type of XML message at Procedure.3.2. In this case, if Application.E.1.2 tries to get a product number from a catalogue, it should download the related information by using the Green Page as well. After that, Application.E.1.2 will send an XML message to Enterprise.n at Procedure.3.3. In this case, there are very few situations required to exchange the master data anymore because all of the master data have already been set with normalized data.

In contrast, we will continue to examine the other case where the business process is controlled by ApplicationS.1.1 deployed in SaaS/ASP.1. In this case, ApplicationS.1.1 also needs to access Yellow and Green Pages in UDDI to get API and the type of XML message and to download the related information at Procedure.3.4. After that, Application.S.1.1 will send an XML message to ApplicationS.m.2 deployed in SaaS/ASP.m. In this case, there are also few cases that new master data are needed. However this procedure could not be carried out, if this activity executed by a request from Enterprise.1 would not be authenticated.

As for (2), we need to consider the quality of the current data stored at UDDI and other repositories. As mentioned before, we assume that the Green Page will be accessed when downloading the related information at Procedure.3.4. However, it is generally difficult and rare to treat the business data with confidentiality such as service life cycle information, service quality and quality assurance information on the public UDDI in a general security level. It is usually impossible to assure the quality of registered information. Therefore, it is necessary to implement these functions by combining the public UDDI with more secure repositories such as private UDDI. In particular most of the major commercial UDDI services had already been closed. It will become an obvious constraint.

5   Implementation and Performance Considerations

When assuming the operation of MDM under the complicated Cloud environment depicted in Fig.4, Fig.5, new operational issues potentially occur as follows;

(1)   In the case where an enterprise adopts MDM as a service provided by an independent SaaS/ASP provider, exchanging master data to another SaaS/ASP provider serving another application must be done before exchanging business XML messages. This means exchanging master data must be done among multiple independent committed providers. In order to avoid needless disclosures of the contracts to other service providers, it is required to develop a method to make multiple service providers invisible to each other. If it is difficult to develop that method, this will lead to a potential operational constraint for MDM.

(2)   As a solution for the above (1), an authentication mechanism and a new protocol should be developed. As a similar story, there is a case where an application deployed at a SaaS/ASP provider must exchange business XML data with other multiple applications at the other SaaS/ASP providers according to requests of the client enterprise. In this case, the procedure could not be carried out if the activity executed by a request from the

enterprise could not be authenticated. However, the request for making multiple service providers invisible might not be necessary.

(3)   When an enterprise discloses identification information data managed by MDM to the outside, especially by registering them to UDDI, the procedures will be divided into multiple parts and become complicated. One part will be done by the client enterprise, whereas another will be done by an independent committed provider. Therefore, a protocol for disclosing the data should be designed.

(4)   When disclosing the identification information of various objects to the public, maintaining the quality of data stored at UDDI and other repositories and their security management are mandatory. However, as it is almost impossible to rely on unpopular public/commercial UDDI, more secure repositories such as private UDDI might be a potential approach. However, this approach might enforce strong constraints for independent operations due to the private use oriented. This might often lead to unavailable cases for small size enterprises.

The above operational issues are not only related to MDM, but related to the individual specific technical areas as well. Thus, it is required to analyze the applicability of solutions with sufficient knowledge on the background when mapping between the above issues and solutions. Therefore, we will only touch the surface in illustrating ways to solve them here.

What we can mention as general items from (1) and (2) are about a risk to define a complicated procedure due to dividing functions into two entities, and a requirement of how to obtain an execution right as a proxy on authentication from the committer. Dreibelbis.A et al. have also pointed out the specific issues of MDM on security and privacy, which are independent from ours [10]. However, the concrete correspondences between their approaches and ours and the verification on their availability have not sufficiently been evaluated yet. That will be looked at as future work along with a protocol design. The issue of (3) could be divided into the two parts, one of them is as an independent issue from (1) (2), and another issue has some dependencies on the solutions for (1) and (2). As for the last (4), there is a certain limitation to be applied when considering the current situation around UDDI. However, as there is another alternative way to provide the equivalent function as a service it is definitely not a crucial matter.

6   Related Studies

MDM has been evolved as a comprehensive solution in industry. It is immature as a research area. Therefore, MDM has been explained under the contexts of other research topics. Studies on MDM could be categorized into two parts. The first is a set of architectural studies, whereas the second is a set of studies related to the frameworks, which have empirically been acquired through learning in many practical projects.

As for the architectural studies, there are several proposals. Krizevnik.M and Juric.M.B mention the importance of data quality to realize SOA, and also propose to deploy MDM function as one of the components of Data service layer [12]. Menet.L, Lamolle.M and Zerdazi.A propose the results of classes' analysis for applying an XML form to manage MDM [13]. Both of the studies [12],[13] give us some hints, but their aims are totally different from ours. Dreibelbis.A et al. also propose the comprehensive architecture in which SOA can be applied [10]. This can be contributed when considering the approach of MDM under a complicated Cloud environment including multiple SaaS/ASP providers. However the study here focuses on the issues caused by the operational conditions of MDM under the complicated Cloud environment. Therefore, their aims are also totally different.

There are also several studies related to the previous frameworks. One of them is the study by Cleven.A and Wortmann.F [14]. They propose a framework for promoting the MDM projects. According to their idea, the strategies for approaching MDM are categorized into four sub areas divided by two axes. The first axis is for issue-oriented/solution-oriented and the second axis is for process-driven/data-driven. Whereas, the study by Otto.B and Reichert.A, reports the results of the scopes and the sizes of MDM projects [15]. The report by Bai.X, et al. gives us an overview summary in regards to MDM projects [16]. As MDM is regarded as a comprehensive solution including various elemental technologies, these studies are useful when thinking about the potential issues related with operations of MDM and considering the strategic approach under the complicated Cloud environment.

7   Summary and Conclusions

In this paper, we have presented the results of the analysis of the prospective new issues which have emerged in the MDM under the complicated Cloud environment such as integrating private Cloud and multi-SaaS/ASPs. And we have clarified that there are four major potential issues. Following that, we also pointed out that, these issues should be solved in combination with other suitable approaches of related technical areas, especially based on their current directions of research. In particular, we mentioned the needs of development of an authentication mechanism and a new protocol in order to make multiple service providers invisible to each other.

In consideration of future work, we need to structuralize suitable approach more by analysing and mapping with existing security and privacy solutions. As a part of this approach, it is better to carry out the formulation of the MDM process model under distributed and centralized environment in order to verify the constraints and limitations. Furthermore, it is required to develop a suitable cost model of MDM operations in order to realize suitable MDM operations. This is one of the long term objectives.

References

1. Vaquero, L.M., Rodero-Merino, L., Caceres, J., Lindner, M.: A Break in the Clouds: Towards a Cloud Definition. The ACM SIGCOMM Computer Communication Review 39(1), 50–55 (2009)
2. ISO/IEC Standard 9594-7, Information technology – Open Systems Interconnection – The Directory: Selected object classes, 5 edn. (2005)

3. Horiuchi, H.: Standardization of Information Resource Dictionary System. IPSJ Magazine 37(7) (1996) (in Japanese)
4. ISO/IEC Standard 19763, Framework for Metamodel Interoperability (2007)
5. W3C Semantic Web Activity, http://www.w3.org/2001/sw/
6. OASIS Universal Business Language v2.0 Committee Specification (2006), http://docs.oasis-open.org/ubl/cs-UBL-2.0/UBL-2.0.html
7. Ma, L., et al.: Semantic Web Technologies and Data Management. In: W3C workshop on RDF Access to Relational Databases (2007)
8. The Chief Information Officers Council: Federal Enterprise Architecture Framework. Version 1.1 (1999), http://www.cio.gov/documents/fedarch1.pdf
9. Kosanke, K., Nell, J.G.: Enterprise Engineering and Integration: Building International Consensus. In: Proceeding of International Conference on Enterprise Integration and Modeling Technology (1997)
10. Dreibelbis, A., Hechler, E., et al.: Enterprise Master Data Management. IBM Press (2008)
11. Halpern, S.: Master Data Management: Extracting Value from Your Most Important Intangible Asset. SAP White Paper (2007)
12. Krizevnik, M., Juric, M.B.: Improved SOA Persistence Architectural Model. ACM SIGSOFT Software Engineering Notes 35(2) (May 2010)
13. Menet, L., Lamolle, M., Zerdazi, A.: Managing Master Data with XML Schema and UML. In: Proceeding of International Workshop on Advanced Information Systems for Enterprises (2008)
14. Cleven, A., Wortmann, F.: Uncovering four strategies to approach master data management. In: Proceedings of the 43rd Hawaii International Conference on System Science (2010)
15. Otto, B., Reichert, A.: Organizing Master Data Management: Finding from an Expert Survey. In: Proceedings of the 2010 ACM Symposium on Applied Computing (2010)
16. Bai, X., Li, P., Li, H., Song, X.: Enterprise Master Data Manage Project Practice. In: Proceeding of 2010 International Conference on Computer Application and System Modeling, ICCASM 2010 (2010)
17. http://www.rosettanet.org/dnn_rose/Standards/RosettaNetStandards/PIPDirectory/tabid/476/Default.aspx

Hiding Data and Structure in Workflow Provenance

Susan Davidson, Zhuowei Bao, and Sudeepa Roy

Department of Computer and Information Science,
University of Pennsylvania, Philadelphia, PA, USA
{susan,zhuowei,sudeepa}@cis.upenn.edu

Abstract. In this paper we discuss the use of *views* to address the problem of providing useful answers to provenance queries while ensuring that privacy concerns are met. In particular, we propose a *hierarchical* workflow model, based on context-free graph grammars, in which *fine-grained* dependencies between the inputs and outputs of a module are explicitly specified. Using this model, we examine how privacy concerns surrounding data, module function, and workflow structure can be addressed.

1 Introduction

Provenance in scientific workflows is of increasing interest, as evidenced by several recent workshops, tutorials, and surveys on the topic [5,6,18,23]. A number of tools for capturing provenance have been developed in workflow systems such as myGrid/Taverna [19], Kepler [7] and VisTrails [13], and a standard for provenance representation called the Open Provenance Model (OPM) [17] has been designed. By maintaining information about the sequence of module executions (processing steps) used to produce a data item, as well as the parameter settings and intermediate data items passed between module executions, the validity and reliability of data can be better understood and results can be made reproducible.

A repository that includes workflow specifications, executions and provenance information – *provenance-aware workflow information* – is clearly useful in many ways. For example, scientists who wish to perform new analyses may search by keyword to find specifications of interest to reuse or modify. They may also search executions associated with a specification to understand the meaning of the workflow, or to correct/debug an erroneous specification. Finding erroneous or suspect data, a user may then wish to ask structural *provenance queries* to determine what downstream data might have been affected, or to understand how the process failed that led to creating the data.

However, authors/owners of workflows may wish to keep some of this provenance information private. For example, intermediate *data* within an execution may contain sensitive information, such as the social security number, a medical record, or financial information about an individual. Although users with the appropriate level of access may be allowed to see such confidential data, making it available to all users through a workflow repository, even for scientific

S. Kikuchi et al. (Eds.): DNIS 2011, LNCS 7108, pp. 41–48, 2011.

purposes, is an unacceptable breach of privacy. Beyond data privacy, a *module* itself may be proprietary, and hiding its description may not be enough: users without the appropriate level of access should not be able to *infer* its behavior if they are allowed to see the inputs and outputs of the module. Finally, details of how certain modules in the workflow are connected may be proprietary, and therefore showing how data is passed between modules may reveal too much of the *structure* of the workflow. **There is thus an inherent tradeoff between the utility of the information shown in response to a search/query and the privacy guarantees that authors/owners desire.**

One technique that can be used to hide details of a workflow is to create *composite modules* which encapsulate subworkflows. Composite modules can be combined to create *views* of a workflow and its associated executions, showing users a subset of provenance information and hiding the rest within unexpanded composite module executions. Originally proposed in [4] as a technique for focusing user attention on relevant provenance, views can also be used to hide private information, which may include the intermediate data and modules within a composite module as well as the dependencies between the inputs and outputs of the composite module.

In this paper, we examine the use of views to implement workflow provenance privacy. We start in Sec. 2 by describing a model for workflow specifications, executions, and views. We continue in Sec. 3 by describing initial results on module and structural privacy, and discuss the connection to views. We close by pointing to future directions for research.

2   Workflow Model

Our workflow model has several components: specifications, runs, execution graphs, port dependencies, and provenance graphs. A workflow specification describes the design of a workflow, while a workflow run (together with information about the data and processes) describes a particular execution of the given specification. Following [3], a specification is given by a context-free graph grammar and the runs corresponding to the specification are given by the graphs in the language generated by that grammar. Port dependencies are used in the definition of data provenance graphs, and model fine-grained dependencies between the inputs and outputs of a module. Rather than giving full details of the model, we illustrate via an example (see [2] for a more formal treatment).

Workflow Specifications. A sample *workflow specification* is given in Fig. 1. The workflow estimates disease susceptibility based on genome-wide SNP array data for an individual as well as information about lifestyle, family history, and physical symptoms, and outputs a prognosis for the patient along with recommended lifestyle changes [25]. In the graph, boxes labeled $M0, \ldots, M16$ indicate *modules* with *input ports* indicated by solid circles and *output ports* indicated by open circles; and the labeled arrows between output and input ports of different modules indicate potential *data flow*. Some of the modules in this workflow are *atomic* ($M5, \ldots, M16$). The rest of the modules ($M0, \ldots, M4$) are *composite*,

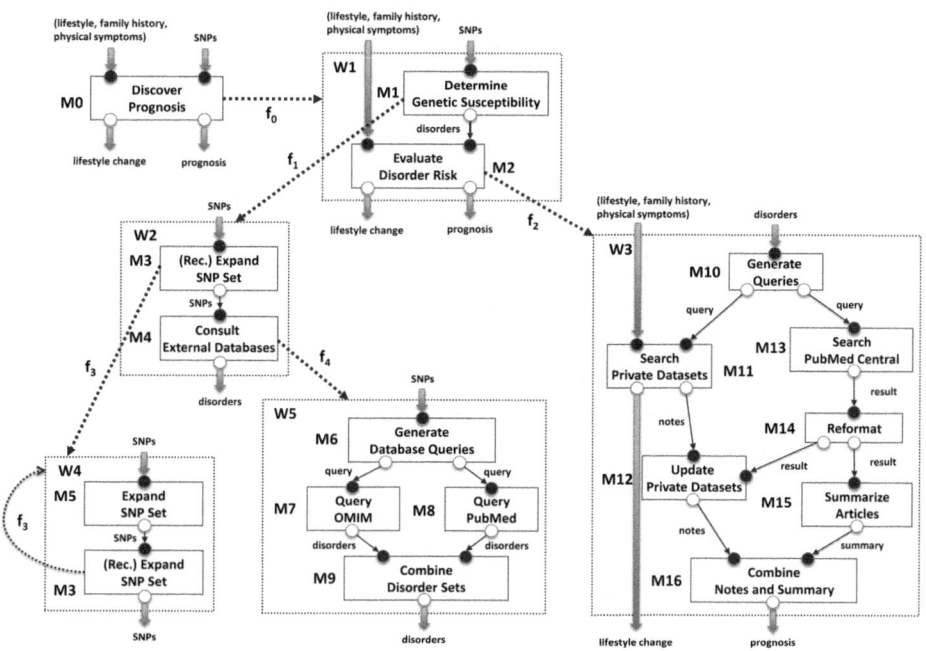

Fig. 1. Disease Susceptibility Workflow Specification

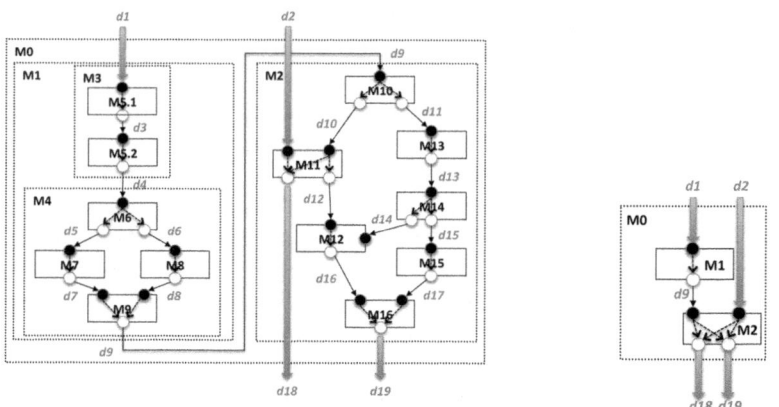

Fig. 2. Sample Workflow Execution   **Fig. 3.** View of Provenance Graph, $V1$

and their expansion to a subworkflow is shown by dotted edges labeled f_i (the name of the production rule). In particular, the root of the workflow is $M0$, which expands via f_0 to $W1$. The correspondence between inputs/outputs of a composite module and the subworkflow to which it expands is indicated in this figure by reusing names. For example, the initial inputs to the workflow are (lifestyle,...) and SNPs, and the final outputs are lifestyle change and prognosis, indicated by double arrows into and out of $M0$, and those names are reused within $W1$. There is also *intermediate* data within subworkflows $W1,\ldots,W5$, e.g. disorders, query, and result.

Note that composite module $M3$ is recursive, indicated by a cycle, and that therefore in an execution the atomic module $M5$ may be executed multiple times. For simplicity, we have dropped from the figure the alternate termination condition for this expansion ($M3 \longrightarrow^{f_5} M5$).

Workflow Executions. The set of all possible *runs* of a specification is modeled as the graph language of the corresponding graph grammar. More precisely, it consists of all simple workflows that can be derived from the start module and contain only atomic module. A *workflow execution* is a run in which each module is given a unique process id and data flows over the edges. One execution of our sample specification is given in Fig. 2, in which we reuse the name of the module as the process id unless the module occurs multiple times in the run, e.g. we use $M5.1$ and $M5.2$ for the two executions of module $M5$. Data items represent instances of the abstract data in the specification, e.g. $d1$ represents the initial input of SNPs.

Provenance Graphs. Data provenance in workflows is typically considered to be *coarse-grained* [9], i.e., the data coming out of each output port of a module depends on the data that entered *all* input ports of the module. However, the ability to capture fine-grained dependencies is increasingly important in a number of workflow systems, e.g., Taverna 2 [24] and COMAD-Kepler [22], so we allow the modeling of *fine-grained* provenance. That is, as part of the specification we assume that each atomic module has an associated *port dependency matrix* $\delta(M)$ showing which inputs are connected to which outputs. This is illustrated in our sample execution in Fig. 2 as an edge between input/output ports within a module execution, which we will call a *dependency* edge. For example, in $M11$ the output $d12$ depends only on $d10$ as there is no edge from $d2$ to $d12$. The information contained in an execution allows us to capture *provenance* for data items (such as $d18$ and $d19$), so we will call them *provenance graphs*. Note that the provenance graph for this relatively simple workflow is already complex. Note also that dependency matrix for composite modules in an execution can be inferred from the dependency matrices of atomic modules as *paths* of dependency and dataflow edges between input and output ports for the composite module.

A provenance query such as "What data does $d18$ depend on?" can be answered by finding all data items at the origin of a path of dependency and data flow edges that ends at $d18$. For our example, this would include data items $d1$, $d2$,..., $d10$, but not $d11$,..., $d17$. In contrast, $d19$ depends on all data items $(d1, d3, \ldots, d17)$ but not $d2$, since there is no dependency between the first input port and second output port in $M11$.

Views. As noted earlier, certain modules in this execution are *composite*, indicated by boxes containing subworkflow executions (e.g., $M0$, $M1$, $M2$). Controlling the expansion to subworkflows can be used to create *views*, such as the one of our sample workflow execution in Fig. 3. In this view $(V1)$, users can only see the expansion of $M0$ and therefore have no access to any intermediate data except for $d9$, and cannot see what modules were executed in the implementation of modules $M1$ and $M2$. For example, the answer to the provenance query "Does the prognosis $d19$ depend on the output of a PubMed search?" (where PubMed search matches modules $M8$ and $M13$) would be "yes" with respect to the full provenance graph of Fig. 2 but "no" with respect to $V1$ since these modules are not visible .

Views may also alter *fine-grained dependencies* between the input and output ports of a module, as illustrated by module $M2$ in Fig. 3. Here, there is a dependency between the first input port and second output port (the given dependency matrix for $M2$ in the view) that does not exist as a path within $M2$ in Fig. 2. In this view, the output of the provenance query "What data does $d19$ depend on?" would therefore include $d2$ and exclude all intermediate data except for $d9$ (i.e., $d1$, $d2$, $d9$).

Finally, we may hide data on edges in a view of an execution (for data privacy) or delete connections between modules in a specification and its executions (for structural privacy).

3   Privacy

Privacy concerns are tied to the workflow components: data, modules, and the structure of a workflow. To illustrate them, consider again the sample workflow in Fig. 1.

Data Privacy. Certain data in a workflow execution may be confidential. For example, the output of $M1$, i.e. the genetic disorder the patient is susceptible to, should not be revealed with high probability, in any execution, to users without the required access privilege. Such data masking is a fairly standard requirement in privacy-aware database systems, and a variety of well known techniques can be applied, e.g. access control [21]. A key question to consider is whether access to aggregated provenance data (e.g. the most frequent genetic disorder) is allowed and, if so, whether some standard notion of privacy like *differential privacy* (see, for instance, [12]) used in statistical databases is appropriate for our application. For example, often random noise is added to the output of a statistical query to achieve differential privacy in statistical databases, but adding random noise to the data values may prohibit repeatability of scientific experiments performed using a workflow.

Module Privacy. Module privacy requires that the functionality of a private module – that is, the mapping it defines between inputs and outputs – is not revealed to users without the required access privilege. Returning to our example, assuming that $M1$ implements a function f_1, module privacy with respect to $M1$ requires that no adversarial user should be able to guess the output $f_1(\texttt{SNP}, \texttt{ethnicity})$ with high probability for any $\texttt{SNP}$ and $\texttt{ethnicity}$ input. From a patient's perspective, this is important because they do not want someone who may happen to have access to their $\texttt{SNP}$ and $\texttt{ethnicity}$ information to be able to determine what $\texttt{disorders}$ they are susceptible to. From the module owner's perspective, they do not want the module to be simulated by competitors who capture all input-output relationships. It is easy to see that if information about all intermediate data is repeatedly given for multiple executions of a workflow on different initial inputs, then partial or complete functionality of modules may be revealed. The approach that we take in [11,10] is to *hide a carefully chosen subset of intermediate data*, thereby limiting the amount of provenance data shown to the user and guaranteeing some desired level of privacy. Since there may be several different subsets of intermediate data whose hiding yields the desired level of privacy, and certain data may be more useful utility-wise to users than other data, this becomes an interesting optimization problem.

Note that there is an interesting connection between data and module privacy: If a module is *public* (i.e. its function is known), then its output can be simulated if the inputs are public. Therefore, hiding the output of a public module may also require hiding some of its input. Furthermore, if a module is *invertible* then its input can be simulated if the outputs are known. Again, hiding the input of a public module may also require hiding some of its outputs.

Structural Privacy. The goal of structural privacy is to keep private the information that some module M contributes to the generation of a data item d, output by another module M'. For instance, in the execution of the workflow $W3$, we may wish to hide the fact that the reformatted data from PubMed Central (module $M13$) contributes to updating the private DB (module $M12$), and hence to the output of module $M12$. One possible approach is to delete edges and vertices from both the visible specification and its execution so as to eliminate all paths from M to M'; for instance, in this example we can delete the edge $M13 \rightarrow M14$. However, by doing so, we may hide additional provenance information that does not need be hidden (e.g. the existence of a path from $M13$ to $M15$). Another approach would be to avoid altering the structure of the workflow and instead find a view in which $M13$ and $M12$ are hidden in a composite module P, so that the reachability of any pair (u, v) in P is no longer externally visible, but in this case we may introduce some new paths that did not exist before. Since there may be many different views of the same workflow, each of which has a different composite module structure and different dependency matrices, we may need to choose the "best" view. Once again one faces a challenging optimization problem: guaranteeing an adequate level of privacy while minimizing unnecessary loss of information or introduction of spurious information. Techniques from preserving the privacy of *social networks* [14,1,20,8,16] may also be useful.

4   Conclusion

We have presented a model of workflows based on context free graph grammars in which fine-grained dependencies between inputs and outputs of an atomic (non-expandable) module can be explicitly specified. Using this model, a view can be defined using several techniques, including: 1) hiding data in an execution; 2) hiding substructure within composite modules, e.g. enabling only a subset of the workflow productions, thereby allowing only some composite modules expansions; 3) hiding data flow edges in the specification. We also discussed privacy concerns in workflow provenance – data, module and structure. Applying a view to an execution yields a subset of the provenance information, in which module executions and intermediate data of non-expandable modules are not visible, and hidden data or data flow are not revealed. Note that hiding data flow edges may introduce false negatives (data that actually is in the provenance of a given data item is not returned in a provenance query) while using composite modules may introduce false positives (data that is not actually in the provenance of a given data item is returned) and/or false negatives, depending on the fine-grained dependency graph associated with the composite module. The utility of a view to a user can be measured by the number of false positives or false negatives introduced in the view used to answer provenance queries.

Our approach of using a view to answer provenance queries while ensuring privacy of the workflow components is quite different from that used in other areas (statistical databases, data mining, social networks) where random noise is added or other randomized mechanisms are applied to guarantee privacy. These approaches do not seem to be directly applicable to our problem; provenance queries are quite different in nature from aggregate queries, and results of scientific experiments performed using a workflow are expected to be repeatable and accurate over different executions. The chief challenge is have a formal analysis of privacy and a utility guarantee of the solutions we provide, which leads to numerous new research directions. In our initial research for module privacy, we used a weaker notion of privacy called ℓ-diversity [15]. In our current work we are studying whether stronger notion of privacy (such as differential privacy) can be applied meaningfully to our application.

References

1. Backstrom, L., Dwork, C., Kleinberg, J.M.: Wherefore art thou r3579x?: anonymized social networks, hidden patterns, and structural steganography. In: WWW, pp. 181–190 (2007)
2. Bao, Z., Davidson, S., Milo, T.: A Fine-Grained Workflow Model with Provenance-Aware Security Views. In: Proceedings of TaPP (2011)
3. Beeri, C., Eyal, A., Kamenkovich, S., Milo, T.: Querying business processes. In: Proceedings of the 32nd International Conference on Very Large Data Bases, pp. 343–354 (2006)
4. Biton, O., Boulakia, S.C., Davidson, S.B., Hara, C.S.: Querying and Managing Provenance through User Views in Scientific Workflows. In: ICDE, pp. 1072–1081 (2008)

5. Bose, R., Foster, I., Moreau, L.: Report on the International Provenance and Annotation Workshop. SIGMOD Rec. 35(3) (2006)
6. Bose, R., Frew, J.: Lineage retrieval for scientific data processing: a survey. ACM Comp. Surveys 37(1), 1–28 (2005)
7. Bowers, S., Ludäscher, B.: Actor-oriented design of scientific workflows. In: Int. Conf. on Concept. Modeling, pp. 369–384 (2005)
8. Campan, A., Truta, T.M.: A clustering approach for data and structural anonymity in social networks. In: PinKDD (2008)
9. Davidson, S.B., Boulakia, S.C., Eyal, A., Ludäscher, B., McPhillips, T.M., Bowers, S., Anand, M.K., Freire, J.: Provenance in scientific workflow systems. IEEE Data Eng. Bull. 30(4), 44–50 (2007)
10. Davidson, S.B., Khanna, S., Milo, T., Panigrahi, D., Roy, S.: Provenance views for module privacy. In: Proceedings of the 30th ACM SIGMOD-SIGACT-SIGART Symposium on Principles of Database Systems, pp. 175–186 (2011)
11. Davidson, S.B., Khanna, S., Panigrahi, D., Roy, S.: Preserving module privacy in workflow provenance (2010) (manuscript), http://arxiv.org/abs/1005.5543
12. Dwork, C.: Differential Privacy. In: Bugliesi, M., Preneel, B., Sassone, V., Wegener, I. (eds.) ICALP 2006. LNCS, vol. 4052, pp. 1–12. Springer, Heidelberg (2006)
13. Freire, J., Silva, C.T., Callahan, S.P., Santos, E., Scheidegger, C.E., Vo, H.T.: Managing Rapidly-Evolving Scientific Workflows. In: Moreau, L., Foster, I. (eds.) IPAW 2006. LNCS, vol. 4145, pp. 10–18. Springer, Heidelberg (2006)
14. Korolova, A., Motwani, R., Nabar, S.U., Xu, Y.: Link privacy in social networks. In: CIKM, pp. 289–298. ACM, New York (2008)
15. Machanavajjhala, A., Kifer, D., Gehrke, J., Venkitasubramaniam, M.: L-diversity: Privacy beyond k-anonymity. ACM Trans. Knowl. Discov. Data 1(1), 3 (2007)
16. Machanavajjhala, A., Korolova, A., Sarma, A.D.: Personalized social recommendations: accurate or private. Proc. VLDB Endow. 4, 440–450 (2011)
17. Moreau, L., Freire, J., Futrelle, J., McGrath, R.E., Myers, J., Paulson, P.: The Open Provenance Model: An overview. In: Freire, J., Koop, D., Moreau, L. (eds.) IPAW 2008. LNCS, vol. 5272, pp. 323–326. Springer, Heidelberg (2008)
18. Moreau, L., Ludäscher, B. (eds.): Concurrency and Computation: Practice and Experience – Special Issue on the First Provenance Challenge. Wiley (2007), http://twiki.ipaw.info/bin/view/Challenge/
19. Oinn, T., Addis, M., Ferris, J., Marvin, D., Senger, M., Greenwood, R., Carver, K., Pocock, M.G., Wipat, A., Li, P.: Taverna: a tool for the composition and enactment of bioinformatics workflows. Bioinformatics 20(1), 3045–3054 (2003)
20. Rastogi, V., Hay, M., Miklau, G., Suciu, D.: Relationship privacy: output perturbation for queries with joins. In: PODS, pp. 107–116 (2009)
21. Samarati, P., De Capitani di Vimercati, S., Paraboschi, S.: Access control: principles and solutions. Software—Practice and Experience 33(5), 397–421 (2003)
22. Shawn Bowers, B.L., McPhillips, T.M.: Provenance in collection-oriented scientific workflows. Concurrency and Computation: Practice and Experience 20(5), 519–529 (2008)
23. Simmhan, Y., Plale, B., Gannon, D.: A survey of data provenance in e-science. SIGMOD Rec. 34(3), 31–36 (2005)
24. Sroka, J., Hidders, J., Missier, P., Goble, C.A.: A formal semantics for the Taverna 2 workflow model. J. Comput. Syst. Sci. 76(6), 490–508 (2010)
25. Stoyanovich, J., Pe'er, I.: MutaGeneSys: estimating individual disease susceptibility based on genome-wide SNP array data. Bioinformatics 24(3), 440–442 (2008)

Organic Databases

H.V. Jagadish, Arnab Nandi, and Li Qian*

University of Michigan
Ann Arbor, MI, USA

Abstract. Databases today are carefully engineered: there is an expensive and deliberate design process, after which a database schema is defined; during this design process, various possible instance examples and use cases are hypothesized and carefully analyzed; finally, the schema is ready and then can be populated with data. All of this effort is a major barrier to database adoption.

In this paper, we explore the possibility of *organic* database creation instead of the traditional engineered approach. The idea is to let the user start storing data in a database with a schema that is just enough to cove the instances at hand. We then support efficient schema evolution as new data instances arrive. By designing the database to evolve, we can sidestep the expensive front-end cost of carefully engineering the design of the database.

The same set of issues also apply to database querying. Today, databases expect queries to be carefully specified, and to be valid with respect to the database schema. In contrast, the organic query specification model would allow users to construct queries incrementally, with little knowledge of the database. We also examine this problem in this paper.

1 Motivation

Database technology has made great strides in the past decades. Today, we are able to process efficiently ever larger numbers of ever more complex queries on ever more humongous data sets. We can be justifiably proud of what we have accomplished.

However, when we see how information is created, accessed, and shared today, database technology remains only a bit player: much of the data in the world today remains outside database systems. Even worse, in the places where database systems are used extensively, we find an army of database administrators, consultants, and other technical experts all busily helping users get data into and out of a database. For almost all organizations, the indirect cost of maintaining a technical support team far exceeds the direct cost of hardware infrastructure and database product licenses. Not only are support staff expensive, they also interpose themselves between the users and the databases. Users cannot interact with the database directly and are therefore less likely to try less straightforward operations. This hidden opportunity cost may be greater than the visible costs of hardware/software and technical staff. Most of us remember the day not too long ago when booking a flight meant calling a travel agent who used magic incantations at an arcane system to pull up information regarding flights and to make bookings. Today, most of us book our own flights on the web through interfaces that

* Supported in part by NSF under grant IIS-1017296.

S. Kikuchi et al. (Eds.): DNIS 2011, LNCS 7108, pp. 49–63, 2011.

are simple enough for anyone to use. Many enjoy the power of being able to explore options for themselves that would have been too much trouble to explain to an agent, such as willingness to trade off price against convenience of a flight connection.

Search engines have done a remarkable job at directly connecting users with the web. Users can publish documents of any form on the Web. For a keyword query, the user is pointed to a set of documents that are most likely to be relevant to the user. This best-effort nature can lead to possibly inaccurate results, but it allows the users the ability to easily and efficiently get information into and out of the ever-changing Web.

In contrast, the database world has had the heritage of constructing rigid, *precisely* defined, carefully *planned*, explicitly engineered, silos of information based on *predictions* regarding data and queries. It was assumed that information would be clean, rigid and well structured. This has led to databases today being hard to design, hard to modify, and hard to query.

When we look at characteristics of search, we find that there is very low prediction and planning burden placed on users – neither to query nor to publish data. Furthermore, precision, while desirable, is not required. In contrast, users interacting with databases find themselves fighting an uphill battle with the constant flux of the data they deal with in today's highly connected world.

Our goal in this paper is to render database interaction lenient in its demands for prediction, planning, and precision. We call this *organic*, to distinguish from the carefully designed and engineered "synthetic" database and query system used today. The result of an organic query may not be as perfect as the result of an engineered query, but it has the benefit of not requiring precision and planning, and hence being more "natural" for most users. To be able to develop such an organic system, let us first study the precision and planning challenges that users face as they interact with databases.

2   Challenges

2.1   Structure Specification Challenge

Precise specification is challenging for users interacting with a database. Consider an airline database with a basic schema shown in Figure 1, for tracing planes and flights. The data encapsulated is starting location, destination, plane information, and times — essentially what every passenger thinks of as *a flight*. Yet, in our normalized relational representation, this single concept is recorded across four different tables. Such splattering of data decreases the usability of the database in terms of schema comprehension, join computation, and query expression.

First, given the large number of tables in a database, often with poorly named entities, it is usually not easy to understand how to locate a particular piece of data. Even in a toy schema such as Figure 1, there is the possibility of trouble. Obviously, the *airports* table has information about the starting location and the destination. To find what is used by a particular flight, we have to bring up the schema and follow the foreign key constraint, or trace the database creation statements. Neither solution is user-friendly, and thus the current solution is often to leave the task to DBAs.

The next problem users face is computing the joins. We break apart information during the database design phase such that everything is normalized — space efficient

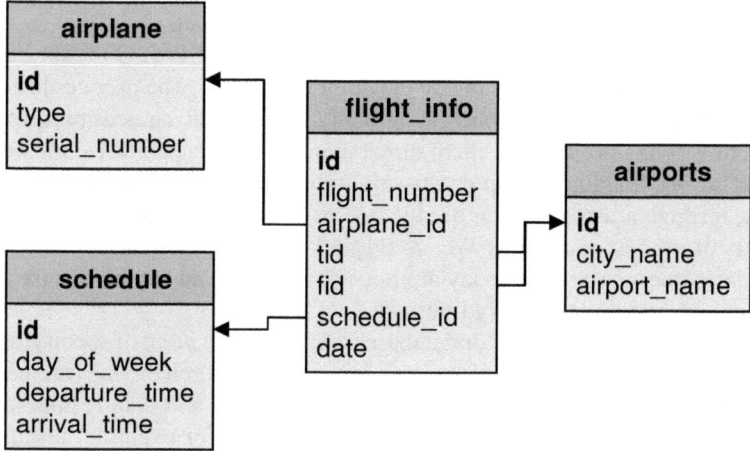

Fig. 1. The base tables needed to store a "flight". A flight contains from location, destination, airplane info and schedule, yet consists of at least four tables. Note that an actual schema for such data is likely to involve many more attributes and tables.

and amenable to updates. However, the users will have to stitch the information back together to answer most real queries. The fundamental issue is that joins destroy the connections between information pertaining to the same real world entities. Query specification is non-intuitive to most normal users in consequence. But even the design is brittle. What if a single flight has multiple flight numbers on account of code sharing? What about special flights not on a weekly schedule? There are any number of such unanticipated possibilities that could render a carefully designed structure inadequate instantly.

2.2   Remote Specification Challenge

Querying in its current form requires *prediction* on the part of the user. In our airline database example, consider the specification of a three letter airport code. Some interfaces provide a drop down list of all the cities that the airline flies into. For an airline of any size, this list can have hundreds of entries, most of which are not relevant to the user. The fact that it is alphabetized may not help — there may be multiple airports for some major cities, the airport may be named for a neighboring city, and so on.

A better interface allows a user to enter the name of the place they want to get to, and then looks for close matches. This cannot be a simple string comparison — we need Narita airport to be suggested no matter whether the user entered Narita or Tokyo or even Tokyu. This does not seem too hard, and some airline web sites will do this. But now consider a user who wants to visit Aizu. No airline search interface today, to our knowledge, can suggest flying into Narita airport in response to a search for Aizu airport even though that is likely to be the preferred solution for most travelers.

On account of difficulty in prediction, it is often the case that the user does not initially specify the query correctly. The user then has to revise her query and resubmit if it did not return desired results. However, essentially all query languages, including visual query builders, separate query specification from output.

Our goal is to enable users to query a database in a WYSIWYG (What You See Is What You Get) fashion. Consider the display of a world map. The user could zoom into the area of interest and select airports geographically from the choices presented. Most map databases today provide excellent direct manipulation capabilities, including pan, zoom, and so on. Imagine a map database without these facilities that requires users to specify, through a text selection of zip code or latitude/longitude, the portion of the map that is of interest each time. We would find it terribly frustrating. Unfortunately, most database query interfaces today are not WYSIWYG and can be compared to this hypothetical frustrating map query interface.

What does WYSIWYG mean for databases? After all, the point of specifying a query is to get information that the user does not possess. Even search engines are not WYSIWYG. A WYSIWYG interface for selection specification and data results involves a constant *predictive* capability on the part of the system. For example, instantaneous-response interfaces (56) allow users to gain insights into the schema and the data during query time, which allows the user to continuously refine the query *as they are typing the initial query*. By the time the user has typed out the entire query, the query has been correctly formulated and the results have returned. Furthermore, if the user then wishes to modify the query, this should be possible by direct manipulation of the result set rather than an *ab initio* restatement of the query.

2.3   Schema Evolution Challenge

While database systems have fully established themselves in the corporate market, they have not made a large impact on how users organize their everyday information. Many users would like to put into their databases (8) information such as shopping lists, expense reports, etc. The main reason for this is that creating a database is not easy.

Database systems require that the schema be specified in advance, and then populated with data. This burdens the user with developing an abstract design of the schema – without any concrete data – a task that we computer scientists are trained to do, but most others find very difficult. Furthermore, careful planning is required as users are expected to predict what data they will need to store in the future, and what queries they may ask, and use these predictions to develop a suitable schema.

Example 21. *Consider a user, Jane, who started to keep track of her shopping lists. The first list she created simply contained a list of items and quantities of each to be purchased. After the first shopping trip, Jane realized that she needed to add price information to the list to monitor her expenses and she also started marking items that were not in stock at the store. A week before Thanksgiving, Jane created another shopping list. However, this time, the items were gifts to her friends, and information about the friends therefore needed to be added to create this "gift list." A week after Christmas, Jane started to create another "gift list" to track gifts she received from her friends. However, the friends information were now about friends giving her gifts. In the end, what started as a simple list of items for Jane had become a repository of items, stores, and more importantly, friends — an important part of Jane's life.*

The above example, although simple, illustrates how an everyday database evolves and the many usability challenges facing a database system. First, users do not have a clear knowledge of what the final structure of the database will be and therefore a comprehensive design of the database is impossible at the beginning. For example, Jane did not know that she needed to keep track of information about her friends until the time had come to buy gifts for them. Second, the structure of the database grows as more information become available. For example, the information about price and out of stock only became available after the shopping trip. Finally, information structures may be heterogeneous. For example, the two "gift lists" that Jane created had different semantics in their friends information and the database needs to gracefully handle this heterogeneity.

In summary, for everyday data, the structure grows incrementally and a database system must provide interfaces for users to easily create both unstructured and structured information and to fluidly manipulate the structure when necessary.

3   Proposed Solution

3.1   Presentation Data Model

We propose the use of a *presentation* data model (36), as a full-fledged layer above the physical and logical layers in the database. Just as the logical layer provides data abstraction and saves the user from having to worry about physical data aspects such as data structures, indices, access methods, etc., the presentation layer saves the user from having to worry about logical data aspects such as relational structure, keys, joins, constraints, etc. To do this, the presentation layer should be able to represent data in a form most suited for the user to easily comprehend, manipulate and query.

3.2   Addressing Structure Specification Challenge

We address the structure specification challenge through the *qunit* search paradigm (57), where the database is translated into a collection of independent qunits, which can be treated as documents for standard IR-like document retrieval. A qunit is the basic, independent semantic unit of information in a database. It represents a quantified unit of information in response to a user's query. The database search problem then becomes one of choosing the most appropriate qunit(s) to return, in ranked order. Users only have to input keywords, which is much simpler than navigating complex database schema and specifying a structured query. In other words, the precision burden is lifted from the user. Consider the flight example in Figure 1. A qunit "flight" can be defined to represent the complete information of what a passenger thinks of as a flight. The qunit includes starting location, destination, plane, and time of travel. This completely relieves users from having to manually performing joins among all the tables. As a user inputs a search criterion, for example "from DTW to LAX, Jan. 2010", qunits are ranked based on the input and the best matches are presented to the user.

We now explain the definition of qunits over a database, and how to search based on qunits. We use a slightly more complex *IMDb* movie database in order to explain more effectively. Figure 2 (a) shows a simplified example schema of a movie database, which

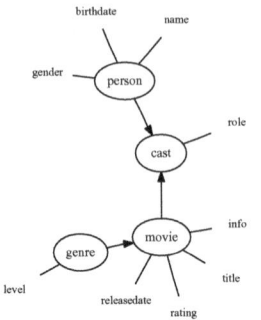

(a) An Simplified database schema

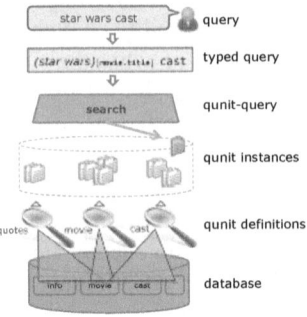

(b) Qunit Search on IMDb

Fig. 2. Qunit Example

contains entities such as movie, cast, person, etc. Qunits are defined over this database corresponding to various information needs. For example, we can define a qunit "cast", as the people associated with a movie. Meanwhile, rather than having the name of the movie repeated with each tuple, we may prefer to have a nested presentation with the movie title on top and one tuple for each cast member. The base data in IMDb is relational, and against its schema, we would write the base expression in SQL with the conversion expression in XSL-like markup as follows:

```
SELECT * FROM person, cast, movie
WHERE cast.movie_id = movie.id AND
cast.person_id = person.id AND
movie.title = "$x"
RETURN
<cast movie="$x">
<foreach:tuple>
<person>$person.name</person>
</foreach:tuple>
</cast>
```

The combination of these two expressions forms our qunit definition. On applying this definition to a database, we derive qunit instances, one per movie.

To search based on qunits, consider the user query, *star wars cast*, as shown in Figure 2 (b). Queries are first processed to identify entities using standard query segmentation techniques (73). In our case one high-ranking segmentation is "[movie.name] [cast]" and this has a very high overlap with the qunit definition that involves a join between "movie.name" and "cast". Now, standard IR techniques can be used to evaluate this query against qunit instances of the identified type; each considered independently even if they contain elements in common. The qunit instance describing the cast of the movie Star Wars is chosen as the appropriate result.

In current models of keyword search in databases, several heuristics are applied to leverage the database structure to construct a result on the fly. These heuristics are often based on the assumption that the structure within the database reflects the semantics assumed by the user (though data / link cardinality is not necessarily an evidence of importance), and that all structure is actually relevant towards ranking (though internal id fields are never really meant for search).

3.3 Addressing Schema Evolution Challenge

In this section we address the schema evolution challenge (Sec. 2.3) by proposing a technique for drag-and-drop modification of data schemas in the spreadsheet-like presentation model, enabling organic evolution of a schema and lifting the planning burden from the user. Consider the example of Jane's shopping list again. Figure 3 shows how Jane can organically grow the schema of the shopping list table. Initially, she has only columns for items to shop (Figure 3 (a)). She later tries to add information about friends to whom the gifts will be given, for instance, by adding a "name" column in "Shopping List". But now, Peter, a close friend of Jane, appears twice since both item Xbox and iPod will be given to him. As a result, Jane may think it makes more sense to group the gifts by person. Jane can do this by dragging the header of the name column and dropping it on the lower edge of the "Shopping List" (Figure 3 (b)). This makes the name attribute a level up; the rest of the columns forms a sub-relation "Gift" (shown in Figure 3 (c)). Now Jane can feel free to add new information, such as an attribute "address", for her friends without worrying that these information would be duplicated (Figure 3 (d)). This process shows how effortless it is for Jane to grow the table about shopping items to include information about friends and structure the table as she desires.

Shopping List			
Item	Quantity	Price	In Stock
Xbox	1	300	N
Swarovski	1	200	Y
iPod	2	180	Y

(a) Initial Shopping List

Shopping List				Name
Item	Quantity	Price	In Stock	Name
Xbox	1	300	N	Peter
Swarovski	1	200	Y	Cathy
iPod	2	180	Y	Peter

(b) Moving Name Column

Name	Shopping List			
	Gift			
	Item	Quantity	Price	In Stock
Peter	iPod	2	180	Y
	Xbox	1	300	N
Cathy	Swarovski	1	200	Y

(c) After Moving Name Column

Name	Address	Shopping List			
		Gift			
		Item	Quantity	Price	In Stock
Peter	2364 Plymouth	iPod	2	180	Y
		Xbox	1	300	N
Cathy	1056 Bishop	Swarovski	1	200	Y

(d) Adding Address Column

Fig. 3. Organic Schema Evolution

Next, we briefly outline the challenges in building a system such as this, and our plans to tackle these challenges.

Specification: Specifying a schema update as in Figure 3 is challenging using existing tools. For example, using conventional spreadsheet software, it is impossible to arrive at a hierarchical schema as shown in Figure 3 (d). To specify the schema update, one has to split the table manually. Alternatively, using a relational DBMS, one has to set up the cross-table relationship, which is not easy for end-users, even with support from GUI tools.

We show how to use a *presentation layer* to address the specification challenge. We design the presentation layer based on a next-generation spreadsheet and it supports easy schema creation and modification through a simple drag-and-drop interface. We call such a spreadsheet *span table* because it is presented in such a way that both table headers and data fields can span multiple cells. The presentation supports four key operations: move an attribute to be part of a sub-relation (e.g., we can move the "Name" column back to "Gift" in Figure 3 (d)), move an attribute out of a sub-relation (the converse of the previous one), create a intermediate sub-relation by moving an attribute *up* one layer (e.g., Jane moves "Name" out to create a new sub-relation under "Shopping List" as in Figure 3 (b)) or *down* a layer (e.g., moving "In Stock" down deepens it by inserting a new immediate level, with only "In Stock" in it; Jane can later add new columns such as "Date" to indicate the timestamp of stocking information).

Data Migration: Once a new schema is specified, there is still a critical task of migrating existing data to the new schema. Because the schema structure is changed, one has to introduce a complex mapping in order to "fit" the old data into the new schema. Even if spreadsheet software supporting hierarchical schema is provided, the user may still have to manually copy data in a cell-by-cell manner to perform such mapping, which is extremely time-consuming and error-prone.

We address this challenge with an *algebraic layer*. Directly below the presentation layer, the algebraic layer must translate drag-and-drops into operations that modify the basic structure of the span table. For this purpose, we have proposed a novel *span table algebra* consisted of three sets of operations. The first set, schema restructuring operators, corresponds to the four aforementioned operations in the presentation layer. We also have a second set of schema modification operators for adding/dropping columns in any sub-relations. Finally, there is a set of data manipulation operators (insert, delete, and update), which extends traditional data edit to our hierarchical presentation. This algebraic layer completely automates the data migration as soon as the the schema modification is performed.

Data Integrity: Expressing and understanding integrity constraints is central to schema design, and thus also critical for an organic database where schema is continuously evolved. Functional dependencies (FD) are often used in database design to add semantics to schemas and to assert integrity constraints for data.

Nested functional dependencies have been studied extensively in the past (32). However, CRIUS presents some new challenges due to its user-centric support for data and schema modification. When a user updates data, or modifies the schema, it is important to understand how the update affects existing dependencies so that we can communicate this information back to the user, and optionally take steps to resolve any resulting inconsistencies.

For this challenge, we consider two specific operations: data value updates and schema updates. For the former case, we show how data value updates and integrity constraints interfere with each other and how we may take advantage of such inference to guide user data entry from a set of appropriately maintained FDs. Specifically, we feature autocompletion for qualified data entry and provide a contextual menu to alert the user each time she issues an update that violates a given FD, in order to preserve data integrity. For schema updates, our hypothesis is that for each schema update operation there is a way to "rewrite" involved FDs to preserve their validity. Precisely how to rewrite the schema is described in detail in (62).

Performance: Schema evolution is usually a heavy-weight operation in traditional database systems. It is not unusual for a commercial database to take days to complete the maintenance required after schema evolution. IT organizations carefully plan schema changes, and make them only infrequently. In contrast, everyday users are unlikely to plan carefully. We would like to develop techniques that support quick schema evolution without giving up on any of the other desirable features.

We address performance challenge with a *storage layer* to implement a practical means of actually storing the data. Conventionally, database systems have been designed with the goal of optimizing query processing. However, schema modifications (e.g., ALTER TABLE) are often time-consuming, heavy-weight operations in current systems. We utilize a vertically partitioned format for the storage layer. Our goal is to significantly reduce the performance penalty incurred due to schema modifications at a very modest cost of overhead in query processing.

Understanding Schema Evolution: When a schema has evolved over an extended period of time, it is difficult for a user to keep track of the changes. A natural need is to concisely convey to the user *how* a database has been evolving. For example, the user may query the relationship between columns in the initial schema and the final schema and how the transformation from old columns to new ones took place over time. We want to show users the gradual organic changes rather than a sudden transformation. We could keep track of all the changes step by step, which requires all changes to be maintained. If such information is not available, which is frequently the case when the user looks at external data sources, we seek to automatically discover such evolution from the data. Challenges involve mining conceptual changes from large amounts of changes to the database (e.g. Inferring the splitting of every "Name" column in each table to two "First Name" and "Last Name" columns, followed by a normalization of the names into a single table). Mining such inferences can be done using either just the data, or a combination of the data and provenance information.

4   Related Work

Database usability started to receive attention more than 25 years ago (23) and gained more momentum lately (36). Research in database usability has been mainly focusing on innovative and effective query interface design, including visual, text (i.e., keyword), natural language interfaces, direct manipulation interfaces, and spreadsheet interfaces.

Visual Interfaces: Query By Example (79), which is the first study on building a query interface not based on a database query language, allows users to implicitly construct queries by identifying examples of desired data elements. This work is followed more recently by QBT (65), Kaleidoquery (55), VISIONARY (9), MIX (54), Xing (27), and XQBE (13). Alternatively, forms-based query interface design has also been receiving attention. Early works on such interfaces include (26; 20), which provide users with visual tools to frame queries and to perform tasks such as database design and view definition. This direction is more recently followed by GRIDS (64) and Acuity (68), and, in XML database systems, by FoXQ (1), EquiX (21), QURSED (60). Adaptive form construction is studied in DRIVE (53), which enables runtime context-sensitive interface editing for object-oriented databases, and in (38), which studies how forms can be automatically designed and constructed based on past query history. Recent work by Jayapandian and Jagadish proposes techniques for automatic construction of forms based on database schema and data (39) and expressive form customization (40).

Text Interfaces: The success of Information Retrieval (IR) style (i.e., keyword based) search among ordinary users has prompted database researcher to study a similar search interface for database systems. The goal is to maintain the simplicity of the search and exploit not only the textual content of the tuples, but also the structures within and across tuples to rank the results in a way that is more effective than the traditional IR-style ranking mechanism. For relational databases, this approach is first studied by Goldman et. al. in (28) and followed by many systems, including DBXplorer (2), BANKS (10), DISCOVER (34), and ObjectRank (7). For XML databases, the inherently more complicated structure within the database content allows the researchers to explore query languages ranging from pure keywords and approximate structural query, and has led to various projects including XSEarch (22), XRANK (29), JuruXML (16), FlexPath (5), Schema-Free XQuery (48), and Meaningful Summary Query (77). A more recent trend in keyword-based search is to analyze a keyword query and automatically discover the hidden semantic structures that the query carries. This trend has influenced the design of projects for both traditional database search (41) and web search (51).

Natural Language Interfaces: Constructing a natural language interface to databases has a long history (6). In particular, (66) analyzed the expressive power of a declarative query language (SEQUEL) in comparison to natural language. Most recently, NaLIX (47) proposed a generic natural language interface to XML database, which is capable of adapting to multiple domains through user feedbacks. However, to this day, natural language understanding is still an extremely difficult problem, and current systems tend to be unreliable or unable to answer questions outside a few predefined narrow domains (61).

Direct Manipulation Interfaces: Direct manipulation (67), although a crucial concept in the user interface field, is seldom mentioned in database literature. Pasta-3 (46) is one of the earliest efforts attempting a direct manipulation interface for databases, but its support of direct manipulation is limited to allowing users to manipulate *a query expression* with clicks and drags. Tioga-2 (4) (later developed into DataSplash (58)) is a direct manipulation database visualization tool, and its visual query language allows specification with a drag-and-drop interface. Its emphasis, however, is on visualization instead of querying. Recent work by Liu and Jagadish (50) develops a direct manipulation query interface based on an spreadsheet algebra.

Spreadsheet Interface: Spreadsheets have proven to be one of the most user-friendly and popular interfaces for handling data, partially evidenced by the ubiquity of Microsoft Excel. FOCUS (71) provides an interface for manipulating local tables. Its query operations are quite simple (e.g., allowing only one level of grouping and being highly restrictive on the form of query conditions). Tableau (30), which is built on VizQL (31), specializes in interactive data visualization and is limited in querying capability. Spreadsheets have also been used for data cleaning (63), logic programming (70), visualization exploration (37), and photo management (43). Witkowski et al (75) proposed SQL extensions supporting spreadsheet-like computations in RDBMS.

Query interface is just one aspect of database usability, there are many other research fields that have direct or indirect impacts on the usability of databases, which we briefly describe below.

Personalization: Studies in this field attempt to customize database systems for each individual user and therefore making them easier to explore and extract information by the particular user, e.g., (24). In addition, studies have also been focusing on analyzing past query workloads to detect the user interests and provide better results tuned to those interests, e.g., (45; 19; 35). It is also worth noting that the notion of personalization has also found interest in the information retrieval community, where the ranking of search results is biased using a certain personalized metric (33; 42).

Automatic Database Management: To alleviate the burden on database administrators, commercial database systems come with a suite of auxiliary tools. The AutoAdmin project (3; 18) at Microsoft, initiated by Surajit Chaudhuri and his colleagues, makes great strides with respect to many aspects of database configuration including physical design and index tuning. Similarly, the Autonomic Computing project (49; 52) at IBM provides a platform to tune a database system, including query optimization. However, none of these projects deal with the user-level database usability that is the focus of this proposal.

Database Schema Design: This has been studied extensively (11; 76; 12; 59). There is a great deal of work on defining a good schema, both from the perspective of capturing real-life requirements (e.g., normalization) and supporting efficient queries. However, schema design has typically been considered a heavyweight, one-time operation, which is done by a technically skilled database administrator, based on careful requirements analysis and planning. The new challenge of enabling non-expert user to "give birth" to a database schema was posed recently (36), but no solution was provided.

Usability Study in Other Systems: Usability of information retrieval systems was studied in (72; 78), which analyzed usability errors and design flaws, and also in (25), which performed a comparison of usability testing methods. Principles of user-centered design were introduced in (44; 74), including how they could complement software engineering techniques to create interactive systems. Incorporating usability into the evaluation of computer systems was first studied in (14). An extensive user study was performed in (17) to identify the reasons for user frustration in computing experiences, while (15) takes a more formal approach to model user behavior for usability analysis. There is also a recent move in the software systems community to conduct serious user studies (69). However, for database systems in particular, these only scratch the surface of what needs to be done to improve usability.

References

[1] Abraham, R.: FoXQ - XQuery by forms. In: IEEE Symposium on Human Centric Computing Languages and Environments (2003)
[2] Agrawal, S., Chaudhuri, S., Das, G.: DBXplorer: A System for Keyword-Based Search over
Relational Databases. In: ICDE (2002)
[3] Agrawal, S., Chaudhuri, S., Kollar, L., Marathe, A., Narasayya, V., Syamala, M.: Database
Tuning Advisor for Microsoft SQL Server 2005. In: VLDB (2004)
[4] Aiken, A., Chen, J., Stonebraker, M., Woodruff, A.: Tioga-2: A direct manipulation database
visualization environment. In: ICDE, pp. 208–217 (1996)
[5] Amer-Yahia, S., Lakshmanan, L.V.S., Pandit, S.: FleXPath: Flexible Structure and Full-Text
Querying for XML. In: SIGMOD (2004)
[6] Androutsopoulos, I., Ritchie, G., Thanisch, P.: Natural Language Interfaces to Databases–an
introduction. Journal of Language Engineering 1(1), 29–81 (1995)
[7] Balmin, A., Hristidis, V., Papakonstantinou, Y.: ObjectRank: Authority-Based Keyword
Search in Databases. In: VLDB (2004)
[8] Bell, G., Gemmell, J.: A Digital Life (2007)
[9] Benzi, F., Maio, D., Rizzi, S.: Visionary: A Viewpoint-based Visual Language for Querying
Relational Databases. Journal of Visual Languages and Computing 10(2) (1999)
[10] Bhalotia, G., Hulgeri, A., Nakhe, C., Chakrabarti, S., Sudarshan, S.: Keyword Searching
and Browsing in Databases using BANKS. In: ICDE (2002)
[11] Biskup, J.: Achievements of Relational Database Schema Design Theory Revisited. In:
Thalheim, B. (ed.) Semantics in Databases 1995. LNCS, vol. 1358, pp. 29–54. Springer,
Heidelberg (1998)
[12] Biskup, J.: Achievements of Relational Database Schema Design Theory Revisited. In:
Thalheim, B. (ed.) Semantics in Databases 1995. LNCS, vol. 1358, pp. 29–54. Springer,
Heidelberg (1998)
[13] Braga, D., Campi, A., Ceri, S.: *XQBE (XQuery By Example)*: A Visual Interface to the
Standard XML Query Language. ACM Trans. Database Syst. 30(2) (2005)
[14] Brown, A.B., Chung, L.C., Patterson, D.A.: Including the Human Factor in Dependability
Benchmarks. In: DSN Workshop on Dependability Benchmarking (2002)
[15] Butterworth, R., Blandford, A., Duke, D.: Using Formal Models to Explore Display-Based
Usability Issues. Journal of Visual Languages and Computing 10(5) (1999)
[16] Carmel, D., Maarek, Y.S., Mandelbrod, M., Mass, Y., Soffer, A.: Searching XML Documents via XML Fragments. In: SIGIR (2003)
[17] Ceaparu, I., Lazar, J., Bessiere, K., Robinson, J., Shneiderman, B.: Determining Causes
and Severity of End-User Frustration. International Journal of Human Computer Interaction 17(3) (2004)
[18] Chaudhuri, S., Weikum, G.: Rethinking Database System Architecture: Towards a Self-
Tuning, RISC-style Database System. In: VLDB (2000)
[19] Chen, Z., Li, T.: Addressing Diverse User Preferences in SQL-Query-Result Navigation.
In: SIGMOD (2007)
[20] Choobineh, J., Mannino, M.V., Tseng, V.P.: A Form-Based Approach for Database Analysis
and Design. CACM 35(2) (1992)
[21] Cohen, S., Kanza, Y., Kogan, Y., Sagiv, Y., Nutt, W., Serebrenik, A.: EquiX–A Search and
Query Language for XML. JASIST 53(6) (2002)
[22] Cohen, S., Mamou, J., Kanza, Y., Sagiv, Y.: XSEarch: A Semantic Search Engine for XML.
In: VLDB (2003)

[23] Date, C.J.: Database Usability. In: SIGMOD. ACM Press, New York (1983)
[24] Dong, X., Halevy, A.: A Platform for Personal Information Management and Integration. In: CIDR (2005)
[25] Doubleday, A., Ryan, M., Springett, M., Sutcliffe, A.: A Comparison of Usability Techniques for Evaluating Design. In: DIS (1997)
[26] Embley, D.W.: NFQL: The Natural Forms Query Language. ACM Trans. Database Syst. (1989)
[27] Erwig, M.: A Visual Language for XML. In: IEEE Symposium on Visual Languages,
[28] Goldman, R., Shivakumar, N., Venkatasubramanian, S., Garcia-Molina, H.: Proximity Search in Databases. In: VLDB (1998)
[29] Guo, L., Shao, F., Botev, C., Shanmugasundaram, J.: XRANK: Ranked Keyword Search over XML Documents. In: SIGMOD (2003)
[30] Hanrahan, P.: VizQL: A Language for Query, Analysis and Visualization. In: SIGMOD, pp. 721–721 (2006)
[31] Hanrahan, P.: Vizql: a language for query, analysis and visualization. In: SIGMOD, p. 721 (2006)
[32] Hara, C., Davidson, S.: Reasoning about nested functional dependencies. In: PODS (1999)
[33] Haveliwala, T.: Topic-Sensitive PageRank: A Context-Sensitive Ranking Algorithm for Web Search. IEEE Transactions on Knowledge and Data Engineering 15(4), 784–796 (2003)
[34] Hristidis, V., Papakonstantinou, Y.: DISCOVER: Keyword Search in Relational Databases. In: VLDB (2002)
[35] Ioannidis, Y.E., Viglas, S.: Conversational Querying. Inf. Syst. 31(1), 33–56 (2006)
[36] Jagadish, H.V., Chapman, A., Elkiss, A., Jayapandian, M., Li, Y., Nandi, A., Yu, C.: Making database systems usable. In: SIGMOD (2007)
[37] Jankun-Kelly, T.J., Ma, K.-L.: A spreadsheet interface for visualization exploration. In: IEEE Visualization, pp. 69–76 (2000)
[38] Jayapandian, M., Jagadish, H.V.: Automating the Design and Construction of Query Forms. In: ICDE (2006)
[39] Jayapandian, M., Jagadish, H.V.: Automated creation of a forms-based database query interface. In: VLDB (2008)
[40] Jayapandian, M., Jagadish, H.V.: Expressive query specification through form customization. In: EDBT (2008)
[41] Jayram, T.S., Krishnamurthy, R., Raghavan, S., Vaithyanathan, S., Zhu, H.: Avatar Information Extraction System. IEEE Data Eng. Bull. 29(1), 40–48 (2006)
[42] Jeh, G., Widom, J.: Scaling Personalized Web Search. In: WWW, pp. 271–279 (2003)
[43] Kandel, S., Paepcke, A., Theobald, M., Garcia-Molina, H.: The photospread query language. Technical report, Stanford Univ. (2007)
[44] Kelley, J.F.: An Iterative Design Methodology for User-Friendly Natural Language Office Information Applications. ACM Trans. Database Syst. 2(1) (1984)
[45] Koutrika, G., Ioannidis, Y.: Personalization of Queries in Database Systems. In: ICDE (2004)
[46] Kuntz, M., Melchert, R.: Pasta-3's graphical query language: Direct manipulation, cooperative queries, full expressive power. In: VLDB, pp. 97–105 (1989)
[47] Li, Y., Yang, H., Jagadish, H.V.: NaLIX: A Generic Natural Language Search Environment for XML Data. ACM Transactions on Database Systems-TODS 32(4) (2007)
[48] Li, Y., Yu, C., Jagadish, H.V.: Enabling Schema-Free XQuery with Meaningful Query Focus. VLDB Journal (in press)

[49] Lightstone, S., Lohman, G.M., Haas, P.J., et al.: Making DB2 Products Self-Managing: Strategies and Experiences. IEEE Data Eng. Bull. 29(3), 16–23 (2006)

[50] Liu, B., Jagadish, H.V.: A spreadsheet algebra for a direct data manipulation query interface. In: ICDE (2009)

[51] Madhavan, J., Jeffery, S., Cohen, S., Dong, X., Ko, D., Yu, C., Halevy, A.: Web-scale Data Integration: You Can Only Afford to Pay As You Go. In: CIDR (2007)

[52] Markl, V., Lohman, G.M., Raman, V.: LEO: An Autonomic Query Optimizer for DB2. IBM Systems Journal 42(1), 98–106 (2003)

[53] Mitchell, K., Kennedy, J.: DRIVE: An Environment for the Organized Construction of User-Interfaces to Databases. In: Interfaces to Databases, IDS-3 (1996)

[54] Mukhopadhyay, P., Papakonstantinou, Y.: Mixing Querying and Navigation in MIX. In: ICDE (2002)

[55] Murray, N., Paton, N., Goble, C.: Kaleidoquery: A Visual Query Language for Object Databases. In: Advanced Visual Interfaces (1998)

[56] Nandi, A., Jagadish, H.V.: Assisted Querying using Instant-Response Interfaces. In: SIGMOD (2007)

[57] Nandi, A., Jagadish, H.V.: Qunits: queried units for database search. In: CIDR (2009)

[58] Olston, C., Woodruff, A., Aiken, A., Chu, M., Ercegovac, V., Lin, M., Spalding, M., Stonebraker, M.: Datasplash. In: SIGMOD, pp. 550–552 (1998)

[59] Papadomanolakis, E., Ailamaki, A.: Autopart: Automating schema design for large scientific databases using data partitioning. In: SSDBM (2004)

[60] Papakonstantinou, Y., Petropoulos, M., Vassalos, V.: QURSED: Querying and Reporting Semistructured Data. In: SIGMOD (2002)

[61] Popescu, A.-M., Etzioni, O., Kautz, H.A.: Towards a Theory of Natural Language Interfaces to Databases. In: IUI (2003)

[62] Qian, L., LeFevre, K., Jagadish, H.V.: Crius: User-friendly database design. PVLDB 4(2), 81–92 (2010)

[63] Raman, V., Hellerstein, J.M.: Potter's wheel: An interactive data cleaning system. In: VLDB, pp. 381–390 (2001)

[64] Sabin, R.E., Yap, T.K.: Integrating Information Retrieval Techniques with Traditional DB Methods in a Web-Based Database Browser. In: SAC (1998)

[65] Sengupta, A., Dillon, A.: Query by Templates: A Generalized Approach for Visual Query Formulation for Text Dominated Databases. In: ADL (1997)

[66] Sheneiderman, B.: Improving the Human Factors Aspect of Database Interactions. ACM Trans. Database Syst. 3(4) (1978)

[67] Shneiderman, B.: The future of interactive systems and the emergence of direct manipulation. Behaviour & Information Technology 1(3), 237–256 (1982)

[68] Sinha, S., Bowers, K., Mamrak, S.A.: Accessing a Medical Database using WWW-Based User Interfaces. Technical report, Ohio State University (1998)

[69] Soules, C., Shah, S., Ganger, G.R., Noble, B.D.: It's Time to Bite the User Study Bullet. Technical report, University of Michigan (2007)

[70] Spenke, M., Beilken, C.: A spreadsheet interface for logic programming. In: CHI, pp. 75–80 (1989)

[71] Spenke, M., Beilken, C., Berlage, T.: Focus: The interactive table for product comparison and selection. In: UIST, pp. 41–50 (1996)

[72] Sutcliffe, A., Ryan, M., Doubleday, A., Springett, M.: Model Mismatch Analysis: Towards a Deeper Explanation of Users' Usability Problems. Behavior & Information Technology 19(1) (2000)

[73] Tan, B., Peng, F.: Unsupervised query segmentation using generative language models and wikipedia. In: WWW (2008)

[74] Wasserman, A.I.: User Software Engineering and the Design of Interactive Systems. In: ICSE. IEEE Press, Piscataway (1981)

[75] Witkowski, A., Bellamkonda, S., Bozkaya, T., Dorman, G., Folkert, N., Gupta, A., Sheng, L., Subramanian, S.: Spreadsheets in rdbms for olap. In: SIGMOD (2003)

[76] Wong, S.K.M., Butz, C.J., Xiang, Y.: Automated database schema design using mined data dependencies. Journal of the American Society for Information Science 49, 455–470 (1998)

[77] Yu, C., Jagadish, H.V.: Querying Complex Structured Databases. In: VLDB (2007)

[78] Yuan, W.: End-User Searching Behavior in Information Retrieval: A Longitudinal Study. JASIST 48(3) (1997)

[79] Zloof, M.M.: Query-by-Example: the Invocation and Definition of Tables and Forms. In: VLDB (1975)

Crowd-Based Data Sourcing
(Abstract)

Tova Milo⋆

School of Computer Science,
Tel Aviv University,
Tel Aviv,
Israel
milo@cs.tau.ac.il

1 Introduction

Harnessing a crowd of Web users for the collection of mass data has recently become a wide-spread phenomenon [9]. *Wikipedia* [20] is probably the earliest and best known example of crowd-sourced data and an illustration of what can be achieved with a crowd-based data sourcing model. Other examples include social tagging systems for images, which harness millions of Web users to build searchable databases of tagged images; traffic information aggregators like *Waze* [17]; and hotel and movie ratings like *TripAdvisor* [19] and *IMDb* [18].

A primary advantage of crowd-based data sourcing is the ability to reach and engage a broader intelligence pool. In the Internet era, this has a great potential of generating information repositories that are otherwise very difficult to construct and for identifying new unforseen solutions and products. The potential for cost-savings associated with crowd data sourcing also provides attractive procurement alternatives to companies bound to tight budgets, particularly during economic downturns.

Yet despite some success stories like the ones mentioned above, the actual realization of the promising advantages from crowd data sourcing are still far from being well-achieved. This comes notably from the difficulty of managing huge volumes of data and users of questionable, ever changing, quality and reliability. Every single initiative built around this concept had to battle - almost from scratch - the same non-trivial challenges. The ad hoc solutions found, even when successful, are application specific and rarely sharable.

To pave the road for successful crowd-based data sourcing, there is a need to develop sound scientific foundations for the management of crowd-sourced data [12,13,7]. We believe that such a principled approach is essential to obtain knowledge of superior quality, to realize the task more effectively and automatically, be able to reuse solutions, and thereby to accelerate the pace of practical adoption of this new technology that is revolutionizing our life. We briefly describe here the requirements from such a model and the research advances that have been

⋆ This research was partially supported by the Israel Science Foundation and the US-Israel Binational Science Foundation.

S. Kikuchi et al. (Eds.): DNIS 2011, LNCS 7108, pp. 64–67, 2011.

done so far in this direction at the Tel-Aviv Databases group [5,4,3]. We sketch below a formal model that we developed for capturing diverse facets of crowd-sourced data. We also describe the reasoning capabilities that are required for managing and controlling data sourcing, cleaning, verification and querying.

2   Declarative Management of Crowed-Sourced Data

To illustrate the main ideas underlying our proposed framework, let us consider one common technique for attracting the crowd to contribute useful facts, namely *games* [16,11]. In the internet era, such techniques have the potential of generating large databases of facts, that is otherwise very difficult to construct. However, the design of games that fulfill this potential is not an easy task, and involves significant challenges. Consider for instance a Web *Trivia* game where user answers to questions are used to create a database of facts in some topic. For instance of capital cities, contributed independently by various Web users. The players are presented with questions on capital cities, and their answers are added to the database. This database can in turn be used to answer queries posed by (a possibly different set of) users. The problem is that some of the facts contributed by users may be wrong, and some may be contradicting, for example two different users claiming different cities to be the capital of England.

Even in this simple settings, several dilemmas arise in designing the data layer of the game: for instance, how to choose the questions that the game poses to users so as to maximize the expected knowledge gain? Which users to pose these questions to? How to settle contradictions in the database when answering queries?

For each of these questions, hard-coded solutions can be employed. But no single solution is guaranteed to always achieve superior results, and the quality of results also depends on the type of data set in hand; and as always, hard-coded solutions are inflexible, hard to adapt and deploy. In contrast, it is desirable to use a *declarative framework for the data layer of crowdsourcing games (and more generally for crowd-sourced data collection and management) which allows for rapid adjustments, modification and optimization.* The development of such framework is our goal. We stress here that we focus on the *data layer* of games. The full design of games involves many additional important issues such as GUI, communication layer and others, that are outside of the scope of the present work.

One may consider using standard declarative data management frameworks for this task. However, as we next observe, practical techniques in this context encounter difficulties that are difficult to address with current frameworks. One such difficulty lies in the *uncertainty* on which data items are correct; this uncertainty is due to the lack of an authoritative opinion, and it is common to capture it with *probabilities*. A related difficulty is due to the *recursive* dependencies between the above two challenges: to identify the questions that should be posed to users, we must first know which data pieces are correct, which require validation, and which are completely missing. On the other hand, in order to know how the data should be cleaned, we need to know which users can be trusted, this depending on their contribution (correct and incorrect) to the aggregated data set introduced into the system.

For instance, one possible solution is based on a set of probabilistic, Pagerank-style rules. A first such rule may randomly decide in which fact to believe, using a distribution that is based upon the credibility of these two users. The credibility of users can then be updated accordingly, via a second rule: for instance, users that supported this fact may now be considered more credible. We may again choose in which facts to believe, based on these new calculated credibility scores, etc. The results of these recursive process can be used for the different tasks listed above. The believed answers can be used to answer queries; the computed credibility of users can be used to identify users that should be asked to gain information; and the questions that they will be asked correspond to facts with high level of uncertainty (close to 50%).

This is only one possible solution, and there are many plausible others. In particular, for settling contradictions, many approaches been proposed in the literature in the context of *data cleaning* [14,1,8,2]. For example, a simple approach decides between two contradicting facts according to their support [14]; another approach suggests the application of "transformation" rules [1] that fix parts of the data. [2] presents a technique to solve key violations using probabilistic choice over possible Database repairs. A recent paper [8] suggests to gradually clean data based on "corroboration", i.e. the trust the system has in the users providing it. This is in fact a non-probabilistic (yet recursive) variant of the PageRank-style policy depicted above. Similarly, the choice of questions to ask users may be based on facts with low entropy, and the users to which these question are posed may be those that gained high credibility in related facts (rather than overall high credibility).

So, we have observed that *recursion and probabilistic data lie at the core of the developed techniques*. However, current declarative frameworks (e.g. [10]) either support only probabilistic rules, or only recursion, but *not both*. Consequently, the development of a novel framework is required. We next briefly explain the principles underlying the one that we propose.

Our framework (described formally in [4,5]) suggests an interface that is based on SQL, but is augmented by a particular operator that allows to introduce probabilities, and supports recursive rule invocation. This syntax allows for a very easy implementation of the various tasks described above. The underlying model is that of *Markov Chain Monte Carlo* (MCMC) [15]. The idea is that we are given probabilistic rules and a query on the data. The former defines probabilistic transitions between possible Database instances, serving as states of the Markov Chain. The query possible results are *sampled* (hence the Monte Carlo algorithm) in each database instance that is defined by the rules to be clean. The output is a set of tuples that appeared in the query results, each accompanied with a probability that intuitively reflects the fraction of its appearance in the observed samples. As it turns out, this provides an expressive and flexible framework to easily capture, declaratively, data cleaning/question selection/answer scoring policies [4].

Several practical issues rise in the development of the framework. In order for the question answering mechanism to be practical, it must return its answers to users in split seconds; However, naturally, running the above sampling algorithm requires much more time to run in practical cases. Therefore, a further effort is thus required for designing preemptive computations that are done in offline and significantly shorten the run-time performance. While we have made some initial advances in this direction [4] much effort is still required and we believe this to be an exiting future research direction.

References

1. Arasu, A., Chaudhuri, S., Kaushik, R.: Learning string transformations from examples. PVLDB 2(1) (2009)
2. Beskales, G., Ilyas, I.F., Golab, L.: Sampling the repairs of functional dependency violations under hard constraints. In: VLDB 2010 (2010)
3. Boim, R., Greenshpan, O., Milo, T., Novgorodov, S., Polyzotis, N., Tan, W.: Asking the Right Questions in Crowd Data Sourcing. To appear in ICDE (2012)
4. Deutch, D., Greenshpan, O., Kostenko, B., Milo, T.: Using markov chain monte carlo to play trivia. In: ICDE, pp. 1308–1311 (2011)
5. Deutch, D., Koch, C., Milo, T.: On probabilistic fixpoint and Markov chain query languages. In: PODS, pp. 215–226 (2010)
6. Dekel, O., Shamir, O.: Vox populi: Collecting high-quality labels from a crowd. In: COLT (2009)
7. Franklin, M.J., Kossmann, D., Kraska, T., Ramesh, S., Xin, R.: Crowddb: answering queries with crowdsourcing. In: SIGMOD (2011)
8. Galland, A., Abiteboul, S., Marian, A., Senellart, P.: Corroborating information from disagreeing views. In: WSDM 2010 (2010)
9. Howe, J.: The rise of crowdsourcing. Wired Magazine - Issue 14.06 (June 2006)
10. Jampani, R., Xu, F., Wu, M., Perez, L.L., Jermaine, C., Haas, P.J.: Mcdb: a monte carlo approach to managing uncertain data. In: SIGMOD 2008 (2008)
11. Ma, H., Chandrasekar, R., Quirk, C., Gupta, A.: Improving search engines using human computation games. In: CIKM 2009 (2009)
12. Parameswaran, A.G., Polyzotis, N.: Answering queries using humans, algorithms and databases. In: CIDR, pp. 160–166 (2011)
13. Parameswaran, A.G., Das Sarma, A., Garcia-Molina, H., Polyzotis, N., Widom, J.: Human-assisted graph search: it's okay to ask questions. PVLDB 4(5), 267–278 (2011)
14. Su, Q., Pavlov, D., Chow, J.-H., Baker, W.C.: Internet-scale collection of human-reviewed data. In: WWW 2007 (2007)
15. Robert, C.P., Casella, G.: Monte Carlo Statistical Methods. Springer Texts in Statistics. Springer, Heidelberg (2005)
16. von Ahn, L., Dabbish, L.: Designing games with a purpose. Commun. ACM 51(8), 58–67 (2008)
17. Free GPS Navigation with Turn by Turn - Waze, http://www.waze.com/
18. The Internet Movie Database (IMDb), http://www.imdb.com/
19. Tripadvisor, http://www.tripadvisor.com/
20. Wikiepdia, http://www.wikipedia.org/

Behavior Capture with Acting Graph: A Knowledgebase for a Game AI System

Maxim Mozgovoy[1,*] and Iskander Umarov[2]

[1] University of Aizu, Tsuruga, Ikki-machi, Aizu-Wakamatsu, Fukushima, 965-8580 Japan
mozgovoy@u-aizu.ac.jp
[2] TruSoft Int'l Inc., 204 37th Ave. N #133, St. Petersburg, FL 33704 USA
umarov@trusoft.com

Abstract. Behavior capture is a popular experimental approach used to obtain human-like AI-controlled game characters through learning by observation and case-based reasoning. One of the challenges related to the development of behavior capture-based AI is the choice of appropriate data structure for agents' memory. In this paper, we consider the advantages of *acting graph* as a memory model and discuss related techniques, successfully applied in several experimental projects, dedicated to the creation of human-like behavior.

Keywords: Behavior capture, learning by observation, case-based reasoning, knowledge representation.

1 Building Believable Game Characters with Behavior Capture

1.1 Believable Behavior: A Key Feature of Game AI

Modern computer games and simulation-and-training applications are often characterized as "virtual worlds". This name emphasizes the growing complexity of game/simulation environments that are able to create higher sense of immersion than ever. This is done not only through hi-quality audiovisual technologies and detailed interactive physical models, but also with the help of modern AI methods.

Many virtual worlds are inhabited both by human-controlled characters and AI agents that serve as world's neutral "native population", allies or enemies. For example, in Unreal Tournament game (Deathmatch mode), independent players try to kill each other in a 3D map, and each player can be controlled either by human or by a computer (in this case it is usually called "a bot"). In general, computer-controlled characters are found in a variety of video games and training simulators. A good example of such simulator (or a "serious game") that involves computer-controlled opponents is Virtual Battle Space 2. This software is a variation of 3D world, specially designed for initial training of soldiers, and includes numerous training scenarios, ranging from vehicle driving in dangerous conditions and team combat to cultural-aware interaction with local population [1, 2].

---

* Supported in part by the Fukushima Prefectural Foundation, Project F-23-1, FY2011.

S. Kikuchi et al. (Eds.): DNIS 2011, LNCS 7108, pp. 68–77, 2011.

Detailed and realistic virtual worlds set high demands on the quality of AI-controlled characters. Relatively simple game environments provide limited acting options for an AI engine, so handcrafted finite-state machine-based scripted decision making systems usually work well. Complex virtual worlds allow computer-controlled agents to exhibit complex behavior patterns, thus making the design of realistic human-like AI behavior an increasingly difficult task.

This trend is well known to both academic researchers and game creators. First, it is widely emphasized that today's AI-controlled game characters should be *believable*, i.e. human-like and virtually indistinguishable from human-controlled characters, in order to increase the overall enjoyability of a game [3, 4, 5]. Second, it is admitted that handcrafted AI systems are hardly able to provide believable behavior: scripted AI is easily recognized by experienced players, especially in complex virtual worlds. For example, even the best systems, participated in 2K BotPrize believability competition among Unreal Tournament bots were unable to deceive human judges [6].

1.2   Behavior Capture

In today's research projects human-like believable behavior is typically constructed by means of analyzing actual human behavior patterns and subsequently implementing them in AI system. Among them, most interest is evoked by the methods that can automatically construct agents' knowledge by observing behavior of human players. This process is known as *behavior capture* [7]. Behavior capture was used, for example, to build Unreal Tournament bots [8, 9], computer-controlled boxers [10, 11], and an AI system for a real-time strategy game [12].

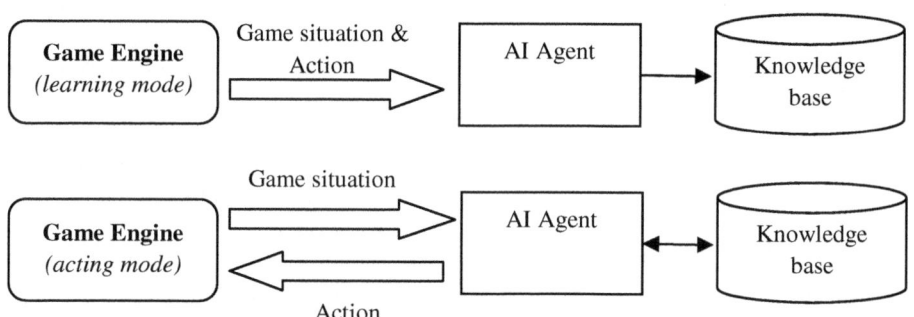

Fig. 1. Learning and acting of a behavior capture-based AI character

While general principles of behavior capture can be described as simply as "watch what the user does and try to reproduce the same patterns" (see Fig. 1), every particular game world sets own challenges. In our works [10, 11, 13] we identified several difficulties, related to practical implementation of behavior capture, common to a wide variety of computer games, and tried to address them in our AI architecture. Currently, our implementation is distributed as a set of tools and libraries under the name of Artificial Contender [14]. Below we will introduce the method of representing agents' knowledge in Artificial Contender.

2   Knowledge Representation with Acting Graph

2.1   Addressing Challenges and Requirements

Our system was designed with the following goals in mind [15]:

- complex, non-repetitive behavior of AI agents;
- distinct personalities of AI characters, exhibiting a variety of skill levels and playing styles;
- the capability to design, edit and adjust AI's behavior (for a game designer).

These requirements served as a basis for our decision to use a variation of finite-state machine that we call *acting graph* as a primary data structure of an AI agent's knowledgebase (see Fig. 2; a similar solution was used in [9]).

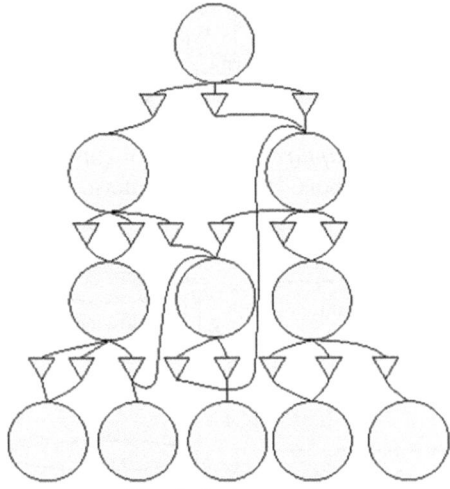

The nodes of this graph correspond to game situations. Game situation is a unique description of the current state of the game world, represented with a set of numerical attributes, defined by the game designer. For example, for the game of boxing such attributes may include the coordinates of both opponents, their directions (where opponents look), body position (standing, leaning, blocking, etc.), health state of each player, and so on.

The edges of the graph correspond to the observed character's actions that introduce changes into the game states. For example, a simple action "move left" connects two game situations that

Fig. 2. Acting graph

have a difference in character's horizontal coordinate. There are no restrictions on incoming and outgoing connections: (a) one action may lead to several new game states (e.g., due to random factors involved in a game, the same action may yield different results); (b) different actions may lead to the same game state; and (c) distinct actions may connect the same pair of game situations (if a character is blocked between two walls, both "move forward" and "move backward" actions yield the same result). Each edge also has an associated probability: while a certain game situation may have numerous outgoing actions, not all of them may be equally preferable.

The ready acting graph represents a complete knowledgebase of a computer-controlled character. Normally it is being constructed automatically during learning by observation phase. A human expert plays the game, and the computer system builds the acting graph on the fly according to the following procedure:

```
wait for the next user action (A)
S = (current game situation)
WHILE game is not finished
    wait for the next user action (A')
    S' = (current game situation)
    find graph nodes for S and S'
    (if a node does not exist, create it)
    establish a link between S and S', and label it with A
    (if this link exists already, increase action probability)
    A = A'; S = S'
END LOOP
```

Let us now consider how the selected data structure helps to achieve the stated goals. The acting graph stores all behavioral patterns, demonstrated by human players. Unlike many knowledge representation mechanisms, such as neural networks, it does not eliminate the noise: even if a certain sequence of actions occurred only once during the training session, it will be still preserved in the graph. Thus an AI agent acquires all idiosyncratic elements of its trainer's style. By asking different human experts to train individual game characters, we obtain separate AI agents with different styles of acting [10].

Another significant advantage of acting graph is the possibility of manual modification. Acting graph can be visualized (we do it with AT&T's GraphViz tool [16]) and edited by the game designer. It is possible to remove unwanted or unintentional sections, to create artificial acting sequences, and to join separate graphs into a single knowledgebase.

Acting graph also lets the AI system to analyze the consequences of applied actions. The game designers might want to increase AI agent's skill level by means of automatic reward-and-punishment schemes (the use of reinforcement learning in behavior capture-based AI is discussed in [11]) or with the help of a heuristic action evaluation function. Such a function can traverse a graph, discover that a certain action is always weak (e.g., it always leads to game states with lower health level of the character), and discard it.

In general, clear and understandable structure of acting graph leaves enough room for new experiments. For example, in one of our research projects we tried to improve adaptivity of AI agents as follows. The agent is programmed to constantly learn new acting sequences from its current opponent. Each action is marked with a timestamp (when it was learned by the system). After certain time interval, old actions are removed from the graph. With this technique, we were able to obtain highly adaptive behavior: an agent tries to learn its opponent's tactics, and quickly changes behavioral patterns when the opponent decides to try another style.

2.2   Decision Making System

While automatic building of a knowledgebase is a rather straightforward process, the use of agent's knowledge for decision making involves more complicated techniques. In order to follow human player's style of behavior, the AI system has to perform case-based reasoning: it needs to identify a node in the acting graph that matches the current game situation, and to apply one of the actions, found in outgoing edges. The complications are caused by heuristic nature of matching algorithm: perfect matches are rare, so the system needs to be able to relax matching conditions gradually until an approximate match is found.

Our system allows the game designer to specify the sequence of search operations and their types, used to find an approximate match. There are two basic options: exact search with attribute exclusion (*static generalization*) and search with attribute variations (*dynamic generalization*).

Exact search finds a node that perfectly matches the given game situation. Since game situations are coded with numbers, this is done in $O(\log n)$ time for a graph, stored as a binary search tree. Attribute exclusions add more flexibility: the game designer can specify game situation attributes that are not taken into account while matching. So if the exact match is not found, we can repeat the search with relaxed conditions. In order to implement this feature, we require the game designer to define all searchable combinations of attributes in compile time. During learning by observation, the system builds additional acting graphs with reduced nodes, and stores them in separate binary search trees (see Fig. 3).

Dynamic generalization is a wrapper around basic search routine. It allows the designer to specify an admissible matching range for each attribute instead of its exact value. For example, if the current game situation is represented with a tuple of three attributes (a_0, b_0, c_0), the use of dynamic generalization on two first attributes with a range $[-1\ldots1]$ will match the following nine tuples:

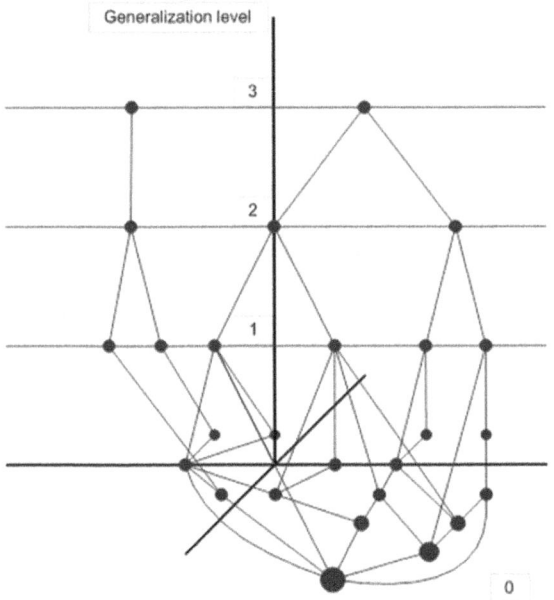

Fig. 3. Static generalization levels

$(a_0 - 1, b_0 - 1, c_0)$ $(a_0, b_0 - 1, c_0)$ $(a_0 + 1, b_0 - 1, c_0)$
$(a_0 - 1, b_0, c_0)$ (a_0, b_0, c_0) $(a_0 + 1, b_0, c_0)$
$(a_0 - 1, b_0 + 1, c_0)$ $(a_0, b_0 + 1, c_0)$ $(a_0 + 1, b_0 + 1, c_0)$

This technique is useful when a certain attribute is important and thus cannot be excluded, but its exact value may slightly vary (as in case of game characters' coordinates). Currently, dynamic generalizations indeed rely on multiple calls to the basic search routine, thus potentially leading to combinatorial explosion of searches. However, in our practical experiments we were able to obtain satisfactory results with minimal use of dynamic generalizations. As a future work, we plan to implement dynamic generalizations with kd-trees, which should result in much lower $O(n^{1-1/k} + m)$ time for each range search, where m is the number of reported points, and k is the dimension of kd-tree [17].

The resulting set of actions, associated with the matching graph nodes, can be further re-ranked or filtered by additional heuristic functions. We use many such functions, both universal and game-dependent. The most important universal ranking function extracts the actions that continue the currently executed acting chain (i.e. the actions outgoing from the target graph node of the last used action). As a rule, such actions should be preferred by the AI. Also, we use weighted random choice in order to take into account action probability, stored in the graph.

3   3D Boxing: An Example Architecture

Our experiments with behavior capture-based AI for a 3D boxing game are described in the papers [10] and [11]. Here we will only discuss basic knowledge configuration for the 3D boxing AI, in order to provide a practical example of a graph-based decision-making system.

3.1   Game State Attributes

Original game states of the boxing game[2] are represented with a set of more than 60 numeric and Boolean attributes for each of the competing players. The most important attributes include:

- the identifier of a boxer's current animation sequence (this attribute describes an actual pose of a boxer);
- distance between the opponents;
- is-player-close-to-knockout-state Boolean flag;
- is-player-on-ropes Boolean flag;
- the direction to nearest ropes (boxing ring edge);
- health and energy values of a player;
- the identifier of a current boxer's animation sequence on the previous frame.

Each action is characterized with the following elements:

- action identifier (a type of an action) — one of 50 built-in action types, such as "move left", "move right", "right jab" or "right-hand high block";
- action duration (in frames).

---

[2] We used a full-fledged commercial boxing game engine.

Not all of game state attributes were considered important, so we have selected a set of 28 most valuable attributes to be stored in the knowledgebase. Additionally, we have performed necessary discretization to ease further retrieval. For example, "distance between the opponents" is measured in pixels, and thus can have hundreds of distinct values. We have scaled this attribute into a range of seven values only ("very far", "far", "not far", "medium", "almost close", "close", "very close"). The same operation was performed with other continuous attributes, such as boxer's health and energy levels.

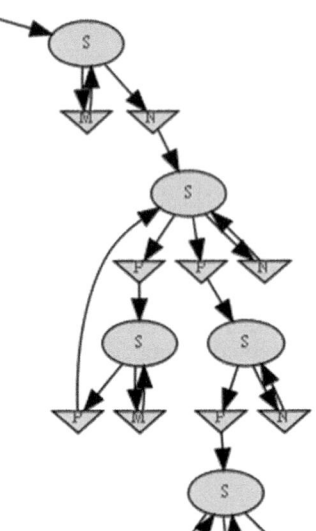

Fig. 4. Acting graph of 3D boxing game (actual fragment of level 2 graph, visualized with GraphViz)

3.2   Generalizations

For the system of static generalizations, we have selected six different sets of attributes. The most accurate set contains all 28 values, while the least accurate set is represented with 9 attributes only (see Table 1 and Fig. 4). So the AI system can find a match for the current game situation on any of these six levels of abstraction.

For the system of dynamic generalizations, the following attributes were chosen:

- distance between the opponents;
- identifier of a boxer's current animation sequence (it can be generalized to possible "neighboring" sequences — e.g., a boxer can be in lean state, then in stand state, or in stand state, then in make-punch state, but it cannot move to the make-punch state directly from lean state);
- (same as above) animation identifier, belonging to the opponent.

Table 1. Configuration of abstraction levels

Level	Attributes	Level	Attributes
0	28	3	15
1	22	4	12
2	17	5	9

3.3   Decision Making

As mentioned above, the game designer can specify any sequence of calls to graph search function in order to achieve desired AI performance. In general, actions found with fewer generalizations, and actions that continue the current acting chain are more preferable.

In our case, the system uses at most 22 invocations of the graph search function. Each invocation is parametered with: (a) level (numerical identifier) of chosen static generalization; (b) Boolean flag indicating whether dynamic generalizations are used; (c) Boolean flag indicating whether the system should extract actions of the current acting chain only (see Table 2).

These 22 parameterizations roughly correspond to different "confidence levels" of case-based reasoning decision maker. The system searches for suitable actions, sequentially relaxing searching conditions according to confidence levels. The first acceptable action is returned as a result.

The 20th confidence level is reserved for a special heuristics: if no actions were found on levels 1-19, the system generates "do nothing" action. The rationale for this decision is simple: if no highly confident actions are available, it might be better just to do nothing and to give the agent the second chance to find a better action on the next request than to proceed directly to less confident "safety levels" 21 and 22.

To make AI less predictable, we also experimented with a slightly modified version of this algorithm. In this version, when the action selection subsystem finds an applicable action, it first extracts all other applicable actions at the current confidence level, and then returns a random action from this actions list.

Table 2. Confidence levels[3]

L	S	D	C		L	S	D	C
1	1	off	True		12	3	off	false
2	1	on	True		13	3	on	false
3	2	off	True		14	4	off	true
4	2	on	True		15	4	on	true
5	3	off	True		16	4	off	false
6	3	on	True		17	4	on	false
7	0	off	false		18	5	off	true
8	1	off	false		19	5	on	true
9	1	on	false		20		WAIT	
10	2	off	false		21	5	off	false
11	2	on	false		22	5	on	false

3.4 Heuristic Filters

As noted earlier, before an action is considered acceptable, it is analyzed with a set of ranking/filtering functions. In our system, we used only four such filters:

---

[3] **L** = confidence level, **S** = static generalization's abstraction level, **D** = dynamic generalizations, **C** = "extract chain actions only" flag.

- "Stumble on ropes". This filter analyzes backward move actions, leading to stumble-on-ropes state (normally they are considered weak), and marks an action as acceptable only if the original move action in the knowledgebase resulted in a similar stumble-on-ropes state in the human-played game (i.e. it really was a human player's intention).
- "Stumble on opponent". Analogously, stumbling on opponent (cinch) is usually a disadvantaged situation, and should not be encouraged. Actions, leading to clinch, are allowed only if the human player tried to initiate clinch in the original learning session.
- "Repeating actions". An action is ranked as weak, if it matches one of the last N (in our experiments, N = 8) used actions. This filter makes boxer's behavior less predictable and less repetitive. Note though, that "same action" means "same action object in the knowledgebase". The boxer can make two identical actions in a row, but they should correspond to distinct objects in the acting graph.
- "Defer non-punches". Punch actions are considered stronger than non-punches. This filter marks all non-punch actions as weak, so punch actions will always be preferred to alternative actions at the same confidence level.

4   Conclusion

The feasibility of our approach has been evaluated and proven in a series of experiments, involving the games of 3D boxing and soccer. We obtained believable and effective characters, able to exhibit human-like behavior style (almost indistinguishable from human actions) and to beat human-controlled opponents.

Our method does not implement reasoning capabilities and long-term planning, so its applicability to virtual worlds that demand these features is still an open question. We believe that our system can be used, at least, as a tactical AI decision maker, while high-level strategic reasoning can be supplied by another AI solution.

The representation of AI agent's knowledge as a game graph provides us with two major advantages: the agent keeps track of all behavioral patterns of its human trainer, and the obtained knowledge is easy to visualize and edit. While the latter point might not seem major from the theoretical point of view, it is an important factor for game developers, who are responsible for AI quality and prefer to have more control over system configuration.

In addition, our case-based reasoning algorithm is fast. We keep a minimal set of expensive operations and achieve our goals with fast search routines. Since game AI systems have to work in realtime conditions, speed and robustness of decision making algorithms are usually among key requirements, set by the game designers.

References

1. VBS Worlds: Cultural Awareness Training Simulation,
   http://www.vbsworlds.com/?page_id=72
2. Hughes, S.: Real Lessons from Virtual Battle. BBC News (August 29, 2008)

3. Taatgen, N.A., van Opplo, M., Braaksma, J., Niemantsverdriet, J.: How to Construct a Believable Opponent using Cognitive Modeling in the Game of Set. In: 5th International Conference on Cognitive Modeling, pp. 201–206 (2003)
4. Choi, D., Konik, T., Nejati, N., Park, C., Langley, P.: A Believable Agent for First-Person Perspective Games. In: 3rd Artificial Intelligence and Interactive Digital Entertainment International Conference (2007)
5. Glende, A.: Agent Design to Pass Computer Games. In: 42nd Annual ACM Southeast Regional Conference, pp. 414–415 (2004)
6. Hingston, P.: A Turing Test for Computer Game Bots. IEEE Transactions on Computational Intelligence and AI in Games 1(3), 169–186 (2009)
7. Funge, J.: Cognitive Modeling for Games and Animation. Communications of the ACM 43(7), 40–48 (2000)
8. Schrum, J., Karpov, I.V., Miikkulainen, R.: UT^2: Human-like Behavior via Neuroevolution of Combat Behaviorand Replay of Human Traces. The University of Texas at Austin (2011)
9. Le Hy, R., Arrigoni, A., Bessiere, P., Lebeltel, O.: Teaching Bayesian Behaviours to Video Game Characters. Robotics and Autonomous Systems 47, 177–185 (2004)
10. Mozgovoy, M., Umarov, I.: Building a Believable Agent for a 3D Boxing Simulation Game. In: 2nd International Conference on Computer Research and Development, pp. 46–50 (2010)
11. Mozgovoy, M., Umarov, I.: Building a Believable and Effective Agent for a 3D Boxing Simulation Game. In: 3rd IEEE International Conference on Computer Science and Information Technology, vol. 3, pp. 14–18 (2010)
12. Ontanon, S., Mishra, K., Sugandh, N., Ram, A.: Case-Based Planning and Execution for Real-Time Strategy Games. In: Weber, R.O., Richter, M.M. (eds.) ICCBR 2007. LNCS (LNAI), vol. 4626, pp. 164–178. Springer, Heidelberg (2007)
13. Mozgovoy, M., Umarov, I.: Believable Team Behavior: Towards Behavior Capture AI for the Game of Soccer. In: 8th International Conference on Complex Systems, pp. 1554–1564 (2011)
14. TruSoft Int'l, Inc., http://www.trusoft.com
15. Mozgovoy, M., Umarov, I.: Behavior Capture: Building Believable and Effective AI Agents for Video Games. International Journal of Arts and Sciences (to appear, 2011)
16. AT&T GraphViz, http://www.graphviz.org
17. Cormen, T., Leiserson, C., Rivest, R.: Introduction to Algorithms, ch. 10. MIT Press and McGraw-Hill (2001)

Personal Genomes: A New Frontier in Database Research

Taro L. Saito

The University of Tokyo,
Department of Computational Biology
leo@cb.k.u-tokyo.ac.jp
http://utgenome.org/

Abstract. Due to the recent technological improvement of the next-generation sequencers, reading genome sequence of individual DNA becomes popular in biology and medical study. The amount of data produced by next generation sequencers is enormous. Today, more than 10,000 people's DNAs are sequenced in the world and tera-bytes of data are being produced in a daily basis. The types of genome information also vary according to the biological experiments used for preparing DNA samples. Biologists and medical scientists are now facing to manage these huge volumes of data with variety of types. Existing DBMS, whose major targets are business applications, is not suited to managing these biological data because storing such large data to DBMS is time-consuming, and also current database queries cannot accommodate various types of bioinformatics tools written in various programming languages. Processing bioinformatics workflows in parallel and distributed manner is also a challenging problem. In this paper, in hope of recruiting database researchers into this rapidly progressing biology and medical research area, we introduce several challenges in genome informatics from the viewpoint of using existing DBMS for processing next-generation sequencer data.

Keywords: Personal genomes, bioinformatics, parallel computing, workflow management.

1 Next-Generation Sequencers

The advent of high-throughput sequencing technology have rapidly changing the world of molecular biology. In 2001, the human genome project [1], a world-wide effort to construct a first human reference genome, spent almost 1 billions dollars to sequence 3 billion base pairs (bp) (3GB of characters comprising of A, C, G and T letters) of the entire human genome. The time needed to finish this project was almost 10 years. In 2011 the cost of sequencing 3 billion base-pairs drops to less than 1,000 dollars in a laboratory equipped with next-generation sequencers (e.g., Illumina HiSeq2000 [12], ABI SOLiD4 [25]). These sequencers can do this sequencing work in a week. Large institutes are equipped with a hundreds of these next-generation sequencers, and have a power to produce several tera-bytes of sequence data in a day.

S. Kikuchi et al. (Eds.): DNIS 2011, LNCS 7108, pp. 78–88, 2011.
© Springer-Verlag Berlin Heidelberg 2011

Although the throughput of sequencing has increased, the individual 'reads', a fragment of DNA sequences generated by sequencers, are worthless by themselves. 800bp is the read length of the Sanger sequencing technology, the older technology used in the human genome project. The next generation sequencers use relatively shorter read length ranging 30bp to 400bp at the expense of increasing the sequencing throughput and lowering the costs. Even though, these short reads have extensive applications after collectively analyzed. For example, mapping the indiviaul reads to the reference human genome tells us the differences of individual DNA sequences from the reference. Some differences of DNA characters, called mutations, can be a cause of diseases. If we can correctly associate these mutations and a disease, it provides us a hint for studying the mechanism of the disease, and hopefully leads to inventing new medicines.

Finding differences of individual DNAs, however, is not sufficient for finding critical mutations. After the emergence of the next-generation sequencers, we have learned that each person has almost 3 million of mutations on average. Among these massive amount of mutations detecting a real cause of diseases is a difficult problem. One clue to squeeze candidate mutations is the knowledge of the common variants that are shared in populations. These common mutations are not likely the cause of rare diseases, e.g., Altsheimer's disease, Parkinson disease, etc., which is less frequent in population. To identify the causal variants of such rare diseases, we need to exclude these common variants from 3 million candidate mutations. The 1,000 genomes project [5] aims to collect the information of these common variants, and is planning to sequence DNAs of 1,000 individuals. Since then the pace of sequencing human genomes has increased; exome sequencing, a targeted sequencing method for reading only gene regions in DNA (called exon), has been widely used to differentiate disease affected people and healthy ones. Recently, several research projects reportedly have sequenced 1,000 to 5,000 persons using exome.

The exome sequencing of one person produces about 10 millions of short-read sequences. For whole-genome sequencing of a person, it is common to read more than billions of reads, 40x-80x fold coverage of 3GB human genome, resulting in 120GB to 240GB of sequences in total. The reason why we need to sequence the human genome more than 3 billion bases, is that the next-generation sequencers have limited accuracy in reading genome sequences. Even with 99% accuracy of the catalog spec of Illumina HiSeq 2000, a top runner of the next-generation sequencers, it still produces 30,000,000 errors if we read 3 billion characters. To distinguish these sequencing errors from real variants, we need to read the same region of the genome multiple times, expecting piles of reads aligned to a close region in the reference genome contain small percentage of sequencing errors (Figure 1). Although the cost of sequencing becomes less expensive, the amount of data we need to process becomes tremendously huge. A whole-genome sequencing of 40x coverage produces 200 millions of short-read sequences. Could you name any RDBMS that can store 200 millions times 1000 (persons) entries at ease?

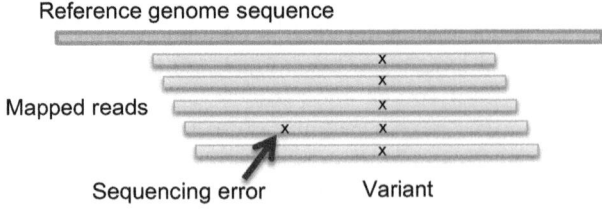

Reference genome sequence

Mapped reads

Sequencing error   Variant

Fig. 1. Read alignment to a reference genome. Piling up read sequences enables us to distinguish sequencing errors and actual mutations (variants) in individual DNA.

Another challenge is that the next-generation sequencers have wide-range of applications in biology. Not only sequencing DNA, these sequencers can be used for sequencing RNA (RNA-Seq [29,28]). RNA is a product inside a nucleus in a cell, transcribed from a DNA using its sequence as a template. RNA is fragile compared to DNA, and may contains more mutations, splicing (cut and paste of DNAs), etc. Since RNA sequences and the reference genome are likely to be more different compared to DNA sequences, alignment algorithms must be tolerant for mismatches and splicing events. RNA-seq is useful to see gene expression in a cell, which is the evidence that some gene regions in DNA sequences are actually used to generate RNAs, subsequently RNAs will be used for generating proteins in our cells. In addition, by capturing the end points of RNA sequences (5'-SAGE [11]), we can know where the transcription of RNA sequences is started. Information of transcription-start sites (TSS) is important in order to learn the function of each gene. With the knowledge of TSSs, we can alter the DNA sequences of model species (e.g., mouse, flys, etc.) so that the transcription of the target genes will be blocked. From the change of phenotypes (e.g., shapes, colors, etc.) we can infer the gene functions.

Surprisingly, the next-generation sequencers can also be used to study physical structure of DNA inside a cell. Nucleosome is a basic unit of DNA packaging. Approximately 147 bp of DNA is wrapped around histones, and creates a folded structure, nucleosome (Figure 2). This three-dimensional structure of DNA has an important role in controlling gene expressions. It is known that if TSS in the upstream region of a gene has a chain of nucleosome structures, its gene expression becomes high. As the nucleosome is loosely structured, the gene expression becomes low. The mechanism of how each gene is expressed has not been fully understood, but by using the next-generation sequencers, we can observe such a structure. Micrococcal nuclease (MNase) is an enzyme which digests nucleic acids around nucleosome structure. By sequencing and mapping the remaining fragments around nucleosome to a reference genome, we can know the nucleosome locations in DNA sequences (MNase-Seq [22]).

The histons forming nucleosomes can be chemically modified, and these modifications can be captured by chromatin immunoprecipitation (ChIP) method. Followed by sequencing DNA regions captured by ChIP experiments (ChIP-Seq [2]), we can observe these modifications mapped onto a reference genome. DNA methylation is another type of modifications affected only to C letters in DNA

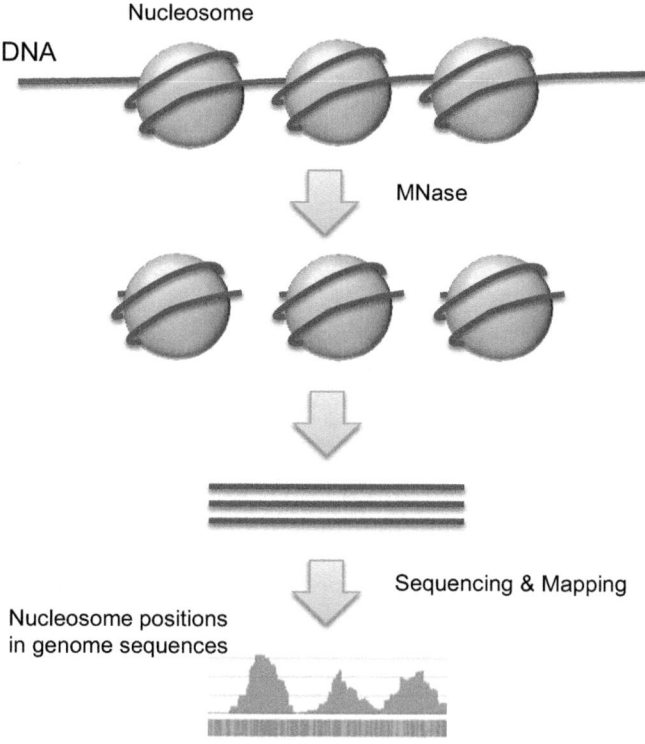

Fig. 2. DNA is folded around nucleosomes. MNase digests sequences around nucleo-somes, so sequences around nucleosomes remain. Sequencing then mapping these DNA fragments to a reference genome can identify the positions of these nucleosomes in the genome sequence. The bottom peaks show nucleosome positioning scores, representing the likelihood of the nucleosome centers positioned there.

sequences. Figure 3 shows ChIP-Seq and DNA methylation states observed by bisulfite sequencing [17]. These modifications is not directly modifies DNA se-quences, but seems to be related to three-dimensional structure and functions of DNA sequences. These superficial changes of DNA are called epigenomic modifi-cations. The next-generation sequencers open a way to these epigenomic studies. Various types of ChIP-seq data is now being produced, and these modification states are different in each tissue (e.g., embryo, liver, somatic cells, etc.). The modENCODE [19] project collects massive amount of these epigenomic data to enhance the knowledge of DNA structures and functions. To see the difference of epigenomic states of each tissue, database that can handle these various types of data is strongly required.

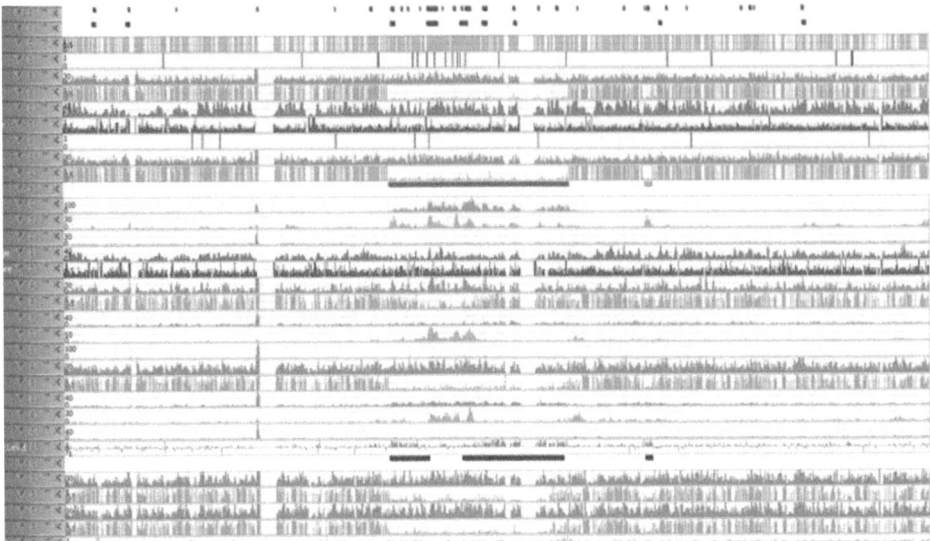

Fig. 3. Epigenetic data, including DNA methylation and ChIP-Seq data for different types of tissues and samples. This picture is a screen shot of the UT genome browser [20] developed in our laboratory.

2   Current DBMS Is Not Usable

We have explained the variations of data that can be produced by the next-generation sequencers. To analyze these large amount of data, however, current DBMS lacks tons of features; How do we store these various data into a single DBMS? Even if databases are federated, how do we efficiently process queries using combinations 100GB of data produced for each individual, tissue and biological experiment? In addition, efficient and scalable data processing is a big problem. Most of the institutes analyzing next-generation sequencer data use cluster-type computer system, and submit hundreds of command-line jobs to a grid engine. For example, write a bioinformatics workflow in Makefile, and let the job management system (e.g., qmake, GXP make [26]) distribute the jobs to multiple nodes in the cluster. This approach works well after we stabilized the workflows. In developing these workflows, however, we need to overcome many trial and error cycles before we can finally reach a stable workflow satisfying the research needs. In these try-and-error cycles, bioinformaticians struggle for increasing throughput of disk I/Os for reading massive amount of sequencer data and generating thousands of output files, filtering out noisy data that is problematic for some programs, and handling various type of data objects in text or binary formats.

In an ideal scenario, every data is stored in a DBMS, and then applying user-defined functions for biological analysis, written in any programming languages, to a specific part of the data retrieved from the database. These program results will be stored in the same DBMS. In reality, however, every data is written in some special purpose formats, developed by sequencer vendors and academic institutes (See how many biological data format exists [27]). The first step for using these data is to write a lexer and parser for translating text-formatted data into objects in a programming language. After that, we code or use third-party programs to analyze next-generation sequencer data. Read data may contain some amount of errors, and may not be usable due to some failures in biological experiments. Thus, we need to evaluate the quality of the data every time. Since the output is written in non-indexed text files, parsing the output (via Unix commands, cut, awk, grep, or using light-weight programming languages, etc.) can be a tedious task. In addition selecting each component of the workflow involves several problems; short-read alignment programs, including BWA [15] and Bowtie [14], have various types of tuning options; the number of mismatches allowed, quality filter of read sequences, etc. To find the best results, we need to test various combinations of the parameter sets. Since the amount of data is huge, each trial takes a lot of hours and days. Hence, simply running bioinformatics programs can be a sort of biological experiments that require enormous amount of time.

Biologists and bioinformaticians has thousands of data needed to be managed in a sophisticated manner. But we cannot find practical usage of current DBMS in this problem other than publishing the analyzed data using genome browsers (e.g., UTGB [20], UCSC Genome browser [8], Ensemble genome browser [7], etc.). These genome browsers store small amount of pre-processed data using RDBMS, and visualize them in web browsers. Making database usable [13] is a serious and demanding problem in genome informatics.

3   Challenges in Bioinformatics

In this section, we concentrate on individual problems in bioinformatics analysis that uses next-generation sequencer data.

3.1   Read Alignment and Assembly

DNA sequences produced by the next-generation sequencers are worthless by themselves. Alignment to a reference genome is the first step where these short reads start to have biological meanings. Two major approaches exist for aligning reads to a reference: hashing and FM-index based alignments. Hashing approach creates a hash table of fixed length fragments of reference genomes, called k-mer hash, where k is the number of fragment length. Since hashing uses non-overlapping k-mer sequences in the reference sequence, the memory consumption tends to be huge. While FM-index based approach uses Burrows-Wheeler transformation (BWT) [3] to create database of the entire human genome. The generated BWT string has the same size of the original sequence, 3GB is sufficient for computing read alignments. Typical FM-index based alignment programs (e.g. BWA [15], Bowtie [14]) uses about 6GB of memory for holding BWT strings of both the forward and reversed sequences of the human genome. Both approaches, however, are weak when reference and individual genome sequence are far different. It has been reported that individual DNA contains various types of structural variations (repetitive sequences, deletion from reference and insertion to reference), and almost 3M bases of sequences are novel, which are not present in the reference genome. Read sequences containing these variations and novel sequences cannot be aligned to a reference.

To compensate these deficits of read alignment, *de novo* assembly of short-read fragments is also used (e.g., ABySS [24], SOAP de novo [16], ALLPATH-LG [9]). Genome assembly programs first construct de Bruijn graphs in order to see the set of reads that has some overlaps. These sets of the short reads can be used to extend the read sequences and create longer 'contig' sequences. However, assembly of human genome sequences is not an easy task due to the presence of repetitive sequences. More than half of the human DNA is said to be repetitive, and un-tangling cycles generated by repeat sequences in de Bruijn graphs has been a difficult problem.

For RNA-seq [29,28], more elaborated alignment and assembly algorithms are required since RNA sequences can be processed in various manners (e.g., splicing, editing). For the summary of RNA-seq alignment and assembly, see [18]. More detailed summary of read alignment and assembly programs can be found in [6].

3.2   Finding Disease-Associated Mutations

Mutations that can be found by the next-generation sequencers vary dependent on the types of the sequencers (Illumina HiSeq 2000, SOLiD4) and characteristics of alignment programs. For example, BWA [15] in the default settings do not find alignments with mismatches more than 4% of the read length, 4 mismatches for 100bp reads. But 5bp or 6bp insertion/deletion in human genome sequences is not rare, and can be a causal variant of diseases.

When squeezing candidate mutations of diseases, databases should be used for filtering common variants. Simply using databases of common variants is vulnerable to the bias of the bioinformatics protocols (e.g., read alignment missed in BWA). False-positive selection of candidates is relatively safe since it can be verified by using more accurate sequencing technology (e.g., Sanger sequencing), but false-negatives must be avoided so as not to overlook causal mutations. The dbSNP [23] and 1,000 genomes data [5] are frequently used for filtering common variants, but the process of these data generation are also must be taken into considerations. Database management system that can save provenance information is strongly required in this application.

3.3   DBMS for Biological Data Objects

Biological analysis tends to vary. Programs for read alignment, assembly, RNA-Seq, ChIP-Seq use different types of data objects. Designing table schema for storing each object in RDBMSs is time-consuming task. We need a quick storage for hierarchically structured data used in these bioinformatics programs. Currently text files or some binary formats (SAM/BAM files for describing short read alignment results [21]) are frequently used to describe biological data, but libraries for parsing these formats are required in each programming language. And also, query operations (e.g., selection, projection, joins) and parallel query processing algorithms must be re-implemented for each data format. A generalized DBMS that can manage various types of biological data formats is in great demand.

3.4   Aggregate Queries

A proverb, not seeing the forests for the trees, applies well when browsing the next-generation sequencer data. The data size is huge, so we often failed to see the global characteristics of the analysis results. Especially there are some biological patterns that is difficult to notice if we are looking the data locally. For example, if we aggregate the nucleosome positioning scores in 1000 bp window and adjusting each score by setting transcription start sites (TSS) of each gene as the 0 point, we can see a clear chain of nucleosome peaks. This result indicates a close relationship between nucleosome positioning and DNA transcription.

3.5   Data Visualization

Visualizing the massive amount of DNA sequencer data is also challenging. Figure 4 shows an example of the visualization of read alignments. Displaying individual alignments is precise, but it easily exceeds the display boundaries when viewing data more than 40x of read depth. A good summary should be generated to grasp the overview of read alignments. We have been developing UTGB [20] as a tool for visualizing next-generation sequencer data using a standard web browsers. Visualization is also important for verifying the results of bioinformatics programs and for sharing the produced results between colleagues and researchers in collaborations.

3.6   Workflow Management

Since the huge amount of time is needed to process next-generation sequencer data, designing and running workflows needs to be done in parallel. Existing programming models, however, follows write-once and run as-many-as you want model. What we need is a workflow management system that can attach a new program to the already running workflows to enable progressive workflow design. And also, to avoid re-computation of the entire workflows caused by minor-case errors that happen only for some exceptional input data, partial evaluation of workflows is necessary. For example, 95% work can be finished in the first phase. After fixing some minor case errors, the remaining 5% of the workflows can be finished in the second phase. Tools supporting this type of progressive workflow development might be useful.

3.7   Parallel and Distributed Data Processing

Institutes that need to process next-generation sequencer data are usually equipped with hundreds of CPU cores and huge-memory machines, ranging

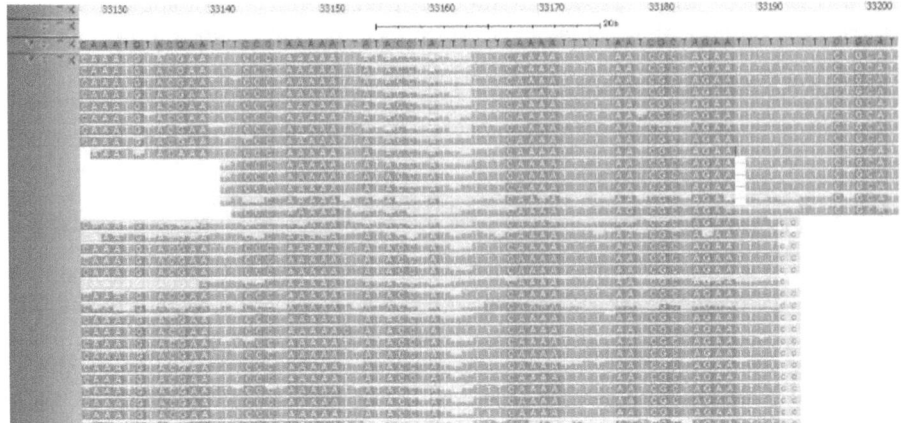

Fig. 4. Visualization of read alignments to a reference sequence (top) using UT Genome Browser [20]

32GB to a few TBs of memory because these high-end machines are necessary for running assembly programs. Current trend in distributed processing, however, is to use commodity hardware with small amount of memory and disks. Hadoop [10], one of the MapReduce [4] implementations, might be a good fit for commodity clusters, but enforcing Hadoop to use abundant memory and CPUs for alignment and biological data processing is not straightforward. We want to control disk I/Os and memory and CPU usage in biological data processing, while Hadoop's map-reduce programming model tries to hide these details from the users. This difference makes difficult to use existing distributed programming platforms, mainly designed for web and business applications. MPI is useful in some applications, for example, when constructing de Bruijn graphs, but it is not fault tolerant and thus not usable for implementing progressive workflows, described in the previous section. Hence, a new parallel and distributed processing model suited to bioinformatics applications needs to be developed.

4   Conclusions

Database systems today are extremely difficult for using in most of the bioinformatics applications, especially for processing next-generation sequencer data. This paper presents existing problems in managing next-generation sequencer data in current DBMS, and the challenges need to be addressed. Biologists and medical scientists are now quite busy in following studies of emerging applications of next-generation sequencers and occupied in analyzing these data. We hope database researchers explore this new field, and tackle the database problems emerging in this new generation of biology and medical studies.

References

1. Initial sequencing and analysis of the human genome. Nature 409(6822), 860–921 (2001)
2. Barski, A., Cuddapah, S., Cui, K., Roh, T., Schones, D.: High-resolution profiling of histone methylations in the human genome. Cell (2007)
3. Burrows, M., Wheeler, D.: A block-sorting lossless data compression algorithm. Technical report 124, Digital Equipment Corporation (1994)
4. Dean, J., Ghemawat, S.: MapReduce: simplified data processing on large clusters. In: Proceedings of the 6th Conference on Symposium on Opearting Systems Design & Implementation, vol. 6, p. 10. USENIX Association, Berkeley (2004)
5. Durbin, R.M., Altshuler, D.L., Durbin, R.M., Abecasis, G.R., Bentley, D.R., et al.: A map of human genome variation from population-scale sequencing. Nature 467(7319), 1061–1073 (2010)
6. Flicek, P.: Sense from sequence reads: methods for alignment and assembly. Nature Methods (2009)
7. Flicek, P., Amode, M., Barrell, D., Beal, K.: Ensembl 2011. Nucleic Acid Research (2011)
8. Fujita, P., Rhead, B., Zweig, A.: The UCSC Genome Browser database: update 2011. Nucleic Acids ... (2011)
9. Gnerre, S., MacCallum, I., Przybylski, D., Ribeiro, F.J., Burton, J.N., Walker, B.J., Sharpe, T., Hall, G., Shea, T.P., Sykes, S., Berlin, A.M., Aird, D., Costello, M., Daza, R., Williams, L., Nicol, R., Gnirke, A., Nusbaum, C., Lander, E.S., Jaffe, D.B.: High-quality draft assemblies of mammalian genomes from massively parallel sequence data. Proceedings of the National Academy of Sciences 108(4), 1513–1518 (2011)
10. Apache, hadoop, http://hadoop.apache.org/
11. Hashimoto, S.-i., Suzuki, Y., Kasai, Y., Morohoshi, K., Yamada, T., Sese, J., Morishita, S., Sugano, S., Matsushima, K.: 5?-end SAGE for the analysis of transcriptional start sites. Nature Biotechnology 22(9), 1146–1149 (2004)
12. Illumina, HiSeq (2000), http://www.illumina.com/
13. Jagadish, H.V., Chapman, A., Elkiss, A., Jayapandian, M., Li, Y., Nandi, A., Yu, C.: Making database systems usable. In: Proceedings of the 2007 ACM SIGMOD International Conference on Management of Data, SIGMOD 2007, pp. 13–24. ACM Press, New York (2007)
14. Langmead, B., Trapnell, C., Pop, M., Salzberg, S.: Ultrafast and memory-efficient alignment of short DNA sequences to the human genome. Genome Biology 10(3), R25+ (2009)
15. Li, H., Durbin, R.: Fast and accurate short read alignment with burrowswheeler transform. Bioinformatics 25(14), 1754–1760 (2009)
16. Li, R., Zhu, H., Ruan, J., Qian, W., Fang, X.: De novo assembly of human genomes with massively parallel short read sequencing. Genome Research (2010)
17. Lister, R., Pelizzola, M., Dowen, R.H., Hawkins, R.D., Hon, G., Tonti-Filippini, J., Nery, J.R., Lee, L., Ye, Z., Ngo, Q.-M., Edsall, L., Antosiewicz-Bourget, J., Stewart, R., Ruotti, V., Millar, A.H., Thomson, J.A., Ren, B., Ecker, J.R.: Human DNA methylomes at base resolution show widespread epigenomic differences.. Nature 462(7271), 315–322 (2009)
18. Martin, J.A., Wang, Z.: Next-generation transcriptome assembly. Nature Reviews Genetics 12(10), 671–682 (2011)

19. Nègre, N., Brown, C.D., Ma, L., Bristow, C.A., Miller, S.W., Wagner, U., Kherad-pour, P., et al.: A cis-regulatory map of the Drosophila genome. Nature 471(7339), 527–531 (2011)
20. Saito, T., Yoshimura, J., Sasaki, S., Ahsan, B., Sasaki, A., Kuroshu, R., Morishita, S.: UTGB toolkit for personalized genome browsers. Bioinformatics (January 2009)
21. Samtools, http://samtools.sourceforge.net/
22. Schones, D.E., Cui, K., Cuddapah, S., Roh, T.-Y., Barski, A., Wang, Z., Wei, G., Zhao, K.: Dynamic regulation of nucleosome positioning in the human genome. Cell 132(5), 887–898 (2008)
23. Sherry, S.T., Ward, M.H., Kholodov, M., Baker, J., Phan, L., Smigielski, E.M., Sirotkin, K.: dbSNP: the NCBI database of genetic variation. Nucleic Acids Research 29(1), 308–311 (2001)
24. Simpson, J., Wong, K., Jackman, S.: ABySS: a parallel assembler for short read sequence data. Genome Research (2009)
25. Applied biosystems, SOLiD4 System, mhttp://www.appliedbiosystems.com/
26. Taura, K., Matsuzaki, T., Miwa, M., Kamoshida, Y.: Design and implementation of GXP make–A workflow system based on make. Future Generation Computer Systems (2011)
27. UCSC, Data File Formats FAQ, http://genome.ucsc.edu/FAQ/FAQformat.html
28. Wang, Z., Gerstein, M.: RNA-Seq: a revolutionary tool for transcriptomics. Nature Reviews Genetics (2009)
29. Wilhelm, B.: RNA-Seq–quantitative measurement of expression through massively parallel RNA-sequencing. Nature Methods (2009)

VisHue: Web Page Segmentation for an Improved Query Interface for MedlinePlus Medical Encyclopedia

Aastha Madaan, Wanming Chu, and Subhash Bhalla

University of Aizu, Aizu-Wakamatsu Shi,
Fukushima-ken, Japan 965-8580
{d8131102,w-chu,bhalla}@u-aizu.ac.jp

Abstract. World Wide Web has become the largest source of information. Consequently web based information retrieval, information extraction; automatic page adaptation and querying deep-web are gaining importance. The need for information retrieval applications is increasing. To address the problems of the ever expanding information over the internet, traditional information retrieval techniques have been applied. Such techniques are sometimes time consuming, and laborious, and the results obtained may be unsatisfactory. This study is an attempt to query web pages like MedlinePlus medical encyclopedia by segmenting the web pages. It summarizes the existing approaches for web page segmentation from the perspective of "structure realization for improved querying" on the web. It proposes a new algorithm *VisHue* for web page segmentation based on visual cues and heuristics and further uses the hierarchical structure generated by it to develop the Query by Segment or Tag (QBT) query interface. This interface is close to the end-user and exploits the relationships among the various content groups within a web page. Such an improved query-interface enables the user to perform in-depth querying. It is a step beyond the page-level search.

Keywords: Web page segmentation, hierarchical structure, advanced querying.

1 Introduction

The World Wide Web has become the most important source of information in the world. The family of algorithms for web focused information retrieval is growing. This is achieved by segmenting the web page, classifying resulting segments. Most information retrieval systems on the Web consider web pages as the smallest and undividable units, but a web page as a whole may not be appropriate to represent a single semantic. Some basic understanding of the structure and the semantics of web-pages could improve people's browsing and searching experience [22]. A web page usually contains various contents such as navigation, decoration, interaction and contact information, which are not related to the topic of the web-page. Furthermore, a web page often contains multiple topics that are not necessarily relevant to each other. Therefore, detecting the semantic content structure of a web page could potentially improve the performance of web information retrieval [1].

S. Kikuchi et al. (Eds.): DNIS 2011, LNCS 7108, pp. 89–108, 2011.

There are a large number of applications which make use of web page segmentation algorithms such as link analysis, topic distillation, focused crawling, improved querying, information accessing, overcoming the limitations of browsing and keyword searching, building wrappers to structure the web data. Such applications exploit the semantic structure within the web page. Furthermore, an acquisition, detection and analysis on web contents are paid more and more attention, web page segmentation algorithms are becoming an important part of them.

There has been plenty of work in this area. Some approaches worked on automating the web page, while some on the learning based splitting of the web page. Kai et al. [1] gave an algorithm that used rule based heuristics to segment the visual layout of a webpage. On the flip side, Kao et al. [13] gave an algorithm for webpage segmentation that relies on content based features. Other notable works used DOM node properties to find webpage segments. While Chakrabarti et al. [12], used template based segmentation for enhanced topic distillation. Chakrabarti et al. [11] also gave an algorithm based on isotonic regression whose by-product is a segmentation of a webpage into informative and non-informative parts [6].

The main aim of this study is to suggest the best approach for web page segmentation algorithm that can generate a hierarchical structure of the web page and improve the queryingfor websites that have pages like web-documents such as the medical encyclopedia entries [14], [15], [16], [17]. The content under these web pages is confined under a main node. In section 2, we introduce the concept of "web-page segmentation" its need and evolution of various approaches for it and explain their categorization.Section 3 presents the characteristics of a good web page segmentation algorithm and describe the features of each of the algorithms their strengths and weaknesses. We draw a detailed comparison of all the existing approaches w.r.t. facilitation in hierarchical structure generation. Among these approaches we mention our on-going work on a new visual cues and heuristic rules-based approach for webpage segmentation*VisHue*. In Section 4 we present the new query interface QBT (Query by Tag or Segment) based on the hierarchical structure constructed by *VisHue* and a qualitative and quantitative analysis of its efficiency in comparison with the keyword search. Section 5 presents the design and scope of improvements of this interface. Section 6 gives the summary and conclusions.

2   Background: Web Page Segmentation

As the amount of information and services available via the web increases, the use of web for accessing information for diverse activities such asshopping and communication is increasing. The changes have resulted in a more sophisticated presentation of content on the web. A web page typically displays a number of different messages to the user, which are usually visually distinct. For example, a web page might contain advertisements and links to other relevant pages in addition to the main content of the page. Thus, an application that intends to re-use content on the web, such as a search engine or a web-to-print application needs to identify the regions of the page that contain distinct information [10]. The presentation of a web page involves placing different pieces of information on it — each serving a different purpose to the end-user — in a manner that appears coherent to users who browse the webpage. These pieces have carefully-placed visual and other clues that cause most users to subconsciously segment the browser-rendered page into semantic regions, each with a different purpose and content [6].

Thus, segmentation of a web page can be defined as dividing a web page into structural blocks, each block may or may not contain templates or may be part of a template. Further, in a segmentation process an area that does not contain templates may be divided into several blocks [7]. It demarcates informative and non-informative content on a webpage; and also discriminates between different types of information. It is very useful in web ranking and web data mining applications. For instance, in a multiword query whose terms match across different segments in a page; this information can be useful in adjusting the relevance of the page to the query [8]. Also the user can be provided with an improved query interface where he can query the semantic groups individually.

2.1 Hierarchical Structure Generation

The hierarchical or logical structure of a document plays an important role in many applications. For example, work presented in [1] exploits the hierarchal structure of a document to carry out anaphora resolution. In [2], the logical structure is used to segment a web document and perform passage retrieval. Other applications that can make use of hierarchical structure include browsers designed for cell phones, PDAs and PCs with non-PC terminals as well as text summarization and data mining applications. However, the hierarchical structure of web documents is not always explicitly represented. Many web designers prefer to use their own styles to represent headings than to use the html heading tags meant to convey a document's logical structure. This limitation can be overcome by a heading detection algorithm and a level detection algorithm through which a document's hierarchical structure can be extracted[18].

Constructing a query interface using the hierarchical structure of the web page is beneficial as it can exploit the various relationships that exist amongst the various content groups and also has additional advantages like:

- In the same domain, there might be a case where important website query interfaces are required to be integrated, to create a unified query interface, if each of these interfaces is generated using a hierarchical structure of the web page, then it is easy to map the attributes.
- It also provides better query interface matching [19].
- Such interfaces are more close to the user's understanding and are qualitatively better than those generated by sources having a flat representation.
- The fields in such an interface are organized in a better manner with appropriate labels.

2.2   Web Segmentation Approaches

Until recently, it has been possible to identify distinct regions and components from the HTML code that generated a web page. The recent trend towards dynamic web technologies implies that the HTML no longer contains sufficient information on the contents of the page. Sometimes it contains almost no information, e.g., in the case of flash presentations where there is no content in the HTML DOM. Such pages however er remain perfectly understandable to the user. Hence, the DOM-based segmentation became obsolete to the new style web pages. They were later replaced by the visual cues based approach, but this approach also used the DOM as an underlying technique. Recent approaches of web page segmentation perform segmentation of a web page by rendering the image of the web page, or creating a graph with the segments as the nodes of the graph but they do not focus on querying applications.Figure 1, consolidates the evolution between the web page generation technologies and segmentation methodologies. It represents evolution of a web-page segment from being a mere syntactical HTML fragment to a well-knit semantic region on the web page. As shown in the figure, the DOM-based techniques can be successfully applied to plain HTML pages.These solutions analyze the HTML DOM and extract information about the appearance of objects on the page and thereby, group HTML objects.These solutions fail with dynamic HTML pages. In case of dynamic HTML pages, the object hierarchy is often available, but it does not describe the layout and components semantically. When we apply the layout algorithm successively, we divide the page to smaller and smaller components, according to the natural visual hierarchy. For such pages, visual cues methods based on generic design heuristicsis a sought solution. The visual cues add to the capability of the algorithm to handle the evolving web page design.

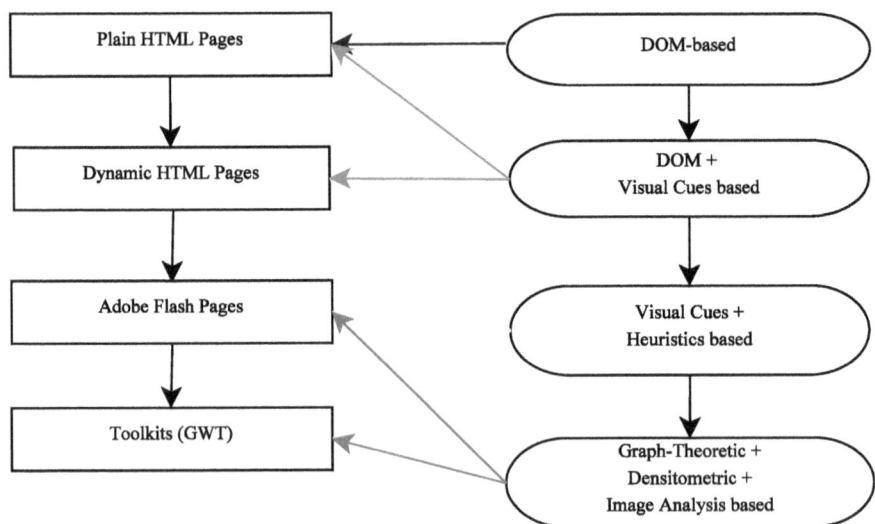

Fig. 1. Evolution of Web Technologies and Web Page Segmentation Methods

3   Web Segmentation Algorithms

3.1   Characteristics of a Good Web Page Segmentation Algorithm

A web page's structure and layout depend on different content type it represents or the taste of designer styling its content. Thereby main content position differs in variety of websites. Even there might be some content in page view that are besides each other but actually in DOM tree they are not in the same level or share same parent node. Finding the main content for querying in this situation where the content doesn't follow any specific rules for arranging and positioning elements needs complicated and expensive algorithms. We list the most desired characteristics in a web-page segmentation algorithm for improved querying:

- Algorithm should be able to simulate a user visiting the website [2].
- It should have high probability to find informative content because in most cases actual users in internet wish to query the informative areas and leave the non-informative segments [2].
- It should be capable to generate the hierarchical structure of a web page.
- The space and time complexity of the algorithm should be reasonable.

Figure 2, displays our target framework in the scenario of human-web interactions. It displays the characteristics desired in a good web-page segmentation algorithm and how they help in generating an improved query interface.

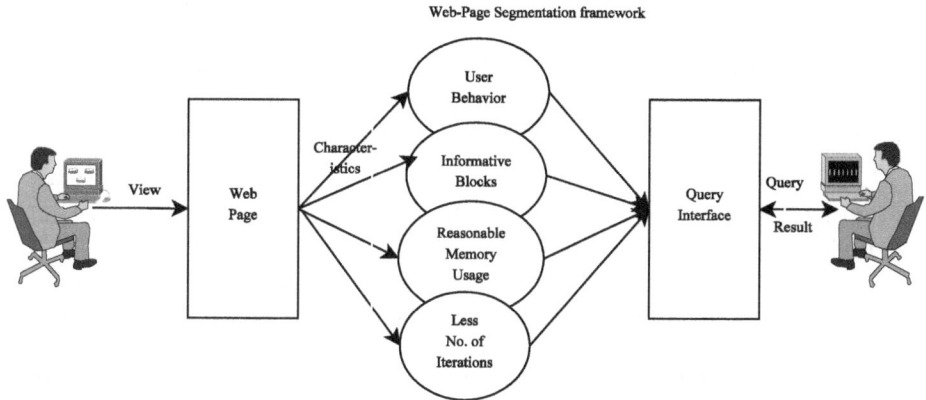

Fig. 2. The Web Page Segmentation and Query Interface Generation Framework

3.2   Classification Criteria

In this sub-section, we classify the various segmentation algorithms based on their underlying approach. The classification tree is captured in Figure 3. These algorithms can be broadly classified into three categories: the DOM-based algorithms, these algorithms are dependent on the rendering of the HTML elements based on the underlying or hidden DOM tree of the web page;methods based on visual cues, these can be further classified into methods keeping the DOM tree in vision and those combining it with heuristic design rules and the modern methodswhich include performing edge analysis over the image of the web-page, constructing a weighted graph that is segmented. Another performs shrinking and dividing operations on the web page. In the following sub-sections we discuss each one of these approaches, highlight the *VisHue* algorithm for web page segmentation and compare it with its counterpart VIPS [1] algorithm. For each of them we discuss the basic approach, existing works utilizing the method, strengths and weaknesses. The comparison is summarized in Table 2.

DOM-Based Algorithms. In general, similar to discourse passages, the blocks produced by DOM-based methods tend to partition pages based on their pre-defined syntactic structure, i.e., the HTML tags. Some simple experiments were performed in [21], where sub-trees tagged with <TITLE>, <P>, <H1>~<H3> and <META>were treated as blocks, but the results were not encouraging.

In some cases this approach can deal with "badly" presented pages. Since almost all blocks share the same length, there are no priorities for short blocks. As windows are overlapped, more blocks are likely to be extracted from a long document than VIPS [1]. However, a lot of web pages do not obey the W3C HTML specifications, which might cause mistakes in DOM tree structure. Moreover, DOM tree was initially introduced for presentation in the browser rather than description of the semantic structure of the web page. Hence, two nodes which may appear to be semantically related actually may not be related. Much recent work [11], [13], [14], and [17] try to extract the structure information from HTML DOM tree [1]. The segmentation by the DOM-based techniques is too detailed [4]. After partitioning, although each block represents some information, it usually does not provide complete information about a single semantic, and thus does not contain good expansion terms [4].

The weaknesses of this approach are:

- DOM is a linear structure, so visually adjacent blocks may be far from each other in the structure and divided wrongly.
- Tags such as <TABLE> and <P> are used not only for content presentation but also for layout structuring. It is difficult to obtain the appropriate segmentation granularity.
- In many cases DOM prefers presentation to content and therefore it is not accurate enough to discriminate different semantic blocks in a web page.
- The number of possible DOM layout patterns is virtually infinite, which inescapably leads to errors when moving from training data to Web-scale [20].

Visual Cues Based Methods. In the sense of human perception, it is always the case that people view a web page as different semantic objects rather than a single object. Actually, when a web page is presented to the user, the spatial and visual cues can help the user to unconsciously divide the web page into several semantic parts. Therefore, it might be possible to automatically segment the web pages by using the spatial and visual cues. Visual cues are very helpful to detect the semantic regions in web pages. Due to the 2-D logical structure, web pages could be partitioned in a 2-D style. A block is assumed to have a rectangle shape and is a closely packed region in the original page.

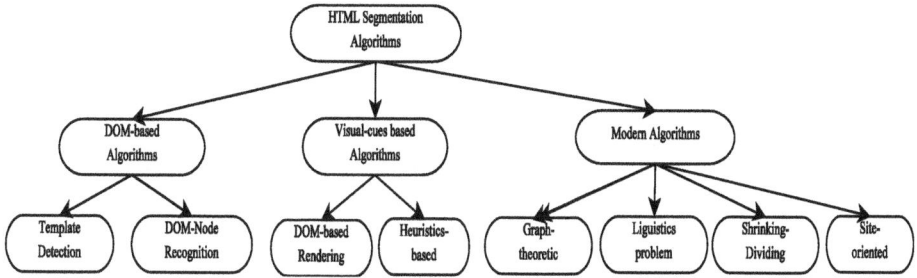

Fig. 3. Classification of Web-Page Segmentation Algorithms

DOM and Visual Cues Based Algorithm (VIPS) [1]. The VIPS (Vision-based Page Segmentation) algorithm extracts the semantic structure of a web page. This semantic structure is a hierarchical structure in which each node corresponds to a block. Each node is assigned a value (Degree of Coherence) to indicate how coherent the content in the block is. The VIPS algorithm makes full use of page layout features: first it extracts all the suitable blocks from the html DOM tree, and then tries to find the separators between the extracted blocks. Here, separators denote the horizontal or vertical lines in a web page that visually cross with no blocks. Finally, based on these separators, the semantic structure for the web page is constructed.

It tries to fill the gap between DOM structure and the conceptual structure of the webpage. The algorithm uses the content structure and tries to simulate how actual user finds a main content based on structural and visual delimiters. The DOM structure and visual information are used iteratively for visual block extraction, separator detection and content structure construction. Finally a vision-based content structure is extracted. In the VIPS method, a visual block is actually an aggregation of some DOM nodes. Unlike DOM-based page segmentation, a visual block can contain DOM nodes from different branches in the DOM structure with different granularities [4].

The blocks obtained from VIPS still have the varying length problem and suffer from lack of normalization factor. More importantly, it remains unclear whether the method would work on passage retrieval and no comparison is provided between this method and traditional passage retrieval methods such as windows, which can be naturally applied to web documents. A web page will first be passed to VIPS for segmentation, and then to a normalization procedure [13]. The blocking result is satisfactory but the algorithm does many loops to reach its desire granularity [2]. We also notice that, for those "badly" presented web pages, VIPS usually fails to partition them into semantic blocks and thus expansion terms are likely to be irrelevant. Also, some relevant long blocks produced by VIPS are ranked low since similarity measure tends to favor short documents.

VisHue Algorithm. The heuristics utilize geometry-related features present on aweb-page, and apply the rules in a greedy fashion to produce the segments. If the heuristics are carefully defined and are generic in nature they prove a strong methodology overcoming weaknesses like the solutions based on heuristics tend to local minima, or they involve a lot of trial and error effort when combined. When combined with the visual cues they give a generic approach for web page segmentation and generate a hierarchical structure for the web pages. Defining heuristics on the base of the web pages can prove more useful rather than the dynamic elements. For e.g.: A heuristic rule stating "headings at same level have same orientation" is more generic and applicable than stating "headings of blue color should be aligned left". Therefore, the former rule has a broader scope of application.

For *VisHue*, we focus on the following key points:

- A method independent of any underlying source code, web standard or web page generation language.
- Web pages may or may not have clear gaps distinguishing the content groups.
- Segmentation need not be too detailed and should be focused on developing an improved query interface.
- The segments that are created should be non-overlapping and capable of constructing a hierarchical structure.

We also assume that (i) Most of the webpages within a website have similar structure and (ii) The geometric patterns can be rendered to derive the inter-content relationship.

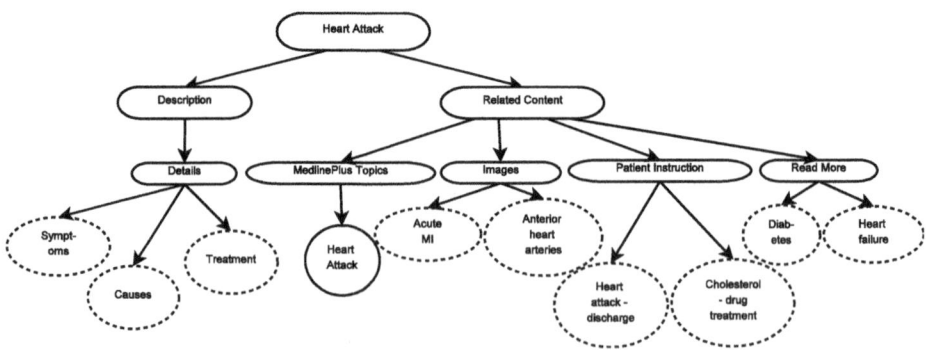

Fig. 4. The Resultant Content Structure

The *VisHue* algorithm creates a hierarchical structure of the web page which is semantically labeled and is suitable for improved querying. The relationships among the content nodes is evident which are perhaps most important for developing a good query interface. The approach constructs two structures; one is a skeleton of the web page called the *domain specific tree* where the domain refers to a website or a group of similar websites, for instance, "MedlinePlus medical encyclopedia". It defines a set of candidate labels for all the possible contents in the domain, renders the tree semantically and assigns labels to the nodes of the tree based on the candidate set to generate a labeled tree termed as the *tree of semantics*.This approach converts the extraction problem to an integration problem. By integrating the two trees we can reproduce the hierarchical structure with subheadings and headings of the page which are the labels of nodes in the tree.Figure 4, shows thehierarchical structure for the MedlinePlus encyclopedia page for the topic "Heart Attack". The dashed lines indicate that the node has more siblings but are not represented due to space constraint. This structure can be mapped to the schema of the web pages directly. We also take into account any differences that might occur amongst the various web pages like missing subheading etc. In the next section we explain how this structure helps in developing a better query interface.

Modern Methods. In this subsection we take up the modern algorithms for web page segmentation.

Graph theoretic segmentation [6]: This approach formulates the segmentation problem in a combinatorial optimization framework. It casts it as a minimization problem on a suitably defined weighted graph, whose nodes are the DOM tree nodes and the edges are the weights expressing the cost of placing the end points in same or different segments. It takes this abstract formulation and produce two concrete instantiations, one based on correlation clustering and another based on energy-minimizing cuts in graphs. Both these problems have good approximation algorithms.

The quality of segmentation in this algorithm depends heavily on the edge weights. The empirical analysis in the paper shows that the energy minimizing formulation performs better than the correlation clustering formulation. It proves that learning edge-weights from labeled data also produce appreciable improvements in accuracy. The segmentation algorithm is applied as a pre-processing step to the duplicate webpage detection problem.

The shortcoming of this approach is the identification of the DOM elements to create the graph. The graph construction is a tedious task, involving a lot of terminology and in-depth understanding. Hence, using such an approach for the purpose of enhancing the querying of a web page will be a complex task where such a high degree of precision in partitioning is not a priority. Moreover, unified query interfaces cannot be constructed as the graph will become more complex when many query interfaces will be considered together.

Site –Oriented Segmentation [7]: Since many pages belonging to a same web site share a common structure, look and feel, this approach hypothesizes that one can achieve a more accurate segmentation by taking all pages of the same web site into account.Based on this idea, the authors of [7] propose and evaluate a segmentation method which segments pages according to properties of the whole web site, instead of just information from a single page. The method adopts a DOM tree alignment strategy proposed for template detection [31, 33]. This method was developed especially for the so called *data-intensive* web sites, such as digital libraries, web forums, news web sites, etc. whose main focus is providing access to a large quantity of data and services [9]. These sites usually contain a large set of web pages which can be organized in a few tens of groups according to the regularity of their structure. This approach focuses on input to web search systems and other similar applications but depends on the DOM tree of each of the different web pages in the website.

Densitomeric Segmentation [20]: This approach builds methods from Quantitative Linguistics and strategies are borrowed from the area of Computer Vision.It utilizes the notion of text-density as a measure to identify the individual text segments of a web page, reducing the problem to a 1D-partitioning task. The distribution of segment level text density follows a negative hyper geometric distribution, described by Frumkina's Law. Their extensive evaluation confirms the validity and quality of the approach and its applicability to the Web. They define an abstract block-level page segmentation model which focuses on the low-level properties of text instead of DOM-structural information. The number of tokens in a text fragment (or more precisely, its token density) is a valuable feature for segmentation decisions.

The strengths of this approach lies in the fact that it reduces the page segmentation problem to a 1D-partitioning problem. It proposes a *Block Fusion algorithm* for identifying segments using the text density metric. It presents an empirical analysis of the algorithm and the block structure of web pages and evaluates the results, comparing with existing approaches. It shows the application of the methodology to the field of near-duplicate detection.

Image analyses of the web page [8, 10]: In this approach a layout for segmentation of the web page is generated by performing edge analysis on the GUI image (or its transformation).It assumes that the main objects are outlined so that there is a border between them. It seeks for areas containing information, and groups them into distinct layout elements. This technique gives a high level layout; thereby segmenting the page to its main components.This approach uses only the visual information and does not apply any semantic analysis to group or ungroup elements. It finds these layouts recursively deeper into the page. The recursive process continues until down to the level of individual elements. Deeper in the hierarchy, this task becomes more difficult because the objects we separate become smaller. Thus, the edges are denser and tend to merge.

After segmentation it uses text detection and applies OCR, which also gives information about the meaning of a layout object. The text information is important for later semantic analysis of the page content. Hence, though the approach segments the web page visually, it does not pay attention to the semantic grouping. Such a technique will fail in case of web-pages with semantically related yet scattered content.

The visual cues and heuristics based method*VisHue*, independent of any standard or model over the web andare applicable to plain HTML pages, dynamic HTML pages, flash pages, or those generated by any of the web toolkits, since it does not depend on any source codes. Since it iterates only till each part of the webpage is covered by some node of the tree, the time complexity of the algorithm is reasonable.The tree stored in the memory comprises of just the headings and subheadings and the height of the tree is directly proportional to the levels of nesting of the subheadings within the page. This number is bounded. The number of leaf nodes is bounded by the distinct blocks in the web page. Hence, the space complexity of the algorithm is reasonable. Moreover, its capability to construct a hierarchical structure makes itappropriate for query interface design. We highlight the strengths of the *VisHue* algorithm in Table 1.

Table 1. Comparison between VIPS and VisHue

Characteristics	VIPS	VisHue algorithm
Underlying technique	Recognition of Visual Cues using basic DOM elements	Visual cues and heuristic rules
Precision	Basic DOM elements	Visible segments on the web page
Application	Block based web search	Advance querying
Authenticity	Non-overlapping blocks.	Better blocks formulation than VIPS
Data structure	Hierarchical tree of all the blocks	Hierarchical tree of headings or labels in the web page
Space complexity	Entire structure needs to be stored	Only the headings of the blocks are stored
Time complexity	Recursive partitioning till the basic DOM elements are found	Less, no attempt to reach the indivisible DOM elements.
Language or standard dependency	DOM dependent	None

Table 2. Comparison Summary Between Various Web Page Segmentation Approaches

	Template Detection	DOM-node Recognition	Graph-theoretic	Image Analysis	Linguistic approach	Shrinking and dividing	Site-oriented
Underlying technique	DOM elements	DOM elements	Weighted graph	Edge analysis on web page image	Token density of a text fragment	Image processing and web page characteristics	DOM tree alignment
Precision	Basic DOM elements	Basic DOM elements	Aggregates at the level of internal nodes	Individual elements	Blocks based on text density	Indivisible sub-images	Basic DOM elements
Application	Link structure analysis	Link structure analysis	Duplicate Detection	Not specified	Near duplicate detection	Phishing page detection	Segment aware web search
Authenticity	Syntactic segments	Syntactic segments	Energy-minimizing cuts	Not specified	Not specified	Not specified	Not specified
Data structure	DOM-tree	DOM-tree	Regions of visual content	GUI image	Statistics: block fusion algorithm	Sub-images of content blocks	Tree combining all the DOM trees
Space complexity	DOM elements are stored	DOM elements are stored	Not specified	Not specified	Minimal	Not specified	Not-specified
Time complexity	Recursive partitioning	Recursive partitioning	Not specified	Recursive partitioning	15ms per page	Serves real time	Not specified
Language or standard dependency	DOM dependent	DOM dependent	Depends on DOM tree	None	None	None	DOM-dependent

VisHue algorithm scores over its counterpart algorithm VIPS on the following features:

- It addresses the visual design heuristics within a web page, whereas the VIPS algorithm gives heuristic rules which are DOM based. For a web page not based on the DOM elements, latter will fail.
- Some of the heuristics of VIPS like,if all the child nodes of a node are text nodes then the node should not be further segmented; implies that a web page where the contents are organized under a single node like MedlinePlus medical encyclopedia this approach will fail.
- *VisHue* labels the hierarchical nodes semantically whereas the VIPS do not assigns labels to the block-hierarchy it constructs.
- The block-based search based on VIPS does not confine the search space for a user query though the blocks are returned as results whereas the labels of the *VisHue* algorithm reduce the search space for user queries significantly.

4   Improved Query Interface Using the VisHue Algorithm

4.1   Web Page Segmentation and Improved Querying

Currently, information on the web may be discovered primarily by two mechanisms: browsers and search engines. Existing search engines such as Yahoo, Google service millions of queries a day. Yet it has become clear that they are less than ideal for retrieving an ever-growing body of information on the Web. This mechanism offers limited capabilities for retrieving the information of interest; still burying the user under a heap of irrelevant information [26]. Also the documents on the web are not well-structured so that a program can reliably extract the routine information that a human wishes to discover. These searches are generic. For example, if a user wishes to find an article authored by a person X. The query results will show all articles with an occurrence of X. Such results are not relevant for the end-users as they do not expect such a generic set of results. Hence, we conclude that there is a need for an in-depth querying of the web pages. And provide users with results that are from specific segments of the web page.

There have been works like the *Block-based Search* [4], where the webpage is segmented into semantic blocks and the importance values of the blocks are labeled using a block importance model [2]. Then the semantic blocks, with their importance values, are used to build block-based Web search engines [1], [3].But these blocks do not improve the query interfaces. In *Object-Level Vertical Search*, all the web information about a real world object or entity is extracted and integrated to generate a pseudo page for this object. These object pseudo pages are indexed to answer user queries, and users can get integrated information about a real-world object in one stop. This object-level vertical search technology has been used to build Microsoft Academic Search (http://libra.msra.cn) and Windows Live Product Search (http://products.live.com).Another type of search called *Entity Relationship Search*deploys an Entity Relationship Search Engine in the China search market called Renlifang (http://renlifang.msra.cn). In Renlifang, users can query the system about people, locations, and organizations and explore their relationships. These entities and their relationships are automatically mined from the text content on the Web. If the query terms scatter at various regions with different topics, it could cause low retrieval precision. It can be argued that a web page with a region of high density of matched terms is likely to be more relevant than a web page with matched terms distributed across the entire page even if it has higher overall similarity.

Keeping the above discussion in mind, and observing the lack of a well formed query interfaces for the encyclopedia like websites, prompted us to utilize the work of segmenting the web page using the *VisHue* algorithm for developing a query interface. Web page segmentation empowers the user to expand his querying horizons by providing him tags or labels of the subtopics within the page that can be queried individually. For instance, a disease name in the user's search criteria will have a web page containing details about it, alongside; it can be a part of the symptoms, causes of another disease or a diagnosis of some test. When an end-user queries the encyclopedia, he is presented with all the results along with the web page about it. All these results may or may not be of relevance to him. Instead, providing him a specific set of results, such as if the query is "heart attack as a symptom", will be more beneficial. Hence, the query is reformulated in terms of occurrence of the queried term within the encyclopedia. Our proposed query interface combines both the object-based as well as the entity-based search. It exploits the relationship between different content segments in a web page and can query specific regions of the web page.

4.2   Query by Segment

Query by Segment is a query interface for the medical encyclopedia by MedlinePlus [3]. We refer Query by Segment as QBT (Query by Tag) in the study. It is an interface for formulating and retrieving query results by various subheadings and headings of different content segments in the web page belonging to the encyclopedia. It utilizes the content structure generated by the *VisHue* algorithm method mentioned in previous section and uses the node labels as query fields within which search can be performed. It allows the user to confine his search to specific regions within a page. It provides only the relevant results for a user query. We compare QBT with standard keyword search available at MedlinePlus [3]. Let us suppose that an end user wants to search "nausea" as a symptom. Using standard search MedlinePlus, displays search results where "nausea" has an occurrence in *side effect of medication* besides in *symptoms*. On the other hand, using QBT, we can just display *nausea* from *symptoms*. Further comparison is given in next subsection.

QBT and the Hierarchical Structure of a Web Page. The node labels of the hierarchical structure are mapped to query fields in the QBT interface. The user can select the sub-heading he wishes to query and also for a keyword can specify scope of search. Once the user selects the subheading or subtitle of a segment to query he or she can also choose to search the related topics, related content, read more etc. Next he or she moves to the second screen where she or he inputs the value of the fields (segment headings) selected in the previous screen. In the figure 5, we see that the user enters the values for "causes" and "title" selections. On this screen the user has the provision to delete an attribute, perform an "OR" or an "AND" operation on the attributes. Once, his or her query is formulated, he or she clicks on the "search" button and is presented with the results that are best fit for his query. In our example displayed in Figure 5, the results are displayed where "Heart Attack" is found in the title and "atherosclerosis" in the "causes" as desired by the user.

We map the design of the QBT from the hierarchical tree of the web page. The child nodes of the description and related content become the search areas within which one can search. Their children define the subspaces that can be searched. For e.g.: If a user wishes to search a symptom X for a disease say "Heart Attack" checks the title to be searched with the keyword "Heart attack" and some keyword for symptom. The content structure enables the interface with a smart search (as required by the above example) by incorporating the following points:

- The left siblings' limit the options for the right siblings in the query interface. If any user selects one sub-heading, it highlights the other sub-headings that co-occur with it in the web pages within the encyclopedia.
- The child nodes of the main content (MC) and related content (RC) define the complete search space for a user and the leaf nodes define the fine lines of search for the user within them.
- The candidate set of labels define an exhaustive list of sub-headings that can define the searchable areas within the encyclopedia.

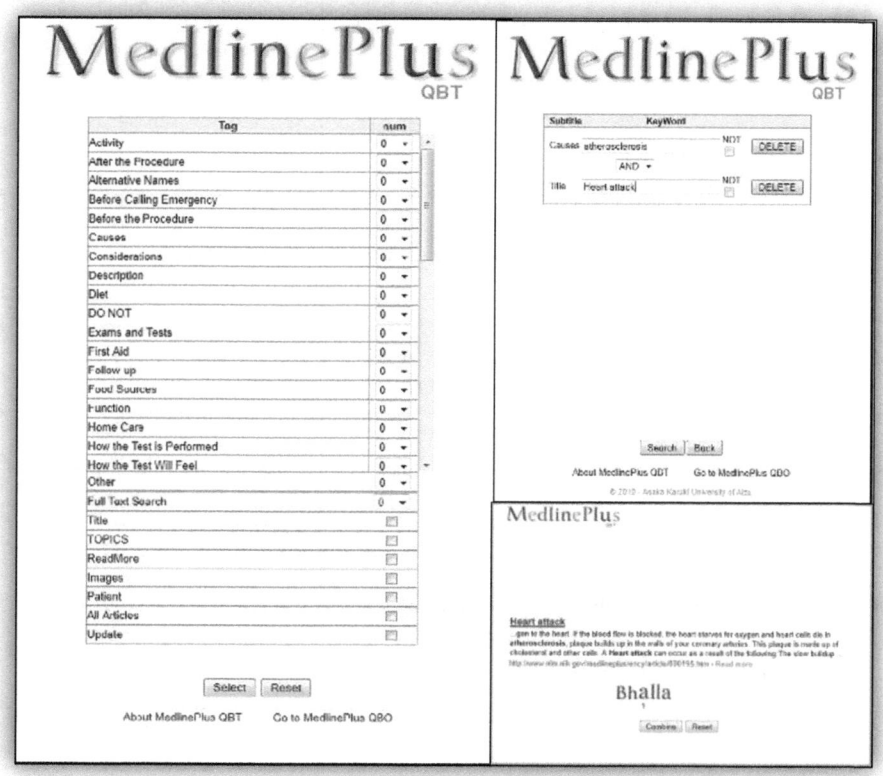

Fig. 5. The MedlinePlus QBT Interface

A Tour of the QBT Interface. We take a brief look at the QBT interface. The interface is composed of three screens, the subtitle selection screen; screen to enter keywords for query and finally the results screen. The initial screen displays a table virtually divided into two parts one describing the various headings or sub-topics of different segments within the encyclopedia page and the other part defines the scope of search in which the user wishes to search a keyword shown in Figure 5 left side. For instance, here the user selects "1" occurrence of "causes" it highlights all the co-occurring segments, the user selects "title" space to search another keyword and clicks "select", he or she is presented with the query formulation screen, where the user enters the values for his or her selections; the user is presented with an exhaustive list of values he or she may enter. The fields have a hint based auto-completion facility. The second and the final screens are shown in Figure 5 right side.

Table 3. Comparison of Querying Features between QBT and Traditional Keyword Search

S.No.	Features	QBT	Keyword Search
1	Direct Answers	Precise, direct answers returned	A set of articles with an occurrence of keyword(s) is returned
2	Query Capability	Focused querying	Limited
3	Retrieval Units	Text snippets along with article URLs	Article URLs
4	Aggregate Queries	Various querying operations like AND, OR and NOT	Not Possible
5	Usefulness	Exact and relevant results	Large number of results are presented which need to be sorted by user
6	Easy to use Interface	Labels are self-explanatory and there is provision of defining the scope of search for a given keyword	Simple and Advanced option for entering the keyword(s)

4.3   Performance of the QBT Interface

In this sub-section we evaluate the performance of the QBT interface, w.r.t the traditional keyword search available for the MedlinePlus medical encyclopedia. We draw a qualitative and quantitative analysis of the performance of the interface and exhibit its efficiency over the existing method to query the encyclopedia. We also differentiate the query formulation of the two methods.

Implementation Details. The QBT interface is implemented on Windows 7, 64-bit OS. Apache HTTP Server is used as a platform to run the application, PHP scripting language is used for user interface (UI) design and IBM DB2 database is used. Table3 presents a qualitative analysis of the QBT interface w.r.t the keyword search. It lists the features of a useful query interface for an end-user to perform efficient information retrieval.

Table 4. Query Formulation in QBT and Traditional Keyword Search

S. No.	User Query	QBT Query	Keyword Search
1	Cases where patient has hypertension but not high blood pressure	Symptom: "Hypertension" Symptom: NOT "High blood pressure"	Search has no provision of negating one of the keywords
2	Cases for patient to stop certain activities before a test (can resume normal activities after it)	Before Procedure: "Stop" After Procedure: "Normal"	Keyword search with "stop" and "normal" keywords
3	Heart attack caused by high blood pressure	Cause: "High blood pressure" Symptom: "heart attack"	Search for keyword "heart attack" and "high blood pressure"
4	Poisoning caused by eating fish	Food Source: "Fish" Side Effect: "Poisoning"	Search all articles for keywords "fish" and "poisoning"

Table 3 shows the QBT interface is a far better approach to query or search the medical encyclopedias. It has the capability to support aggregated queries and complex queries where user can find articles with occurrence of a keyword and negation of another keyword. It is an easy to understand interface that provides the end-user precise answers for his queries. All these features make it a much powerful interface for medical domain.

Table 4 shows how a user query is understood by either of the interfaces. The QBT interface understands the user query in perhaps the most natural way. Whereas the keyword search just picks up the keywords and fails in case of aggregate or negation like queries. We perform a quantitative analysis of the performance of the QBT interface with a small set of queries. We observe the performance of both querying mechanisms on these queries and present the analysis in Table 5. The existing keyword search in MedlinePlus is generic to the entire website. Hence, we enter a keyword and later sort the results belonging to the medical encyclopedia. Table 5 shows a comparison between the number of results and number of relevant results and calculates their relative percentage. We also compare the rank at which a resultdisplayed by QBT occurs in case of the keyword search. Web ranking is critical for information retrieval methods as stated in Section 2. The reduction in the search space is significant in case of the QBT interface whereas the user may not be able to confine his search space in case of simple keyword search. We calculate the percentage of content searched with respect to a total of 4000 web pages within the MedlinePlus medical encyclopedia. Hence, we conclude that QBT narrows down the results and displays only the relevant results to the user and cuts down the processing time of these queries.

Table 5. Quantitative Performance Analysis of the QBT and Keyword Search for User Queries in Table 4

User Query	Parameters	QBT	Keyword Search
1	No. of Results	4	380
	No. of Relevant Results	4	4
	Relative Ranking	All 4	No result in top 10
	Relevant Results (%)	100	1.05
	Contents Searched (%)	0.01	100
2	No. of Results	15	523
	No. of Relevant Results	15	15
	Relative Ranking	All 15	No result in top 10
	Relevant Results (%)	100	2.87
	Contents Searched (%)	2.5	100
3	No. of Results	3	145
	No. of Relevant Results	3	3
	Relative Ranking	All 3	No result in top 10
	Relevant Results (%)	100	2.06
	Contents Searched (%)	2	100
4	No. of Results	3	85
	No. of Relevant Results	3	3
	Relative Ranking	All 3	No result in top 10
	Relevant Results (%)	100	3.53
	Contents Searched (%)	0.5	100

5   Discussion and Future Work

The majority of the existing methods for web-page segmentation compute structural similarity using features derived from HTML codeor DOM tree representation of web pages [1], [5], and [11]. Only little work has been done to compare web pages based on their visual structure [6].From a web user's perspective, however,the visual structure of a web page is more discriminating than the structure of its source code: The fundamental reason is that the process of rendering a web page is a non-injective, and hence lossy mapping is done from a one-dimensional code fragment into a two-dimensional arrangement, where the same visual appearance can be generated by very distinct HTML code fragments. With ever more complex web pages and more available HTML options to create the same design, structural similarity as perceived by web users can be only reliably determined from a web page's visual rendering [18].

The paper summarizes all the existing works in the field and highlights a detailed comparison between them. It gives an account of the on-going work on formulating a generic heuristic design-ruleandvisual cues based *VisHue* algorithm for web page segmentation which is more beneficial than the existing methods for querying purposes and constructs a corresponding hierarchical structure. It discusses the QBT interface which is designed by using this approach. Future work will include improving the QBT interface; making it more generic, dynamic and intelligent in nature. A practical evaluation of the proposed *VisHue* algorithm and a comparison of performance between the QBT and the block based search in terms of reliability and scalability.

6   Summary and Conclusions

The present study considers a detailed account of the existing approaches for web-page segmentation. It gives a comparison among these approaches. Since, the face of the web is continuously changing the need for such approaches are ever growing. By understanding the current techniques, the scope for improvements can be clearly understood. Combining heuristics with the visual rendering of the web page for web page segmentation can prove to be a turning point in the need for language independent solutions for web-page segmentation and for improving existing query interfaces. The medical domain has a need to evolve in terms of making the available information accessible to the end-users in a user-friendly manner. The need for advanced query interfaces that provide an in-depth querying persists. Query by Segment or Tag (QBT) is an attempt in this direction. It aims at returning the users the desired results from the designated parts of the web-page rather than complete web page results.

References

1. Cai, D., Yu, S., Wen, J., Ma, W.-Y.: Extracting Content Structure for Web Pages based on Visual Representation. In: Zhou, X., Zhang, Y., Orlowska, M.E. (eds.) APWeb 2003. LNCS, vol. 2642, pp. 406–417. Springer, Heidelberg (2003)
2. Asfia, M., Pedram, M.M., MasoudRahmani, A.: Main Content Extraction from Detailed Web Pages. International Journal of Computer Applications (IJCA) 11 (2010)
3. http://www.nlm.nih.gov/medlineplus/encyclopedia.html

4. Cai, D., He, X., Wen, J.-R., Ma, W.-Y.: Block-based Web Search. In: Proc. of SIGIR (2004)
5. El-Shayeb, M.A., El-Beltagy, S.R., Rafea, A.: Extracting the Latent Hierarchical Structure of Web Documents. In: SITIS (2006)
6. Chakrabarti, D., Kumar, R., Punera, K.: Graph-Theoretic Approach to Webpage Segmentation. In: WWW 2008 / Refereed Track: Search - Corpus Characterization & Search Performance, Beijing, China (2008)
7. Fernandes, D., de Moura, E.S., da Silva, A.S.: A Site Oriented Method for Segmenting Web Pages. In: SIGIR 2011, July 24-28 (2011)
8. Cao, J., Mao, B., Luo, J.: A segmentation method for web page analysis using shrinking and dividing. International Journal of Parallel, Emergent and Distributed Systems 25(2), 93–104 (2010)
9. Bohunsky, P.: Visual Structure-based Web Page Clustering and Retrieval. In: WWW 2010, Raleigh, North Carolina, USA, April 26-30 (2010) (Poster)
10. Pnueli, A., Bergman, R., Schein, S., Barkol, O.: Web Page Layout via Visual Segmentation. HP Laboratories
11. Chakrabarti, D., Kumar, R., Punera, K.: Page-level template detection via isotonic smoothing. In: 16th WWW, pp. 61–70 (2007)
12. Kao, H.-Y., Ho, J.-M., Chen, M.-S.: WISDOM: Web intrapage informative structure mining based on document object model. TKDE 17(5), 614–627 (2005)
13. Bohunsky, P.: Visual Structure-based Web Page Clustering and Retrieval. In: WWW 2010, Raleigh, North Carolina, USA, April 26-30 (2010) (Poster)
14. Pnueli, A., Bergman, R., Schein, S., Barkol, O.: Web Page Layout via Visual Segmentation. HP Laboratories
15. Chakrabarti, S., Joshi, M., Tawde, V.: Enhanced topic distillation using text, markup tags, and hyperlinks. In: 24th SIGIR, pp. 208–216 (2001)
16. Kao, H.-Y., Ho, J.-M., Chen, M.-S.: WISDOM: Web intrapage informative structure mining based on document object model. TKDE 17(5), 614–627 (2005)
17. http://adam.about.net/encyclopedia/
18. http://www.drugs.com/medical_encyclopedia.html
19. http://www.mgo.md/encyclopedia.cfm
20. http://www.umm.edu/ency/
21. Hong, J., He, Z., Bell, D.A.: An evidential approach to query interface matching on the deep Web. Information Systems Journal 35(2) (2010)
22. Kohlschütter, C., Nejdl, W.: A Densitometric Approach to Web Page Segmentation. In: CIKM 2008, October 26-30 (2008)
23. Crivellari, F., Melucci, M.: Web Document Retrieval Using Passage Retrieval, Connectivity Information, and Automatic Link Weighting. In: TREC-9 Report, In The Ninth Text Retrieval Conference (TREC 9), (2000)
24. Nie, Z., Wen, J.-R., Ma, W.-Y.: Webpage Understanding: Beyond Page-Level Search. Sigmod Record 37(4) (2008)

Dynamic Generation of Archetype-Based User Interfaces for Queries on Electronic Health Record Databases

Shelly Sachdeva, Daigo Yaginuma, Wanming Chu, and Subhash Bhalla

Graduate Department of Computer and Information Systems,
University of Aizu, Fukushima, Japan
{d8111107,m5151102,w-chu,bhalla}@u-aizu.ac.jp

Abstract. Standardized Electronic Health Records (EHRs) make use of archetypes for representation of data. In combination with terminologies, the archetypes enable powerful possibilities for semantic querying of repository data. Such querying enables longitudinal processing of health data, regardless of the originating system. The semantics of data is better understood by viewing the data in the context of the user interface (UI). The paper demonstrates the feasibility of creating a query interface. It introduces a general purpose database transformation channel. It will shorten the application development process and increase the quality of the software by automatically generating software artifacts that are often made manually (and are prone to errors). It is possible to know the locations of each leaf datum within information conforming to an archetype. The tool helps in the inspection of an archetype in advance, which can yield a set of path fragments. It can be used to query instances which conform to an archetype for intelligent querying.

Keywords: Electronic Health Records, Querying, User-Interfaces, Improving Information Quality, Archetype-Based EHR.

1   Introduction

Electronic Health Records (EHRs) are the paperless solution to healthcare world that runs on a chain of paper files. These former Electronic Medical Records (EMRs) have bad record design and shallow support of user interfaces to fill in and extract data, leading to incomplete and incorrect data records. In contrast, the standardized EHR record design is based on clinical investigator recording process [5]. These ensure Data Quality (DQ). Its two key principles are data accuracy and data validity. To communicate effectively, data must be valid and conform to an expected range of values. To be useful, data must be accurate. As the recording of data is subject to human error, there need to be built-in control measures to eliminate errors, in manual recording and computer entry. DQ also includes reliability, completeness, legibility, timeliness, accessibility, usefulness, confidentiality and security [27]. Data quality is proportionate to the attainment of achievable improvements in health care.

Thus, the proposed Electronic Health Records (EHRs) have a complex structure that may include data of about 100-200 parameters, such as temperature, blood-pressure, heart rate and body mass index. Individual parameters have their own

S. Kikuchi et al. (Eds.): DNIS 2011, LNCS 7108, pp. 109–125, 2011.
© Springer-Verlag Berlin Heidelberg 2011

contents (Figure 1). In order to serve as an information interchange platform, EHRs use archetypes to accommodate various forms of contents [16]. The components within EHR data have multitude of representations. The contents can be structured, semi-structured or unstructured, or a mixture of all three. These can be plain text, coded text, paragraphs, measured quantities with values and units, date, time, date-time, and partial date/time, encapsulated data (multimedia, parsable content), basic types (such as boolean, state variable), container types (list, set) and uniform resource identifiers (URI).

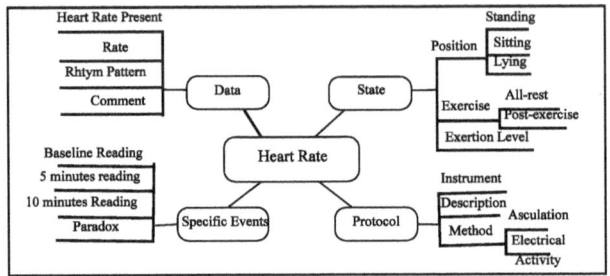

Fig. 1. Heart Rate Archetype

1.1   Archetype-Based EHRs

Standardized EHRs provided by openEHR [24], HL7 [13] and CEN TC/251[10] aims to use archetypes. Archetypes allow describing specific clinical concepts (for example, blood pressure, and ECG measurements) as constraint rules that constrain the possible types, relationships and values of the record components in an ISO 13606 'Composition' [15]. A 'Composition' corresponds to one clinical document. Thus, archetype is an agreed formal and interoperable specification of a re-usable clinical data set which underpins an electronic health record (EHR). It captures as much information about a particular and discrete clinical concept as possible. An example of a simple archetype is WEIGHT, which can be used in multiple places, wherever is required within an EHR. ISO 13606-2 [16] has defined an Archetype Definition Language (ADL) [16], [6], i. e., a formal language that is related to the ISO 13606-1 [15] reference model. Archetypes expressed in this language will be convertible to HL7 Refined Message Information Models (R-MIMs) and Common Message Element Types (CMETs). It is intended to harmonize the ISO/openEHR 'archetype' concept with the HL7 Clinical Document Architecture [14] and HL7 Templates.

An archetype definition basically consists of three parts: descriptive data, constraint rules and ontological definitions (Figure 2). The descriptive data contains a unique identifier for the archetype, a machine-readable code describing the clinical concept modeled by the archetype and various metadata such as author, version, and purpose. The constraint rules are the core of the archetype and define restrictions on the valid structure, cardinality and content of EHR record component instances complying with the archetype (represented by definition section). The ontological part defines the controlled vocabulary (i. e., machine readable codes) that can be used in specific places in instances of the archetype. It may contain language translations of code meanings and bindings from the local code values used within the archetype to external vocabularies such as SNOMED or LOINC. It may also define additional constraints on the relationship between coded entries in the archetype based on the code value. The ADL for the archetype 'heart rate' is given in Figure 6. ADL is path addressable in a similar way, as data in XML.

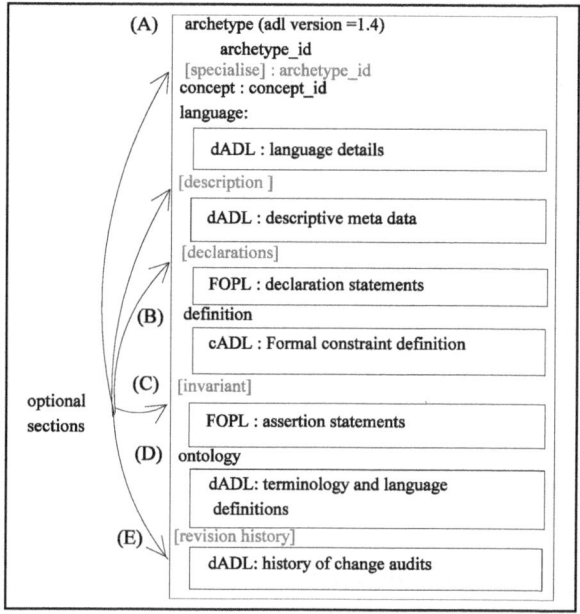

Fig. 2. Structure of Archetype

At the storage level, the EHR components use a Reference Model (RM) [5] for the physical structure. The archetype defines constraints on the structure, types and values of instances of the RM. It enables archetypes to have different granularity levels according to the different classes defined in the RM. Thus, there are different categories of archetypes such as 'Composition', 'Section', 'Entry' and 'Item-Structure'. Each category may have a different structure. Archetypes are stored in common agreed repositories that allow both sides, source and receptor, to identify the semantic links and relationships between the concepts included within an EHR Extract. EuroRec[1] requirements include recommendations for repositories [11]. There are the public archetypes repositories [9] across the world such as openEHR Clinical Knowledge Manager (CKM), NHS repository, Minas Gerais repository and Swedish CKM.

The current research indicates the need for building user interfaces (UI) on the top of qualitatively designed archetypes, thus helping to obtain correct and

---

[1] The European Institute for Health Records or EuroRec Institute [11] is a non-profit organization that promotes the quality of EHR systems.

complete records. The rest of paper is organized as follows. Section 2 describes the context of archetypes related to improving quality aspects. Section 3 describes querying EHR data with emphasis on high-level user-interfaces for semi-skilled users. The dynamic generation of a user-interface based on archetype is discussed in Section 4. Section 5 describes the system configurations. Section 6 presents related work and discussions. Finally, section 7 presents the summary and conclusions.

2   User- Interfaces for Improving Information Quality

2.1   Motivation and Background

Often, the data quality problem is actually a data misinterpretation problem [21]. The data source may not have any "error," within the data that it provided. However, the content may not convey the meaning that the receiver expected. The issue is about how data in one context can be used in a different context. This is a desirable goal. It is sought through standardization efforts [21]. The current research addresses the problem of semantic heterogeneity in EHR domain. The archetypes created through domain knowledge governance and developing technologies, provide data that is consistent with receiver preference (service layer), thereby improving the data quality at the receiver end. A prototype query interface has been implemented at the service layer for the EHRs that follow the openEHR standard.

2.2   Improving Data and Information Quality

Table 1 gives various DQ requirements [37] and their aspects in archetypes. High quality archetypes with high quality clinical content are the key to semantic interoperability of clinical systems [12]. They aid in decision support. Archetypes may define compositional relationships to other archetypes by using 'Slots'. A 'Slot' sets constraints in the archetype nodes to define which archetypes can be allowed or excluded. These increase the reusability of archetypes because these follow the definition of hierarchical structures between archetypes. Terminologies also help in achieving semantic interoperability. Terms within archetypes are linked (bound) to external terminologies like SNOMED-CT [32]. Thus, archetypes have been chosen in current study for resolving the problem of semantic heterogeneity in EHR domain.

3   Intelligent Querying through Archetypes

Considering the challenges faced by today's health record systems (the need to record more data, the need to analyse more data and the need to share more data), querying plays a vital role in enhancing the information quality of EHR systems. The hindrances to querying are detailed knowledge of schema and specialized knowledge of query language.

Table 1. Data Quality Requirements and Aspects

Data Quality Requirements	Aspects in Archetypes
Accuracy and Validity	Business rules defined in archetypes
Believability	Archetypes developed by domain experts
Accessibility	Sharable Archetypes (through common repository)
Timeliness	New and modified archetypes are developed as clinical knowledge expands
Completeness	Standardized data definitions, content and structure
Interpretability	Fine granularity of data in archetypes and Linkage to terminology standards
Ease of Understanding	Translatable to different languages without language primacy
Concise Representation	Rich health data definitions
Consistency	Ontology-based archetype transformation process (e.g. openEHR archetypes to HL7 CDA archetypes or CEN 13606 archetypes)

The Agency for Healthcare Research and Quality (AHRQ) has found low EHR adoption rates for physician groups [2]. Need of high-level query language interface (as a need) has been identified for improving information quality gains and ease of access in EHR domain [29]. In order to achieve information quality, the current research identifies the use of generated user interfaces for the purpose of querying. It allows querying data at the finest level of granularity (providing flexibility).

3.1 Schema Analysis

EHRs allow multiple representations [5]. In principle, EHRs can be represented as relational structures (governed by an object/relational mapping layer), and in various XML storage representations.

The schema of the EHR consists of set of archetypes along with their parameters and the relationships they have with one another (Figure 3). Archetypes in our data model correspond to an entity set. The parameters of the archetype include not only simple and multi-valued attributes, but also complex-typed attributes. Unlike ER model, our model does not support relationship attributes nor does it distinguish between strong and weak attributes.

EHR has a hierarchical structure. An archetypable data instance in an openEHR standard based EHR is either a 'composition', or a 'section' (which must be contained in a composition or section), or an 'entry' (which must be contained in a composition or section), or an 'item structure' (which must be contained within an entry or item structure). The hierarchical structure of EHR and categories of archetypes based on openEHR standard is shown in Figure 4.

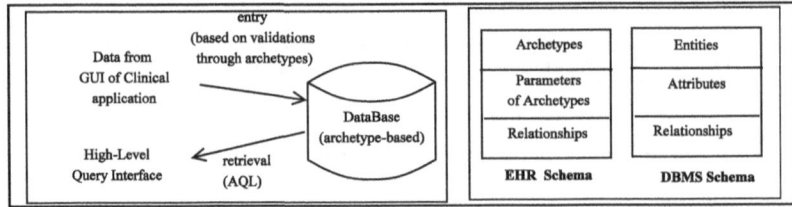

Fig. 3. Querying archetype-based EHR based on analogy of EHR Schema and DBMS Schema

The archetype paradigm (containing categories) is more flexible and easily scalable because it provides the means to handle the knowledge evolution. This technology avoids reimplementation of systems, migrating databases and allows the creation of future-proof systems. Also, these categories are based on the clinical investigator recording process [5], hence improving data quality improvement.

In order to create a data instance of a parameter of EHR, we need different archetypes in ADL, and also these archetypes may belong to different categories of archetypes. For example, to create a data instance for Heart Rate, we need two different archetypes-namely, encounter and heart rate. These archetypes belong to different categories viz., 'composition' and 'observation' (having different structure). At the time of query, a user faces this problem- which archetypes must be included in querying?

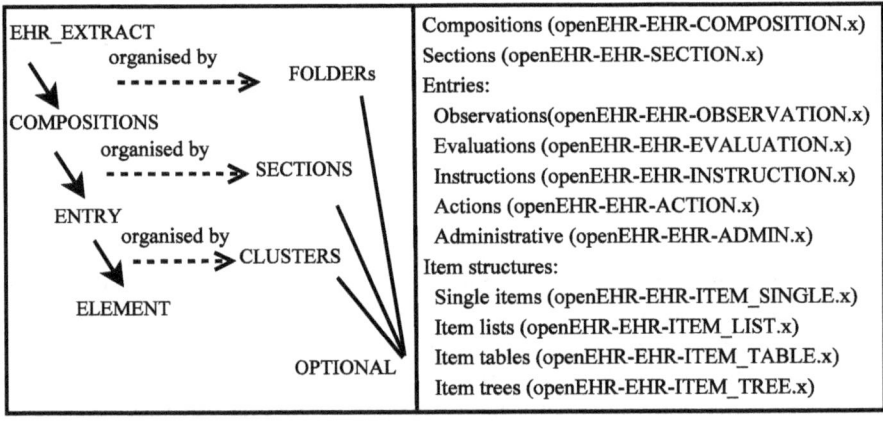

Fig. 4. Hierarchical structure of EHR and categories of archetypes

3.2   Data Analysis

Relatively few archetypes are used to construct quite large slabs of data; a clinical example would be 'ECG results', where one archetype corresponds to 10 leads' worth of time-series data, with possibly hundreds of samples. Consider a simple EHR of health encounter consisting of SOAP (subjective, objective, assessment, plan), which further consists of blood_pressure and heart_rate. The instance data of such an EHR is very large. The archetype map is much smaller than its data as shown in Figure 5. It is a suitable basis for optimized querying [7].

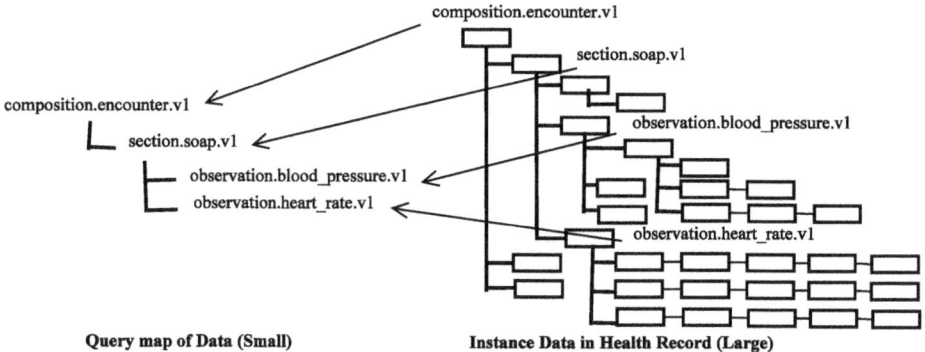

Fig. 5. Data analysis of an EHR transaction [based on 7]

4   Dynamic Generation of User-Interfaces

Recent research emphasizes that good graphical user interfaces that support customization and data validation play a decisive role for user acceptance and data quality [31]. It shows the feasibility of generation of user interfaces from openEHR archetypes. However the use of Mozilla XML User Interface Language (XUL) revealed some problems (e.g., implementation bugs, inconsistencies, lack of modern development environment). Thurston [35] mentions that the presentation of EHR data must be flexible to support a variety of access needs and should be extensible to support the presentation/viewing needs of various clinical and administrative institutions. The opereffa project is the real model of practical EHR use (which is based on openEHR standard) [26]. It makes use of archetype-based user interfaces for the purpose of data entry and validation. Our proposed study implements the tool for generating user interfaces. It shows its usage for the purpose of intelligent querying, and for improving information quality aspects. This is the first initiative taken in this regard.

4.1   User-Interfaces for EHRs

The generated user interfaces records the maximal data about the physiological measurements (Figure 6). For example, blood pressure is higher if a person is lying down than if they are sitting or standing. The reading itself has little meaning without detailed information about the context in which it was taken. This leads to data quality enhancements. Further, the generated UI provides runtime validation of data input - thus improving data entry quality. For example, ADL for archetype 'heart rate' (Figure 6 (left) , line 20) defines the constraint that rate should be greater than 0.

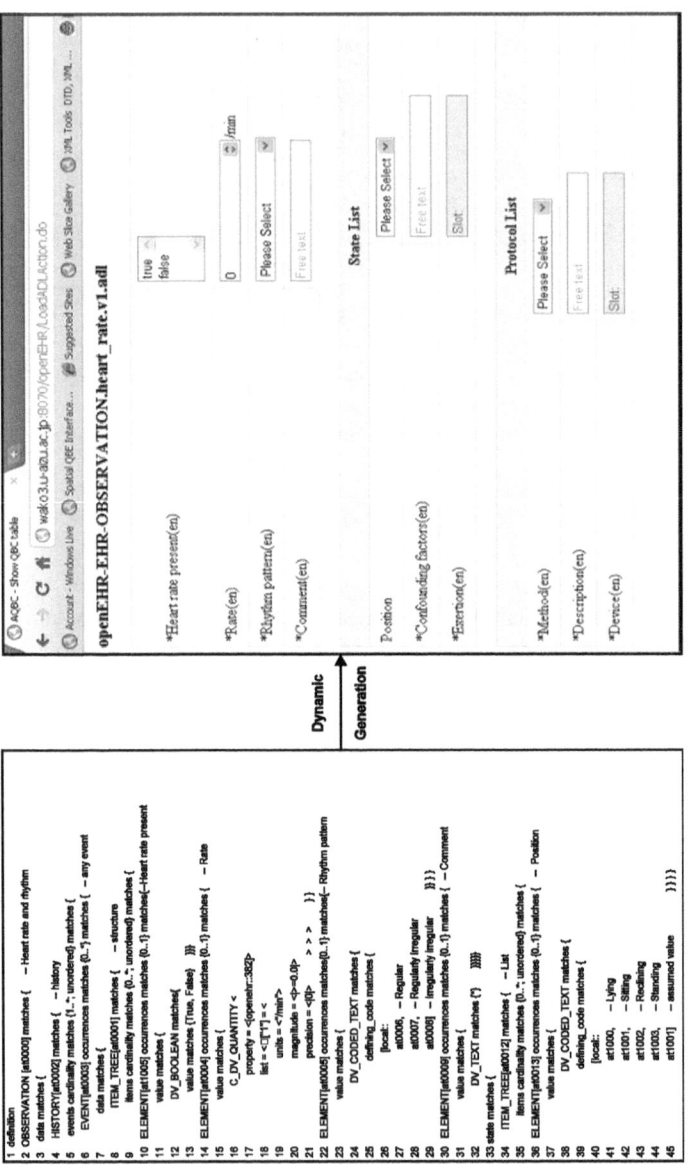

Fig. 6. Dynamic Generation of User Interface for archetype 'heart rate'

This constraint has been represented as shown under 'rate' field in the generated UI (second graphical widget in Figure 6 (right) shows value of '0' and permits the data value only greater than it).

4.1.1 Challenges Encountered

The challenges during automatic generation of user-interfaces are dealing with:

(i) Multitude of representations.
(ii) Different categories of archetypes having different structures.

The prototype deals with the multitude representations. A little difficulty is being faced while dealing with the link type ('reference') object and multimedia ('media-type') object. For example, in case of link type object, the module needs first to search for finding the corresponding object (it may be quantity, text, date), followed by returning the link path. Consider another example, in case of 'media-type' object; it is described by referring to a URL according to openEHR Java API. However, URL is mentioned but is stated through codes. ADL has codes such as '[425, 426, 427,...]', which imply that data should be displayed as [image/cgm, image/gif, image/tiff,...]. The software has been coded with a conversion table (for instance, change of '425' to 'image/cgm').

Archetypes belong to any one among following categories (composition, section, entry and item-structure). There are five sorts of entries (observation, evaluation, action, instruction, administrative) and four types of item-structures - single entities (e.g. weight, height), lists (e.g. blood test results), tables (e.g., visual acuity results) and trees (e.g., biochemistry results) (Figure 4). During implementation, it has been observed that 'action' category completely has another structure. A different presentation model according to each category of archetype has been being built. Thus, all the concepts (279 developed till date) can be represented by using these small number of presentation models.

For current research, the archetypes have been downloaded from openEHR CKM [23]. The corresponding ADLs are stored as an archetype repository. The process of user interface generation involves the following:

(i) 'LoadADL file' module loads the ADL archetype.
(ii) The category of the archetype is being checked.
(iii) The ADL archetype is read using openEHR Java ADL Parser reference implementation which generates Archetype Object Model representation of the archetype.
(iv) These are further pushed to the browser in the form of HTML, using HTML, JavaScript and JavaScript libraries (jQuery and jQuery UI), which turns simple components into more capable components.
(v) User sees a capable, dynamic HTML based UI.

Our approach is dynamic in the sense that whenever clinical knowledge expands, a new archetype is being developed by domain expert without changing the underlying schema. So, we automatically generate a new user interface based on the newly developed archetype. These can be used further for the purpose of intelligent querying, leading to quality enhancements for end-users.

4.2   Querying EHRs

The current research is an effort towards the archetype-based high-level query interface (Figure 3). In contrast to a traditional setting, where users express queries against the database schema, we assert that the semantics of data can often be understood by viewing the data in the context of the user interface (UI) of the software tool used to enter the data. The conceptual model of the user interface of a data-entry application may bear little or no resemblance to the schema of the underlying database. User's view of data in the application is heavily influenced by how the data appears in the user interface. Our goal is to allow domain experts with little technical skill to understand and query data.

We propose that intelligent querying is possible through the use of

(i) Archetype user-interface (Figure 6) and
(ii) Archetype query maps (Figure 5).

When data is committed, its "archetype query map" [7] is computed, and stored separately to aid efficient querying. The map is simply a list of archetypes used to construct the data, keyed by the actual paths in the data where they are used (Figure 5).

The query interface for heart rate is defined by the contents of its archetype. The availability of automatic generation of user-interface on the top of archetypes is effectively a service interface for data. The tool helps in the inspection of an archetype in advance, which can yield a set of path fragments which can be used to query instances which conform to an archetype. The detailed design specifications with sample query examples are a topic for future consideration. The current research presents the implementation issues and details. The study considers QBE (Query-by-Example) [38] as a model which can support many levels of user skills and many types of functional requirements. It can provide an interface that accepts user's intent and communicates well-formed formulas (W.F.Fs) for computations. The proposed approach is implemented on the basic SQL style data operations for queries (relational algebraic operations/set-theoretic operations). The various query examples have been implemented against the functionality, which includes the basic operations - project, select, rename, negation and join (Table 2). It can be further enhanced to include full query language operations. Most of the healthcare worker's needs are met by the single table style queries (i.e., single archetype based). However, the approach is simple for queries involving multiple archetypes, as it is facilitated by the archetype query map. QBE is a relationally complete language [38]. The proposed approach is a relationally complete language as it is built as an extension to QBE. Thus, QBE can be used for archetype-based EHR data. For querying, it provides archetype as a view which provides user-defined subset of a large database. The implementation snapshots for the following query example are shown in Figure 7. In future, the authors propose to test the functionalities of querying through the described approach for semi-skilled users.

Example: Get the heart rate values where the rate is equal to 120 beats per minute and the heart rhythm is regular.

AQL Expression:
SELECT obs/data[at0002]/events[at0003]/data[at0001]/items[at0004]/value[at0017],
FROM EHR [ehr_id/value=$ehrUid]

CONTAINS COMPOSITION [openEHR-EHR-COMPOSITION.encounter.v1]
CONTAINS OBSERVATION obs openEHR-EHR-OBSERVATION.heart_rate.v1]
WHERE
obs/data[at0002]/events[at0003]/data[at0001]/items[at0004]/value[at0017]=120 AND
obs/data[at0002]/events[at0003]/data[at0001]/items[at0005]/value = 'regular'

Query interface:
   Step 1. The concept 'heart_rate' is known and selected by the health worker for a specified patient. (Figure 7(a)).
   Step 2. The required archetypes connected with 'heart_rate', that is, 'encounter' and 'heart_rate' are prompted to the user in the form of tabular data. (Figure 7(b)).
      (archetype description of 'heart_rate' presented by the system)
      (archetype description of 'encounter' presented by the system)
      [Restrict] and [project] single patient data

The system support facilities for specifying restrict operation (rate=120 AND rhythm= 'regular'). (Figure 7(c)).

5   System Configurations and Architecture

Client-server architecture has been used as shown in Figure 8. The prototype system has been implemented using Java 6 [17], Struts 1.3.10 [33]. A tomcat 6.0 [36] server has been used. The libraries from openEHR Java API 1.0.1 [25] have been incorporated. The other components used are JavaScript (JS) libraries such as, jQuery 1.6.2 [19] and jQuery UI 1.8.16 [20]. jQuery UI provides abstractions for low-level interaction and animation, advanced effects and high-level, themeable widgets, built on top of the jQuery JavaScript Library, that you can use to build highly interactive web applications.

   The current prototype has been implemented based on standardized openEHR specifications. To standardize the representation of an international electronic health record, the abstract specifications are defined using the UML notation and formal textual class specifications [5]. The prototype makes use of the archetypes downloaded from a public repository named openEHR CKM [23]. It has 279 numbers of archetypes developed through domain-knowledge governance till date. The prototype has been tested by generation of user-interfaces for a selected list of archetypes. A sample is presented in Figure 9. It consists of examples taken from each category of the archetypes.

   Requirement of specific user interface elements and screen design for medical applications have been studied in a wider extend recently. There are many research initiatives by Microsoft such as, Microsoft Health Common User Interface (MS CUI) [22] trying to produce UI elements which would serve better than the usual text box, combo box and other well known UI elements. However, investing into strong UI technologies does not solve the problem, because standardized EHR implementations (openEHR) heavily rely on models, in other words composition of RM classes described by ADL [34]. Joining the UI to these models is an architectural challenge.

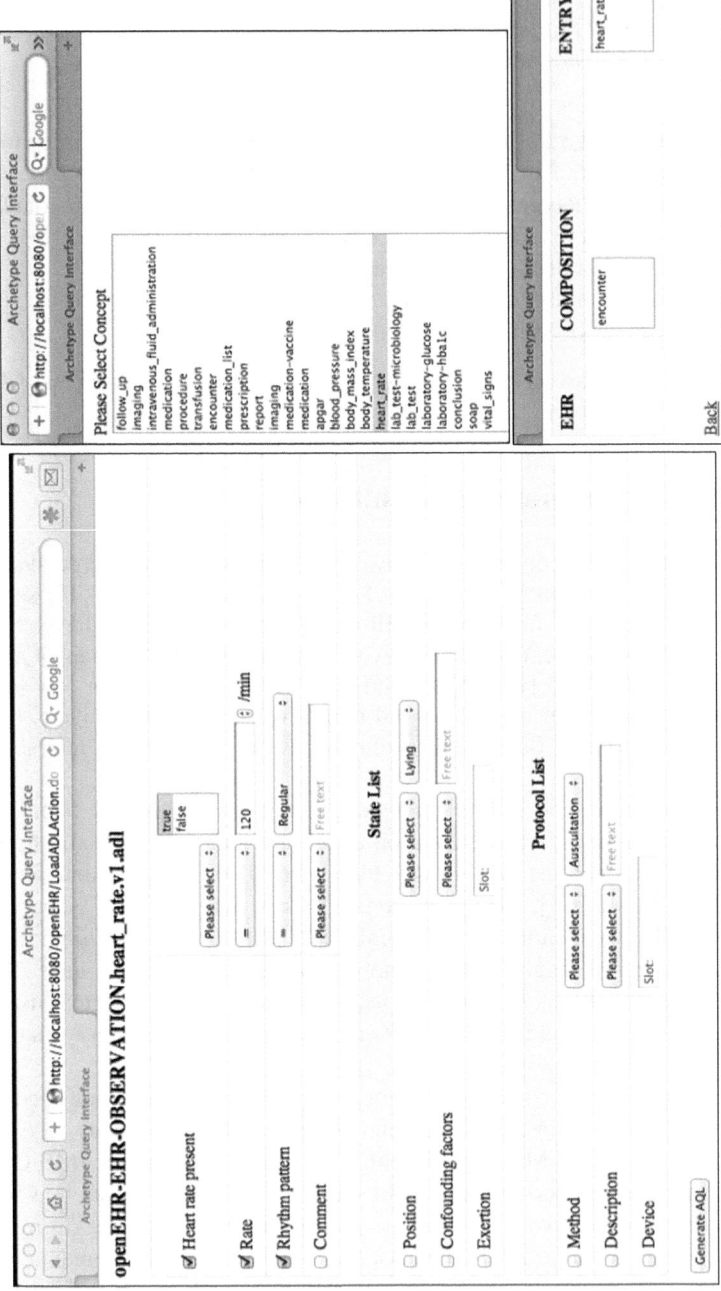

Fig. 7. Snapshots for query example. (a) Snapshot for selecting clinical concept (top-right), (b) Based on chosen concept by user in (a) the related concepts for querying presented by the system (below-right), and (c) Interface for specifying query conditions.

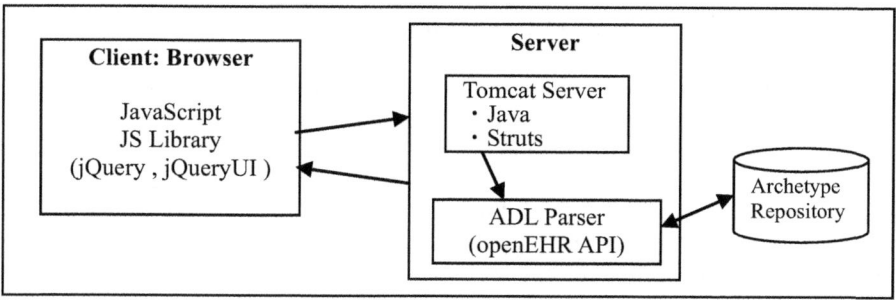

Fig. 8. System Configurations for Generation of User-Interfaces

openEHR-EHR-COMPOSITION.report.v1
openEHR-EHR-COMPOSITION.prescription.v1.adl
openEHR-EHR-EVALUATION.problemdiagnosis.v1
openEHR-EHR-OBSERVATION.laboratory-hba1c.v1
openEHR-EHR-OBSERVATION.blood_pressure.v1
openEHR-EHR-OBSERVATION.body_mass_index.v1
openEHR-EHR-OBSERVATION.heart_rate.v1
openEHR-EHR-OBSERVATION.lab_test-microbiology.v1.adl
openEHR-EHR-ITEM_TREE.medication-vaccine.v1
openEHR-EHR-ITEM_TREE.imaging.v1
openEHR-EHR-ACTION.procedure.v1.adl

Fig. 9. Sample List of Archetypes

Table 2. Relational operations for querying

Query Languages→ QL Functionality↓	SQL	AQL	Proposed approach
Project	√	√	√
Restrict	√	√	√
Rename	√	√	√
Negation	√	√	√
Join	√	√	√
Relational operators/ Boolean Operators	√	√	√
Rename	√	√	√
Disjunction	√	√	√
Union	√	√	√
Difference	√	√	√

6   Related Work and Discussions

Archetype Query Language (AQL) [3] has been developed by openEHR for querying archetype-based EHRs. AQL is used by developer level users (skilled users). Its syntax is complex. It requires more skills than SQL and XQuery, which are at application level. It also requires the knowledge of ADL path. Ocean informatics provides query builder tool for building AQL queries [28]. It often limits the query expressiveness. A common challenge of many query building tools is a case of a complex query. The limitation may be because the chosen graphical metaphor or the tool's native modeling paradigm cannot support all necessary query criteria; or there is limited capability to combine interim solution layers within the tool (e.g., output of one query criterion is input for another criterion). In comparison, the EHR system must have an appealing and responsive high-level query interface that provides a rich overview of data and an effective query mechanism for patient data. It should support semi-skilled users at clinics or hospitals.

All of the form-based query interfaces share two characteristics in common, besides their form-based nature. First, they are all intended to hide some complex query operations from the user. In most cases, the complex query operation in question is the join operator. Second, these techniques typically expose only a subset of the data available in a database. For instance, an application may have a search form for building complex queries to find medical providers in a database, but that form was custom-built by a developer anticipating a certain class of query; one cannot then use the same query form to search for patients. In recent research, one of the metrics that they use to evaluate their generated search forms is coverage of schema elements (tables and foreign keys) because they generate forms only for the most frequently accessed tables and the most frequently issued queries (to keep the number of generated forms low) [18].

Jayapandian and Jagadish [18] proposed tools that generate forms-based query interfaces based on the schema of the database (and the profiles of executed queries). The query interface generation in the current study is through the EHR schema, presented in section 3.1. It uses the bottom-up approach for the query interface generation. In our proposal, the user's view is incorporated despite the use of actual database schema tables, which is more user-friendly. The current research treats the user interface itself as a view schema and constructs the query interface. It does not require users to specify complex operators such as joins. The query interface exposes all the data that is available in the user interface of the application in a similar way, as the QBE approach. It generates a query interface from the conceptual model. The interface poses limitation in the kinds of queries that it can express relative to SQL.

FoxQ [1] and EquiX [8] help end users rather than form developers to build forms to query a database. These approaches provide graphical view of the database schema and allow users to specify predicates on schema attributes to build queries incrementally. We provide a tabular view of archetype map (archetypes involved in querying) and allow users to specify predicates on archetype attributes to build queries incrementally.

Earlier, the use of XQBE (XQuery-by-Example) interface directly over the XML description of archetype has been examined [30]. The XQBE interface requires some knowledge of tree or graphs on the part of users, whereas QBE interface is quite simple and intuitive to use. In the current approach, the archetype query map in combination with archetype user interfaces provide the information of what items will be available in any actual data, enabling complex queries to be served easily.

6.1   Information Quality Requirements

The keyword and form-based interfaces have limitations for EHR domain, where obtaining accurate and qualitative data is very important for medical users. Suitable query language capable interfaces enhance information quality. Many previous studies have identified the need of high-level query language interface for improving information quality gains in EHR domain [29] [32].

Various information and data quality issues have been reported in data integration systems [4]:

(i) Technological heterogeneity
(ii) Schema heterogeneity due to
    - Different data model and
    - Different data representations, and
(iii) Instance-level heterogeneity (caused by different conflicting data values provided by distinct sources for the same objects). These are caused by quality errors such as accuracy, consistency, completeness and currency errors.

The recent research studies highlight the handling of these issues through the use of abstract specifications (defined using UML), adherence to a single Reference Model and adoption of international set of archetypes developed through domain knowledge governance. Thus, this paper contributes in following ways. First, it demonstrates that information and data quality can be included as an integral part during the user-interface generation. Secondly, it offers a perspective for the migration from today's focus on the EHR domain towards a broader concern for enhancing information quality. The research highlights the need for Quality of the content being accessed from EHR repositories. It is related to topics like "structuring" the data, information sources, modeling and encoding, and consolidating redundant data. It focuses on how the method of data capture (through archetypes) plays an important role in shaping what is possible to measure in an electronic environment.

The generated user-interfaces specify the design of the clinical data that a health care professional needs to store in a computer system. Thus, we show how the generation of UI can be used to capture context knowledge and improve information access and its quality by automatically reconciling semantic differences between the sources and the receivers. The proposed interface meets a key requirement for semantic interoperable EHR systems which is the key to information and data quality in healthcare domain.

7   Summary and Conclusions

Keeping in mind, the ultimate goal of data engineering, which is to put high quality data in the hands of users, this study has explored the generation of user interfaces from archetypes (which are powerful representations of clinical knowledge). The current research treats the user interface itself as a view schema and constructs the query interface against it that may be more user-friendly. The efforts are undergoing for implementation to further test the approach with sample set of queries for all database operations with medical users. The graphical interface would complement efforts by the openEHR foundation, Microsoft, ISO 13606 and CEN/TC251 (European committee for standardization), which are working on semantic interoperable EHRs, making use of archetype-based EHRs. Thus, querying in an environment, where all sources and all receivers of data always have the same meanings, will reduce the problem of semantic heterogeneity.

In contrast to the old message paradigm, the archetype paradigm is more flexible and easily scalable because it provides a means to handle knowledge evolution. This technology avoids reimplementation of systems, migrating databases and allows the creation of future-proof systems. The study explores the aspects of archetypes considering the DQ attributes of wholeness, discrete, specialization, simple, generic and re-usable.

References

1. Abraham, R.: FoXQ – XQuery by Forms. In: Proceedings 2003 IEEE Symposium on Human Centric Computing Languages and Environments (2003)
2. Agency for Healthcare Research and Quality (AHRQ). Research Finds Low Electronic Health Record Adoption Rates for Physician Groups. Press release (September 14, 2005)
3. Archetype Query Language Description, http://www.openehr.org/wiki/display/spec/Archetype+Query+Language+Description
4. Batini, C., Scannapieco, M.: Data Quality: Concepts, Methodologies, and Techniques. Springer, Berlin (2006)
5. Beale, T., Heard, S.: openEHR Architecture: Architecture Overview in The openEHR release 1.0.2. In: Beale, T., Heard, S. (eds.) openEHR Foundation (2008)
6. Beale, T., Heard, S.: The openEHR Archetype Model-Archetype Definition Language ADL 1.4. openEHR release 1.0.2 (December 12, 2008)
7. Beale, T.: Archetypes Constraint-based Domain Models for Future proof Information Systems. The OpenEHR Foundation (August 21, 2001)
8. Cohen, S., Kanza, Y., Kogan, Y., Sagiv, Y., Nutt, W., Serebrenik, A.: EquiX—A search and query language for XML. Journal of the American Society for Information Science and Technology 53, 454–466 (2002)
9. Conde, A.M.: Towards best practice in the Archetype Development Process. Master thesis, Trinity College Dublin, Center for Health Informatics, Department of Computer Science (September 2010)
10. European committee for Standardization, Technical committee on Health informatics, Standard for EHR communication, http://www.cen.eu
11. EUROREC. European Record Institute (2010), http://www.eurorec.org/
12. Garde, S., Hovenga, E.J.S., Gränz, J., Foozonkhah, S., Heard, S.: Managing Archetypes for Sustainable and Semantically Interoperable Electronic Health Records. Electronic Journal of Health Informatics (2007)
13. HL7 (Health Level 7), http://www.hl7.org (retrieved November 10, 2010)
14. HL7 CDA (Clinical Document Architecture), Release 2, http://www.hl7.org/v3ballot/html/infrastructure/cda/cda.htm

15. ISO 13606-1, Health informatics - Electronic health record communication - Part 1: Reference Model (2008)
16. ISO 13606-2, Health informatics - Electronic health record communication - Part 2: Archetype interchange specification (2008)
17. Java 6, http://www.oracle.com/technetwork/java/javasebusiness/downloads/java-archive-downloads-javafx-419431.html#jdk-6u23-javafx-1.3.1-oth-JPR
18. Jayapandian, M., Jagadish, H.V.: Automated Creation of a Forms-based Database Query Interface. In: VLDB 2008, Auckland, New Zealand, August 25-28, pp. 695–709 (2008)
19. jQuery 1.6.2, http://jquery.com/
20. jQueryUI 1.8.16, http://jqueryui.com/
21. Madnick, S., Zhu, H.: Improving Data Quality through Effective Use of Data Semantics. Journal of Data & Knowledge Engineering - Special issue: WIDM 2004 59(2) (November 2006)
22. Microsoft Health Common User Interface (MS CUI), http://www.mscui.net/
23. openEHR Clinical Knowledge Manager version 1.0.5, http://www.openehr.org/knowledge
24. openEHR Foundation, http://www.openehr.org
25. openEHR Java API, http://www.openehr.org/wiki/display/projects/Java+Project+Download
26. Opereffa Project, http://opereffa.chime.ucl.ac.uk/introduction.jsf
27. Orfanidis, L., Bamidis, P.D., Eaglestone, B.: Data Quality Issues in Electronic Health Records: An Adaptation Framework for the Greek Health System. Health Informatics Journal 10(1), 23 (2004)
28. Query builder, Ocean Informatics, http://www.oceaninformatics.com/Solutions/ocean-products/Clinical-Modelling/Ocean-Query-Builder.html (accessed April 4, 2011)
29. Sachdeva, S., Bhalla, S.: Electronic Health Record- A Framework for Standardization and Semantic Interoperability, Technical Report, University of Aizu, Technical Report 2010-001 (November 29, 2010)
30. Sachdeva, S., Bhalla, S.: Implementing High-Level Query Language Interfaces for Archetype-Based Electronic Health Records Database. In: International Conference on Management of Data (COMAD), pp. 235–238 (December 2009)
31. Schuler, T., Garde, S., Heard, S., Beale, T.: Towards automatic generation of GUIs from archetypes. Studies in Health Technology and Informatics 124, 221–226 (2006)
32. SNOMED (Systematized Nomenclature of Medicine) Clinical Terms, http://www.snomed.org/documents/snomed_overview.pdf
33. Struts 1.3.10, http://struts.apache.org/download.cgi
34. Technology and architecture challenges in UI implementation, http://www.openehr.org/wiki/display/projects/Technology+and+architecture+challenges+in+UI+implementation
35. Thurston, L.M.: Flexible and Extensible Display of Archetyped Data: The openEHR Presentation Challenge. In: Proceedings of HIC 2006 and HINZ 2006, Brunswick East, Vic.: Health Informatics Society of Australia, pp. 28–36 (2006)
36. Tomcat 6.0, http://tomcat.apache.org/download-60.cgi
37. Wang, R.Y., Zaid, M., Lee, Y.W.: Book on "Data Quality". Kluwer Academic publishers (2001)
38. Zloof, M.M.: Query-By-Example. In: AFIPS 1975: Proceedings of the National Computer Conference and Exposition, May 19-22 (1975)

Exploring OLAP Data with Parallel Dimension Views

Mark Sifer

University of Wollongong,
School of Information Systems and Technology,
Wollongong, Australia
msifer@uow.edu.au

Abstract. Existing OLAP user interfaces typically explore hierarchical multi-dimensional data through tabular data cube views. Aggregation is supported by dimension hierarchy level selection and filtering by slice and dice operations. Aggregation determines the size of data cube cells while filtering determines the cells in the view. Table based interfaces provide views that typically include two or three dimensions at a chosen level of aggregation. This paper describes an interface that is based on an alternative paradigm, parallel coordinates. However, instead of parallel axis, we use parallel dimension trees. The interface supports data aggregation and filtering operations. It supports both proportional and fixed value dimension scales. It supports a range of exploration tasks including viewing data distribution, comparing data distributions and viewing correlation. The main benefit of our interface is its support for rapid and flexible overviews across many dimensions and multiple hierarchy levels at the cost of less detailed views.

Keywords: OLAP, data exploration, visualisation, user interface.

1   Introduction

OLAP (OnLine Analytical Processing) [2] is the interactive exploration of hierarchical multi-dimensional data. For example sales data can be analysed along product category, price, location and date dimensions. Multiple aggregation levels can be defined for each dimension. For example dates can be aggregated by day, month, quarter and year. The standard OLAP data models is a data cube with hierarchies over each dimension. A data cube is formed by aggregating n-dimensional data facts into n-dimensional base cube cells where cells can contain fact counts or the sum of a fact measure such as sales value. The dimension hierarchy's lowest levels determine base cube cells. Views over a base cube are facilitated by two transformations (i) a cube operator applied to add subtotals [4] and (ii) further aggregation of base cells into larger cells (that sum base cell values) determined by higher dimension tree levels.

Table based OLAP interfaces such as pivot tables [6,9,10] support all possible tabular views over a data cube at varying granularities. A user can slice and dice to restrict the cube to tabular subsets and can drill-down or roll-up though dimension hierarchies to view the cube at different granularities. These operations apply equally to cells containing aggregated facts and subtotals.

S. Kikuchi et al. (Eds.): DNIS 2011, LNCS 7108, pp. 126–136, 2011.

An OLAP interface supports a variety of user exploration tasks: looking up the value of a specific data cube cell, observing and comparing data distributions across a dimension for a chosen subset, and looking for association and correlation. For example a user may wish to see the distribution of hat sales by location and then break this down by quarter to compare the first and second quarter sales' distributions. A user may also want to check if there is an association between product type hat and particular locations. Table based interfaces have two major limitations. First, as the number of dimensions increases initial exploration can become more difficult. Table views typically contain 2 or 3 dimensions along which data distribution can be easily read. If there are many dimensions, say five or more, the user must choose a subset of these dimensions to display and pivot. If there are even more dimensions, there are even more choices to be made. Second, if the data is sparse, views over the base cube and lower aggregation levels become unusable as most cells are empty. Examples of sparse data include web log and network traffic particularly when small time slices are used.

We have developed an OLAP interface that targets these issues. It provides data cube views that are less sensitive to the number of dimensions and to data sparsity, while still providing aggregation and filtering capabilities to support standard OLAP user tasks. It is implemented in our SGViewer (Structured Graph Viewer) tool. The interface is based on (i) parallel coordinates rather than cartesian coordinates to support 5-8 dimension views and (ii) proportional hierarchical dimension scales rather than fixed scales to support both dense and sparse data. The tradeoff for our systems benefits is that each individual dimension view is less detailed, containing 1 or 2 dimensions. We expect our approach can compliment traditional tabular approaches, particularly for early exploratory data analysis of new data where viewing 1-D distributions for each dimension is a natural starting point.

Our system has been presented [8] from an information visualisation perspective. This paper builds on that work by providing an OLAP perspective and describing support for fixed scale dimension views and correlation views.

The next section presents related work. Section 3 presents a mapping from data-cube to parallel dimension views, our hierarchical proportional dimension view visualisation and our division and restriction query operators. Section 4 presents a sales data use case and data preparation, Section 5 presents our systems support for association and correlation views and Section 6 discusses limitations.

2   Related Work

The standard interface for OLAP is the pivot-table. To setup a pivot-table a user first decides on the axis for their table by dragging dimensions from a list of dimensions onto X and Y-axis. If more than one dimension is dragged onto the X-axis a nested table is formed. Colours can be allocated to a dimension. Users choose from a wide variety of charts, such as bar charts, to present their tables.

Tableau [10] based on Polaris [9] is leading pivot-table software. Its unique feature is support for nested tables that can show a grid of charts. When used in combination with a colour legend a single table can show five dimensions of data. Tableau also allows dashboards of coordinated tables and filters to be created. Microsoft has recently innovated their pivot-table offering with Power Pivot [6], which supports dimension sliders that act as global filters on a dashboard of up to four charts.

Parallel coordinate charts [5] typically show n-dimensional data using n vertical axis where each axis has an annotated scale. Each data point is shown by plotting it on each axis, then drawing a path through these axis positions. The biggest advantage of parallel coordinates is they easily scale to 10 or more dimensions. Unlike bar charts, which are designed to present aggregated data, parallel coordinates work best when presenting distinct points. However, a range of parallel coordinate systems have been developed that support some aggregation through the use of density map style blurring [3] or explicit aggregation in the case of parallel sets [1]. Our work is not table based like Tableau, it is parallel axis based. Rather than supporting a single level of aggregation [5], our system supports the multiple levels of aggregation that are implicit in a dimension hierarchy.

OLAP is part of what is now called BI (business intelligence), which is concerned with integrating manual data exploration with statistical and heuristic analysis to find patterns and make predictions. Our focus in this paper is with the traditional OLAP task of supporting manual data exploration via interactive charts.

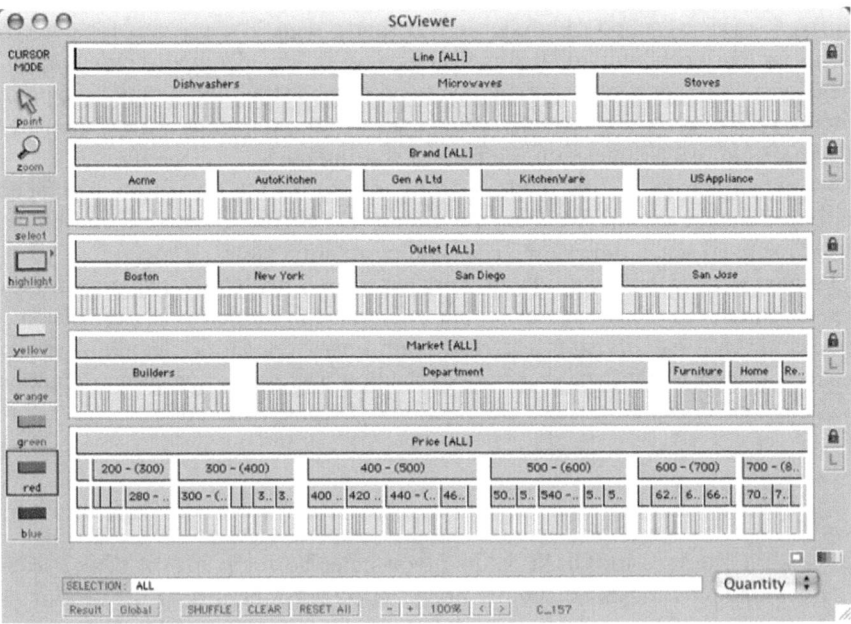

Fig. 1. Startup screenshot of SGViewer presenting sales data in: line, brand, outlet, market and price dimensions. Parallel dimensions are stacked vertically while widths indicate proportions.

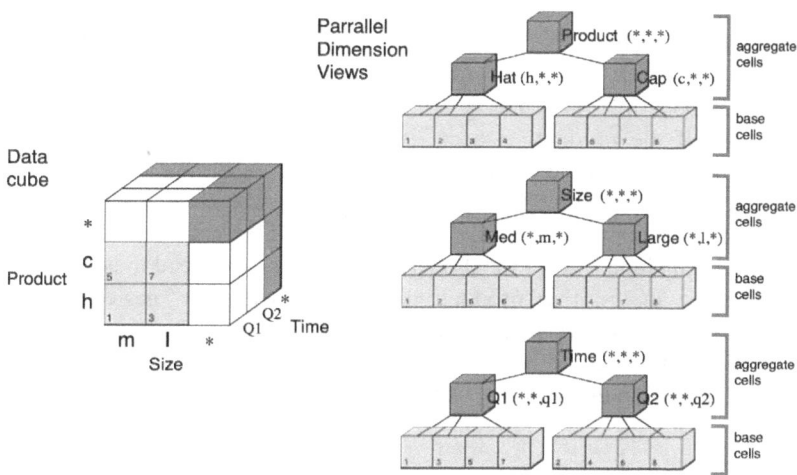

Fig. 2. Sales data cube with subtotals above dimension views containing some aggregate cells and all base cells

3   Parallel Dimension Views

This section presents our interface design based on parallel dimension views. Fig. 1 shows our interface presenting each dimension in a separate parallel view. Here we define which data cube cells appear in an initial view, and then present a hierarchical proportional visualisation for each dimension view. Finally two ways of evolving views to present additional portions of a data-cube are described.

Table 1. A fact table of sales data with product, size and time dimensions and sales counts

	Product	Size	Time	Sales
1	hat	med	Q1	100
2	hat	med	Q2	50
3	hat	large	Q1	150
4	hat	large	Q2	250
5	cap	med	Q1	120
6	cap	med	Q2	160
7	cap	large	Q1	110
8	cap	large	Q2	200

Table 1 presents a fact table of sales data that has been aggregated in three dimensions: product, size and time. The eight facts appear in fig. 2 as the eight yellow base cube cells. The remaining cube cells contain subtotals. Each cell in the cube is a tuple (p,s,t). Dimension totals are denoted with '*'. For example, (h,*,*) denotes the total sales for hats over all combinations of size and time while (*,*,*) denotes the total of all sales. The latter cell appears at the top-right-back of the cube.

The overall total and one dimensional subtotals (those tuples with two *'s such as (h,*,*) are the red cube cells. These cells form the top of each parallel dimension view. The product view is a tree with root (*,*,*) and children hat (h,*,*) and cap (c,*,*) placed above all base cube cells. Size and time dimension views are built in the same way. If the product, size or time dimension hierarchies contained more levels the extra levels would also be included. Note each base cube cell is placed under its appropriate subtotal, so the order of base cube cells is different in each dimension view. The three views only show a subset of the subtotal cells; there are 12 cells that are not included. Additional operators will be introduced to access them.

Fig. 3 (top) shows the product dimension with our nested proportional visualisation. Cell values are represented by relative widths. The cap cell with value 590 is slightly wider that the hat cell with value 550. The highest valued base cube cell (with value 250) is the widest. Overall the dimension view shows a tree of nested proportions.

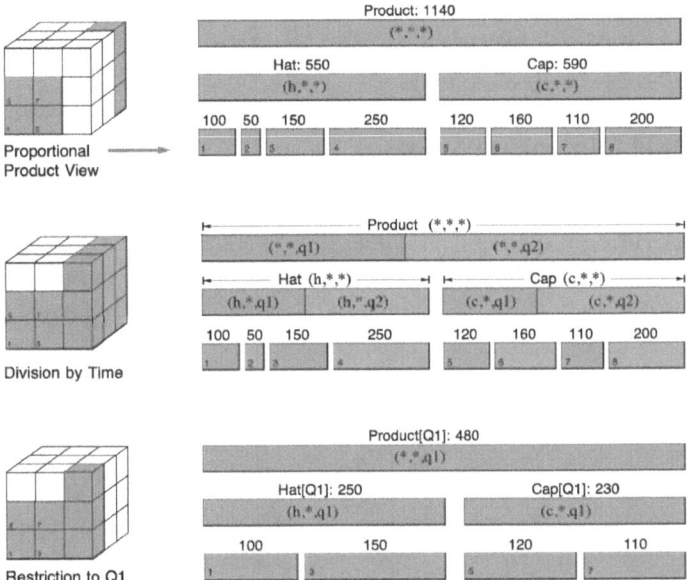

Fig. 3. The initial proportional product view, the view after division by time and view after restriction to Q1

Views can be divided or restricted to see more detail. Fig. 3 (middle) shows the effect of dividing the product view by time. The top box shows three values: the overall total (*,*,*) and its division into (*,*,q1) and (*,*,q2) parts. Hat and cap boxes have been divided in a similar way. The (h,*,*) cell has been divided into (h,*,q1) and (h,*,q2) proportional parts. The eight base cube cells are now coloured according to quarter. The divided view presents nine subtotal proportions. Fig. 3 (bottom) shows the effect of restricting the product view to the first quarter, that is to the subtotals (*,*,q1), (h,*,q1) and (c,*,q1) and four base cells.

Our design coordinates dimension views. Division and restriction are applied by making selections in one or more views to effect other views. A colour partition of the time view divides the other dimension views into slices. A filter selection of Q1 in the time view restricts the other dimensions to the Q1 slice. Division can be applied once while restriction can be applied repeatedly. Restricted views can be coordinated in a variety of ways [7]. The default coordination is progressive querying; when a selection is made in a dimension view, later selections do not change that view. Division and repeated restriction can be used in combination to view and compare distributions across any part of a data cube.

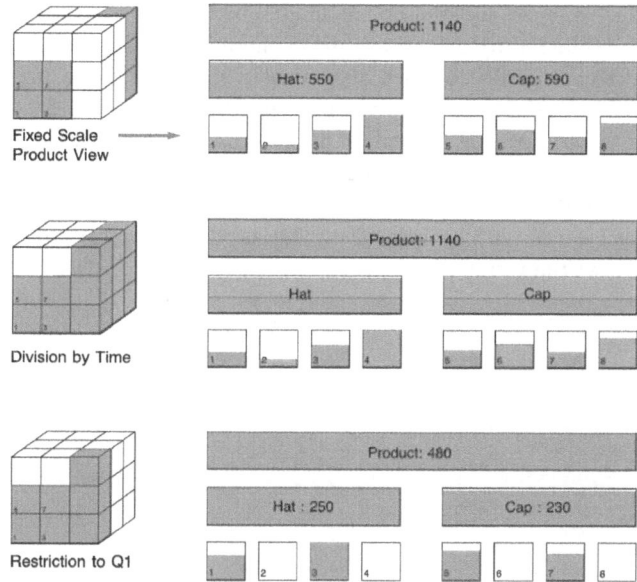

Fig. 4. Fixed scale views of the product dimension: the initial view, the view after division by time and view after restriction to Q1

Dimensions can also be shown with a fixed tree rather than a proportional tree scale. Fig. 4 shows an example. The leaves of each dimension tree view are base cube cells that have a fixed width, where fill area is varied to reflect varying counts or measure values. Cell and category box fill areas are relative, that is, they are relative to the highest value on each tree level. For example in the initial view, the highest cell value is 250, so cell 1 with a value of 100 is shown 40% filled. Query operations no longer change the visible structure of dimension trees. Division by time, then filtering by time, change cell and category box fill areas rather than change cell and category box widths, where the latter can have the effect of excluding cells and categories from view.

4   System Usage

4.1   Exploring Sales Data

Fig. 1 showed an initial view of an electrical appliance distributor's sales data, a small dataset of 365 orders (for 5254 items in total) with five dimensions and two measures: quantity and profit per order. Fig. 1 showed most sales were by department stores rather than specialty furniture or home stores. The overall distribution of sales across the other dimensions can also be read. Sales were evenly divided among three appliances while there were more sales to San Diego and San Jose than to Boston and New York. Sales were evenly split above and below the 500-dollar price point.

We wish to explore further. We are most interested in department stores as they were the largest contributor, but we also wanted more detail on the breakdown of sales from Boston and New York versus San Diego and San Jose. We selected department stores to restrict the other dimension views to department sales and applied green and orange to Boston and New York respectively to divide the other dimensions by these outlets. Finally we shuffled the dimension views placing the selected market view at the bottom and the coloured view at the top to make reading easier. Fig. 5 shows the result.

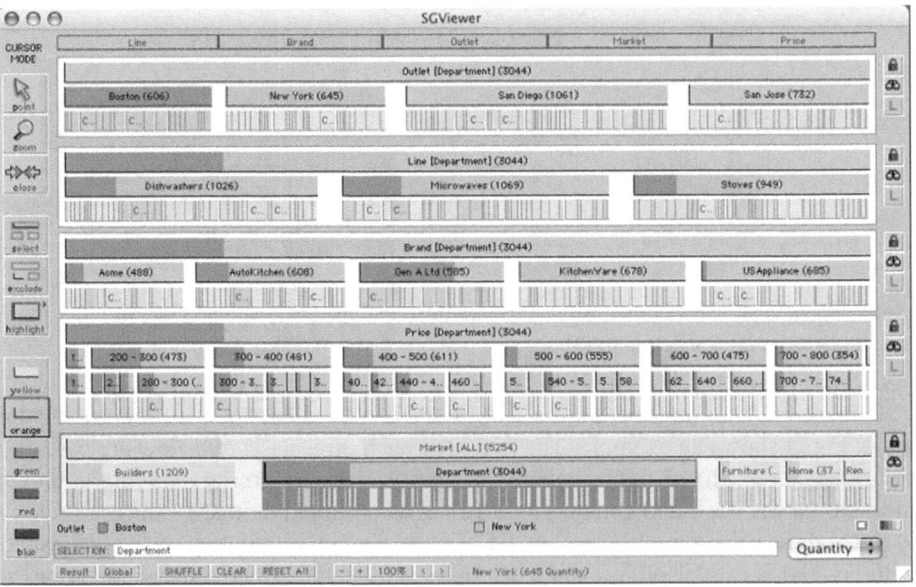

Fig. 5. Exploring sales data with SGViewer. Outlet, Line, Brand and Price dimension views have been restricted to department while all dimensions have been divided into Boston, New York and other outlet sales.

The distribution of sales from department stores for Boston, New York and other outlets are shown in the line, brand and price point views. The line view shows each location's sales are evenly spread across the three appliances. However the brand view shows divergence. Most Boston sales are Gen A brand while most New York sales are for AutoKitchen or KitchenWare brand items. The price dimension view shows most Boston sales are below the 500-dollar price point while most New York sales are above the 500-dollar price point. It would be interesting to breakdown the line dimension view further by brand to see how the KitchenWare and Gen A brands associate with individual appliance types. This would require a further division of the line view. SGViewer supports a second division operator, pattern mask that could be used for this task.

Colour division and pattern division can only be applied in one dimension view. Restrict selections can be made in many dimension views. For example to see the line and brand breakdowns for sales to Boston department stores costing less than 300 dollars we would select Boston, Department and both 100-200 and 200-300 price intervals. This would restrict the line and brand views to Boston and Department and (100-200 or 200-300) sales. SGViewer supports three restriction coordination modes: default, result and global. In the default progressive query mode a selection restricts only those dimension views that have not been selected. In result mode all views are restricted. In global mode no views are restricted instead box borders are highlighted.

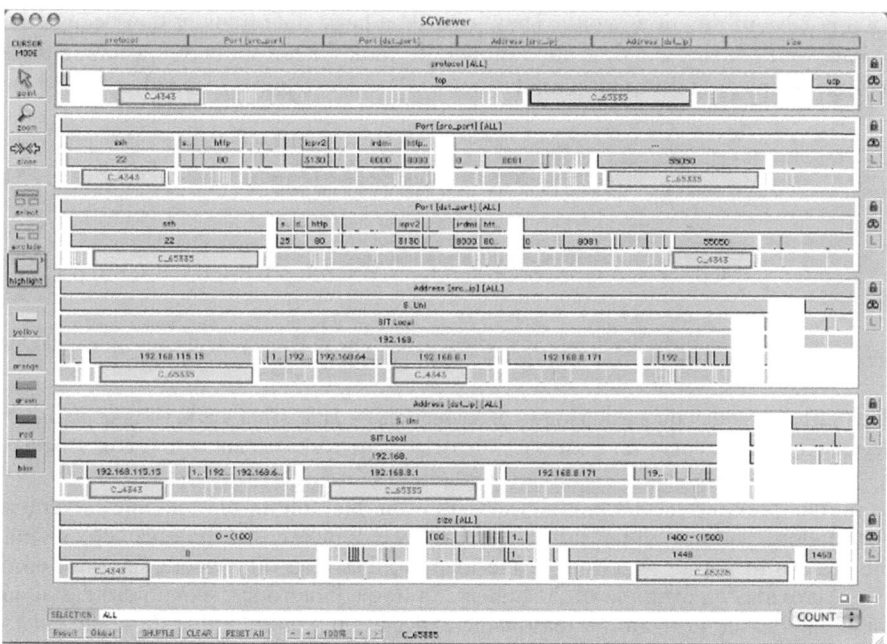

Fig. 6. Network data with six dimensions. A sparse data cube of 100,000 non-empty cells with two hot spots.

4.2   Data Preparation

We used a supporting tool MakeSGF to convert our example sales data from a spreadsheet into an SGF (Structured Graph Format) XML document that SGViewer loads. MakeSGF is a Java application while SGViewer is a Java application/applet. MakeSGF's input is a fact table and dimension tables (as tab or comma delimited text files). Numeric scales like prices can be defined without a dimension table. Facts and dimensions are joined by ID matching, interval value matching, prefix text matching or tree path text matching.

5   Association and Correlation Views

This section presents two interface features for showing the relationship between dimensions: hot spots and spectrum colouring. Hot spots are individual base cube cells that have such high values they are visible even when the cube is very large. For example Fig. 6 shows 1 million network message headers that were processed into a sparse data cube of about 100,000 non-empty cells. Given a display width of one thousand pixels, 100 base cells on average will fit into each pixel width. However in Fig. 6 there are two major exceptions, highlighted cells C_4343 and C_65335 that occupy 20% of the view width. They indicate a large data transfer that occupied a lot of bandwidth during the time slice shown. To look for hot spots or clusters in a subset of dimensions or at different granularities SGViewer requires recalculated cube input.

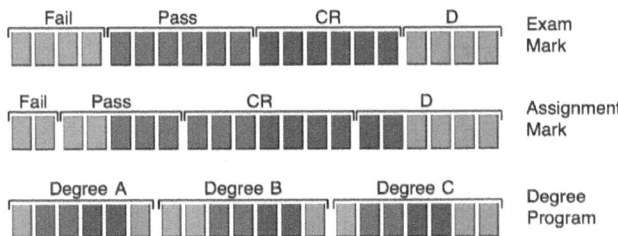

Fig. 7. Three parallel dimension views of student result data: exam mark, assignment mark and degree program. Exam marks correlate with assignment marks but not with degree program.

In the previous sections we used division by colour to compare several data distributions within a dimension view. Here we compare distributions across multiple dimensions to get an overview of the mapping between dimensions for selected data. Fig. 7 provides an example of 20 students in three dimensions: exam mark, assignment mark and degree program. A reasonable expectation would be that those students who did assignments well would also do well in the exam. That is, each student's exam mark rank would match their assignment mark's rank. This is shown in Fig. 7 where assignment mark colour sequence matches the exam mark colour sequence. In contrast each exam grade has been spread equally across each degree program indicating no association. Note that this visualisation checks for correlation between the top-most dimension exam-mark and the other two dimensions, rather than between adjacent pairs of dimensions.

Fig. 8 shows some real student data. We restricted the view to the two best performing tutorials to see how exam mark, assignment mark and degree programs are related. Exam and assignment marks appear to correlate as their colouring is mostly in sequence though with some breaking up at the lower end of the scale. While the degree program dimension shows a mostly even distribution of exam performance across degrees. Finally note that in Fig. 8 (unlike in Fig. 7) colour alignment and dispersion is read between dimension categories rather than cells. This ensures our colouring technique will work for arbitrary sized datasets.

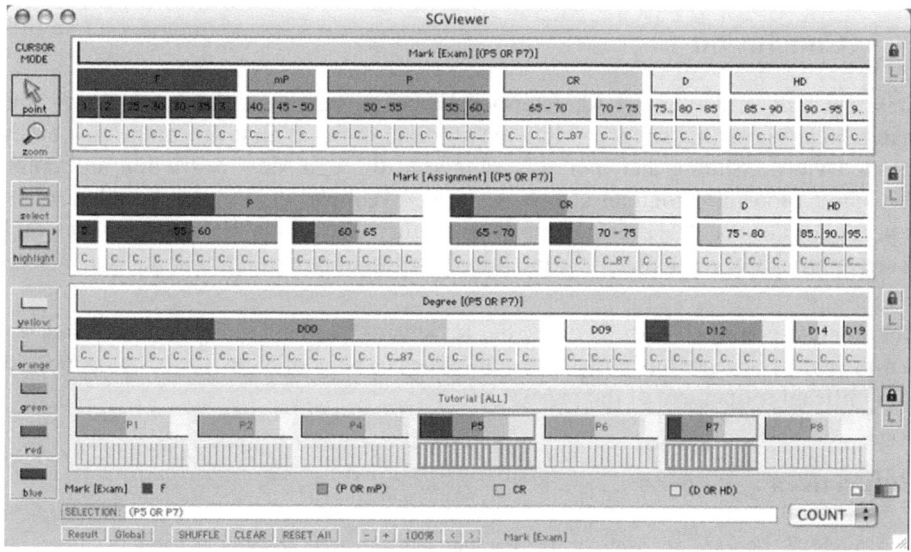

Fig. 8. View of student data showing a partial correlation between exam and assignment mark

6 Limitations

This section briefly discusses limitations of our system with respect to scalability and visual clutter. SGViewer is a memory bound component, requiring about 1GB of memory per 200K non-empty data cube cells. Supporting larger datasets may require using less dimensions or shallower dimension trees to reduce the number of base cube cells. There is no strict limit on the number of dimensions that can be loaded by SGViewer; the limitation is on how many can be displayed. About 8 - 12 dimensions can be shown on a display with a height of 800 - 1200 pixels, depending on the depth of each dimension tree.

Colour division can contribute to visual clutter. A careful comparison between Fig. 5 and 8 shows how our system addresses this. When the color spectrum operation is applied to a dimension, setting each top-level category to a different colour from a palette, root category and leaf cell colours are suppressed to reduce visual clutter. In contrast, when colours are applied manually as shown in Fig. 5, root categories and leaf cells are coloured. Use of an appropriate colour scheme can reduce visual clutter.

Our system supports heatmap palettes of 5, 7 and 9 colours. A heatmap palette is based on two colours and graduated intensities, for example, red, light red, white, light blue and blue. However, heatmap palettes are more suitable for dividing numeric rather than categorical dimensions as their intensity scale implies a left-to-right ordering of categories in the dimension to which they are applied. Visual clutter can also be moderated by careful choice of dimension tree fan out factors, when such a choice is possible. A fan out of 5 - 10 children, particularly for the root category in each dimension, aligns well with our colour palettes' 5 - 9 colours.

7   Conclusion

This paper describes an OLAP interface based on parallel dimension views rather than tabular views that supports showing all dimensions at all levels at the cost of less detailed views. Slicing and dicing is supported through view restriction and colour division. Colour division can also be used to reveal association and correlation. We expect our interface design is a complement rather than an alternative to existing table based approaches, particularly for the initial exploration of unfamiliar datasets.

Acknowledgement. I wish to thank the reviewers for their thoughtful feedback and comments, while time has not allowed all issues to be addressed, the reviews have led to significant refinement of the paper.

References

1. Bendy, F., Kosara, R., Helwig, H.: Parallel sets: a visual analysis of categorical data. In: IEEE InfoVis. MN, USA, October 23-25, pp. 133–140 (2005)
2. Chaudhuri, S., Dayal, U.: An Overview of Data Warehousing and OLAP Technology. ACM SIGMOD Record 26(1), 65–75 (1997)
3. Fua, Y., Ward, M., Rundensteiner, E.: Structure based brushes: a mechanism for navigating hierarchically organised data and information spaces. IEEE Trans. on Visualization and Computer Graphics 6(1), 150–159 (2000)
4. Gray, J., Chaudhuri, S., Bosworth, A., et al.: Data Cube: A relational aggregation operator. Data Mining and Knowledge Discovery 1, 29–53 (1997)
5. Inselberg, A.: The plane with parallel co-ordinates. The Visual Computer 1(2), 69–92 (1985)
6. PowerPivot, http://www.powerpivot.com/
7. Sifer, M.: A visual interface technique for exploring OLAP data with coordinated dimension hierarchies. In: Proceedings ACM CIKM 2003, New Orleans, pp. 532–535 (2003)
8. Sifer, M.: User interfaces for the exploration of hierarchical multi- dimensional data. In: Proc. IEEE Symposium on Visual Analytics Science and Technology, Maryland, pp. 175–182 (2006)
9. Stolte, C., Tang, D., Hanrahan, P.: Analysis, and Visualization of Hierarchically Structured Data using Polaris. In: Proceedings ACM SIGKDD 2002 (2002)
10. Tableau, http://www.tableausoftware.com/

Improving the Performance of Recommender System by Exploiting the Categories of Products

Mohak Sharma[1], P. Krishna Reddy[1], R. Uday Kiran[1], and T. Ragunathan[2]

[1] International Institute of Information Technology Hyderabad,
Hyderabad, India
{mohak.sharma,uday_rage}@research.iiit.ac.in, pkreddy@iiit.ac.in
[2] ACE Engineering College, Hyderabad, India
ragunathan@research.iiit.ac.in

Abstract. In the literature, collaborative filtering (CF) approach and its variations have been proposed for building recommender systems. In CF, recommendations for a given user are computed based on the ratings of k nearest neighbours. The nearest neighbours of target user are identified by computing the similarity between the product ratings of the target user and the product ratings of every other user. In this paper, we have proposed an improved approach to compute the neighborhood by exploiting the categories of products. In the proposed approach, ratings given by a user are divided into different sub-groups based on the categories of products. We consider that the ratings of each sub-group are given by a virtual user. For a target user, the recommendations of the corresponding virtual user are computed by employing CF. Next, the recommendations of the corresponding virtual users of the target user are combined for recommendation. The experimental results on MovieLens dataset show that the proposed approach improves the performance over the existing CF approach.

Keywords: Electronic commerce, Recommender systems, Collaborative Filtering, Mass-customization, Classification, Customer loyalty, Cross-sell, Up-sell.

1 Introduction

A recommender system for an E-commerce site receives information from a customer about which products he/she is interested in, and recommends products that are likely to fit his/her needs. Today, recommender systems are deployed on hundreds of sites, serving millions of customers. For example, recommender systems are employed to suggest books on Amazon™(www.amazon.com). Currently, recommender systems have become a key component of modern E-commerce applications. Several research efforts are going on to investigate efficient algorithms for building recommender systems [1,2,3].

In the literature, collaborative filtering (CF) approach has been proposed to build recommender systems [4]. There are two types of CF approaches: memory-based and model-based. Model-based CF approaches compute predictions by

S. Kikuchi et al. (Eds.): DNIS 2011, LNCS 7108, pp. 137–146, 2011.
© Springer-Verlag Berlin Heidelberg 2011

Table 1. Sample of transactions in a book store

User/Category	S_1	S_2	S_3	S_4	C_1	C_2	C_3
U_1	1	1	1	0	1	1	0
U_2	1	0	0	0	1	1	1
U_3	1	1	0	1	0	0	0
U_4	1	0	1	1	0	0	1
U_5	0	1	0	0	1	1	1
U_6	0	0	1	0	1	1	0

modeling user and item and memory-based CF approaches compute recommendations based on the purchase history of products and users. Improving the performance of CF approach is one of the research issue [1].

In this paper, we make an effort to propose the improved memory-based CF approach by exploiting the categories of products.

The CF approach works by building a database of product ratings given by customers. It recommends products to the customer based on the ratings of other customers who gave similar product ratings. To recommend products to a target user, finding other users who have similar preferences with the target user is an important step. In CF, the recommendation for a target user is computed based on the ratings of k nearest neighbours. Under CF, the product ratings of the target user are compared with the product ratings of other users, and the nearest neighbours are computed based on the similarity values. We have observed the fact that there is an opportunity to improve the performance of CF if we process the ratings of the user by grouping them category-wise. In CF, during the neighbourhood formation step, the similarity values of the product ratings between two users are computed by considering the product ratings of each user as one unit. Normally different sub-groups, based on categories, exist in the set of products rated by a user. It means that users may rate products similarly with respect to certain categories and dissimilar with respect to other categories. In this situation, if we carry out comparison at the user-user level, there is a possibility to miss the close neighbours with respect to categories. So, if we find the neighbourhood by comparing the ratings at the category-level, there is an opportunity to improve the performance of CF. We explain the proposed idea through Example 1.

Example 1. Let U_1, U_2, U_3, U_4, U_5 and U_6 be the users and S_1, S_2, S_3, and S_4 are story books and C_1, C_2 and C_3 are the books related to computer science. Table 1 shows the user-book matrix where the value '1' indicates that the user has purchased the corresponding book (rating = 1) and a '0' indicates that the user hasn't purchased the book (rating = 0). Let U_1 be the target user. If we find the similarity of other users with U_1, the top two neighbours selected for U_1 will be U_2 and U_5. The similarity is computed based on the number of common books purchased. If we compare category-wise, the neighbours of U_1 computed by considering only story books are U_3 and U_4. In this way, the notion of neighbourhood changes if we find the similarity by considering entire user as one unit and each category as one unit.

In the proposed approach, each user ratings are divided into different sub-users by exploiting the categories of products. We consider that the ratings of each sub-group are given by a virtual user. For a target user, the recommendations of the corresponding virtual user are computed by employing CF. Next, the recommendations of the corresponding virtual users of the target user are combined for recommendation. The experimental results on MovieLens dataset show that the proposed approach improves the performance over the existing CF approach.

The rest of the paper is organized as follows. In the next section, we discuss the related work. In section 3, we briefly explain CF. We present the proposed approach in Section 4. Experimental results are presented in Section 5. The last section consists of summary and conclusions.

2   Related Work

A survey on the approaches used for building recommender systems is carried out in [1]. The survey paper discusses various limitations of recommendation methods and suggests possible extensions. These extensions include, among others, an improvement of understanding of users and items, incorporation of the contextual information into the recommendation process, support for multi-criteria ratings, and a provision of more flexible and less intrusive types of recommendations.

The CF approach is a popular recommendation approach and several variations have been proposed in the literature. The user-based CF is proposed in [4] and the item-based CF is proposed in [5,6]. A fusion framework of both user-based and item-based approaches have been proposed in [2]. Wang [7] has shown how the development of CF can gain benefits from information retrieval theories and models, and proposed probabilistic relevance CF models. Horting [8] is a graph-based recommendation technique in which nodes are consumers, and edges between nodes indicate degree of similarity between two consumers. Bell and Koren [9] have used a comprehensive approach to improve the performance of CF by removing global effects in the data normalization stage of the neighbour-based CF and working with residual of global effects to select neighbours. A user-based CF which is based on an analysis of prediction errors is presented in [10].

A rate-item-pool-based (RIP-based) approach has been proposed in [11]. The RIP-based approach refines the contribution of the global neighbourhood by weighing the impact of global neighbours with a fine-grained similarity metric based on RIPs, and subsets of item ratings in the active user's profile. Ensemble method has been proposed to improve the performance of CF algorithms [12] which combines the predictions of different algorithms (the ensemble) to obtain the final prediction.

In [13], two approaches based on CF namely latent factor models and neighbourhood models are exploited to propose an effective recommendation algorithm. A recursive prediction algorithm is proposed in [14] which suggests that if a nearest-neighbour user has not rated the given item, it's value is estimated based on his/her own nearest neighbourhood. Next, the the estimated rating value is used in the the prediction process for the final active user.

An alternative method to find neighbourhood by exploiting lower-bound similarity is proposed in [15]. A preference-based organization technique has been proposed in [16] to accelerate users' decision process. It suggests that rather than explaining each item one by one, a group of products can be explained together by a category title, provided that they have shared tradeoff characteristics compared to a reference product. A prediction algorithm is discussed in [17] which predicts the ratings of items that they have not rated for every user. The algorithm proposed in [18] visualizes the problem as node selection on a graph, giving high scores to nodes that are well connected to the older choices, and at the same time well connected to unrelated choices.

In this paper, we have made an effort to propose an improved recommendation approach by exploiting the categories of products. The proposed idea is different from the preceding approaches as it exploits a notion of "virtual user" for finding efficient neighbourhood.

3   Collaborative Filtering Framework

In this section we explain CF. It [4] consists of three sub-tasks: data representation, neighbourhood formation and recommendation generation.

1. *Data representation*
   The input data is a collection of products purchased or rated by a user. Assume that there are m users and n products. It is usually represented as a $m \times n$ user-product matrix, R, such that $r_{i,j}$ is '1' if the ith user has purchased the jth product, and '0', otherwise.

2. *Neighbourhood Formation*
   The main goal of neighbourhood formation is to find, for each user u, an ordered list of k users N={$N_1,N_2,...,N_k$} such that u $\notin$ N and sim(u,N_1) is maximum, sim(u,N_2) is the next maximum and so on. The most extensively used similarity measures are based on correlation and cosine-similarity [5,19,20]. After computing the proximity among users, the next task is to actually form the neighbourhood. Different kinds of neighbourhood formation approaches can be employed. The *Center-based* [4] approach forms a neighbourhood of size k for a particular user c by simply selecting the k nearest other users.

3. *Generation of Recommendation*
   In this step, top-N recommendations ($N > 0$) are computed for a given user. For this, *Most-frequent Item Recommendation* method can be used. The procedure is as follows. It looks into the neighbourhood and scans through the ratings data for each neighbour and performs a frequency count of the products rated. After sorting the products according to their frequency count, it returns the N most frequent products that have not yet been purchased by the target user as recommendation.

4   Proposed Approach

It can be observed that the neighbourhood formation process plays a key role in improving the performance of recommender system. Under CF, a fixed number of neighbours for the target user are selected by considering the ratings of the one user as a single unit. This is appropriate if a typical user rates/purchases the products in all categories in a uniform manner. However, a user may not purchase or rate the products in all categories in a uniform manner in certain kinds of applications. That is, a typical user rates more number of products in certain categories and rates few products among other categories. So, if we consider the ratings of one user as a single unit and find similar users, there is a possibility of missing genuine neighbours. There is a scope to improve the performance, if we divide the user ratings into sub-groups by exploiting categories and build an algorithm by computing neighbourhood at category level.

Similar to CF, the proposed category-based CF (CCF) consists of the following steps: data representation, neighbourhood formation, and generation of recommendation.

The CCF approach divides a target user into several virtual users by considering that each category of products of user are rated by a virtual user. We find neighbours for each virtual user of a target user by employing CF. Next, the recommendations to the target user are computed by combining recommendations of the corresponding virtual users. We explain these steps in detail.

1. *Data representation in CCF*
   In CCF, a user is fragmented into virtual users on the basis of the categories of the purchased products. For instance, a particular user u has purchased n products which can be classified under c categories. The transaction of a user u is divided into c virtual users. Let m, p, c, and v represent the number of real users, products, categories and virtual users respectively. Then, $v = m \times c$. So, $(v \times p)$ virtual user-product matrix will be formed.
2. *Neighbourhood Formation in CCF*
   In CCF, neighbourhoods are formed by processing the ratings of virtual users. For a given real user, neighbourhood is formed for all the corresponding virtual users. The proximity and neighbourhood methods of CF can be used.
3. *Generation of recommendation in CCF*
   The process of recommendation generation in CCF is different from CF. At first, we have to generate recommendation for each virtual user of the corresponding target user. We can follow the most-frequent item recommendation method for this step. Next, recommendations have to be combined to generate final recommendations to the target user. Several options are possible. We present two approaches.

   (a) *Random Approach*: We combine all the recommended products into one set. To find *top-N* recommendations for a particular user, we randomly select N recommendations from this set.

(b) *Ranking Approach*: In this algorithm, we select top ranked P $(P > 0)$ virtual users and follow random approach. The ranking approach is as follows. At first, the virtual users of a target user are ranked based on the number of products rated. The virtual user who rates the large number of products receives higher rank. To find *top-N* recommendations for a particular user, we randomly select $\lfloor \frac{N}{P} \rfloor$ recommendations from the corresponding *top-P* virtual users.

5   Experimental Results

We conducted experiments on the data set provided by MovieLens (http://www.grouplens.org/) project. We selected 943 users to obtain 10,0000 ratings on 1682 movies. All ratings follow the 1 (bad) - 5 (excellent) numerical scale. The data set was converted into a user-movie ratings matrix R that had 943 rows (i.e., 943 users) and 1682 columns (i.e., 1682 movies). There are total 18 genres available. The initial dataset was divided into five distinct splits. All the experiments are performed on each of the five splits and average value is reported.

Dataset (each split) was divided into two parts: the training set and the test set. Experiments have been done on the training set, and generated a set of recommendations, we call the *top-N* set. We then look into the test set and match products with our *top-N* set. Products that appear in both sets are members of a special set, we call the *Hit Set* and each match is known as a *Hit*.

We employed recall, precision, and F1-metric [3] as performance metrics. The definitions of precision, recall and F1-metric are as follows.

– Precision. It is defined as the ratio of hit set size to the *top-N* set size, i.e., $precision = \frac{size\ of\ hit\ set}{size\ of\ top - N\ set}$ which can be written as

$$precision = \frac{|test \bigcap top - N|}{|N|}. \tag{1}$$

– Recall. It is defined as the ratio of hit set size to the test set size, i.e., $recall = \frac{size\ of\ hit\ set}{size\ of\ test\ set}$ which can be written as

$$recall = \frac{|test \bigcap top - N|}{|test|}. \tag{2}$$

– F1-metric. It is a combined effect of both recall and precision.

$$F1 = \frac{2 * recall * precision}{recall + precision}. \tag{3}$$

Using the genres of a movie as the categories of a product, 943 users have been fragmented into several other virtual users. The neighbours of a virtual user have been formed using *center-based* neighbourhood method. The *most-frequent item recommendation* is used for generating recommendations to the virtual users. The total number of recommendations for a virtual user and to a target user has been set at 10, i.e., $N = 10$.

We have conducted experiments by fixing k=70 (number of neighbours for virtual users) and varying the number of virtual users from 1 to 18 (there are only 18 genres in the dataset). So each virtual user can only be split into maximum of 18 virtual users. Figures 1(a), 1(b), and 1(c) show the precision, recall and F1-metric performance of CF, CCF with random and CCF with ranking approaches respectively. It should be noted that the performance of both CF and CCF with random method does not vary with the number of virtual users. The performance curve of CCF with random method indicates the recommendation performance obtained by selecting final recommendations randomly from the recommendations of 18 virtual users. It can be observed that CCF with random method improves the performance over CF. It is due to the fact that by

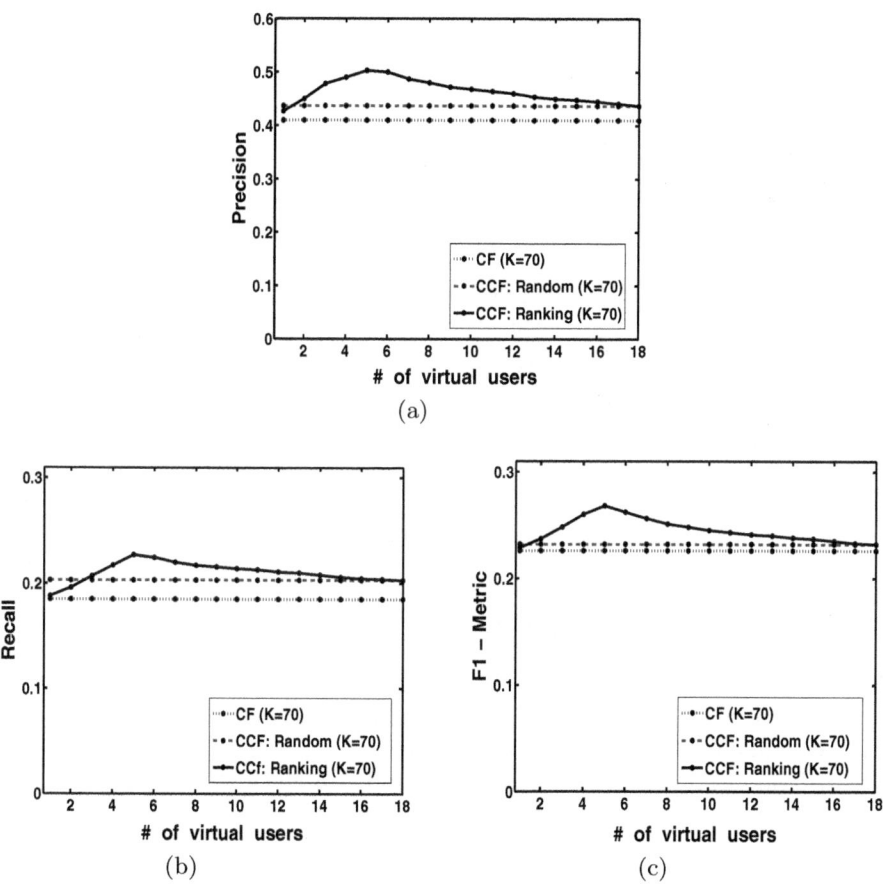

Fig. 1. Performance results of # of virtual users vs (a) Precision, (b) Recall and (c) F1-metric

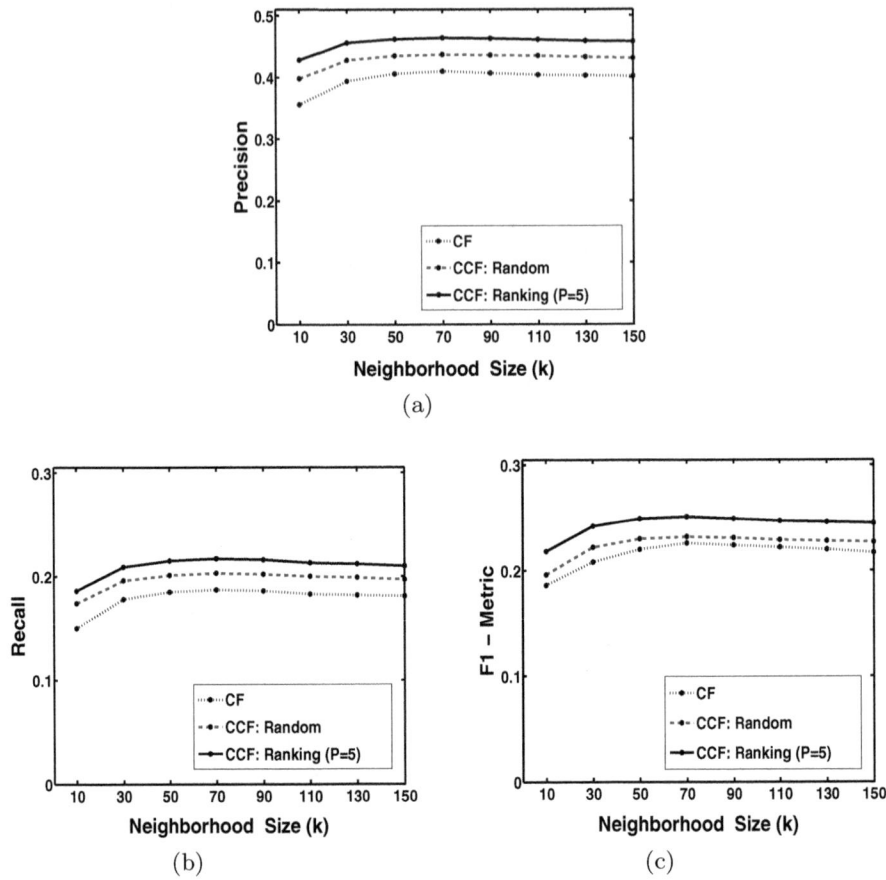

Fig. 2. Performance results of k vs (a) Precision, (b) Recall and (c) F1-metric

computing neighbourhood at the category level, the proposed approach is able to get the efficient neighbourhood as compared to CF. It can be noted that the performance of CCF with ranking method varies based on the number of virtual users. As we increase the number of virtual users, the performance increases gradually to the peak. It then gradually decreases and coincides with the random approach as expected. The results show that the performance of CCF with ranking method is significantly higher than CF. It indicates that by computing the recommendations from the top ranked virtual users, it is possible to capture the neighbourhood based on user interests in an efficient manner.

We have also conducted experiments by fixing number of virtual users to five and varying number of neighbourhood virtual users from 10 to 150. Figure 2(a), 2(b), and 2(c) shows the precision, recall and F1-metric performance respectively. As we increase the number of virtual users in neighbourhood, the performance of CF, CCF with random, and CCF with ranking approaches increases gradually and saturates. It can be observed that CCF with random method improves the performance over CF. Also, the results show that the performance CCF with ranking method is higher than the other two approaches.

Overall, the experiment results show that the proposed approach improves the performance over CF.

6   Conclusion and Future Work

Recommender system is the main component in E-commerce systems. In this paper, we made an effort to improve the performance the CF approach which is being used to build recommendation systems. We have proposed a framework in which each user is divided into virtual users based on the categories of the products rated. The proposed approach divides each user into corresponding virtual users, computes recommendations for each virtual user and combines these recommendations to give recommendations to the target user. Through experimental results, it has been shown that it is possible to improve the performance of recommender systems using the proposed approach.

As a part of future work, we are planning to conduct extensive experiments by employing different neighbourhood formation and similarity methods. We are planning to investigate improved methods to combine the recommendations computed for virtual users for giving final recommendations to the user. We are also planning to investigate how the notion of virtual user improves the performance of item-based, model-based and other variations of CF approaches.

References

1. Adomavicius, G., Tuzhilin, A.: Toward the Next Generation of Recommender Systems: A Survey of the State-of-the-Art and Possible Extensions. IEEE Trans. Knowl. Data Eng., 734–749 (2005)
2. Wang, J., de Vries, A.P., Reinders, M.J.T.: Unifying user-based and item-based collaborative filtering approaches by similarity fusion. In: Proc. of 29th Annual Int. ACM SIGIR Conf. on Research and Development in Information Retrieval (2006)
3. Roy, S.B., Amer-Yahia, S., Chawla, A., Das, G., Yu, C.: Constructing and exploring composite items. In: Proc. of the 2010 International ACM SIGMOD Conference on Management of Data, pp. 843–854 (2010)
4. Sarwar, B.M., Karypis, G., Konstan, J.A., Riedl, J.: Analysis of recommendation algorithms for e-commerce. In: ACM Conference on Electronic Commerce, pp. 158–167 (2000)
5. Sarwar, B.M., Karypis, G., Konstan, J.A., Riedl, J.: Item-based collaborative filtering recommendation algorithms. In: Proc. of World Wide Web Conference, pp. 285–295 (2001)
6. Deshpande, M., Karypis, G.: Item-based top-n recommendation algorithms. ACM Transactions on Information System, 143–177 (2004)
7. Wang, J., de Vries, A.P., Reinders, M.J.T.: Unified relevance models for rating prediction in collaborative filtering. ACM Transaction on Information Systems 26 (2008)

8. Wolf, J., Aggarwal, C., Wu, K.-L., Yu, P.: Horting hatches an egg: A new graph-theoretic approach to collaborative filtering. In: Proc. of the ACM SIGKDD International Conference on Knowledge Discovery and Data Mining (1999)

9. Bell, R., Koren, Y.: Improved neighbourhood-based collaborative filtering. In: Proc. of Knowledge Discovery and Data Mining Cup and Workshop (2007)

10. Ding, S., Zhao, S., Yuan, Q., Zhang, X., Fu, R., Bergman, L.D.: Boosting collaborative filtering based on statistical prediction errors. In: Proc. of the 2008 ACM Conference on Recommender Systems, pp. 3–10 (2008)

11. Shi, Y., Larson, M., Hanjalic, A.: Exploiting user similarity based on rated-item pools for improved user-based collaborative filtering. In: Proc. of the 2009 ACM Conference on Recommender Systems, pp. 125–132 (2009)

12. Jahrer, M., Töscher, A.: Combining Predictions for Accurate Recommender Systems. In: Proc. of the 16th ACM SIGKDD International Conference on Knowledge Discovery and Data mining, pp. 25–28 (2010)

13. Koren, Y.: Factorization meets the neighborhood: A multifaceted collaborative filtering model. In: Proc. of 14th ACM SIGKDD Knowledge Discovery and Data mining (2008)

14. Zhang, J., Pu, P.: A recursive prediction algorithm for collaborative filtering recommender systems. In: Proc. of 2007 ACM Conference on Recommender Systems (2007)

15. Sharma, M., Reddy, P.K.: Using lower-bound similarity to enhance the performance of recommender systems. In: Proc. of ACM Bangalore Compute Conference (2011)

16. Chen, L., Pu, P.: A cross-cultural user evaluation of product recommender interfaces. In: Proc. of the 2008 ACM Conference on Recommender Systems (2008)

17. Schclar, A., Tsikinovsky, A., Rokach, L., Meisels, A., Antwarg, L.: Ensemble methods for improving the performance of neighborhood-based collaborative filtering. In: Proc. of the 2009 ACM Recommeder Systems, pp. 261–264 (2009)

18. Onuma, K., Tong, H., Faloutsos, C.: TANGENT: a novel, 'Surprise me', recommendation algorithm. In: The Proc. of 15th ACM SIGKDD Knowledge Discovery and Data mining (2009)

19. Herlocker, J.L., Konstan, J.A., Riedl, J.: An empirical analysis of design choices in neighborhood-based collaborative filtering algorithms. In: Proc. of 25th Annual International ACM SIGIR Conference on Research and Development in Information Retrieval (2002)

20. McLaughlin, M.R., Herlocker, J.L.: A collaborative filtering algorithm and evaluation metric that accurately model the user experience. In: Proc. of 27th Annual Int. ACM SIGIR Conference on Research and Development in Information Retrieval (2005)

Detecting Unexpected Correlation between a Current Topic and Products from Buzz Marketing Sites

Takako Hashimoto[1], Tetsuji Kuboyama[2], and Yukari Shirota[3]

[1] Commerce and Economics, Chiba University of Commerce, Chiba, Japan
takako@cuc.ac.jp
[2] Computer Center, Gakushuin University, Tokyo, Japan
kuboyama@tk.cc.gakushuin.ac.jp
[3] Department of Management, Faculty of Economics, Gakushuin University, Tokyo, Japan
yukari.shirota@gakushuin.ac.jp

Abstract. This paper proposes a method to detect unexpected correlation from between a current topic and products word of mouth in buzz marketing sites, which will be part of a new approach to marketing analysis. For example, in 2009, the super-flu virus spawned significant effects on various product marketing domains around the globe. In buzz marketing sites, there had been a lot of word of mouth about the "flu." We could easily expect an "air purifier" to be correlated to the "flu" and air purifiers' shipments had grown according to the epidemic of flu. On the other hand, the relatedness between the "flu" and a "camera" could not be easily expected. However, in Japan, consumers' unforeseen behavior like the reluctance to buy digital cameras because of cancellations of a trip, a PE festival or other events caused by the epidemic of flu had appeared, and a strong correlation between the "flu" and "camera" had been found. Detecting these unforeseen consumers' behavior is significant for today's marketing analysis. In order to detect such unexpected relations, this paper applies the dynamic time warping techniques. Our proposed method computes time series correlations between a current topic and unspecified products from word of mouth of buzz marketing sites, and finds product candidates which have unexpected correlation with a current topic. To evaluate the effectiveness of the method, the experimental results for the current topic ("flu") and products ("air purifier", "camera", "car", etc.) are shown as well. By detecting unexpected relatedness from buzz marketing sites, unforeseen consumer behaviors can be further analyzed.

Keywords: Data mining, Marketing analysis, Web Intelligence, Dynamic time warping, Social media analysis.

1 Introduction

Data mining techniques for product marketing to analyze word-of-mouth in social media such as blogs and buzz marketing sites have recently become an active area of

S. Kikuchi et al. (Eds.): DNIS 2011, LNCS 7108, pp. 147–161, 2011.

research[3-6, 11]. In analyzing product reviews or reputation in social media, almost all existing research focuses first on specific products, and extracts typical evaluation expressions such as "favorite," "dislike," "expensive," and "useful." They then calculate positive/negative degrees of extracted expressions. We have also researched data mining techniques on home electrical appliances such as air purifiers and front loading washing machines with automatic drying systems, and proposed a reputation analysis framework for buzz marketing sites[13]. It may be easy to analyze a specific product's reputation, because the target product's characteristics can be illustrated by the ontology for the product, which is constructed with relatively little effort.

On the other hand, for buzz marketing sites, it is very difficult to analyze unexpected consumer behavior for "unspecified products" which is caused by current topics such as an epidemic of flu and a great disaster. Because the target product is not explicit, it is not possible to prepare a specific ontology in advance. To detect unexpected consumer behavior, we also have proposed the graph-based consumer behavior analysis framework [15, 16]. Our previous proposed framework visualizes time series variation of unforeseen relations between a current topic and unspecified products from buzz marketing sites. In our previous experiments concerning the super-flu spawn in 2009, we could find an unexpected consumer behavior as follows; in threads about digital cameras, we discovered that many persons wrote that the flu made them cancel plans of children's PE festivals and trips during Golden Week in Japan, since people had to be confined at home. The flu pandemic made consumers hold off buying digital camera, since people who had been planning to take photos at those events were reluctant to buy digital cameras due to the flu pandemic. The reluctance in buying digital cameras because of the flu was not something we'd expect. On the contrary, we could easily expect more air purifiers to be sold because of the flu pandemic. We can say that the relation between the flu and digital cameras can be recognized as an unforeseen and unexpected relationship.

The problem for finding unexpected relations between a current topic and unspecified products is how we can easily find the target unspecified products. To address the problem, this paper proposes a method to detect correlations between a current topic and unspecified products from buzz marketing sites. For detecting unexpected correlations, this paper applies the dynamic time warping techniques. Our method computes time series correlation based on the occurrence patterns of both a current topic and products, and selects product candidates which may cause consumers' unexpected behavior. By detecting unexpected correlation, unforeseen consumer behaviors can be further analyzed. Our proposed method will be part of a new approach to marketing analysis. This is the novel point in this paper.

The following section explains our previous method "Graph-based Consumer Behavior Analysis." Section 3 refers to existing research. In section 4, our proposed method using the dynamic time warping technique is described. Section 5 shows experimental results. Finally, section 6 gives concluding remarks and describes the direction of future work.

2   Graph-Based Consumer Behavior Analysis

This section briefly explains our previous proposed method "Graph-based Consumer Behavior Analysis[15,16]." Our previous proposed method consists of the following six steps (Fig.1):

Step1. Crawling
Step2. Language processing
Step3. Graph transformation
Step4. Visualization
Step5. Graph edit distance calculation
Step6. Consumer behavior detection

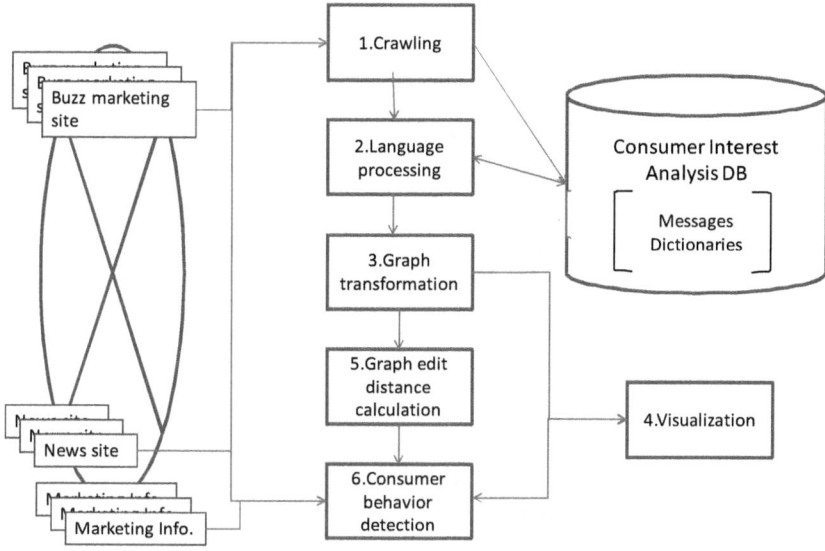

Fig. 1. Consumer behavior analysis framework

In Step1, word-of-mouth in buzz marketing sites is crawled according to the given query which is a term of a current topic like "flu." As the target buzz marketing site, we have selected the online bulletin board of kakaku.com[2], that is the most popular buzz marketing site in Japan.

In Step2, the crawling results of Step1 are analyzed by language processing technique. We've defined one word-of-mouth as one document. This step extracts keywords that are nouns, verbs, adjectives, and adverbs from one document using morphological analysis. Then the score of an individual keyword is calculated. As score calculation method, the step uses RIDF(residual IDF), LSA(latent semantic analysis), and tf-idf(Term Frequency- Inverse Document Frequency). According to our examination, at the moment, RIDF is appropriate for extracting keywords which indicate the document content.

In Step3, we construct directed graphs to show consumer behavior structure from the output of Step2, which is a matrix between message id and keyword id with high score. As a directed graph, we use the concept graph due to Hirokawa[1], which makes relevance hypernym relations of keywords appearing in a set of documents based on co-occurrence frequencies. In our framework, the posted date is delimited by appropriate period (e.g. monthly, weekly, or daily) and the graph structures are formed according to the period.

Step4 is a visualization module to show concept graph structures which is made by Step3. Fig.2 illustrates an example of the concept graph visualization related to the "flu" in 2009 from the kakaku.com BBS sites. There is a large island structure discussing digital camera and air purifier.

Our hypothesis is that major changes of the concept graph structures show consumers' behavior changes. To detect the consumers' behavior change, we employ graph topology-based distance for measuring changes in concept graph topology over time. In Step5, the graph edit distance[14] is calculated from a set of concept graph data (the outputs of Step3). By analyzing time series variation of the graph edit distance, people interest changes can be detected and unexpected consumer behavior can be analyzed.   Fig.2 shows the results of the graph edit distance calculation as well. In Fig.2, graph structures about digital cameras are recognized in the concept graphs of January, May, July, August, September and October of 2009. With the plots in Fig.2, we recognize that the major structure changes happened in May and July, and a part of substructure emerged in July is preserved until October. Compared to real sales of digital cameras, sales increased in June (after May) and October (after September). We can guess, therefore, that the structure change in May and October illustrates consumer behavior change.

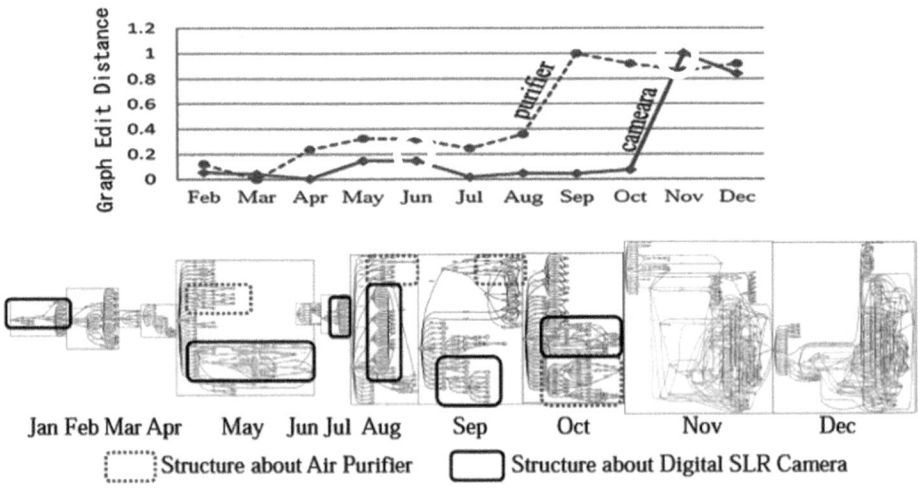

Fig. 2. Monthly concept graphs related to "flu" in 2009, and substructures related to "air purifier," "digital camera"

The problem for our previous method is how the pair of a current topic and unspecified products that would have unexpected relationship can be easily found. In our previous method, we've detected the unexpected correlation manually. However, to increase efficiency, the automatic detection method is needed. To address the problem, this paper proposes an unexpected correlation detection method using the dynamic time warping.

3   Related Work

3.1   Research on Reputation Analysis

Various researchers have analyzed product reviews and reputation from social media [3,4,5,6]. Nagano et. al[3] propose the word-of-mouth engine to present product reputation on the Web. In their system, users first specify the products by taking pictures using cell-phone cameras. The system then retrieves word-of-mouth information and extracts typical evaluation words like "favorite," "dislike," "expensive," and "useful" about the specific product. It also calculates positive/negative degrees. Kobayashi et. al[4] define the main portions of an opinion as (object, attribute, opinion). Asano et. al[5] also define the basic element of reputation as (object, evaluation point, expression). To extract reputation from word-of-mouth information, both propose a technique for efficiently building an object name dictionary, an attribute expression dictionary (ontology), and an opinion word dictionary for the specific object domain. Spangler et. al[6] propose an automated way to monitor social media to analyze the specific corporate brand, reputation, consumer preferences and buying habits. They also offer a mechanism for developing the ontology, near-real-time gathering of word-of-mouth information and the calculation of positive/negative measures. This related work targets specific products, extracts evaluation expressions from word-of-mouth in social media and calculates sentiment orientations of extracted expressions to analyze product reviews and reputation. They require specific ontology. Our proposed method, however, does not target specific products, and a specific ontology is not needed. We focus on a current topic and visualize the unforeseen relations between a current topic and unspecified products from buzz marketing sites. Through the visualization, we can detect unexpected consumer behavior.

3.2   Research on Analyzing Correlation over Time

Various researchers have analyzed correlation over time. Zhu et. al[7] propose a mechanism for finding a song by humming part of the tune. They use the dynamic time warping (DTW) technique and improve both the retrieval precision and speed by introducing existing dimensionality reduction to DTW indexes. Our approach is also based on the dynamic time warping technique, but focuses on word correlation over time. Word correlation is not relatively complicated in comparison with the hum tune, so that we can concentrate on how to utilize the result of detecting word correlation.

Otanto et. al[8] propose the Dynamic Conditional Correlation model, which uses the idea of distance between dynamic conditional correlations, and the classical Wald test, to compare the coefficients of two groups of dynamic conditional correlations. They apply their method to a set of financial time series. Loy et. al[9] propose an approach to understanding activities from their partial observations monitored through multiple non-overlapping cameras separated by unknown time gaps. They use a new Cross Canonical Correlation Analysis (xCCA) to formulate to discover and quantify the time delayed correlations of regional activities observed within and across multiple camera views in a single common reference space. Unlike existing approaches, we focus on word correlation over time to detect the unexpected correlation between a current topic and unspecified products. Our target data is different from existing approaches' target data.

3.3   Research on Detecting Word Relation over Time

Regarding research on detecting word relation over time, Radinsky et. al[10] propose a semantic relatedness model, Temporal Semantic Analysis (TSA) which captures the words' temporal information. It targets words in news archives (New York Times, etc.) and utilizes the dynamic time warping technique to compute a semantic relatedness between pre-defined words. Our approach is also based on the dynamic time warping technique. But, our aim is to detect the unexpected correlation between a current topic and unspecified products. Wang et al[11] propose time series analysis which has been used to detect similar topic patterns. They focus on specific bursty topic patterns in coordinated text streams and try to find similar topics. Their aim is to detect similar topic patterns.

While our work also makes use of temporally evolving statistics, our target data is word of mouth in buzz marketing sites and the goal is different in that we seek unspecified products that consumers show unexpected behavior for the products. We do not pre-define the products which have unexpected correlation with a current topic. We propose a new marketing research framework. This is the novel point of our work.

4   Detecting Correlation between a Current Topic and Products Using Dynamic Time Warping

As we mentioned above, the problem for our previous proposed framework is that how we can easily find the unspecified products which have unexpected correlation with a current topic. To address the problem, this paper proposes the unexpected correlation detecting method using the dynamic time warping. Our proposed method targets buzz marketing sites and try to find unforeseen correlation between a current topic and unspecific products. This method will be inserted into the previous proposed framework as "Step3-2. Correlation calculation" after Step2 (Language processing) (Fig. 3).

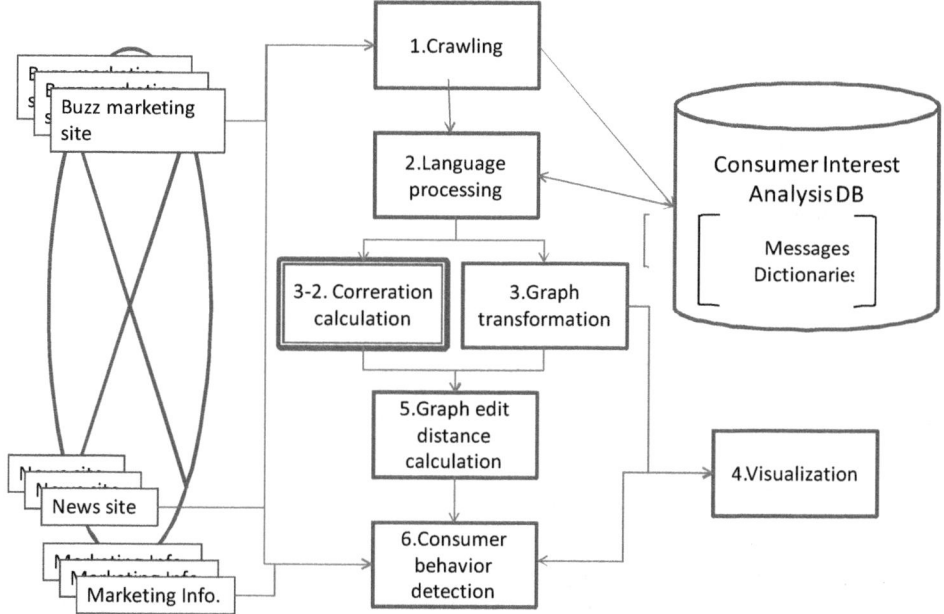

Fig. 3. New consumer behavior analysis framework including our proposed method

4.1   Dynamic Time Warping

This section explains the dynamic time warping (DTW) definition.

The dynamic time warping distance measures the similarity [17] between two time series that may differ in time scale, but similar in shape. For example, in speech recognition, this method is used to identify similar sounds between different speakers whose speech speed and pitch might be different. We use this technique to detect the correlation between a current topic and products. The influence by a current topic sometimes follows the development of the current topic. To address this time lag, DTW which can measure similarity between two sequences that may vary in time or speed is appropriate.

The standard definition of dynamic warping distance is as follow;

- **Definition 1.** Local cost matrix $C \in R^{|ts_1| \times |ts_2|}$ between two time series ts_1, ts_2 as

$$C_{i,j} \in \left\| ts_1[i] - ts_2[j] \right\|, i \in \langle 1..|ts_1| \rangle, j \in \langle 1..|ts_2| \rangle \tag{1}$$

where $\left\| ts_1[i] - ts_2[j] \right\|$ is a distance metric between two points of the time series.

Given this cost matrix, DTW constructs an alignment path that minimizes the cost over this cost matrix. This alignment p is called the "warping path," and defined as follows;

- **Definition 2.** Sequence of points pairs as

$$Pair_l = \left(pair_1, ... pair_k \right) \tag{2}$$

where $Pair_l = (i, j) \in \langle 1..|ts_1| \rangle \times \langle 1..|ts_2| \rangle$ is a pair of indexes in ts_1 and ts_2 respectively. Each consequent pair preserves the ordering of the points in ts_1 and ts_2, and enforces the first and last points of the warping path to be the first and last points of ts_1 and ts_2. For each warping path p we compute its cost as follows;

- **Definition 3.** Cost of warping path p as

$$c(p) = \sum_{i=1}^{k} c(pair_l) \tag{3}$$

The DTW is defined to be the minimum optimal warping path as follows;

- **Definition 4.** *DTW* between two time series ts_1, ts_2 as

$$DTW(ts_1, ts_2) = min\left\{ c(p) | p \in P^{|ts_1| \times |ts_2|} \right\} \tag{4}$$

where P are all possible warping paths. A dynamic programming algorithm (similar to the one in Fig. 6) is usually applied to compute the optimal warping path of the two sequences.

4.2   Step3-2: Correlation Calculation

Our proposed method will be inserted into the previous proposed framework as "Step3-2." Inputs for the step are results of Step2. The method will be done in parallel with Step3 and find product candidates as unspecified products that would have unexpected relationship with the current topic. In order to detect unexpected correlations, the method applies the above-mentioned dynamic time warping techniques for analyzing word correlation over time. The following is the process of our method.

1. At first, as for the results of Step2, the number of occurrences of a target current topic w such as "flu", "great earthquake", etc. in buzz marketing sites is counted according to the appropriate period (daily, weekly, monthly, etc.) delimited in advance.

2. We've decided products categories in kakaku.com as the products for calculating correlation with a current topic. It is not possible to calculate correlation for all existing products. Kakaku.com provides around 2000 product category list on their sites. Since the product categories provided by kakaku.com are well-organized and reliable, we've supposed that they are appropriate for calculating correlation. As for the results of Step2, we count the number of occurrences of these 2000 product categories, as well as the current topic. The number of occurrences is counted according to the appropriate period delimited in advance.

3. For both the current topic and each product category, we've calculated the occurrence pattern based on the following formula.

$$C_{tl} = \frac{n_{tl}}{\sum_{i=1}^{n} n_{ti}} \tag{5}$$

$$C_{pjl} = \frac{n_{pjl}}{\sum_{i=1}^{n} n_{pji}} , \quad \left\{ n_{pj} \in 2000 \; product \; categories \; in \; kakaku.com \right\} \tag{6}$$

Where n_{tl} is the number of occurrence for the lth period of the current topic and n_{pjl} is the number of occurrence for the lth period of the jth product.

4. Using dynamic time warping technique, we calculate correlations between the current topic occurrence pattern and each product occurrence pattern, then compute distances $D_{t\text{-}pj}$ for each correlation.

5. Products with high distance ($D_{t\text{-}pj} \leq T$) will be extracted as product candidates which has a strong correlation with the current topic. Where T is a threshold for the distance.

These product candidates will be the result of this Step3-2 (Correlation calculation). As for the product candidates, in Step5, we seek substructures which include terms of product candidates from the concept graph structures. If there are substructures, they will be extracted, and the graph edit distance between substructures will be calculated. This graph edit distance calculation will be done based on our previous proposed method. Products with major graph structure changes will be recognized unspecified products which cause unexpected consumer behavior. Then, Step6 (Consumer behavior detection) refers a marketing data such as product shipments as an evidence of unexpected consumer behavior to confirm whether there are correlation between the product occurrence pattern and a marketing data.

5   Experimental Result

Based on our method, we conducted the experiments. This section shows the results of our experiment.

In our experiment, we set $w=$"flu" and $T=1.0$. The delimited period is one week. At first, we retrieve post documents from January 2009 to December 2009 in buzz marketing sites of kakaku.com by the query "flu." As a result, 857 documents were retrieved. As for these 857 documents, we calculate the correlation between the "flu" and product categories of kakaku.com.   To calculate the correlation based on the dynamic time warping, we used R[18] which is a free software environment for statistical computing and graphics.   As an example, we select main products, "camera", "air purifier", "car", "printer", "mobile" and "television." Table 1 shows the distance calculation results between the "flu" and example products based on our calculation.

Fig. 4 shows the occurrence pattern of "flu", "air purifier" and "camera". And Fig. 5 shows the occurrence pattern of "flu", "car", "printer", and "television."

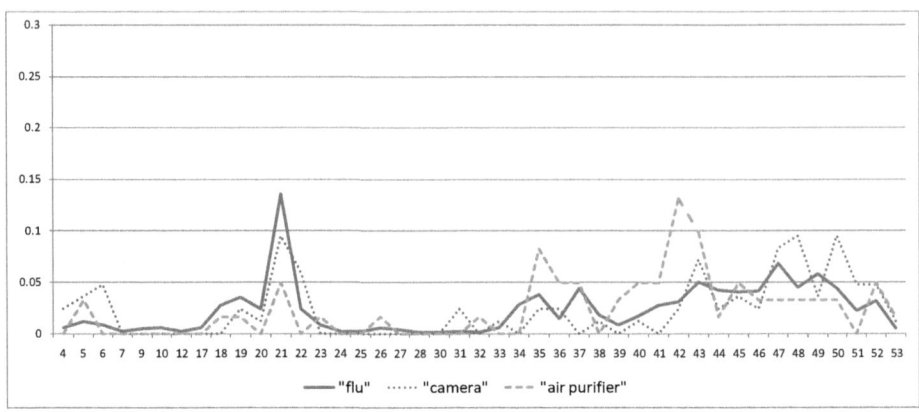

Fig. 4. Occurrence pattern of "flu", "air purifier", "camera", "car", "printer", and "television"

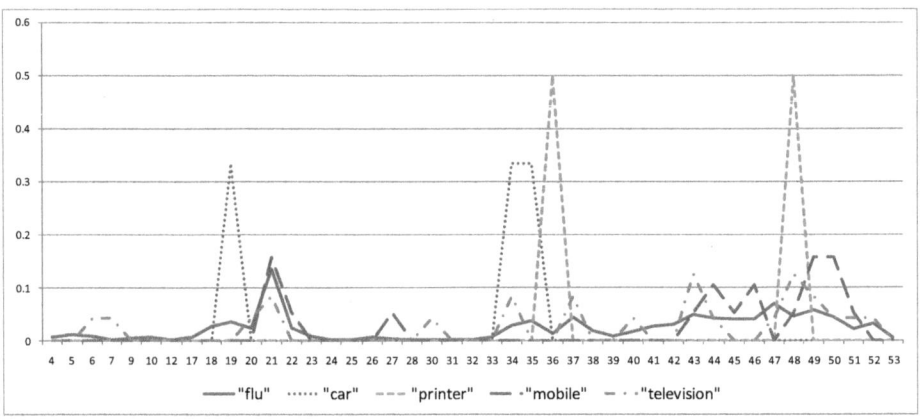

Fig. 5. Occurrence pattern of "flu", "air purifier", "camera", "car", "printer", and "television"

In Fig.4 and Fig.5, the horizontal axises show the number of week in 2009. The vertical axises show the occurrence ratio for each product derived by the formula (5) and (6). According to Fig.4, there seem correlations between the "flu" and the "camera"/ the "air purifier." On the other hand, in Fig.5, there seem less correlations between "flu" and other products. By computing the dynamic time warping paths, we confirm these correlations.

Fig. 6-11 show the warping path of each pair ("flu" and "camera", "flu" and "air purifier", "ful" and "car", "ful" and "printer", "ful" and "mobile", and "ful" and "television") in a time warping grid.   Warping path distances of Fig.6 ("ful" and "camera"), and Fig. 7 ("flu" and "air purifier") are short. This means that both the relation between "ful" and "camera", and the relation between "flu" and "air purifier" are correlated. On the contrary, warping path distances of other products are longer. This means these products are not correlated with the "ful."

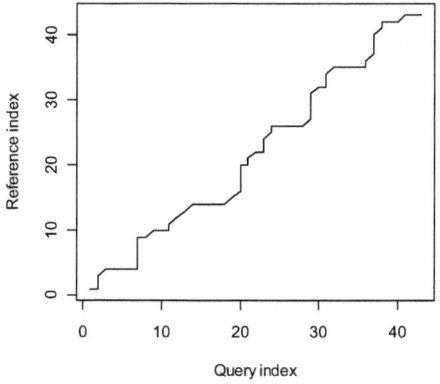

Fig. 6. Dynamic time warping path between the "ful" and the "camera"

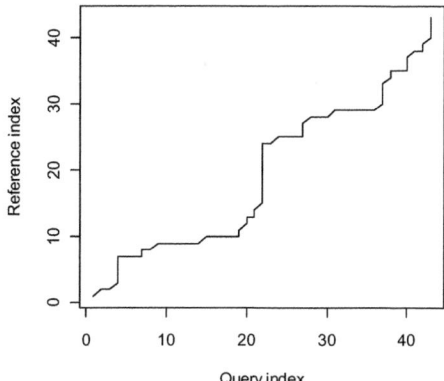

Fig. 7. Dynamic time warping path between the "ful" and the "air purifier"

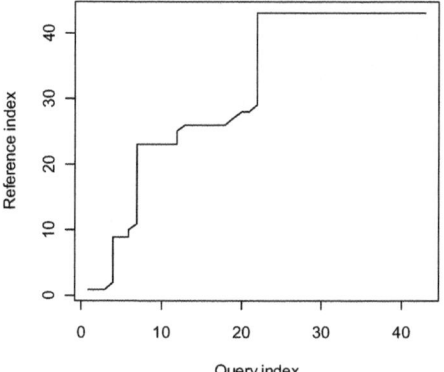

Fig. 8. Dynamic time warping path between the "ful" and the "car"

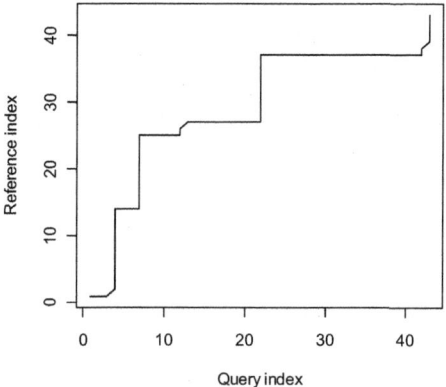

Fig. 9. Dynamic time warping path between the "ful" and the "printer"

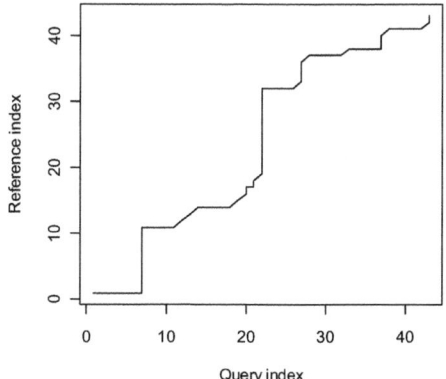

Fig. 10. Dynamic time warping path between the "ful" and the "mobile"

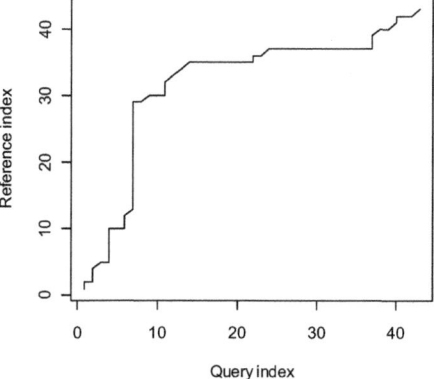

Fig. 11. Dynamic time warping path between the "ful" and the "television"

Table 1 shows the distance derived from the dynamic time warping for each pair. The distance of "camera" and "air purifier" are less than T (=1.0). On the other hand, the distance of "car", "printer", "mobile" and "television" are larger than T. Therefore, both "camera" and "air purifier" seem to correlate with the "flu." Based on the results, we can recognize "camera" and "air purifier" as product candidates which have correlations with the "flu."

Table 1. The distance based on dynamic time warping between "flu" and major products

	"camera"	"air purifier"	"car"	"printer"	"mobile"	"television"
"flu"	0.821	0.870	1.816	1.948	1.049	1.027

To confirm our result, we compare the occurrence pattern of product candidates with the real product shipments. Fig. 12 shows the volume of shipments for digital single-lens reflex camera in 2008 and 2009 and the occurrence pattern of camera in kakaku.com BBS sites. In 2008, an ordinary year, the lack sales in March, April, May, September and November do not exist. On the contrary, in March to May and September to November 2009, the volume of shipments in 2009 is negatively correlated with the occurrence pattern of camera. We can say that for a camera, consumers' unexpected behavior appears. On the other hand, Fig. 13 also illustrates the volume of shipments for air purifiers in 2009 and the occurrence pattern of air purifiers in kakaku.com BBS sites. We easily detect a correlation between the volume of shipments and the occurrence pattern. We recognize this kind of explicit relationships as expected consumer behavior.

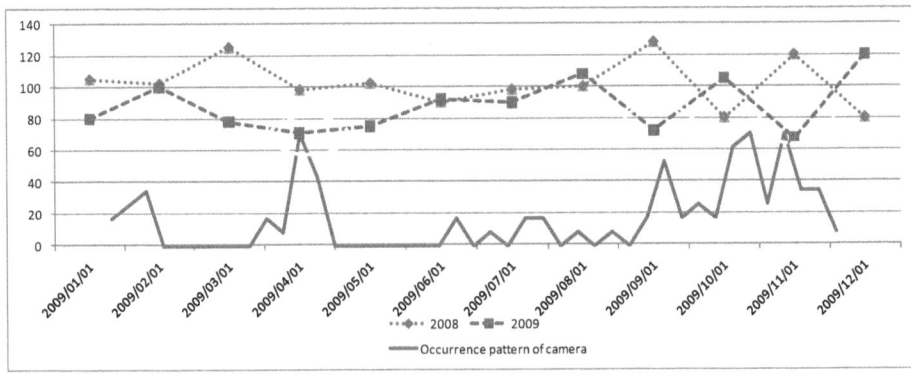

Fig. 12. The occurrence pattern of camera and the volume of shipments for digital single-lens reflex camera in 2008 & 2009. (Cited: The Camera Information Center: Camera information Center Report, http://www.camera-info.net/index.htm).

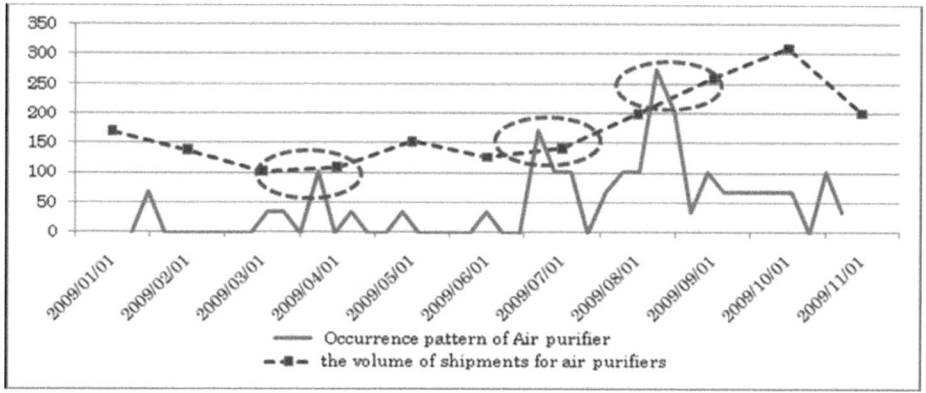

Fig. 13. The occurrence pattern of air purifier and the volume of shipments for air purifier in 2009. (Cited: : GfK Marketing Services Japan Ltd., http://www.gfkjpn.co.jp/).

Regarding the scalability, we have not applyed our proposed method for a large data yet.   In fact, our method does not need to evaluate all time series data to find the optimal alignment. We plan to detect the specific bursty topic patterns , and then find correlations between the current topic and products. As for the algorithm for detection bursty structures in data streams, there are several researches[19, 20].   And there are also several proposals to improve the computational efficiency of the dynamic time warping[21, 22]. Especially, Salvador et. al[21] proposed FastDTW, an approximation of DTW that has a linear time and   space complexity. We are going to evaluate these algorithms and introduce appropriate algorithms into our method.

6   Conclusion

In this paper, we proposed a method to detect correlations between a current topic and unspecified products from word of mouth in buzz marketing sites. For detecting unexpected correlations, this paper applies the dynamic time warping techniques to analyze over time. Our method computes time series correlation based on the occurrence patterns of both a current topic and products, and selects product candidates which may cause consumers' unexpected behavior. Our proposed method uses the dynamic time warping technique to compute time series correlation between a current topic and products. The method calculates the dynamic time warping paths for the 2000 product categories, which are classified in kakaku.com, and extracts product candidates which will have a unexpected correlation with a current topic. According to our method, we conducted the experiments and confirm the effectiveness. By our method, we could detect the unforeseen correlation between the "flu" and "camera", while there are no relatedness between the "flu" and "car", "printer", and "television." Of course, we confirmed expected correlations between "flu" and "air purifier." We indicated the real marketing data about the "camera" as an evidence of unexpected consumer behavior to confirm unforeseen correlation.

As future work, we will acquire other data examples that can express unexpected consumer behavior from buzz marketing sites, and evaluate the effectiveness of our proposed method using the dynamic time warping. In addition, at the moment, from the product candidates which have correlations with the current topic, we manually decide products which have unexpected correlations. To automatically detect products with unexpected correlations, we investigate the measure for judging unexpected correlations.

Our proposed method is part of a marketing analysis framework which can detect unexpected correlation between a current topic and products. We can say that by detecting unexpected correlation, unforeseen consumer behaviors can be further analyzed and we can achieve the new marketing analysis.

References

1. Shimoji, Y., Wada, T., Hirokawa, S.: Dynamic Thesaurus Construction from English-Japanese Dictionary. In: The Second International Conference on Complex, Intelligent and Software Intensive Systems, pp. 918–923 (2008)
2. kakaku.com, http://kakaku.com/
3. Nagano, S., Inaba, M., Mizoguchi, Y., Iida, T., Kawamura, T.: Ontology-Based Topic Extraction Service from Weblogs. In: IEEE International Conference on Semantic Computing, pp. 468–475 (2008)
4. Kobayshi, N., Inui, K., Matusmoto, Y., Tateishi, K., Fukushima, S.: Collecting evaluative expressions by a text mining technique. IPSJ SIG NOTE 154(12), 77–84 (2003)
5. Asano, H., Hirano, T., Kobayasi, N., Matsuno, Y.: Subjective Information Indexing Technology Analyzing Word-of-mouth Content on the Web. NTT Technical Review 6(9), 1–7 (2008)
6. Spangler, W.S., Chen, Y., Proctor, L., Lelescu, A., Behal, A., He, B., Griffin, T.D., Liu, A., Wade, B., Davis, T.: COBRA - mining web for COrporate Brand and Reputation Analysis. Web Intelligence and Agent Systems (WIAS) 7(3), 243–254 (2009)
7. Zhu, Y., Shasha, D.: Warping Indexes with Envelope Transforms for Query by Humming. In: Proceedings of the 2003 ACM SIGMOD International Conference on Management of Data, pp. 181–192 (2003)
8. Otranto, E.: Identifying financial time series with similar dynamic conditional correlation. Journal of Computational Statistics & Data Analysis archive 54(1), 1–15 (2010)
9. Loy, C., Xiang, T., Gong, S.: International Journal of Computer Vision 90(1), 106–129 (2010)
10. Radinsky, K., Agichtein, E., Gabrilovich, E., Markovitch, S.: A Word at a Time: Computing Word Relatedness using Tremporal Semantic Analysis. In: WWW 2011, pp. 337–346 (2011)
11. Wang, G., Araki, K.: A Graphic Reputation Analysis System for Mining Japanese Weblog Based on both Unstructured and Structured Information. In: AINA Workshops 2008, pp. 1240–1245 (2008)
12. Iino, Y., Hirokawa, S.: Time Series Analysis of R&D Team Using Patent Information. In: Velásquez, J.D., Ríos, S.A., Howlett, R.J., Jain, L.C. (eds.) KES 2009. LNCS, vol. 5712, pp. 464–471. Springer, Heidelberg (2009)

13. Hashimoto, T., Shirota, Y.: Semantics Extraction from Social Computing: A Framework of Reputation Analysis on Buzz Marketing Sites. In: Kikuchi, S., Sachdeva, S., Bhalla, S. (eds.) DNIS 2010. LNCS, vol. 5999, pp. 244–255. Springer, Heidelberg (2010)

14. Bunke, H.: On a relation between graph edit distance and maximum common subgraph. Pattern Recognition Letters 18(8), 689–694 (1997)

15. Hashimoto, T., Kuboyama, T., Shirota, Y.: Graph-based Consumer Behavior Analysis from Buzz Marketing Sites. In: Proc. of 21st European Japanese Conference on Information Modelling and Knowledge Bases, pp. 60–71 (2011)

16. Kuboyama, T., Hashimoto, T., Shirota, Y.: Consumer Behavior Analysis from Buzz Marketing Sites over Time Series Concept Graphs. In: Proc. of 15th International Conference on Knowledge-Based and Intelligent Information & Engineering Systems, pp. 73–83 (2011)

17. Berndt, D., Clifford, J.: Using dynamic time warping to find patterns in time series. In: Proc. of Advances in Knowledge Discovery and Data Mining, pp. 229–248. AAAI/MIT (1994)

18. R, a language and environment for statistical computing and graphics, http://www.r-project.org/

19. Zhu, Y., Shasha, D.: Efficient Elastic Burst Detection in Data Streams. In: Proc. of the Ninth ACM SIGKDD International Conference on Knowledge Discovery and Data Mining, pp. 336–345 (2003)

20. Kleinberg, K.: Bursty and hierarchical structure in streams. In: Proc. of the Eighth ACM SIGKDD International Conference on Knowledge Discovery and Data Mining, pp. 91–101 (2002)

21. Salvadore, S., Chan, P.: FastDTW: Toward accurate dynamic time warping in linear time and space. In: Proc. of 3rd Workshop on Mining Temporal and Sequential Data, pp. 561–580 (2007)

Understanding User Behavior through Summarization of Window Transition Logs

Ryohei Saito[1,3], Tetsuji Kuboyama[2],
Yuta Yamakawa[1,3], and Hiroshi Yasuda[3]

[1] Hummingh Heads, Inc.,1–2–13 Tukishima, Chuo-ku, Tokyo, Japan
[2] Gakushuin University,1–5–1 Mejiro, Toshima-ku, Tokyo, Japan
[3] Tokyo Denki University, 2–2 Kandanisikicho, Chiyoda-ku,Tokyo, Japan
{ryouhei-s,yamakawa}@hummingheads.co.jp,
kuboyama-DNIS2011@tk.cc.gakushuin.ac.jp,
yasuda@mpeg.im.dendai.co.jp

Abstract. This paper proposes a novel method for analyzing PC usage logs aiming to find working patterns and behaviors of employees at work. The logs we analyze are recorded at individual PCs for employees in a company, and include active window transitions. Our method consists of two levels of abstraction: (1) task summarization by HMM; (2) user behavior comparison by kernel principle component analysis based on a graph kernel. The experimental results show that our method reveals implicit user behavior at a high level of abstraction, and allows us to understand individual user behavior among groups, and over time.

Keywords: user behavior analysis, PC usage patterns, pattern extraction, hidden Markov model, graph kernel, kernel principal component analysis.

1 Introduction

Computers with window-based user interface are nowadays common and vital tools for everyday business activities in most companies. Workers use their own computers in the workplaces, and open a number of windows for applications such as word processor, spreadsheet, web browser, and email client on their computer displays. Computer systems are capable of recording window transitions, which are changes of active/focused windows, into log files. These window transition data potentially provide a rich source of user behavior information on computers, and allow us to extract knowledge of the usage patterns of applications and to generate user behavior models. Furthermore, we expect that these models lead to evaluation and improvements of job performance and productivity, and to the application of anomaly detection of user behavior on computers.

Since the raw log data are, in general, too massive to handle, and too microscopic to interpret usage patterns, they are needed to be summarized at a higher level of abstraction. To summarize the data into an understandable form of user behavior, there are several sub-problems to be addressed, i.e., identifying

S. Kikuchi et al. (Eds.): DNIS 2011, LNCS 7108, pp. 162–178, 2011.

task segments, modeling user behavior based on task segments, and comparing and clustering user behavior models. In this paper, we address the following two problems.

1. Many workers are involved with various tasks on computers, and usually switch a number of application windows in a task. We, thus, assume that a segment of consecutive window transitions is supposed to correspond to a task. First, we identify each task segment in a long window transitions, and make a generative model of user behavior.
2. Next, we compare generative models among users to investigate user behavior from a group viewpoint.

To tackle the first problem, we employ a hidden Markov model (HMM), and engineer our model to HMM. The resulting models are in the form of ergodic Markov models of tasks. In the second problem, we apply a graph kernel and kernel principal component analysis to comparing the structural differences among these models.

Contributions. Our contributions in this paper are as follows: (i) we propose a task summarization method from active window transition logs based on hidden Markov model, and generate user behavior models from the summarization; (ii) we also propose a comparison method among user behavior models based on a graph kernel; and (iii) we empirically examine our method by using real world data. We emphasize that our method consists of two levels of abstraction: (1) task summarization by HMM; (2) user behavior comparison by kernel Principle Component Analysis based on a graph kernel. To the best of authors' knowledge, our method is a novel approach for extracting knowledge from log data. The analysis results show that our method reveals implicit task patterns at a high level of abstraction for gaining a better understanding of user behavior.

Related Work. There are a vast amount of studies related to the task or event summarization from log data [1,2,3,4,5,6,7,8]. For example, Kiernan and Terzi proposed an algorithm for generating event summaries based on hidden Markov Models [9]. Our method strongly relies on this algorithm in the first step, but the resulting summaries are not enough for understanding user behavior in the level of abstraction. Our method aims at a higher abstraction. Renaud and Gray made an analysis of user activities from the log data of key strokes, mouse clicks, and windows focuses [10]. Also Brdiczka et al. introduced a novel method for characterizing routine tasks from the active window transition [11]. However, in both studies, the comparison method among user behavior over time are not proposed. Ferreira et al. [12] proposed a mining method from sequential data, and obtained process transition models. This method focuses on the common event patterns shared in all users, whereas our method sheds light on the differences among user behavior patterns.

Organization. This paper is organized as follows. In Section 2, we describe the method for summarizing window transition patterns from the active window transition logs based on the hidden Markov model. In Section 3, we propose a novel method for comparing user behavior models generated by the method in the previous section. In Section 4, we conduct the analysis based on the proposed methods, and discuss the results. Finally, we conclude this paper in Section 5 with future work.

2   Summarizing Window Transition Patterns

The window transition log is regarded as a sequence of events. It appears reasonable that existing sequence mining methods, such as frequent episode/pattern mining [8], are applicable to modeling user behavior through the event sequence. However, even just flipping two consecutive events in the log makes the pattern different in these sequence mining methods. It is too sensitive to the order of events for modeling user behavior. This is because tasks on computer are not so strictly related to the order of window transitions. Hence, we model each task as the rate of events in a disjoint segment of the sequence after the event summarization method by Wang et al. [13].

2.1   Window Transition Logs

A window transition log contains a sequence of process names corresponding to active windows such as Excel, Word, Explorer, and Outlook with interval timestamps and user IDs. This sequence of process names is at a low level of abstraction from which it is hard to interpret the workflow. Therefore, it is helpful for a better understanding of user behaviors to segment the sequence into meaningful chunks so that the boundaries of chunks implicitly indicate the changes of tasks on computers at a higher level of abstraction.

Table 1. Active Window Transition Logs

Application	Start Time	Duration (sec)
Web	2010-04-01 8:00:30	403
Mail	2010-04-01 8:07:13	165
Word	2010-04-01 8:10:15	503
Web	2010-04-01 8:18:38	386
Excel	2010-04-01 8:25:04	303
Word	2010-04-01 8:30:20	440
$\vdots$	$\vdots$	$\vdots$
Word	2010-04-01 9:04:30	328

Observations from Log Data. We formulate the window transition log as a sequence of event sets. Let $\mathcal{E}$ be the set of events $\{e_1, \ldots, e_m\}$ observed in the log such as Excel and Word. We assume that time is measured in equal discrete intervals $t \in \{0, 1, \ldots, T\}$, and what we observe is just the set of events occurring in the interval $[t-1, t)$ for each $t \in \{0, \ldots, T\}$, where $[t-1, t)$ denotes the duration t' such that $t - 1 \leq t' < t$. We denote by o_t the set of events observed in the time interval $[t-1, t)$, i.e. $o_t = \{e \in \mathcal{E} \mid e \text{ occurs in } [t-1, t)\}$. Therefore, we have an event set sequence as our observation

$$\boldsymbol{O} = (o_1, \ldots, o_T), \text{ where } o_t \subseteq \mathcal{E} \text{ for } t \in \{1, \ldots, T\}.$$

Example. Here, we have the active window transition log as shown in Table 1. Then, we obtain the following sequence of event sets for $\mathcal{E} = \{\text{web,excel,word,mail}\}$:

$$\boldsymbol{O} = (\{\text{web,mail}\}, \{\text{web,word}\}, \{\text{word,excel}\}, \{\text{word,mail}\},$$
$$\{\text{web,word,mail}\}, \{\text{excel,word}\}, \{\text{excel,word,mail}\}).$$

Note that we discretize time with a constant interval as in Fig. 1.

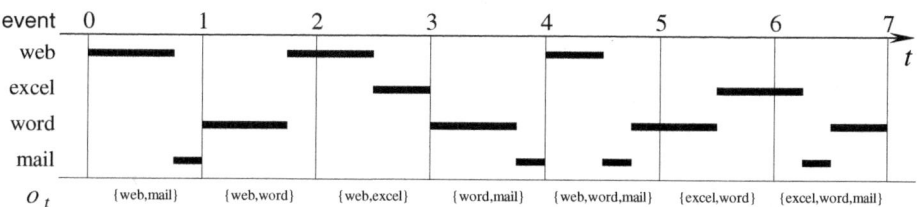

Fig. 1. Observations obtained from log data

2.2   User Behavior Modeling

We first construct probabilistic generative models of the sequence of event sets with hidden Markov Model (HMM). To model user behavior at a higher abstraction, we segment the sequence of event sets $\boldsymbol{O} = (o_1, \ldots, o_T)$ into the sequence of chunks $\mathcal{I} = (I_1, \ldots, I_\tau)$ as follows

$$\underbrace{o_1, \ldots, o_{t_1-1}}_{I_1}, \underbrace{o_{t_1}, \ldots, o_{t_2-1}}_{I_2}, o_{t_2}, \ldots, o_{t_\tau - 1}, \underbrace{o_{t_\tau}, \ldots, o_T}_{I_\tau},$$

where $t_1 < t_2 < \cdots < t_\tau \leq T$ and $I_i = (o_{t_i}, \ldots, o_{t_{i+1}-1})$ for $i \in \{1, \ldots, \tau\}$. Note that let $t_{\tau+1} - 1$ be T for consistency.

Table 2. Notations used in the paper

$0, \ldots, T$	discrete time sequence
$\mathcal{E} = \{e_1, \ldots, e_m\}$	set of events
$\boldsymbol{O} = (o_1, \ldots, o_T)$	sequence of event sets
$o_t \subseteq \mathcal{E}$	set of events observed at time t
$\boldsymbol{I} = (I_1, \ldots, I_\tau)$	sequence of segments
$S = \{s_1, \ldots, s_K\}$	set of states of tasks
$\boldsymbol{S} = (\sigma(1), \ldots, \sigma(\tau))$	sequence of states corresponding to $\boldsymbol{I}$
$a(s_i, s_j)$	transition probability from s_i to s_j
$b_s(o)$	probability observing o in state s
π_s	initial probability of state s
$M_s = (P_s(e_1), \ldots, P_s(e_m))$	task summary of state s

Task Transition. We assume that users have K states of tasks. Henceforth, we regard that each task corresponds to state $s_i \in \{s_1, \ldots, s_K\}$. Hence, the set of tasks is denoted by the set of states $S = \{s_1, \ldots, s_K\}$. Also, we assume that each segment I_i in the sequence $\boldsymbol{I}$ corresponds to a task $\sigma(i) \in S$ for $i \in \{1, \ldots, \tau\}$. Thus, a user starts work with state $\sigma(1)$ at segment I_1, and ends with state $\sigma(\tau)$ at segment I_τ with a task transition $\boldsymbol{S} = (\sigma(1), \ldots, \sigma(\tau))$.

A transition probability from state s_i to s_j is denoted by $a(s_i, s_j)$ for any two states $s_i, s_j \in S$, and represented by the matrix $A = \{a_{ij}\}$, where $a_{ij} = a(s_i, s_j)$. The initial probability of state s is denoted by π_s, which is the probability of a user starting with state $s \in S$, and Π denotes the set of initial probabilities $\{\pi_{s_1}, \ldots, \pi_{s_K}\}$.

Task Summary. In our modeling, each task s determines the probabilities of window applications observed. From the intuitive point of view, it is a natural modeling of tasks since, for example, when we are in the task of making web pages, we activate the windows of web browser and HTML editor more often than the windows of other applications. Therefore, we assume that a user engaged in the task $s \in S$ activates a set of windows $o \subseteq \mathcal{E}$ with the output probability $b_s(o)$. Let B be the set of $b_s(o)$ for any $s \in S$ and $o \subseteq \mathcal{E}$.

Given the set B, the probability that the window e is activated in a state s is denoted by $P_s(e)$ for $e \in \mathcal{E}$, and estimated as follows.

$$P_s(e) = \sum_{o \subseteq \mathcal{E} \text{ such that } e \in o} b_s(o).$$

Hence, a user in task s activates the windows of applications $e_1, \ldots, e_m$ with the probabilities $P_s(e_1), \ldots, P_s(e_m)$, respectively, where m is the number of applications considered, i.e. $m = |\mathcal{E}|$. We denote the m-tuple of probabilities for task s by

$$M_s = (P_s(e_1), \ldots, P_s(e_m))$$

and regard it as the *task summary* of s.

2.3   Inferring User Behavior Models

The HMM is defined with the parameters $\lambda = (\Pi, A, B)$. Each hidden state of HMM corresponds to the task which generates a combination of applications with the probability B, starts with the probability Π, and transits to another with the probability A. In our method, summarizing user behavior is regarded as the estimation of the parameters λ from the sequence of observation O.

We apply the Baum-Welch algorithm [14] to estimating HMM parameters λ. Since the HMM here is attributed to the ergodic model(all states can be connected from any states), the initial parameter setting is significant.

In this paper, we introduce a specific initialization method based on k-means clustering as follows.

1. Segmenting the sequence of observations O into L segments by connecting similar neighbor observations.
2. Clustering segments by k-means clustering algorithm.
3. Assigning each cluster as a distinct state, and estimating HMM parameters in this setting of segmentation and states.

At Step 1, we start with setting each observation in the sequence O as one segment, i.e. $I = (o_1, \ldots, o_T) = (I_1, \ldots, I_T)$. For each segment I_i, the cost for merging it to the next segment is estimated, and two adjacent segments with the minimal cost are merged. Let $I_i \circ I_{i+1}$ be the segment mering I_i and i_{i+1}. The merge cost is defined as follows:

$$\text{cost}(I_i, I_{i+1}) = -\log_2(P(I_i \circ I_{i+1} \mid M'_{i,i+1}))$$
$$+ \log_2(P(I_i \mid M'_i)) + \log_2(P(I_{i+1} \mid M'_{i+1})),$$

where $-\log_2(P(I_i \mid M'_i))$ is the number of bits required to describe the segment I_i under the model M'_i. The model M'_i is the tuple of probabilities $(P_i(e_1), \ldots, P_i(e_m))$ estimated from segment I_i. (Note that M' is similar to the task summary M introduced in the previous section, but these are not the same.) Each $P_i(e_j)$ is estimated by $P_i(e_j) = n(e_j, I_i)|/|I_i|$, where $n(e, I)$ denotes the number of time points at which event e occurs in the segment I, and so does $n(\bar{e}, I)$ the number of time points at which event e does not occur in I. (The model $M'_{i,i+1}$ is also estimated from the segment $I_i \circ I_{i+1}$.)

$$P(I_i \mid M'_i) = \prod_{e \in \mathcal{E}} P_i(e)^{n(e, I_i)}(1 - P_i(e))^{n(\bar{e}, I_i)}$$

This merging operation is repeated until a minimal merge cost is greater than a given threshold.

At Step 2, each segment I_i is labeled with a state $s \in S$ using k-means clustering algorithm. In clustering, the distance function between two segments I_i and I_j is measured by symmetrized Kullback-Leibler divergence between corresponding models M'_i and M'_j.

$$\text{dist}(I_i, I_j) = \sum_{e \in \mathcal{E}} P_i(e) \log \frac{P_i(e)}{P_j(e)} + \sum_{e \in \mathcal{E}} P_j(e) \log \frac{P_j(e)}{P_i(e)}.$$

Now, we can assume that each observation o_t is labeled with a state $c_t \in S$ for $t \in \{1, \ldots, T\}$ as the result of clustering.

At Step 3, now for each time point $t \in \{1, \ldots, T\}$, the observation o_t belongs to a cluster $s \in S$ due to Step 2. Let $D(s)$ be the set of observations attributed to the cluster s, and let $n(e, D(s))$ be the number of observations in $D(s)$ including event e.

Now, we can estimate the task summary $M_s = (P_s(e_1), \ldots, P_s(e_m))$ for a task $s \in S$, where $P_s(e) = n(e, D(s))/|D(s)|$. Let $C(s)$ be $\{t \in \{1, \ldots, T\} \mid c_t = s\}$. Then, we estimate the initial parameters of HMM as follows:

$$\pi_s = \frac{D(s)}{T}, \quad a(s_i, s_j) = \frac{|C(s_i) \cap C(s_j)|}{|C(s_i)|}, \quad b_s(o) = \prod_{e \in \mathcal{E}} q_s(e, o),$$

where

$$q_s(e, o) = \begin{cases} P_s(e) & \text{if } e \in o \\ 1 - P_s(e) & \text{otherwise.} \end{cases}$$

Starting with these initial parameters, we apply the well-known Baum-Welch algorithm [14] to estimate HMM parameters. In addition, to extract the most likely hidden state sequence, i.e. task transition, from the refined HMM, we also employ Viterbi algorithm [14].

3   Clustering User Behavior

Now we have the user behavior models in the form of ergodic Markov models through the method in the previous section. We want to compare user behavior at the level of this abstraction. In this section, we present a method for measuring similarity between two models for visualizing and clustering user behavior.

3.1   Similarity Measure between Two User Behavior Models

The user behavior models inferred by the previous section are regarded as directed graphs in which each vertex is labeled with task summary and each (directed) edge is labeled with the transition probability from one task to another. This graph is also referred to as a *task transition graph* in this paper.

As the similarity measure between two task transition graphs, we employ the marginalized kernel between labeled graph proposed by Kashima et al. [15] since the random walk model in the graph kernel is appropriate for the task transition model. Intuitively, this kernel compares two random walkers' trails on two graphs. A random walker starts from a vertex and moves on to the next vertex according to transition probabilities on edges. After τ-steps, the walker finishes a sequence of τ tasks. Each task sequence is weighted with the production of all the transition probabilities of tasks. The kernel computes the similarity between any possible pairs of weighted sequences of the same length in two graphs, and sum them up from length one to infinity.

A task transition graph is denoted by $G = (S, E)$, where S is the set of vertices and $E \subseteq S \times S$ is the set of directed edges. Each vertex corresponds to a task summary in the task transition graph. (We abuse the notation by identifying each vertex $s \in S$ to both its label and a hidden state inferred by the previous section.) A *task sequence* of length τ is denoted by $\boldsymbol{S} = (v_1, \ldots, v_\tau)$, where $v_1, \ldots, v_\tau$ are vertices in S, the consecutive vertices v_i and v_{i+1} in $\boldsymbol{S}$ are connected by the edge $(v_i, v_{i+1}) \in E$. By $\boldsymbol{S}^\tau(G)$, we denote the set of all task sequences of length τ in graph G.

The probability of task sequence $\boldsymbol{S} \in \boldsymbol{S}^\tau(G)$ generated by the random walk on G is

$$P(\boldsymbol{S} \mid G) = \pi_{v_1} \left(\prod_{i=2}^{\tau} a(v_{i-1}, v_i) \right) \pi_{v_\tau},$$

where the random walker starts from vertex v_1 with probability π_{v_1}, ends at v_τ with π_{v_τ}, and $a(v_{i-1}, v_i)$ is the transition probability from v_{i-1} to v_i. In our case, we assign the start and end of office work to two states $v_1 = s_1$ and $v_\tau = s_K$ in S, respectively.

Then, the similarity between two task transition graphs G_1, G_2 is denoted by $K(G_1, G_2)$ and given as follows:

$$K(G_1, G_2) = \sum_{\tau=1}^{\infty} \sum_{\boldsymbol{S}_1 \in \boldsymbol{S}^\tau(G_1)} \sum_{\boldsymbol{S}_2 \in \boldsymbol{S}^\tau(G_2)} P(\boldsymbol{S}_1 \mid G_1) P(\boldsymbol{S}_2 \mid G_2) k(\boldsymbol{S}_1, \boldsymbol{S}_2),$$

where $k(\boldsymbol{S}_1, \boldsymbol{S}_2)$ is the similarity (subkernel) between two sequences $\boldsymbol{S}_1$ and $\boldsymbol{S}_2$ without transition probability, and $\delta(\boldsymbol{S}_1, \boldsymbol{S}_2) = 1$ if $\boldsymbol{S}_1$ is equal to $\boldsymbol{S}_2$, otherwise $\delta(\boldsymbol{S}_1, \boldsymbol{S}_2) = 0$.

Kashima et al. [15] proposed a simple and efficient algorithm for computing the similarity measure based on a fixpoint computation. This type of similarity measure is called a kernel function which is a class of functions implicitly represented as the cross product of two feature vectors, and is applicable to a wide range of multivariate analysis and machine learning methods.

As the similarity between two sequences $\boldsymbol{S}_1 = (v_1, \ldots, v_\tau)$ and $\boldsymbol{S}_2 = (v'_1, \ldots, v'_\tau)$, we design the following simple kernel function:

$$k(\boldsymbol{S}_1, \boldsymbol{S}_2) = \prod_{i=1}^{\tau} k_s(v_i, v'_i),$$

where $k_s(v_i, v'_i)$ is the similarity between two task summaries $M_s = (P_s(e_1), \ldots, P_s(e_m))$ and $M_{s'} = (P_{s'}(e_1), \ldots, P_{s'}(e_m))$. Here, we assume that the states s and s' correspond to v_i and v'_i respectively. Also we design $k_s(v, v')$ as the cosine similarity:

$$k_s(v, v') = \frac{M_s \cdot M_{s'}}{\|M_s\| \, \|M_{s'}\|}.$$

4   Analysis and Discussion

We conducted an analysis of active window transition logs for a real IT corporation. Our analysis consists of two states: (i) the task summarization for each
user, (ii) the comparison among users and visualizations.

4.1   Target Log Data

The target log data are provided by a software company that designs, develops,
markets, and support softwares. Most employees work from 9:00 to 17:00 with
one hour lunch break, five days a week, and the majority of employees use
their own desktop computers running Microsoft Windows. The company has
six departments for Administrative, Sales Office, Marketing, Technical Support,
Research and Development, and Quality Control. In this study, we target the
log range from 8:00 to 21:00.

We employ the following nine categories for applications regarded as events,
where the category "Others" includes any other applications except for the major
applications used in the company.

$$\mathcal{E} = \{\text{Mail, Web, Explorer, Word, Excel, PowerPoint, Editor, Viewer, Others}\}$$

In particular, the category "Mail," "Web," "Editor," and "Viewer" respectively
indicate the groups of applications with the same role at work. For example,
the category "Web" includes web browsers such as Internet Explorer, Firefox,
Chrome.

4.2   Task Transition Inferred by HMM

In inferring task transition models from the log data by HMM, we set the number of hidden states as twelve including the starting (state 1) and ending states
(state 12) of everyday work, and the null state (denoted by "nop", state 12) for
no-operation. The states are shared over all users for comparing among user behavior models. Figure 2 shows the task transition for four months for an employee
(USER1). In this figure, each task state is expressed by color. USER1 joined the
company and started basic training at the end of August. After that, USER1
received on-the-job training and involved in handover practice till October. At
November, USER1 started practical work.

As shown in Fig. 2, in September, most assigned states are state 7, 8 and 11;
in October are state 5, 7, 10 and 11; and in November and December are state
5, 7 and 10. We can confirm that, for each working period of basic training,
on-the-job training, and practical working, the patterns of task transitions are
different. Since the state 7 occurs beyond these three periods, it appears to be
a fundamental work unit of USER1. In contrast, the state 11 occurs exclusively
in September and October, especially at the start and end of each working day.
Since we do not observe the state 11 within such a long duration in the other
months, we can guess that this state is related to training, for example, writing
planning documents or reports about training.

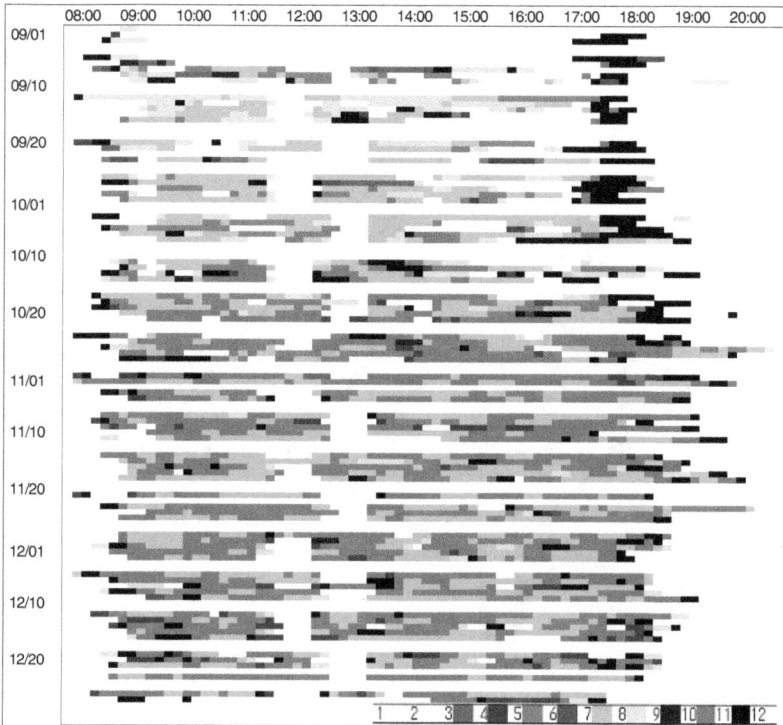

Fig. 2. The task transition of USER1 for four months: the horizontal axis indicates working time, and the vertical axis indicates the date in the form of (MM/DD); the twelve states of tasks are expressed by colors

Figure 3 shows the task transition as the Markov model inferred by HMM (upper in Fig. 4), and two task summaries for top two steady-states (lower 3) from the stationary distribution of the Markov model. Figure 4 shows the steady-state distribution of the Markov model in Fig. 3(upper).

We show the task transition and its steady-state distribution in Figure. 4 and Figure 3 from the estimated HMM.

For USER1, the ration of two steady-states 7 and 10 are exclusively high except for the null state 2 (State 2 stands for no operation on a computer). Thus, USER1 is mainly involved in the tasks implied by state 7 and 10, and mutually switches between these tasks.

The difference between two states 7 and 10 lies in the frequency of mail application usage. In these states, Explorer and Excel are mainly used. Hence, we can guess that USER1 usually uses Explorer and Excel, and occasionally uses a mail application at practical work. In addition, the observation that state 10 appears after the end of September, and does not in September, suggests that USER1 starts exchanging e-mail after the training period.

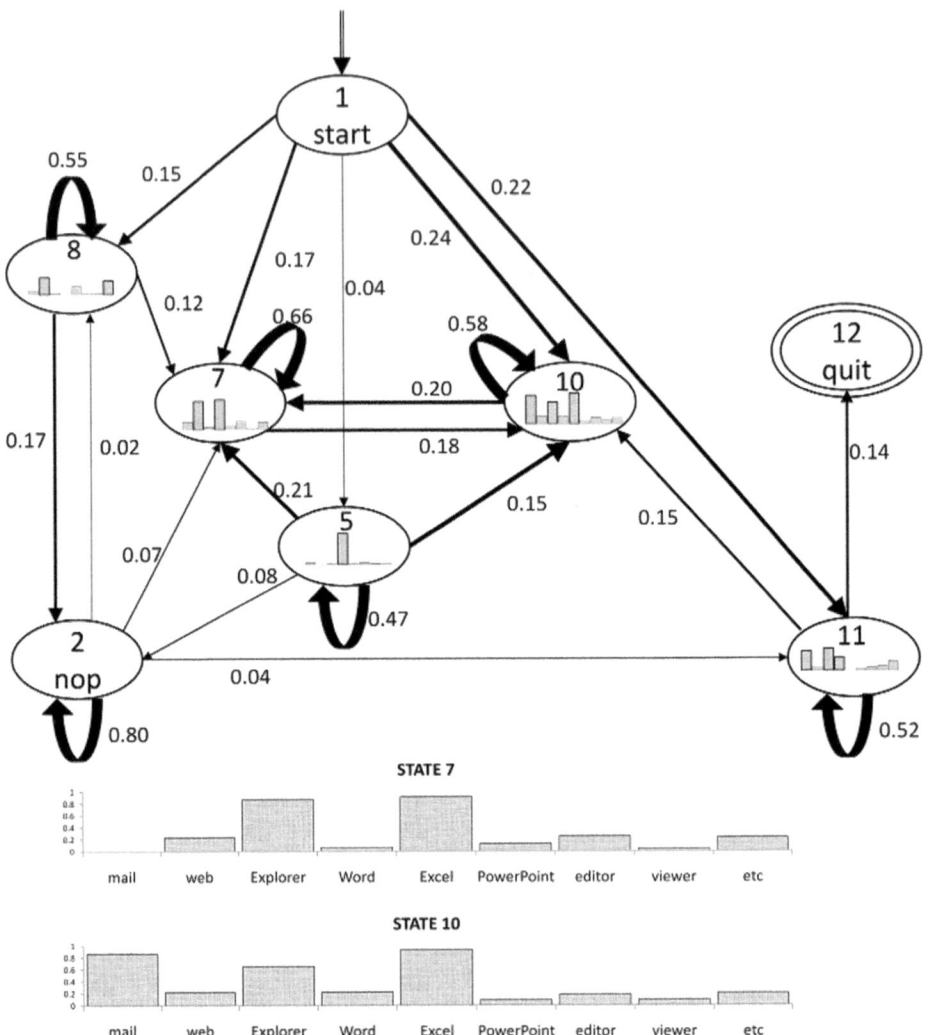

Fig. 3. (i) Task transition inferred by HMM (upper); (ii) Top two steady-states from the stationary distribution(lower)

4.3 User Behavior Clustering by Static State Distributions

To confirm the validity of our modeling method, we conduct the hierarchical clustering for user behavior by measuring the distance between the stationary distribution for all users. The results are shown in Fig. 5. We exclude state 2 (null state) from the input of clustering since the probability staying at the null state does not have direct effect over the working patterns on computers, and

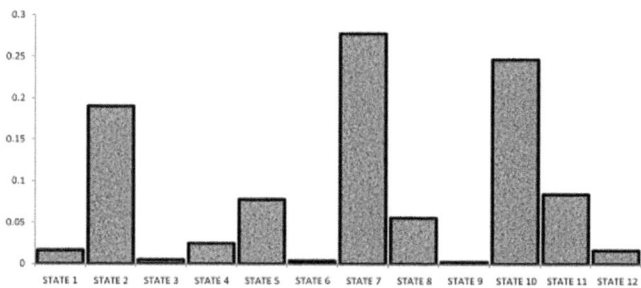

Fig. 4. The steady-state distribution of the task transition in Fig. 3(upper)

the ratio of the null state depends on the users leaving seat, having meetings, or working at their own desk. In Table 3, we show the number of users in each department recorded in logs.

Table 3. Department

Department	Abbreviation	Number of users
Marketing	marketing	7
Quality Control Assurance	qa	8
Research&Development	rd	17
Sales	sales	9
Sales Office	sales_office	2
Technical Support	tech_support	16

We can confirm that the users in the same department are clustered very closely, especially in Marketing(marketing), Research&Development(rd), and Quality Control Area(qa). Also, we observe that the pairs of (sales02, sales09), (tech_support05, tech_support09), and (sales_office01, sales_office02) are respectively clustered very closely. According to a hearing, these pairs of users are involved in the same tasks respectively in a complementary style. In general, it is natural assumption that the working patterns of the users in the same department are more similar than the patterns in the different departments. Our experiment supports this conjecture and the validity of our method. On the other hand, the users in Technical Support are divided into multiple clusters. We verify the result by confirming that these users are actually involved in the different tasks from each other.

4.4   User Behavior Clustering by Graph Kernel

We apply kernel Principle Component Analysis(kernel PCA) [16] based on the graph kernel described in the previous section to generating monthly task

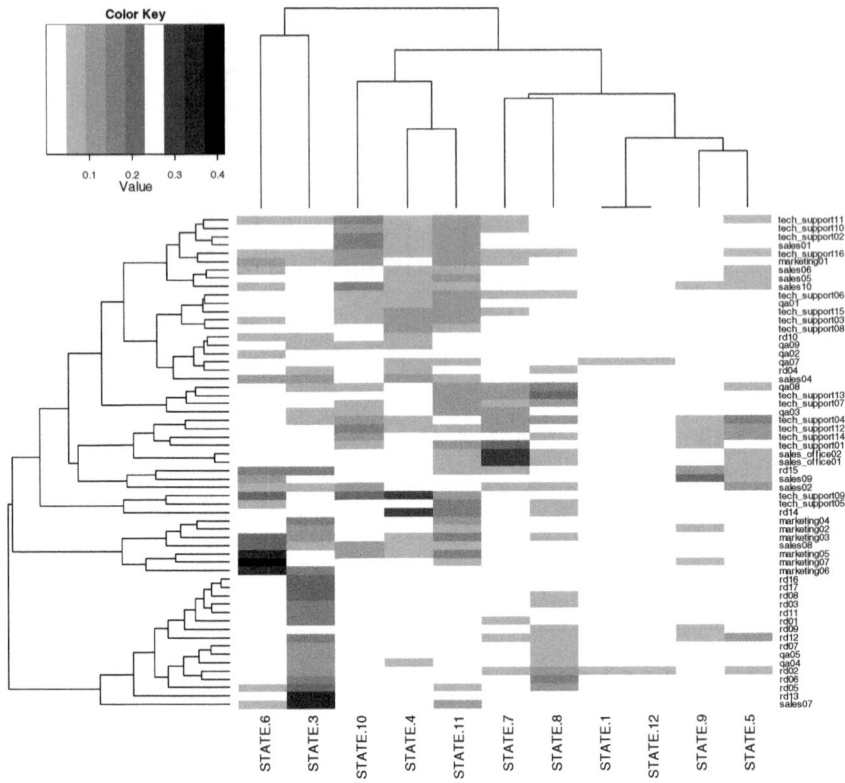

Fig. 5. Hierarchical clustering based on the distance between stationary distributions for all users

transition models. These models are generated from the logs for four months of 60 users.

We show the scatter plot of principal component scores obtained by kernel PCA for monthly task transition models of all users in Fig. 6. In Fig. 7, we extract a pair of users in Sales Office, and plot the monthly models from Fig. 6. As shown in Fig. 7, these users are closely plotted except for October. They both joined the company in September. Following initial training in September, they received on-the-job training in October, and then they started working from November. They have been working together sharing the same tasks from the initial training. This fact is also supported by our method using the graph kernel. The result implies that our method using kernel PCA is capable of detecting the change of working patterns over time.

Figure 8 shows the plot of all user in Technical Support and Marketing. The points of users can be divided into two groups according to the departments by a line. This fact shows that task patterns in the two departments are recognizable, and the users of two departments can be classified from logs without the department information.

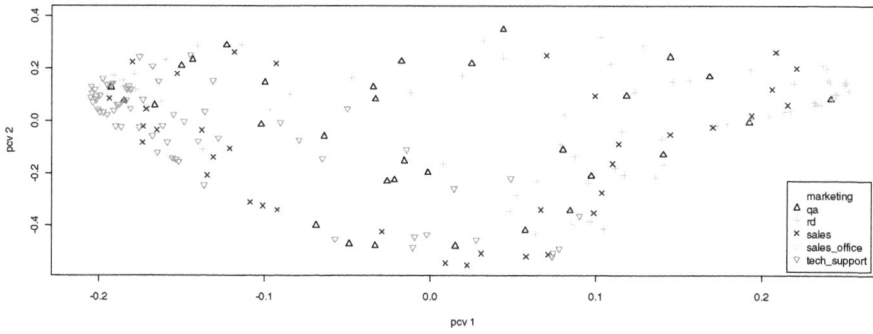

Fig. 6. Scatter plot of all users by kernel PCA

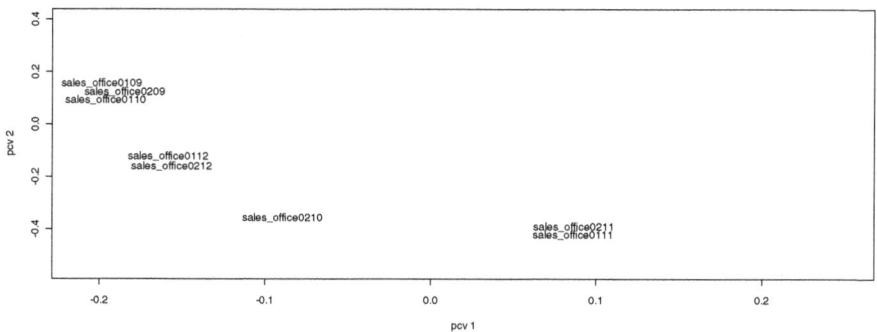

Fig. 7. Scatter plot of two users working together by kernel PCA

In the last analysis, we infer the task transition models on the daily basis for USER2 for four months, i.e. about 80 days, and apply kernel PCA to these models. Figure 9 shows the scatter plot of the models with the first and third principal component. We can confirm that the task transition models are clearly divided into four clusters. USER2 is engaged in atypical(non-routine) work, and this observation shows effectively that USER2 has four patterns of work. For many users, clear clusters are confirmed, while for many others clusters are not confirmed.

We conducted a hearing for USER2 to confirm the relationship between our results and actual working patterns of USER2. Table 4 shows the summary of the investigation (the date is in the form of MM/DD). "General work" includes several tasks, and USER2 did not concentrate on a specific one task. "Proofreading" and "Writing manuscript" respectively indicate that USER2 spent on the same tasks throughout the day. According to Table 4, Cluster 3 and 4 respectively

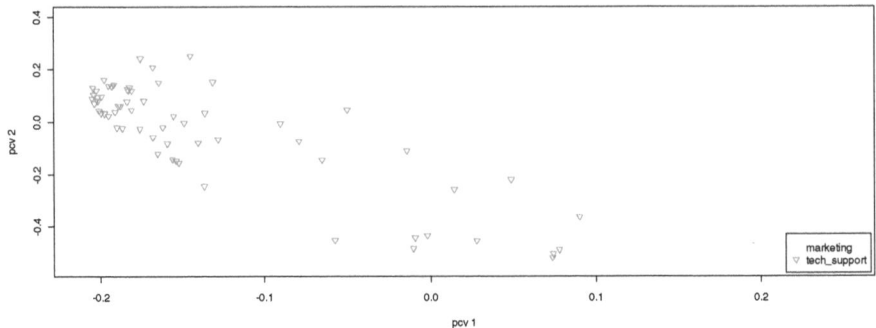

Fig. 8. Scatter plot of users in Technical Support and Marketing

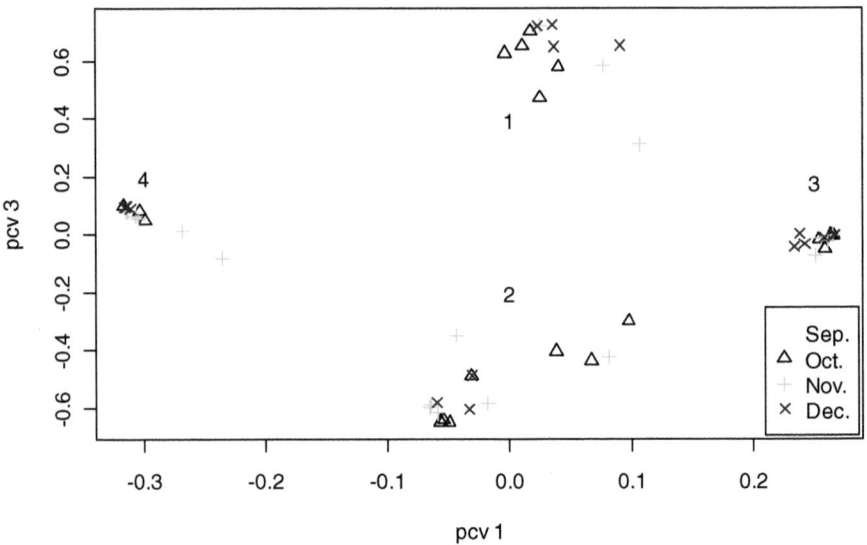

Fig. 9. Scatter plot of user's daily behavior by kernel PCA

correspond to "Proofreading" and "Writing manuscript." The two exceptions in
11/22 and 11/30 are considered that these models also mainly include "Writing
manuscript." The other "General work" models are divided into two clusters 1
and 2. We observe that most days in the cluster 1 are Monday or Friday also for
the other months besides November. According to the hearing, USER2 attends
regular meetings, and has outside jobs especially on Monday and Friday.

Table 4. Cluster number and actual work

Cluster number	Date		Hearing results
1	11/01	Mon	General work
1	11/05	Fri	General work
1	11/26	Fri	General work
2	11/02	Tue	General work
2	11/08	Mon	General work
2	11/12	Fri	General work
2	11/18	Thu	General work
2	11/24	Wed	General work
2	11/29	Mon	General work
3	11/04	Thu	Proofreading
3	11/10	Wed	Proofreading
3	11/11	Thu	Proofreading
3	11/19	Fri	Proofreading
3	11/25	Thu	Proofreading
4	11/09	Tue	Writing manuscript
4	11/15	Mon	Writing manuscript
4	11/16	Tue	Writing manuscript
4	11/17	Wed	Writing manuscript
4	11/22	Mon	General work
4	11/30	Tue	General work

From these observations, we can show that our method reveals implicit task patterns at a high level of abstraction from the active window transition logs.

5   Conclusions and Future Work

In this paper, we propose a new method for understanding user behavior on computer from active window transition logs. The method is based on inferring generative models of window transitions using hidden Markov model, and comparing these models using kernel principal component analysis for graph structures. The analysis for the real world logs in a company shows that our method allows us to understand user behavior at a high level of abstraction, and enables us to compare the user behavior among groups and over time.

In future work, from the technical point of view, we plan to introduce a more sophisticated method for estimating HMM parameters including the number of states using Bayesian nonparametric HMM. To evaluate and show the effectiveness of our method, we need much more information other than computer operation logs by conducting questionnaires and hearings to compare the low level abstraction of user behavior in computer logs with the high level abstraction of behavior such as questionnaire results. Also, we plan to apply our method to the anomaly detection of user behavior among groups or the change detection of it over time.

References

1. Hilbert, D., Redmiles, D.: Extracting usability information from user interface events. ACM Computing Surveys (CSUR) 32(4), 384–421 (2000)
2. Karlson, A., Meyers, B., Jacobs, A., Johns, P., Kane, S.: Working overtime: Patterns of smartphone and pc usage in the day of an information worker. Pervasive Computing, 398–405 (2009)
3. Begole, J., Tang, J., Smith, R., Yankelovich, N.: Work rhythms: analyzing visualizations of awareness histories of distributed groups. In: Proceedings of the 2002 ACM Conference on Computer Supported Cooperative Work, pp. 334–343. ACM (2002)
4. Beauvisage, T.: Computer usage in daily life. In: Proceedings of the 27th International Conference on Human Factors in Computing Systems, pp. 575–584. ACM (2009)
5. Safer, I., Murphy, G.: Comparing episodic and semantic interfaces for task boundary identification. In: Proceedings of the 2007 Conference of the Center for Advanced Studies on Collaborative Research, pp. 229–243. ACM (2007)
6. Singh, N., Tomar, D., Roy, B.: An approach to understand the end user behavior through log analysis. International Journal of Computer Applications IJCA 5(11), 9–13 (2010)
7. Shen, J., Li, L., Dietterich, T.: Real-time detection of task switches of desktop users. In: Proc. of IJCAI, vol. 7, pp. 2868–2873 (2007)
8. Zaki, M.: Sequence mining in categorical domains: incorporating constraints. In: Proceedings of the Ninth International Conference on Information and Knowledge Management, pp. 422–429. ACM (2000)
9. Kiernan, J., Terzi, E.: Constructing comprehensive summaries of large event sequences. ACM Transactions on Knowledge Discovery from Data (TKDD) 3(4), 21 (2009)
10. Renaud, K., Gray, P.: Making sense of low-level usage data to understand user activities. In: Proceedings of the 2004 Annual Research Conference of the South African Institute of Computer Scientists and Information Technologists on IT Research in Developing Countries, pp. 115–124. South African Institute for Computer Scientists and Information Technologists (2004)
11. Brdiczka, O., Su, N., Begole, J.: Temporal task footprinting: identifying routine tasks by their temporal patterns. In: Proceeding of the 14th International Conference on Intelligent user Interfaces, pp. 281–284. ACM (2010)
12. Ferreira, D., Zacarias, M., Malheiros, M., Ferreira, P.: Approaching Process Mining with Sequence Clustering: Experiments and Findings. In: Alonso, G., Dadam, P., Rosemann, M. (eds.) BPM 2007. LNCS, vol. 4714, pp. 360–374. Springer, Heidelberg (2007)
13. Wang, P., Wang, H., Liu, M., Wang, W.: An algorithmic approach to event summarization. In: Proceedings of the 2010 International Conference on Management of Data, pp. 183–194. ACM (2010)
14. Rabiner, L.: A tutorial on hidden markov models and selected applications in speech recognition. Proceedings of the IEEE 77(2), 257–286 (1989)
15. Kashima, H., Tsuda, K., Inokuchi, A.: Marginalized kernels between labeled graphs. In: Proceedings of 20th International Conference on Machine Learning (ICML), pp. 321–328 (2003)
16. Schölkopf, B., Smola, A., Müller, K.: Kernel Principal Component Analysis. In: Gerstner, W., Hasler, M., Germond, A., Nicoud, J.-D. (eds.) ICANN 1997. LNCS, vol. 1327, pp. 583–588. Springer, Heidelberg (1997)

Information Filtering by Using Materialized Skyline View

Yasuhiko Morimoto, Md. Anisuzzaman Siddique, and Md. Shamsul Arefin

Hiroshima University
1-7-1 Kagamiyama, Higashi-Hiroshima, 739-8521, Japan
`morimoto@mis.hiroshima-u.ac.jp`
`http://www.morimo.com/morimo-ken`

Abstract. We consider information filtering methods that use materialized skyline view. Skyline query contains data objects that are preferable for each user even though users' preference is different for each. We propose various kinds of skyline queries such as skyline on relatively high-dimensional numerical databases, skyline on spatial databases, and skyline set. We materialize such skyline information to make concise answer for each query. We also considered methods for maintaining materialized skyline view up to date to handle an update for a numerical database.

Keywords: Information Filtering, k-Dominant Skyline, Skyline Sets, Spatial Skyline, Temporal Skyline.

1 Introduction

With rapid growth of information technology, we can collect information and can construct databases easier than ever. As a result, there are too many information to find necessary answers quickly. In such situation, information filtering methods are important.

Skyline query function is one of promising information filtering methods. Given a k-dimensional database DB, an object p is said to be in skyline of DB if there is no object q in DB such that q is better than p in all k dimension. If there exist such object q, then we say that p is dominated by q or q dominates p. Figure 1 shows a typical example of skyline. The table in the figure is a list of hotels, each of which contains two numerical attributes "distance" and "price".

Preference of each user of the hotel database is different. For example, one user wants to find the cheapest one, while another wants to find the nearest one. Skyline of the database is $\{h_1, h_3, h_4\}$ (See Figure 1 (b)). In general, each user can find the optimal hotel of her / his preference in the skyline. Therefore, information filtering by using skyline queries is useful to filter unnecessary information. A number of efficient skyline algorithms have been reported in the literature [1,2,3,4,5].

S. Kikuchi et al. (Eds.): DNIS 2011, LNCS 7108, pp. 179–189, 2011.

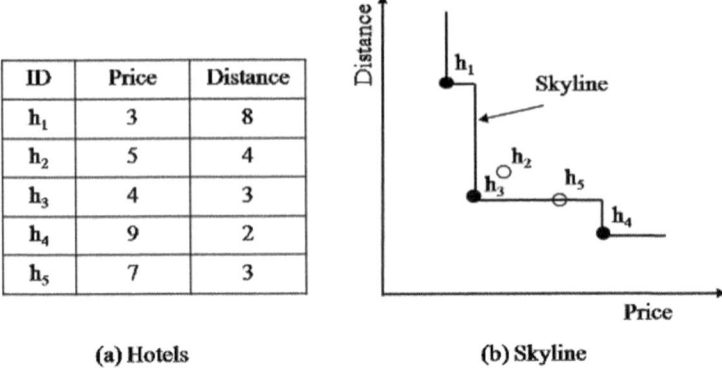

ID	Price	Distance
h_1	3	8
h_2	5	4
h_3	4	3
h_4	9	2
h_5	7	3

(a) Hotels   (b) Skyline

Fig. 1. Skyline Example

2   General Numerical Database

The skyline query can greatly help user to filter information. It is always assumed that all the attributes are involved in the skyline queries, that is, the dominating relationship is evaluated based on every dimensions of the dataset. However, a major drawback of skylines is that, in datasets with many dimensions, the number of skyline objects becomes large and no longer is an effective for filtering information.

To deal with this dimensionality curse, Chan, *et al.* considered k-dominant skyline query [6]. They relaxed the definition of "dominated" so that an object is more likely to be dominated by another.

2.1   Preliminary of k-Dominant Skyline

Assume there is an n-dimensional database DB and $D_1, D_2, \cdots, D_n$ be the n attributes of DB. Let $O_1, O_2, \cdots, O_r$ be r objects (tuples) of DB. We use $O_i.D_s$ to denote the s-th dimension value of O_i. Without loss of generality, we assume smaller value is better in each dimension.

An object $O_i \in DB$ is said to dominate another object $O_j \in DB$, denoted as $O_i \prec O_j$, if (1) for every $s \in \{1, \cdots, n\}$: $O_i.D_s \leq O_j.D_s$; and (2) for at least one $t \in \{1, \cdots, n\}$: $O_i.D_t < O_j.D_t$.

The skyline of DB is a set of objects that are not dominated by any other objects. For example, skyline query for Table 1 dataset returns five objects: O_2, O_3, O_5, O_6, and O_7. Objects O_1 and O_4 are not in skyline because they are dominated by O_7.

An object O_i is said to k-*dominate* another object O_j, denoted as $O_i \prec_k O_j$, if (1) $O_i.D_s \leq O_j.D_s$ in k dimensions among n dimensions and (2) $O_i.D_t < O_j.D_t$ in one dimension among the k dimensions. We call such O_i as k-*dominant object* and such O_j as k-*dominated object* between O_i and O_j.

Table 1. Symbolic Dataset

Obj.	D_1	D_2	D_3	D_4	D_5	D_6
O_1	7	3	5	4	4	3
O_2	3	4	4	5	1	3
O_3	4	3	2	3	5	4
O_4	5	3	5	4	1	2
O_5	1	4	1	1	3	4
O_6	5	3	4	5	1	5
O_7	1	2	5	3	1	2

An object $O_i \in DB$ is said to be a *k-dominant skyline object* of DB if O_i is not k-dominated by any other object in DB. We denote a set of all k-dominant skyline objects in DB as $Sky_k(DB)$. Note that conventional skyline objects are n-dominant objects and are in $Sky_n(DB)$.

In Table 1, for example, if $k = 5$, the 5-dominant skyline query returns two objects: O_5 and O_7. Objects O_1, O_2, O_3, O_4, and O_6 are not in 5-dominant skyline because they are 5-dominated by O_7. The 4-dominant skyline query returns only one object, O_7, and the 3-dominant skyline query returns empty. Like this example, we can control the selectivity by changing k.

The k-dominant skyline has following property [7]. Any object in $Sky_{k-1}(DB)$ must be an object in $Sky_k(DB)$ for any k such that $1 < k \leq n$. Any object that is not in $Sky_k(DB)$ cannot be an object in $Sky_{k-1}(DB)$ for any k such that $1 < k \leq n$. Similarly, every object that belongs to the k-dominant skyline also belongs to the skyline, i.e., $Sky_k(DB) \subseteq Sky_n(DB)$.

The conventional skyline is the k-dominant skyline where $k = n$. If we decrease k, more objects tend to be k-dominated by other objects. As a result, we can reduce the number of k-dominant skyline objects. Using above properties, we can compute $Sky_{k-1}(DB)$ from $Sky_k(DB)$ efficiently. For example, O_1 and O_4 of Table 1 are not in $Sky_6(DB)$ because they are 6-dominated by O_7. Therefore, they cannot be a candidate of k-dominant skyline object for $k < 6$. We can prune such non-skyline objects for further procedure of the k-dominant query. If we consider 5-dominant query, then O_2, O_3, and O_6 are 5-dominated objects. Therefore, we can prune all of those five objects in 4-dominant query computation. Thus, by decreasing k, more dominated objects can be pruned away.

2.2   *k*-Dominant Skyline View

In order to compute k-dominant skyline efficiently, we compute *domination power* of each object. We say an object O_i has δ-*domination power* if there are δ dimensions in which O_i is better than or equal to all other objects of DB. We sort objects in descending order by domination power. If more than one objects have same domination power then sort those objects in ascending order of the sum value. This order reflects how likely to k-dominate other objects.

Table 2 is the sorted object sequence of Table 1, in which the column "DP" is the domination power and the column "Sum" is the sum of all values. In the sequence, object O_7 has the highest domination power 4. Note that object O_7 dominates all objects lie below it in four attributes, D_1, D_2, D_5, and D_6.

After computing the sorted object sequence, we compute dominated counter (DC) and dominant index (IDX). The dominated counter (DC) indicates the maximum number of dominated dimensions by another object in DB. The dominant index (IDX) is the strongest dominator. That means IDX keeps the record of the corresponding strongest dominator for each object.

Table 2. Ordered Domination Table

Obj.	D_1	D_2	D_3	D_4	D_5	D_6	DP	Sum	DC	IDX
O_7	1	2	5	3	1	2	4	14	3	O_5
O_5	1	4	1	1	3	4	3	14	4	O_7
O_4	5	3	5	4	1	2	2	20	6	O_7
O_2	3	4	4	5	1	3	1	20	5	O_7
O_6	5	3	4	5	1	5	1	23	5	O_7
O_3	4	3	2	3	5	4	0	21	5	O_7
O_1	7	3	5	4	4	3	0	26	6	O_7

$Sky_k(DB)$ is a set of objects whose DC is less than k. In Table 2, for example, according to the dominated counter, we can see that $Sky_6(DB) = \{O_7, O_5, O_2, O_6, O_3\}$, $Sky_5(DB) = \{O_7, O_5\}$, and $Sky_4(DB) = \{O_7\}$. Since there is no object whose DC value is less than 3, thus $Sky_3(DB) = \{\emptyset\}$. Using this table, we can quickly answer the k-dominant skyline query for a given k.

2.3   View Maintenance and Remarks

In order to maintain the ordered domination table up to date, we have to re-calculate the table if necessary. The IDX column in Table 2 is used for the maintenance procedure for database updates. The detailed procedures are given in [7].

To deal with the dimensionality curse of skyline query, another popular counter measure is to reduce the number of dimensions and provide skyline for the reduced space. Subspace Skyline and Skycube [8,9,10] materialize all possible subspace skyline. Users can choose their preferred subspace and can retrieve corresponding skyline from the materialized subspace skyline. However, to compute skylines on every subspace required prohibitive cost.

Instead of materialize all subspace skyline, we are now considering using the ordered domination table to answer the subspace skyline query. Though the response time is worse than the materialized subspace skyline method, we can utilize the domination power and the sum to compute subspace skyline efficiently.

3 Additional Distance Attributes

There are many spatial entities such as hotels, stations, restaurants, convenience stores, supermarkets, and so on. Each of such spatial entities has location information. Using the location information, we can add important distance attributes to databases such as distance to the nearest hotel, distance to the nearest station, and so on, which we call "nearest attributes".

In order to add the nearest attributes for each pair of spatial entities efficiently, we construct a Voronoi diagram for each spatial entity.

3.1 Voronoi Diagrams and the Point Location Problem

We use a Voronoi diagram for finding the nearest point (instance) of a spatial entity. A Voronoi diagram is an efficient data structure for this purpose [11]. Figure 2 shows an example of a Voronoi diagram. Assume that we have a set of n points, $P = \{p_1, ..., p_n\}$, in a plane, then the Voronoi diagram of P, $Vor(P)$, is the subdivision of the plane into n regions, called "Voronoi regions," one for each point, called a "Voronoi point."

Let $p_i \in P$ be a Voronoi point of $Vor(P)$ and $Reg(p_i)$ be the corresponding Voronoi region. The Voronoi diagram has the following property.

A point q lies in the region $Reg(p_i)$ if and only if $dist(q, p_i) \geq dist(q, p_j)$ for each $p_j \in P$ with $j \neq i$.

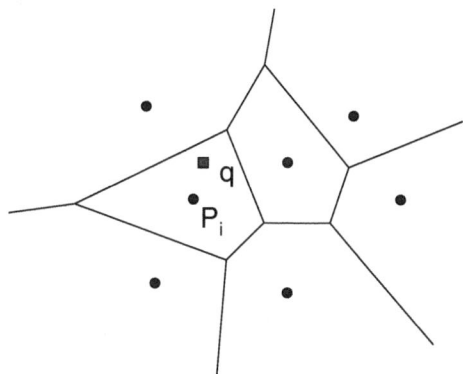

Fig. 2. Voronoi Diagram

We can find the nearest point $p_{nearest} \in P$ from a point q efficiently by using this property of the Voronoi diagram $Vor(P)$. Algorithm 3.1, often called *point location*, is one such algorithm.

Though the worst case time complexity of Algorithm 3.1 is $O(n)$, the expected running time is approximately constant if we can start the algorithm from a Voronoi point that lies close to the nearest point in Step [1].

Algorithm 3.1. *Point Location in Voronoi Diagram*

Input 1: q (a point)

Input 2: $Vor(P)$ (the voronoi diagram of a set of points P)

Output: $p_{nearest}$ (the point in P nearest to q)

01. Choose an arbitrary starting point $p_i \in P$.
02. Initialize the distance value as $d_{min} = dist(p_i, q)$.
03. For each Voronoi region $Reg(p_j)$ that is adjacent to $Reg(p_i)$:
04.   If $dist(p_j, q) < d_{min}$, then set the values of $d_{min} = dist(p_j, q)$, $p_i = p_j$.
05.   Go to Step [3].
06. Return p_i as $p_{nearest}$.

3.2   Quaternary Tree Indexing

A quaternary tree like Figure 3 is often used for indexing a two dimensional plane. We used a quaternary tree for indexing sets of points of each spatial entity. As the root note of the tree, we use a large rectangle that covers all the points in a database. Then, we divide the rectangle into four equal-sized subrectangles. We continue this division procedure for each rectangle, recursively. Since the width and depth of each leaf node of the tree is fixed, we can find a leaf node for each point in a constant time.

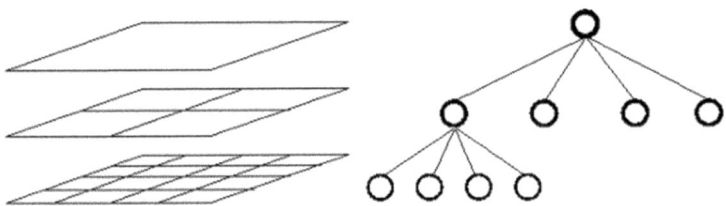

Fig. 3. Quaternary Tree

For each spatial entity, we assign a representative point to each node as a label of the node. A label of a leaf node is chosen arbitrary from all points that belong to the node. A label for an ancestor node is chosen from the labels of its child nodes. If there is no point in a leaf node, we label the node null.

For example, assume a leaf node, say $node_1$, contains three restaurants ($restaurant_1$, $restaurant_2$, and $restaurant_3$), one hotel ($hotel_1$), and no station. In this case, we choose a restaurant from those tree arbitrary as the "restaurant" label of $node_1$. The "hotel" label of $node_1$ is $hotel_1$ since it is the only one hotel in the node. The "station" label of $node_1$ is *null* since there is no station in the node.

In Step [1] of Algorithm 3.1, we search for the nearest point from the label of the leaf node that the point q lies in. If the label is null, we use the non-null label of its closest ancestor node.

For example, there is a record of a database that lies in $node_1$ whose "restaurant" label, "hotel" label, and "station" label are $restaurant_1$, $hotel_1$, and $null$, respectively. Assume we are now computing "nearest restaurant", "nearest hotel", and "nearest station", for the record. For the nearest restaurant and the nearest hotel, we start the point location algorithm from $restarant_1$ and $hotel_1$, respectively. For the nearest station, we climb the tree since the "station" label of $node_1$ is $null$ until we can reach a node that has non-null station label. Then, we start the point location algorithm from the station label of the ancestor node.

This quaternary tree indexing of Voronoi points and the heuristics for labeling of the nodes in the tree significantly improves the expected running time of Algorithm 3.1. As a result, the expected running time for finding the nearest instance of a spatial entity will be approximately constant.

3.3   Voronoi Diagram Construction and Maintenance

We construct the Voronoi diagram for each spatial entity. Algorithms for constructing Voronoi diagrams have been investigated intensively. The problem is proved to be $\Omega(n \log n)$ where n is the number of Voronoi points [11]. There is a known algorithm whose worst time complexity is $O(n \log n)$, which is the optimal complexity.

Ohya et al invented an efficient algorithm whose average time complexity is $O(n)$, though the worst time complexity is $O(n^2)$ [12,13]. In general, most applications prefer to an algorithm whose average running time is fast. Therefore, we used this efficient method.

Once we construct the Voronoi diagram for each spatial entity, we save them as the index data structure for computing the nearest attribute of the spatial entity. In order to maintain the nearest attributes up to date, we have to update Voronoi diagram if an insertion or a deletion occurs to a spatial entity.

If a point p is inserted or deleted from a Voronoi diagram, we, first, find the Voronoi region $Reg(p)$ that contains p, which takes constant time by using Algorithm 3.1 together with the quaternary tree index. Then, we update the affected regions that are adjacent to $Reg(p)$.

4   Skyline Sets

We also consider a skyline query for sets of objects in a database. Let s be the number of objects in each set and n be the number of objects in the database. There are $_nC_s$ sets in the database. We consider an efficient algorithm for computing convex skyline of the $_nC_s$ sets, which we call "convex skyline sets".

Figure 4 (a) is a list of 3-sets, in which all of the combinations of three hotels, which are in Figure 1, are listed. The "h_{123}" denotes a set of $\{h_1, h_2, h_3\}$. "Distance" and "price" of "h_{123}" are the sum of the "distance" and "price" of respective hotels in the set. Skyline of the sets of three hotels are $\{h_{123}, h_{135}, h_{235}, h_{234}, h_{345}\}$. Our *convex skyline sets query* efficiently computes those convex skyline sets. Detailed algorithm of the skyline sets is presented in [14]. By materializing skyline sets, we can make concise answers for group selection problems.

Recently, to preserve the individuals' privacy is one of the important data management issues. In many databases, we have to hide individual record's values to preserve privacy even though there is no ID information. In such situation, convex skyline sets query can be utilized.

Convex skyline sets query does not disclose individual values of an object. Instead, it discloses aggregated values of s objects. It will be one of the most promising alternatives for decision making in a privacy aware environment.

If one wants to know the cheapest hotel, she/he can find that the cheapest set is h_{123} from the skyline and can easily imagine that the price of the cheapest hotel is around 4, since price of the cheapest 3-set h_{123} is 12. Similarly, if one prefers cheaper and closer, she/he may choose h_{235} from the skyline and can easily imagine the value of the preferable choice from the aggregated values.

In another case, we have to choose a set instead of individual data record. For example, an event organizer might want to reserve rooms in three different hotels around the event venue. Our skyline set query can provide preferable set for her/him.

ID	Price	Distance	ID	Price	Distance
h_{123}	12	15	h_{145}	19	13
h_{124}	17	14	h_{234}	18	9
h_{125}	15	15	h_{235}	16	10
h_{134}	16	13	h_{245}	21	9
h_{135}	14	14	h_{345}	20	8

(a) Sets of 3 Hotels

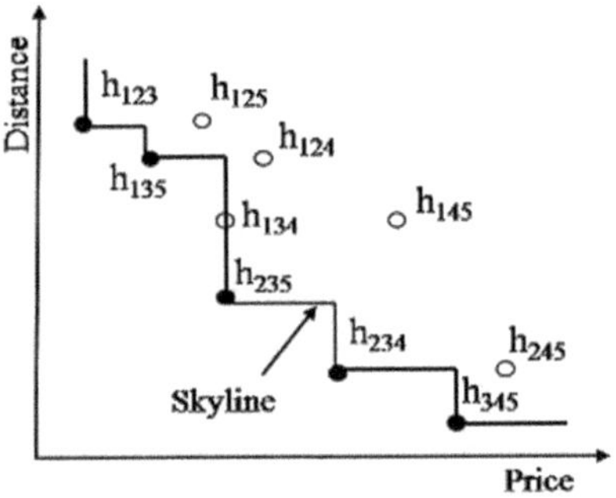

(b) Skyline of 3 Hotels

Fig. 4. Skyline of 3-Set

4.1 Spatio-Temporal Skyline Set

We can expand the idea of skyline query into spatio-temporal data for the skyline sets problem. Table 3 is an example of such spatio-temporal database. The "time" column shows an attribute that contains a time stamp information. The "lat." and "lon." are latitude and longitude of each object's location, respectively.

Table 3. Spatio-Temporal Database

obj.	time	lat.	lon.	att_1	att_2 ...
o_1	2	35.742	135.221	3	8
o_2	5	38.421	134.822	5	4
o_3	6	39.012	138.500	4	3
o_4	3	35.985	138.159	9	2
o_5	9	36.058	133.318	7	3

Assume we are considering $_5C_3 = |S|$ 3-sets in the database containing 5 objects as in Table 3. Following table is the projected aggregated list of 3-sets.

3-set	Twidth	att_1	att_2 ...	3-set	Twidth	att_1	att_2 ...
o_{123}	4	12	15	o_{145}	7	19	13
o_{124}	3	17	14	o_{234}	3	18	9
o_{125}	7	15	15	o_{235}	4	16	10
o_{134}	4	16	13	o_{245}	6	21	9
o_{135}	7	14	14	o_{345}	6	20	8

In the list, "o_{123}" denotes a set of $\{o_1, o_2, o_3\}$. "Twidth" is width of 3 time stamps of each 3-set. And, "att_1" and "att_2" is the sum of "att_1" and "att_2" of each 3-set, respectively.

Temporal skyline 3-set query outputs convex 3-sets of the list for the database in Table 3. Temporal skyline set query is able to give a clue, for example, what is the best portfolio that gained profit in a small period of time, what is the best group of players that performed best within a short period of time, and so on.

By using spatial information such as "lat." and "lon." in Table 3, we can compute spatial skyline sets. Following table is the projected aggregated list of 3-sets for spatial skyline sets.

3-set	area	att_1	att_2 ...	3-set	area	att_1	att_2 ...
o_{123}	13.53	12	15	o_{145}	1.53	19	13
o_{124}	8.94	17	14	o_{234}	11.13	18	9
o_{125}	5.10	15	15	o_{235}	15.31	16	10
o_{134}	11.78	16	13	o_{245}	11.79	21	9
o_{135}	16.95	14	14	o_{345}	15.69	20	8

In the list, "area" is the area of the minimum bounding rectangular of 3 locations of each 3-set. Spatial skyline 3-set query outputs convex 3-sets of the list. Spatial skyline set query is able to give a clue, for example, where are places that have a lot of crimes, where are places that contains a lot of customers, and so on.

5   Conclusion

Information filtering methods are more important than ever since there are too many information to find necessary answers quickly. We consider information filtering methods that use materialized skyline view. Skyline query contains data objects that are preferable for each user even though users' preference is different for each.

We propose various kinds of skyline queries such as skyline on relatively high-dimensional numerical databases, skyline on spatial databases, and skyline set. We materialize those skyline information to make concise answers for each query.

We also considered methods for maintaining materialized skyline information up to date to handle an update for a numerical database. Currently, we are now considering methods for handling updates for spatial skylines and skyline sets.

Acknowledgments. This work was partially supported by KAKENHI (23500180) Grants-in-Aid for Scientific Research, Japan Society for the Promotion of Science (JSPS). Md. A. Siddique and Md. S. Arefin were supported by the scholarship of The Ministry of Education, Culture, Sports, Science and Technology (MEXT) Japan.

References

1. Borzsonyi, S., Kossmann, D., Stocker, K.: The skyline operator. In: Proc. of ICDE, pp. 421–430 (2001)
2. Kossmann, D., Ramsak, F., Rost, S.: Shooting stars in the sky: An online algorithm for skyline queries. In: Proc. of VLDB Conference, pp. 275–286 (2002)
3. Papadias, D., Tao, Y., Fu, G., Seeger, B.: Progressive skyline computation in database systems. JACM 30(1), 41–82 (2005)
4. Tan, K.L., Eng, P.K., Ooi, B.C.: Efficient progressive skyline computation. In: Proc. of VLDB Conference, pp. 301–310 (2001)
5. Li, C., Ooi, B.C., Tung, A.K.H., Wang, S.: DADA: A data cube for dominant relationship analysis. In: Proc. of ACM SIGMOD Conference, pp. 659–670 (2006)
6. Chan, C.Y., Jagadish, H.V., Tan, K.L., Tung, A.K.H., Zhang, Z.: Finding k-dominant skyline in high dimensional space. In: Proc. of ACM SIGMOD Conference, pp. 503–514 (2006)
7. Siddique, M.A., Morimoto, Y.: Efficient maintenance of all k-dominant skyline query results for frequently updated database. IARIA International Journal on Advances in Software 3(3) (2010)
8. Yuan, Y., Lin, X., Liu, Q., Wang, W., Yu, J.X., Zhang, Q.: Efficient computation of the skyline cube, 241–252 (2005)
9. Tao, Y., Xiao, X., Pei, J.: SUBSKY: Efficient computation of skylines in subspaces. In: Proc. of ICDE (2006)
10. Pei, J., Yuan, Y., Lin, X., Jin, W., Ester, M., Liu, Q., Wang, W., Tao, Y., Yu, J., Zhang, Q.: Towords multidimensional subspace skyline analysis. ACM Trans. on Database Systems 31(4), 1335–11381 (2006)

11. de Berg, M., van Kreveld, M., Overmars, M., Schwarzkopf, O.: Computational Geometry, Algorithms and Applications. Springer, Heidelberg (1997)
12. Ohya, T., Iri, M., Murota, K.: A fast voronoi diagram algorithm with quaternary tree bucketing. Information Processing Letters 18(4), 227–231 (1984)
13. Ohya, T., Iri, M., Murota, K.: Improvements of the incremental method for the voronoi diagram with computational comparison of various algorithms. Journal of the Operations Research Society of Japan 27(4), 306–337 (1984)
14. Siddique, M.A., Morimoto, Y.: Algorithm for computing convex skyline objectsets on numerical databases. IEICE Trans. on Information and Systems (10), 2709–2716 (2010)

Summary Extraction from Chinese Text for Data Archives of Online News

Nozomi Mikami and Lukáš Pichl

International Christian University
Osawa 3-10-2, Mitaka, Tokyo, 181-8585, Japan
lukas@icu.ac.jp
http://www.icu.ac.jp/

Abstract. Electronic news media consistently use a specific language frame for efficient knowledge delivery and opinion formation. Since machine representation of logographs, and their derived forms, such as ideograms, and the Chinese characters in general, enumerates to a large set of symbols, the information content of particular text sequence interconnects context patterns across various scope ranges. Here we concern with the enumerated form of sinogram reflecting on the characters not only historically and culturally, but also educationally. Logographs visually invoke mutual functional relations by design and through their usage in overlapping scopes. Here we study the procedural summarization of text originally intended for online news distribution and the preferable evaluation method of its usability. Sinogrammatic electronic news sentences are analyzed for mutual similarity patterns both inward and outward, in order to facilitate sentence extraction for summary inclusion while reflecting on the principle of characters. Traditional partition of linguistic knowledge representation is aided by invocation of bypass routes in logographic text similar to software pictograms, for which design and usage frames are coeducational. Machine extracted summaries are compared with human chosen sentences while employing the Turing test to ascertain cohesion of Human - Human and Human - Machine comparison. The implementation of popularity-based summarization algorithm is available as a Java program.

1 Introduction

Recent research developments in summarization algorithms, which extract or abstract substances from a range of text data including information designed for online distribution, have been in part motivated by increase of electronic commerce (e.g. automatic abstracting of product manuals) and online search engines (e.g. to decrease volume of text to be indexed for cataloguing) [1,2,3,4,5,6,7,8,9,10,11,12]. It is especially in such technological area that new words and collocations are frequently introduced, tested, commercially and technically framed for multiple usage, and balanced with product economics and usage fashion. Some of such neologies are eventually admitted into broader linguistic existence (as defined

S. Kikuchi et al. (Eds.): DNIS 2011, LNCS 7108, pp. 190–202, 2011.

by sizable usage statistics throughout the population, standardization as intellectual property, or recognition for use in education). Inversely, current words and collocations can be analyzed back for such formative meaning substance (following historical data or implied routes based on the prevalent usage in the past or typical context). Whereas English information is still dominant subject of the research papers, other languages, such as those of Asia, increasingly gain importance.

In accord with the increase of online data, number of internet users worldwide has risen dramatically [13], decreasing in turn the ratio of English speaking population due to Asian countries, and especially sinogram readers. Here we analyze the specifics of the popularity based concept to the extraction of document summaries in case of Chinese language, and using major online news repositories. The method, in case of the English language, has been formulated by P. Arun Kumar et al. [7]. Following the general outline, the potential of the popularity based aggregation concept in general is recognized and proved natural for logographs, and in particular for the Chinese online newspaper articles. In brief, it is the natural language frame of sinogram that allows us to meaningfully postulate sentence filtering through popularity [8] as a direct summarization method, which is programmable via statistical ranking of ideographic character occurrences dynamically interpreted through the current popularity of aggregating sentence clusters throughout all stages of extraction.

Our work is organized as follows. Elements of popularity-based approach are briefly reviewed in the next section. In particular, the clustering algorithm for selecting the most popular text sentences is reviewed along with the definitions of local and global similarity coefficients. It is shown that in case of newspaper articles, popularity concept can naturally include explicit importance weights, which are allocated to various parts of newspaper articles by design. Section 3 explains specific features of sinogram text processing, and outlines the implementation of present approach. Integration of our algorithm with representative online news text is assured in Section 4 by means of Turing test for the computer program and a group of human volunteers. In contrast to standard information retrieval measures unsuited for small and diverse samples, we are thus able to meaningfully calibrate summarization framework via indistinguishability of human and machine summarization actions. Concluding remarks in the last section summarize our main findings.

2   Popularity Based Abstract Extraction

The concept of popularity has been established for search engine application areas, such as Hyperlink-Induced Topic Search [6] and PageRank [10] approaches to document cataloguing and dynamic contents provision. For instance, the former algorithm builds on concepts of authority and hub value. Authority and hub values are mutually related based on the number of links pointing to or out from a particular webpage. Authority value of document is computed as the sum of scaled hub values that point to it. Hub value of document is the sum of scaled

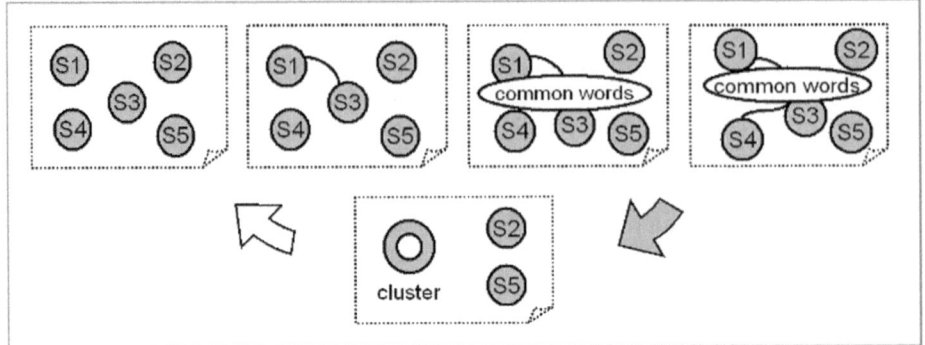

Fig. 1. Basic steps in constructing textual similarity graph

authority values of documents it points. We emphasize in this context that sino-gram offers a palette of culturally established context tools beyond counting of vertex in-degree and out-degree as the number of explicit links, due to several levels of context hierarchy. The potential of linked information containers for knowledge framing is however vast, and not fully exploited, such as in case of encyclopedia assembly [1], in broader procedural framework of what could be named in our viewpoint as socioformatics.

In case of text summarization, sentence popularity is defined by number of similar sentences that appear in the same document. Similarity of two sentences is correspondingly defined as a relative ratio of *words* common to both of them. Due to linguistic complexity of most languages, it is not *a priori* obvious what kind of text preprocessing is suitable for extracting good summaries or abstracts, which is the most important obstacle and ambiguity source for text summa-rization. For instance, if *words* were used to define the similarity, then "old," "age," and "oldster" would appear as unrelated units. If morphemes were used, then "crown" could appear ambiguous depending on the context, while "point," "pointless" and "pointy" could appear similar. Here we make use of the fact that a fully logographic writing system has morphemes consistently standardized as characters, which reduces grammatical (program) processing load via extended vocabulary (larger data base). Enumeration of similarity in terms of character popularity thus naturally provides most representative sentences into resulting document summary.

The key element of popularity-based summarization is an iterative construc-tion of similarity graph from all sentences in the document. The vertices of the graph are formed by clusters of similar sentences. Weights assigned to graph edges quantify the vertex connection links measured in the similarity space. Whether a sentence should be a part of a particular sentence cluster at one ver-tex, or not, is decided by the similarity value of the sentence and the cluster. To that aim, a threshold value τ for the global similarity coefficient (GSC), and the local similarity coefficient (LSC) is defined [7]. Both coefficients can take any number between 0 and 1 as given below. In what follows, a "word" will mean one sinogram character by definition (cf. Section 3).

2.1 Elementary Algorithm for Abstract Extraction

Figure 1 shows the flow of sentence clustering when building text similarity graph. Initially, every document sentence is represented by one graph vertex. The most similar sentences are merged to build a cluster, and then replaced by an artificial sentence representing common words in the newly created graph vertex. The parental vertices are deleted at the same time. Finally, all other sentences, not yet assigned to the clusters, are screened for similarity with the new vertex (higher than the threshold value), and possibly merged to it. The clustering procedure then restarts again, until all sentences over a certain similarity threshold are exhausted.

In constructing the similarity graph, there are two key functions taking a pair of sentences on input: the global similarity coefficient (GSC), the local similarity coefficient (LSC), and one parameter: the threshold value τ to determine the binary-valued similarity relation.In the following, we denote the total number of sentences in the source document text as N.

Global Similarity Coefficient. The global similarity coefficient between every two sentences S_i and S_j is defined as follows,

$$\text{GSC}(S_i, S_j) = \frac{2 \times n(\text{common words of } S_i \text{ \& } S_j)}{n(S_i) + n(S_j)} \tag{1}$$

$\forall i \neq j \leq N$
$n(X)$: number of words in vertex X, $0 \leq GSC \leq 1$.

Here GSC is used to form a cluster seed (e.g. vertices S_1 and S_3 in the particular example in Fig. 1).

Local Similarity Coefficient. After the $n(C)$ common words of the two most similar sentences S_{i_0} and S_{j_0} are stored in the cluster $C(S_{i_0}, S_{j_0})$, the LSC is calculated for all sentences except S_{i_0} and S_{j_0}. The local similarity coefficient is defined as follows,

$$\text{LSC}(S_k, C) = \frac{2 \times n(\text{common words of } S_k \text{ \& } C)}{n(S_k) + n(C)} \tag{2}$$

$\forall k \neq i_0, j_0$
C: cluster, $0 \leq \text{LSC} \leq 1$.

LSC is used to grow the clusters (cf. e.g. the vertex S_4 in Fig. 1 added to the cluster of S_1 and S_3).

Since the GSC decreases with similarity of shortened sentences constructed by common words, the iterative algorithm eventually stops when the threshold value is reached (at most after N steps).

Clustering and Threshold Values. The threshold value specifies whether a certain graph vertex (sentence or cluster) should be connected to another graph vertex (sentence or cluster). The threshold values of 0 and 1 correspond to the case of one or N graph vertices, respectively. Setting up a proper threshold value facilitates the separation of the main themes in the text and facilitates capture of diverse content aspects [7].

Process of Abstract Extraction. The process of abstract extraction generally consists of four parts: Preprocessing, Building Text Graph, Clustering into Themes and Sentence Choice.

1. Preprocessing
   Generally, all stop words with high frequency and negligible relevance should be removed from the source text before summarization. Since logographic text reasonably dissolves weight of such problem, we do not preprocess sinogram document text sources. This allows for more objective evaluation of popularity-based summarization in this work.
2. Building Text Graph
   In the initial stage for building the text graph, words that separate each sentence are used as delimiters, in order to recognize text sentences as new graphvertices. This work adopts "○" (as "." equivalent to sentence period), "?" and "!" as delimiters. Then the document text is initially represented as an undirected graph which consists of single-sentence vertices.
3. Clustering into Themes
   Clustering is the most important part of the algorithm. The procedure is based on the the two types of similarity coefficients.
4. Sentence Choice
   After all sentences fall into the thematic groups represented by clusters, resulting groups are sorted in decreasing order based on the number of sentences merged together in each group. A group with a larger number of sentences has the higher priority to be included in the summary. The number of groups to be selected is at most the number of sentences required by the user for the summary. From each selected group, one representative sentence is extracted, as discussed subsequently.

Thematic groups selected by above algorithm result from the popularity-based selection. On the other hand, in weight-based methods, representative sentences are typically selected according to features such as cues or location in the article. A hybrid approach is likely to improve effectiveness of summary extraction. Therefore in case of newspaper articles, such hybrid approach naturally comes into play when selecting the final representative sentence for each cluster.

Cluster Selection of Representative Sentence. The weight-based approach for news articles is applied implicitly in present work. Among the original sentences merged into each cluster[1], the one with upmost position in the news article is selected into the summary. Such particular choice corresponds to the implicit contents ranking common in the news, which can therefore be considered as an application of the weight-based approach. The weight-based approach also naturally comes into play when the number of sentences included in two or more clusters is the same. The cluster with a representative sentence located in the upper part of the article is set to have a larger priority to enter the final summary.

2.2 Logographic Features of Sinogram Text

Sinogram characters are different from English letters in whether each character is logogram or phonogram. Every sinogram character carries a meaning in itself. Therefore, in this work, every single character is counted as a word, resulting in easy preprocessing and low summarization cost. For instance, there is no need to recognize and distinguish the past form, adjectives or adverbs, such as "clean" and "cleanly," "help" and "helped."

Figure 2 shows several illustrative examples of sinogram characters; (1)

河   river   (1)

干净   clean   (2)

净水   clean water   (3)

奥林匹克(àolínpǐkè) Olympic   (4)

Fig. 2. Examples of sinogram characters

is the basic symbol meaning a river, simple example of one character, which is regarded as a word. In addition, there are strings consisting of two or more characters. For instance, example (2) in Fig. 2 means clean, while example (3) means clean water. Example (2) consists of two characters, but when these characters are used separately such as in example (3), the second character of example (2) still keeps its meaning as "clean" in the first character of example (3). Therefore, in example (2), little effect is expected even when several characters are separately counted as words, along the lines of present approach. In the example (3), the first character indicates "clean" and second character means "water". As every character has a morpheme connotation, it seems suitable to regard each character as a word, yet still in very good harmony with dynamic multi-character meaning (de)composition in sequential order.

---

[1] The original sentences are stored in a linked list array labeled by the order of inclusion and the particular graph vertex. A heap of vertex pairs is created to maintain the GSC priority queue.

Naturally, there are sinogram characters grouped together to indicate a word, yet in complete absence of particular meaning for all of them. The example (4) in Fig. 2 shows such case. The four Chinese characters have no traditional meaning. They are used for the word "Olympic" to represent the sound of western word. The letters in the brackets show the pin-yin transliteration into Roman alphabet. The individual characters do not traditionally function as logograph; the separated meaning appears void, at least in traditional cultural context.

However, compared to phonetic transcription alphabets in other languages, sinogram has a much larger set of available symbols. When representing the sound "ya", for example, there exist 32 characters expressing the same sound. From this point of view, even if characters with void meaning are used to represent a sound, it is plausible to expect that selected characters do not significantly overlap with other words; in fact they are used in semantically consistent way for most adopted foreign words, wherever possible. Therefore, even in the case of example (4), the logographs are not, in fact, meaningless. That is also why no word or character is omitted in the preprocessing of sinogram text document source.

Let us also mention that there exist two main written forms of sinogram text, namely the simplified one and the traditional one. Since we deal with extracting summaries from independent documents, such fact does not pose any difficulty: it is uncommon to mix both types in one document. Our java implementation deals with both traditional and simplified document encoding. The program is briefly outlined in the following two subsections.

2.3   Sinogram Encoding in Text Summarization

In dealing with sinogram, java is one of the appropriate programming language tools because it supports Unicode. CJK Unified System [14] has the range from U+4E00 to U+9FBB (19968 to 40891) in the Unicode Standard, Version 4.1, which supports both the simplified and traditional versions. All characters in the input article are converted into the integer data type and stored as a numerical array. By subtracting 19968 from the Unicode character table, the values in the integer data array range from 0 to 20923. In order to separate article sentences, only three delimiters, "。", "？" and "！", have been used. The program is implemented as a Java application.

3   Evaluation and Results

In order to evaluate the efficiency of machine text summarization rigorously, we have collected a representative set of newspaper articles, and gathered a 10-member volunteer group. Human-extracted abstracts are compared to the abstracts extracted by the computer program. To compare between the two, we calculate the relevance score (RS) between all pairs of extractors (human vs. human, or human vs. computer in the sense of Turing test).

The source text was distributed to human extractors as follows.

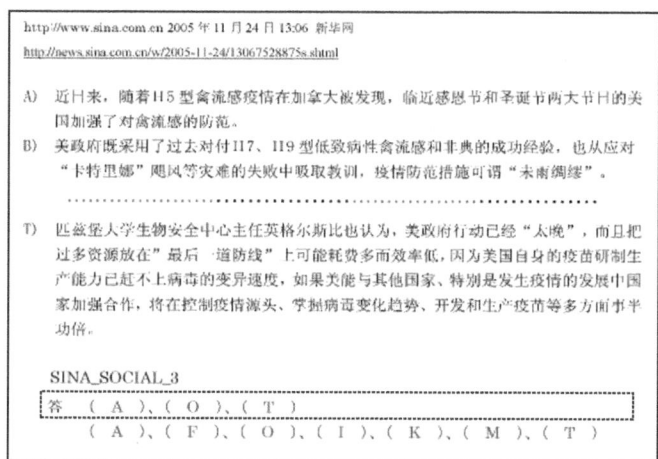

Fig. 3. Human extraction format for evaluation

1. Ten native speakers
2. Each person extracts summaries from ten articles
3. Among the ten articles, five articles are common for all people
   The other five articles are unique to each human extractor
4. Number of different articles: $5 \times 10 + 5 = 55$
5. Article length: 20 to 25 sentences (labeled by Latin alphabet letters)
6. Number of sentences to be extracted: three
7. Article type: international, domestic, education, finance, social
   eleven articles for each type: $11 \times 5 = 55$
8. Articles from five thematically different websites (eleven articles for each): $11 \times 5 = 55$. The sources are SINA (international, C_1) [15], CCTV (domestic, C_2) [16], RENMIN (finance, C_3) [17], TOM (education, C_4) [18], and XINHUA (social, C_5) [19].
9. Each person extracts summaries from every article type
10. Each person extracts summaries from all five websites

The abstract extraction results for the common articles are used to calculate the spread of summarization within human reference group. Since the summarization is performed by selecting appropriate sentences, the results were readily collected by using questionnaire forms shown in Fig. 3.

3.1 Calibration: Human vs. Human Extraction

In order to compare the computer vs. human summarization, the pairwise relevance score (RS) must be computed. It is defined as the ratio of the number of matched sentences between human summary and human summary, or human summary and the computer system summary, to the total number of sentence retrieved. By calculating the RS between human and human (a control subset of

Table 1. Summaries by ten people (A to J) and the computer program for five common articles

	C_1	C_2	C_3	C_4	C_5
A	a, d, t	b, q, t	k, r, u	a, c, o	m, o, s
B	a, b, x	a, b, e	a, d, w	a, c, o	p, q, r
C	a, d, u	a, j, p	a, f, k	a, c, o	b, m, x
D	a, l, u	b, h, p	a, r, u	a, b, e	d, x, s
E	a, c, u	e, j, w	a, r, t	b, d, g	b, d, s
F	a, l, w	a, h, q	b, d, n	a, e, g	d, l, v
G	a, d, w	a, d, o	a, g, o	a, g, s	d, o, x
H	a, d, e	j, k, u	a, t, w	a, b, c	b, c, d
J	a, b, w	a, b, h	a, g, n	a, b, c	a, c, g
$\tau=0.40$	a, d, i	a, b, c	k, b, d	a, b, e	a, d, g
$\tau=0.35$	a, i, m	a, b, e	f, k, u	a, c, e	d, g, m
$\tau=0.30$	a, i, q	a, e, f	f, k, s	a, d, e	d, g, m
$\tau=0.25$	a, d, i	e, f, s	f, k, u	d, e, p	d, g, m

five articles distributed to the human group), the variance of abstract extraction among humans can be assessed. In order to evaluate the machine summarization, the RS of the control human group should be compared with the RS of human and computer in the sense of Turing test.

Be A and B the set of sentences retrieved by two extractors (whether human or computer), and M the set of sentences common to both A and B. The relevance score is then defined as

$$RS(A, B) = \frac{2 \times n(M)}{n(A) + n(B)} \tag{3}$$

$n(X)$ = number of sentences in X.

First, we compare the RS in the control human group and asses the spread of human summarization. To this aim, ten native speakers extracted summaries from five common articles (length of 20 to 25 sentences each). Every article was taken from a different website in a different category. Table 1 shows the results. The computer program results for various values of τ are included in the bottom part for comparison.

From the data collected in Table 1 the RS values for all pairs of human extractors were obtained.

Table 2 then shows the average RS value for each extractor obtained by averaging over the five control articles and the ten members of human control group. The maximum RS value reached is 0.37 (0.05 above the average) for human C, while the minimum is 0.22 (0.1 below the average) for human A.

The RS values comparing the five abstracts extracted by each human and the computer are listed in Table 3 for all common articles. The total average has a maximum at about the threshold value $\tau = 0.35$, which is higher than the total average RS of 0.32 for the human control group. This proves that the machine

Table 2. Relevance score for ten people and five common articles

A 0.222	B 0.326	C 0.370	D 0.348
E 0.270	F 0.289	G 0.341	H 0.348
I 0.267	J 0.348	total average: 0320	

Table 3. Relevance score between the human and computer summarization for 5 common articles without normalization (total average is 0.3)

threshold	relevance score	threshold	relevance score
0.40	0.33	0.35	0.340
0.30	0.313	0.25	0.213

summarization reaches quality of human control group. We consider such result to be remarkably good, since the only parameter in the present method is the threshold value τ. Note that the interval of $\tau \in < 0.25, 0.4 >$ spans the range of the human RS values in Table 2, and that the computer RS value of 0.3 (Table 3) averaged over such broad range of τ values still compares well to the total average RS of 0.32 in the human control group (Table 2). The optimal value of $\tau = 0.35$ is still a way below the limit $\tau \to 1$, at which an L-sentence long summary would simply consist of the first L sentences. This demonstrates very good applicability of the popularity based approach in the present work.

3.2   Evaluation: Human vs. Computer Extraction

In addition to the analysis of summary extraction for the set of common articles, each of the ten people extracted five summaries from other newspaper articles uniquely assigned to him. Same as before, the five articles were taken from different websites in different categories. The human extracted summaries for the total of 50 articles were then used to calculate the RS score between human and computer summarization. Representative extracted summaries (alphabetical sentence labels) are listed in Table 4.

In addition to the human-extracted summaries, the data in Table 4 include computer-extracted summaries using four threshold values of τ. Both the publisher of the newspaper and type of the article are indicated. The numbers attached to publisher names discriminate between the same category group (e.g. domestic) from the same website (e.g. RENMIN). Sentences denoted in brackets such as "(a)" were selected in case of a tie by emphasizing their upper location in the article (a weight-based feature).

Table 5 shows the relevance scores for ten human extractors evaluating different articles. The average RS values are shown as as a function of the article type and the threshold value τ. The machine summarization worked best for articles in education; the lowest agreement was achieved for domestic articles. This may well reflect the existence of an opinion bias in education along with more opinion diversity on domestic matters, rather than a drawback of the extraction algorithm. A slightly higher threshold value of $\tau = 0.4$ worked best for computer

Table 4. Representative summaries of 5 people for different articles

selector	international	domestic	finance	education	social
	SINA1	RENMIN1	XINHUA1	CCTV1	TOM1
A	a, s, t	a, i, k	a, c, k	p, u, v	a, c, d
threshold τ =0.40	(a), (b), (c)	(a), (b), l	b, e, c	(b), (c), n	(a), (b), (c)
threshold τ =0.35	(a), (b), l	a, k, n	b, c, d	e, n, p	(a), (b), (c)
threshold τ =0.30	(a), m, l	c, k, l	b, c, d	e, n, o	(a), (b), (c)
threshold τ =0.25	b, f, m	k, l, s	b, c, g	c, e, n	a, (b), d
	CCTV1	TOM1	SINA1	RENMIN1	XINHUA1
B	a, b, d	a, c, u	a, b, w	a, d, v	d, f, l
threshold τ =0.40	a, c, n	(a), (b), q	(a), b, (c)	(a), (b), f	(a), q, m
threshold τ =0.35	a, c, n	b, o, q	(a), b, c	(a), c, f	k, m, q
threshold τ =0.30	a, c, n	b, o, q	b, c, m	c, f, m	k, m, q
threshold τ =0.25	a, f, n	b, o, q	b, f, m	c, f, p	b, m, q
	RENMIN1	XINHUA1	CCTV1	TOM1	SINA1
C	a, l, p	a, c, k	c, e, o	b, i, q	b, n, t
threshold τ =0.40	(a), d, j	(a), f, j	(a), j, p	d, e, m	b, c, p
threshold τ =0.35	d, i, j	i, j, l	h, j, p	b, e, l	a, b, m
threshold τ =0.30	a, d, j	f, i, j	b, h, p	b, e, m	a, b, j
threshold τ =0.25	d, k, n	b, f, j	b, f, p	b, m, q	a, m, p
	TOM1	SINA1	PEOPLE1	XINHUA1	CCTV1
D	a, c, e	a, l, x	a, d, x	a, b, t	a, l, x
threshold τ =0.40	(a), l, o	b, e, h	a, (b), i	(a), f, b	(a), (b), g
threshold τ =0.35	(a), l, o	d, e, h	a, i, k	a, b, f	b, g, n
threshold τ =0.30	d, l, o	d, e, h	a, e, i	a, b, q	e, g, n
threshold τ =0.25	e, l, u	a, e, o	a, b, q	b, f, q	g, n, r
	XINHUA1	CCTV1	TOM1	SINA1	RENMIN1
E	e, i, w	a, g, t	b, r, v	b, c, v	b, o w
threshold τ =0.40	(a), (b), (c)	(a), (b), (c)	a, i, j	b, c, l	(a), (b), d
threshold τ =0.35	(a), e, l	b, h, k	a, i, (c)	a, c, l	(a), b, n
threshold τ =0.30	(a), e, l	b, h, k	b, i, j	a, b, c	d, e, n
threshold τ =0.25	a, e, l	b, h, k	b, (c), i	b, c, m	d, e, n

*Sentences are grouped in two clusters, thus only two sentences are selected.

Table 5. Human and computer relevance score for 50 articles

Article type	Threshold				Average
	0.40	0.35	0.30	0.25	over τ
International	0.367	0.300	0.333	0.233	0.308
Domestic	0.333	0.267	0.167	0.233	0.250
Finance	0.300	0.333	0.300	0.233	0.292
Education	0.333	0.400	0.300	0.300	0.333
Social	0.367	0.300	0.267	0.200	0.283
τ-average	0.347	0.320	0.273	0.240	0.295

summarization of the entire set of 50 articles. It is remarkable that average RS for $\tau = 0.35$ is 0.32, which exactly equals the value for human summaries in the control group (cf. the total average in Table 2). This again demonstrates the good efficiency limited *only* by the natural spread in human summary extraction.

4   Conclusion

We have developed a popularity based approach for the summarization of sinogram text, in particular newspaper articles. Popularity of a sentence is established as the number of similar sentences in the document [7]. Based on the logographic nature of sinogram text, we have defined two-sentence similarity as the relative ratio of common characters. The summarization algorithm is based on iterative construction of similarity graph for sentence clusters. Our approach has been validated by using a control group of native speakers, several online news providers, and several types of news articles. It was shown that for the threshold value of $\tau = 0.35 \sim 0.40$, computer summarization is as good as human summarization in electronic news segment. The results were normalized with respect to the spread of text summaries extracted by human control group. The work is generally applicable in the area of archival and annotation of Chinese text; it is also a rather rare study into such kind of subject as compared to the major research on English text [7].

References

1. He, X., Ding, C.H.Q., Zha, H., Simon, H.D.: Automatic Topic Identification Using Webpage Clustering. In: ICDM 2001, pp. 195–202 (2001)
2. DiCesare, F., Sahnoun, Z., Bonissone, P.P.: Linguistic summarization of fuzzy data. Information Sciences 52, 141–152 (1990)
3. Guo, Y., Stylios, G.: An intelligent summarization system based on cognitive psychology. Information Sciences 174, 1–36 (2005)
4. Hahn, U., Mani, I.: The challenges of automatic summarization. IEEE Computer 33(11), 29–36 (2000)
5. Kacprzyk, J., Zadrozny, S.: Linguistic database summaries and their protoforms. Information Sciences 173, 281–304 (2005)
6. Kleinberg, J.M.: Authoritative sources in a hyperlinked environment. Journal of the ACM 46(5), 604–632 (1999)
7. Kumar, P.A., Kumar, K.P., Rao, T.S., Reddy, P.K.: An Improved Approach to Extract Document Summaries Based on Popularity. In: Bhalla, S. (ed.) DNIS 2005. LNCS, vol. 3433, pp. 310–318. Springer, Heidelberg (2005)
8. Mani, I.: Automatic Summarization. John Benjamins Publishing Company, Amsterdam (2001)
9. Myaeng, S.H., Zhou, M., Wong, K.-F., Zhang, H.-J. (eds.): AIRS 2004. LNCS, vol. 3411. Springer, Heidelberg (2005)
10. Page, L., Brin, S., Motwani, R., Winograd, T.: The PageRank Citation Ranking: Bringing Order to the Web. Stanford Digital Libraries Working Paper (1998)
11. Radev, D.R., McKeown, K.R.: Generating natural language summaries from multiple on-line sources. Computational Linguistics 24(3), 469–500 (1998)

12. Strzalkowski, T. (ed.): Natural Language Information Retrieval. Kluwer Academic Publishers (1999)
13. Global Reach, Evolution of Online Linguistic Populations (December 11, 2005), `http://global-reach.biz/globstats/evol.html`
14. Unicode, CJK Unicode (October 14, 2005), `http://www.unicode.org/charts/PDF/U4E00.pdf` (January 12, 2006)
15. `http://news.sina.com.cn/`
16. `http://www.cctv.com/news/`
17. `http://www.people.com.cn/GB/news/`
18. `http://www.tom.com/`
19. `http://www.xinhuanet.com/newscenter/`

GEOSO – A Geo-Social Model:
From Real-World Co-occurrences to Social Connections[*]

Huy Pham, Ling Hu, and Cyrus Shahabi

Integrated Media Systems Center,
University of Southern California (USC),
Los Angeles, California, USA
{huyvpham,lingh,shahabi}@usc.edu

Abstract. As the popularity of social networks is continuously growing, collected data about online social activities is becoming an important asset enabling many applications such as target advertising, sale promotions, and marketing campaigns. Although most social interactions are recorded through online activities, we believe that social experiences taking place offline in the real physical world are equally if not more important. This paper introduces a geo-social model that derives social activities from the history of people's movements in the real world, i.e., who has been where and when. In particular, from spatiotemporal histories, we infer real-world co-occurrences - being there at the same time - and then use co-occurrences to quantify social distances between any two persons. We show that straightforward approaches either do not scale or may overestimate the strength of social connections by giving too much weight to coincidences. The experiments show that our model well captures social relationships between people, even on partially available data.

Keywords: Data mining, geospatial, spatiotemporal, social network.

1   Introduction

Nowadays, a significant amount of social interactions are gathered from various online activities of Internet users. These virtual social events provide important cues for inferring social relationships, which in turn can be used for target advertising, recommendations, search customization, etc., the main business model of Internet giants. However, an important aspect of the social network is overlooked – the fact that people play active social roles in the physical world in their daily lives. However, as most social interactions and events that take place in the physical world are not as well documented as the ones that can be acquired from an online social network application, it is necessary to seek for alternative methods to infer social relationships from people's behavior in the physical world.

With the popularity of GPS-enabled mobile phones, cameras, and other portable devices, a large amount of spatiotemporal data can easily be collected or is already

---

[*] This paper is a full version of a poster paper appeared in ACMGIS'2011 [19].

S. Kikuchi et al. (Eds.): DNIS 2011, LNCS 7108, pp. 203–222, 2011.

available. Those data in their simplest form capture people's visit patterns, i.e., *who has been where and when*. However, we believe that the information hidden behind those data is a strong indicator of the social connections between people in their real lives [5,6]. Intuitively speaking, if two people happen to be at the same place around the same time for multiple occasions, it is very likely that they are socially involved in some way.

One area of related work includes a number of recent studies [20,21,22,23,24] that investigate similarity between objects' (e.g., people, cars) locations in time, represented as trajectories, for various reasons (e.g., to identify moving convoys, to recommend carpool partnerships). In particular, the similarity between trajectories can be used to infer social connections among people as shown by Li et al. [3]. The concept of trajectories in these studies usually indicates a shorter duration of time (in the order of hours) in which the sequence/order of visits is important. However, in our case co-occurrences refer to longer-term shared locations (in the order of months) in which the sequence of visits has no significance. Hence our "vector" model that captures "frequency" of co-visits and our various distance measures (used between the vectors) are very different than those suggested by these related studies.

One of the few papers that study the inference of social connections from real-world co-occurrences is by Crandall *et al.* [1]. They applied a probabilistic model to infer the probability that two people have a social connection, given that they co-occurred in space and time. Their method not only takes into account both spatial and temporal features but also handles sparsely distributed spatial data. However, they do not consider the frequency of co-occurrences in space and time, which we argue that it is an important indicator of social connections. Moreover, to render the problem tractable, Crandall *et al.* made the simplifying assumption that each person has one and only one friend, generating a sparse graph of M vertices and M/2 edges, where M is the total number of the users. Unfortunately, this assumption may not hold in many cases, as the social connection network can be quite dense in real world. For example, consider a group of people, who work for the same company; they are all socially connected to each other as co-workers.

In this paper, we take an entirely different approach to this problem by trying to estimate the strength of people's relationships based on the similarity of their visit patterns (i.e., *who has been where and when*). Hence, the questions we focus on are how to represent people's visit patterns (in space and time) and how to measure the distance between these visit patterns.

One intuitive solution is to represent the visit patterns as time-series (by transforming 2-D space to 1-D location ID's on the y-axis), and then apply a cross-correlation integral to measure the similarity between two time-series of two users. Besides the fact that this approach would not scale due to the eternity of time, in Section 2.2, we show that a more important problem with this approach is that the y-axis (representing the 2D space) of the time-series reflects a false notion of continuity of space, resulting in misrepresentation of the visit information in time intervals between two visits.

Alternatively, a person's visit pattern can be modeled as a vector where each dimension corresponds to a fixed location ID (again, by transforming 2-D space to

1-D), and the values capture the frequency of visits. Consequently, we can apply distance metrics, such as the cosine similarity [2] to calculate the distance between two patterns represented by vectors. However, we show in Section 2.2 that there are two major drawbacks with this approach. That is, it does not preserve the temporal feature and it cannot differentiate a vector $\vec{v}$ with its scaled counterpart $k\vec{v}$, both of which are crucial to our problem.

Since straightforward representations and distance measures do not work, in this paper, we propose a new representation along with a corresponding distance measure. In addition, and more importantly, we identify two properties, *commitment* and *compatibility*, that any distance measure should have in order to correctly infer social strengths from co-occurrences. We call this collection of contributions as a new model, dubbed Geospatial Social Model (*GEOSO*), towards integrating real-world spatiotemporal data with social-networks.

Our representation of visit patterns is a slight modification of the vector representation with time information captured at each dimension of the vector. However, we show in Section 4.3 that the simple cosine or Euclidean distance measures on this new representation cannot capture both of our properties, resulting in wrong estimation of social connectivity. Therefore, we discuss various auxiliary representations such as *co-occurrence vector* and *master vector,* to enable an accurate distance computation.

We experimentally evaluate the *GEOSO* distance model using data from the Internet Movie Database-IMDB (for co-occurrence events and social connections) and Wikipedia (for social connections). We compute the social distances based on co-occurrence events of celebrities, and validate the results with the social connection information available from their Bio on IMDB and Wikipedia. That is to verify whether user pairs with small social distances in our model have close social relationships in reality, e.g., close friends, siblings, life partners, etc. Our experiments show that the precision of our distance model is over 80% for user pairs with distance values less than 0.5.

The remainder of this paper is organized as follows. Section 2 formally defines the problem and shows why existing similarity metrics do not apply to our problem. In Section 3, we introduce the *GEOSO* model which quantifies the social distances between user pairs. In Section 4, we prove that GEOSO captures our two social properties. We validate our model through extensive experiments and report the results in Section 5. Finally, we conclude the paper with future directions in Section 6.

2   Problem Definition

2.1   The Problem

Given a set of users $U = (u_1, u_2, ..., u_M)$, a set of places $P = (p_1, p_2, ... p_N)$, and a set of spatiotemporal social events, the problem is how to infer the social connections between each pair of users and how to measure the social connections based on certain quantitative values. As part of the input data, social events are represented by a set of triplets $< u, p, t >$ stating *who (u) visited where (p) and when (t)*. The temporal feature of the event can be either a time-stamp or a time interval, whichever is available. We term the event triplets as W^3 events.

Intuitively speaking, people who are socially close to each other have higher chances of visiting same places at the same time (co-occurrences in both space and time). For example, a couple who lives together probably visits same grocery shops, restaurants, and vacation destinations at the same time. Furthermore, people who repeatedly visit the same location at the same time are socially connected with higher probability. For example, co-workers go to work on every weekday. Subsequently, we declare the following observations for the ease of discussion and refer to them later.

Observation 1. The more places two users visited together at the same time, the more likely these two users are socially close to each other.

Observation 2. The more often two users visited same places at the same time, the closer the two users are socially connected.

2.2   Candidate Similarity Metrics

As discussed earlier, the W^3 event history of any person can be easily represented as a vector or a time-series. Therefore, applying existing similarity metrics to our problem appears to be promising. In this section, we discuss two existing similarity metrics and point out why these candidate solutions do not apply to our problem.

2.2.1   Cross-Correlation Integral

Cross-correlation integral is frequently used in signal processing [4,7] to measure the similarity of two waveforms as a function of time. It also applies to pattern recognition problems [8,15] to find the similarity between two patterns. We can use cross-correlation integral to measure the visit patterns of two users in space and time. Particularly, let the x-axis be time and y-axis the geo-spatial locations, e.g., the label of grid cells if we consider the whole 2D space as a grid and number the cells in row-order. Each W^3 event corresponds to a point in the coordinate system and points are connected chronically using linear interpolation. Consequently, we have one time-series for each user as shown in Fig. 1. Next we compute the cross-correlation integral based on the time-series of two users and use the result as the similarity measure of the two users.

However, there are two major problems with this approach when applied to our problem. First, as the time-series is a function of time, it does not scale well. When the time axis is continuously growing, it results in a linear increase in time complexity of any possible similarity function. This shows that representing user visit patterns as a function of time and space is not appropriate for our problem. Second, the space is discretized as non-overlapping cells and the cells on the y-axis may be numbered in an arbitrary way (in row order or Hilbert curve order). Thus, being in two cells, for example, cell x and cell z, at two time instances does not indicate that the user was ever in any intermediate cells that lie spatially between cell x and cell z. Therefore, the time-series can misinterpret the visit pattern of the user, and the cross-correlation integral over time-series of two users may lead to imprecise results and hence incorrect social distance measurements.

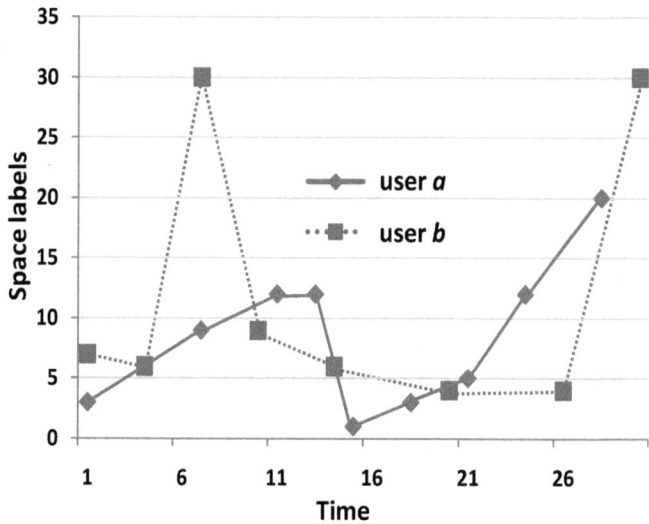

Fig. 1. Cross-correlation integral of two user visit patterns

2.2.2 Cosine Similarity

Cosine similarity measures the similarity between two vectors based on the cosine value of the angle between them. In the field of information retrieval, cosine similarity is often used to compare the similarity between two documents [9,10]. If we consider the user visit patterns as vectors, the cosine similarity metric can be adopted to solve our problem. Let V_a be a vector which records the number of times that user a visits a geo-location in the space and V_b be the same vector for user b. We can compute the cosine similarity between the two vectors V_a and V_b, which is then used to measure the social distance between a and b. However, there is a major drawback in this approach because the time dimension is overlooked in the vector representation of the visit history. For example, if both user a and user b have visited the same geo-locations, but on different days, they are considered similar in this approach but they are not similar in reality as they have never been at the same place *at the same time*. Obviously, the simple vector representation cannot handle the time dimension, which is an important factor in measuring social distances.

Furthermore, cosine similarity essentially measures the cosine of the angle between two vectors, therefore, the scalar of the vectors are not measured or considered. That is, the cosine similarity between a vector $\vec{v}$ and $\vec{u}$ is the same as the cosine similarity between $k\vec{v}$ and $\vec{u}$. This is not appropriate in measuring social distances based on visit patterns as the number of visits is an important indication of social closeness.

3   The GEOSO Model

To better capture the relationship between spatiotemporal co-occurrences and social ties between people, we propose a geo-social data model, called *GEOSO*.

3.1   Data Representation

Assume that the data input to the problem is a sequence of triplets in the form of *<user, location, time >*, specifying who visited where and when. Following the storage model in [1,11], the 2D space, formed by latitude and longitude, is partitioned into disjoint cells. For example, the space could be divided by a grid consisting of X x Y rectangular cells. The size of the cells is application-dependent and we discuss it later in the experiment section.

3.1.1   Visit Vector

A **visit vector** is a data structure that records the movement history of a user. We consider the grid as a matrix and then store it in row-first order as a vector. Subsequently, for each user, a **visit vector** is constructed to record the visit history of that user within a period of time. Specifically, each dimension of the visit vector represents one cell of the grid, and the value of the dimension is a list of time showing when these visits to the cell happened. If the user has not visited a cell within the time period of interest, the value of that cell is 0. For example, in Fig. 2, the visit vectors of user a and user b are:

$$V_a = (0, < t_1, t_2, t_3 >, < t_4, t_5 > ,0,0,0)$$

$$V_b = (0,0, < t_4, t_5, t_6 >, t_7, t_8, t_9)$$

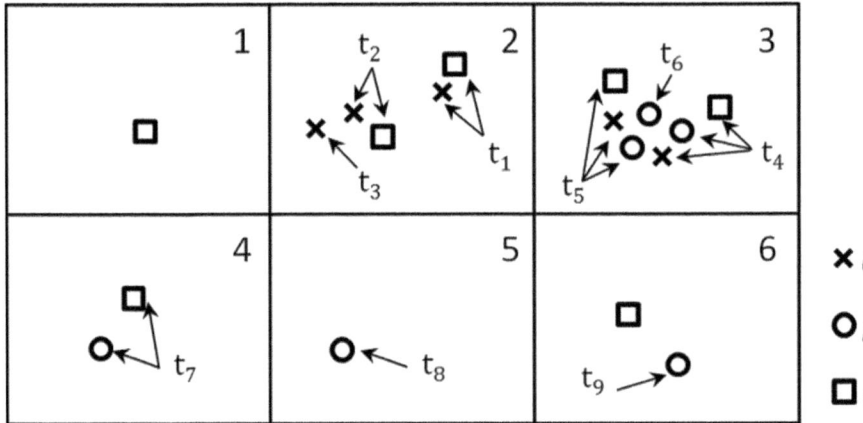

Fig. 2. Visit history of user a, b and c

As most users only visit a fairly small number of cells compared to the total number of cells in the space, the visit vector for a single user may contain mostly zeros and a few non-zero values. For storage and computation efficiency, we can eliminate all zeros and only store the non-zero values together with their cell IDs. For example, the visit vector of user a in Fig. 2 can be stored as $V_a = (2: < t_1, t_2, t_3 > ,3: < t_4, t_5 >)$, which represents that user a visited cell 2 for three times and cell 3 two times. For ease of presentation, we still use the original representation of the visit vector throughout the rest of the paper but keep in mind that the vectors can be stored and computed in a more efficient way.

3.1.2 Co-occurrence Vector

Next, we define a data representation to capture the commonalities between two users. The **co-occurrence vector** states the common visits of two users for the time period of interest. Each dimension of the vector still corresponds to a cell in the grid. However, the value of each dimension does not record the time of the visits but the number of times that the two users visited the same cell at *roughly the same time*, that is, the time spans of the visits of the two users at the same cell overlap. Note the length of the time overlap is application dependent and can be an input parameter to our model, for example, 20 minutes or two hours. Consider users a and c in Fig. 2, both a and c visited cells 2 and 3 at the same time. In particular, a and c visited cell 2 two times and cell 3 two times together. The co-occurrence vector between user a and c is $C_{ac} = (0,2,2,0,0,0)$. We formally define the co-occurrence vector as follows:

$$C_{ij} = (c_{i1,j1}, c_{i2,j2}, \ldots, c_{iN,jN}) \tag{1}$$

In Eq. 1, a term $c_{ik,jk}$ denotes the number of times that user i and user j both visited cell k while k ranges from 1 to the total number of cells N. Note that co-occurrence vectors can also be stored in a compact form, while only non-zero values are stored and maintained. In the next section, we discuss how to perform computation efficiently on these compact vectors.

3.1.3 Master Vector

As two co-occurrence vectors can considerably differ from each other, we need to normalize co-occurrence vectors so that the distance measurements are comparable. Consider that two users i and j have visited every cell in the space at the same time, and the number of visits to each cell is the maximum among any pair of users in the group of users of interest. Let C_{ij} be the co-occurrence vector of i and j. Undoubtedly, user i and user j have the highest similarity, hence, the smallest distance between each other. Furthermore, the more similar the co-occurrence vectors of any user pair to C_{ij}, the closer the two users are in terms of social distance. Following this intuition, we define the **master vector** for a group of users. A master vector contains the maximum pair-wise co-occurrences in each cell for a group of users of interest. For instance, the co-occurrence vectors of users a, b and c in Fig. 2 are as follows:

$$C_{ab} = (0,0,2,0,0,0)$$
$$C_{ac} = (0,2,2,0,0,0)$$
$$C_{bc} = (0,0,2,1,0,1)$$

The master vector of the three users is $M = (0,2,2,1,0,1)$ where the value of each dimension of M is the maximum value of the three co-occurrence vectors at the corresponding dimension. Note that only one master vector is constructed for a given set of users. Computing the master vector is simple and can be done efficiently. The definition of the master vector is shown in Eq. 2, where U stands for the total number of users and N is the total number of cells.

$$M = (m_1, m_2, \ldots, m_k, \ldots, m_N) \qquad (2)$$

$$m_k = \max_{1 \le i < j \le U, 1 \le k \le N} c_{ik,jk}$$

3.2 The GEOSO Distance Measure

The goal of our problem is to efficiently compute the social connections among all pairs of users and report those users who are strongly bonded. For any given set of users and their W^3 events, we first compute the co-occurrence vectors for every pair of users and the master vector for the entire set of users. Next, we compute the social distance between each pair of users.

The social distance d_{ij} between user i and user j is defined by the Pure Euclidean Distance (PED) between the co-occurrence vector C_{ij} and the master vector M. The similarity s_{ij} between two users is the inverse of the distance metric.

$$d_{ij} = \sqrt{\Sigma_k(c_{ik,jk} - m_k)^2}, \qquad s_{ij} = \frac{1}{d_{ij}} \qquad (3)$$

Consider a simple example consisting of two cells and three users shown in Fig. 3. The x-axis shows the number of co-occurrences in cell 1 and the y-axis shows the number of co-occurrences in cell 2. The co-occurrence vectors are plotted as thinner arrowed lines and the master vector is plotted with a solid bold arrowed line. The co-occurrence vector of user a and b is (2,2), the co-occurrence vector of users a and c is (0,3), and the co-occurrence vector of users b and c is (0,2). The master vector of the three users is $M = (2,3)$.

Next, the PED distances between all user pairs are computed as follows:

$$d_{ab}^2 = (2 - 2)^2 + (3 - 2)^2 = 1$$

$$d_{ac}^2 = (2 - 0)^2 + (3 - 3)^2 = 4$$

$$d_{bc}^2 = (2 - 0)^2 + (3 - 2)^2 = 5$$

The smaller the distance between two users, the closer they are. Therefore, we know that users a and b are the closest user pair in the example shown in Fig. 3.

As co-occurrence vectors contain mostly zeros, they are stored in a compact form. That is, all zeros are eliminated from the vector. Subsequently, we can improve the computation efficiency by employing the Projected Pure Euclidean Distance (**PPED**) proposed in [2].

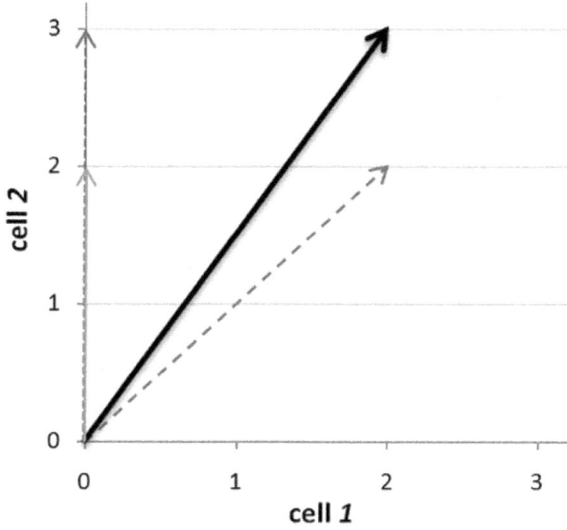

Fig. 3. Vector view of GEOSO distance measurements

4   Properties of the GEOSO Measure

In this section, we introduce two important properties of the *GEOSO* model and how our model captures the properties quantitatively.

4.1   Compatibility

According to the first observation in Section 2.1, the more common cells two users visit, the higher the likelihood that these two users are socially closer. Now, we show that our social distance measure is consistent with this observation. First, let us temporarily not consider the number of co-occurrences in one cell between two users, but only the fact whether two users co-occurred in that cell. In the co-occurrence vector, if two users both visited a cell at the same time (co-occurred), we use the value *1* for that cell. Otherwise, we assign *0* to that cell. Note that the dimensionality of the vector stays the same. In the extreme case, if two users visited every cell together, their co-occurrence vector contains only ones in all dimensions. Generally, suppose we have two pairs of users, i.e., (i, j) and (p, q). Users i and j both visited k cells together, while users p and q both visited $k + a$ cells together ($a > 0$). The co-occurrence vectors of the two user pairs are:

$$C_{ij} = (1,1, ... ,1,0,0,, ...   ,0)$$

$$C_{pq} = 1,1, ... ,1,1, ... 1,0, ... ,0)$$

Without loss of generality, suppose all co-occurrences happened in the first several cells. Clearly, the social distance between the user pair (p, q) is closer because p and

q has more overlap in space and time. We define the total number of dimensions with non-zero values in the co-occurrence vector as the **compatibility** between the two users. Then, compatibility property says that the more compatible two users are in their social relations, the closer they are. Next, we prove that our distance model captures the compatibility property.

Consider a new master vector that is represented as $M' = (m, m, ..., m)$ where m is the maximum value of all dimensions in the original master vector in Eq. 2. Note that the new master vector M' changes the absolute distance values but does not change the relative values between two distances. That is, if d_{ij} is greater than d_{pq} with regard to the original master vector M, it is still greater than d_{pq} with regard to the new master vector M'. Consequently, we use M' instead of M as the master vector in the following discussions where only the relative distance values are of concern. Hence, the distances between user i and j, p and q are as follows:

$$d_{ij} = \sqrt{k(m-1)^2 + (N-k)m^2}$$

$$d_{pq} = \sqrt{(k+a)(m-1)^2 + (N-k-a)m^2}$$

Next, consider the difference between the two distances:

$$d_{ij}^2 - d_{pq}^2$$

$$= k(m-1)^2 + (N-k)m^2 - (k+a)(m-1)^2 - (N-k-a)m^2$$

$$= -a(m-1)^2 + am^2 = a(2m-1) > 0 \text{ as } m > 0$$

Hence d_{ij} is greater than d_{pq}. Consequently, user p and q are more socially connected than user i and j. Note that if m equals to zero, it is a trivial case where no two users visited the same cell and their distances are all set to infinity. Therefore, our model has the compatibility property.

4.2   Commitment

As stated in our second observation, if two users repeatedly visited the same places together, they are more likely socially close to each other. For examples, the fact that students go to the same classroom twice a week is a strong indication that they are classmates. To show that our distance model is consistent with this observation, we need to take into account the number of co-occurrences between two users which we left behind in the previous section. That is, the value of each dimension in the co-occurrence vector corresponds to how many times two users co-occurred in space and time. Then the second observation states that the more two users committed to a certain place, the closer they are. We call it the **commitment** property of social relations. Next we prove how the model captures the commitment property.

Suppose that the co-occurrence vectors of two pairs of users (i,j) and (p,q) are identical except in one dimension.

$$C_{ij} = (k, \quad c_2, c_3, ..., c_N)$$

$$C_{pq} = (k + a, c_2, c_3, \dots, c_N) \ (a > 0)$$

The distances between the two pairs of users are:

$$d_{ij} = \sqrt{(m - k)^2 + \beta}$$

$$d_{pq} = \sqrt{(m - k - a)^2 + \beta}, \beta = \Sigma_{2 \leq l \leq N}(m - c_l)^2$$

Next, consider the difference of the two distances:

$$d_{ij}^2 - d_{pq}^2 = (m - k)^2 - (m - k - a)^2 > 0$$

Hence d_{ij} is greater than d_{pq}. Therefore we conclude that p and q are more socially connected than i and j. This shows that our model has the commitment property.

4.3   Compatibility vs. Commitment

We have shown that both compatibility and commitment properties play important roles in measuring social distances and they are captured by our *GEOSO* model. As the next step, we analyze the relationship between the two in the model and show which of the two properties are more important.

Assume user i and j have x co-occurrences in one cell (say cell 1), user p and q have y co-occurrences all of which happened in different cells. Without loss of generality, suppose that y co-occurrences happened at the first y cells. The co-occurrence vectors are:

$$C_{ij} = (x, 0, 0, \quad \dots, 0)$$

$$C_{pq} = (1, 1, \dots, 1, 0 \dots, 0)$$

The distances functions are:

$$d_{ij} = \sqrt{(m - x)^2 + (N - 1)m^2}$$

$$d_{pq} = \sqrt{y(m - 1)^2 + (N - y)m^2}$$

Let $d_{ij} = d_{pq}$ and we have the relationship between x and y as the quadratic function shown in Eq. 3.

$$y = f(x) = \frac{2mx - x^2}{2m - 1} \tag{4}$$

In the equation above, m is a constant. The relationship between the variable x and variable y is plotted in Fig. 4 (m is set to 20).

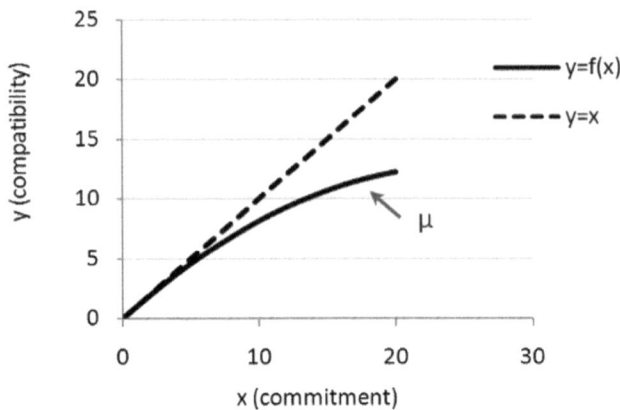

Fig. 4. Commitment vs. compatibility

The figure of the relationship between commitment and compatibility gives two important insights. First, as the curve of $y = f(x)$ is always below the line of $y = x$, our models shows that the commitment property has less importance on the distance function than the compatibility property. This is consistent with some intuitive examples. Consider the activities of two students on campus. If their W^3 event history shows that they went to the cafeteria *10* times together, the gym *10* times together and the same classroom *4* times together in the past month (high compatibility), this is a strong indication that these two students are close friends. On the other hand, if two students have been to the library at the same time for 30 times (high commitment), it does not necessarily show that the two are friends. In fact, there might be hundreds of students who go to the library every day. However, most of them do not know other students who also study in the same library.

Second, it is shown in the Fig. 4 that as commitment (x) increases, compatibility (y) also increases, however, with a much slower speed. We can increase either the commitment or the compatibility to yield a certain social distance. However, it requires less change in compatibility than commitment. When commitment reaches its upper limit (the saturation point) μ, further increasing commitment only very insignificantly affects the social distance of our model. This also confirms the fact that a spike of large commitment value only implies a coincidence in our social lives and does not bring closer the social distances.

The *GEOSO* model captures both compatibility and commitment properties of social behaviors by applying both the co-occurrence vectors and the master vector collectively. Without these data representations, applying the simple cosine or Euclidean distance measures on the simple visit vectors of users will lead to wrong estimation of social connectivity, in particular, the commitment property will overestimate social distances and weaken the influences of compatibility. For example, two users that co-occurred in the same places together for k times will have the same social distance as two users that co-occurred in k different places but only once in each place in both cosine similarity or Euclidean distance measure.

5   Experiment

5.1   Dataset

Ideally, we want to first compute the social distances between user pairs by applying the *GEOSO* distance model to a dataset of visit patterns (*who has been where and when*), Subsequently, we compare our results with the real social distances of the same set of users and measure the *precision and recall* of results. However, data that include both spatiotemporal information and real social connections among the same set of people are often considered sensitive and private. One can easily find either a spatiotemporal dataset (e.g., extracted from photos on Flickr [12]) or a dataset with social connections (e.g., LiveJournal [13]) separately. However, to the best of our knowledge, datasets with the combination of the two are not fully available for public or research uses.

Consequently, we seek an alternative solution and decide to use data from the Internet Movie Database (IMDB) [14] because it resembles the data requirements of our experiments for two reasons. First, the dataset contains spatiotemporal data of people. For example, if two actors/actresses acted in the same movie/episode, we consider that two persons co-occurred in space and time. If they performed in more than one movie/episode, we consider that they co-occurred in space and time multiple times as an indicator of compatibility, and if they performed in multiple episodes of the same TV series, it is considered an indicator of commitment. The social distance d (see Eq. 3) is calculated for each pair of people. Second, social connections of these actors/actresses are available publicly. For example, the Bio sections on IMDB and/or the Wikipedia [18] web pages usually contain the social relationships of that actor/actress, such as parents, siblings, spouses, best friends, long-time acting partners, etc. These data of social connections can be used to verify if two people with short social distance d is indeed socially connected. One might argue that the fact of two actors/actresses performing in the same movie does not necessarily suggest that they are related. This is a valid argument. However, the same thing is also true in a real spatiotemporal dataset, that is, two persons appearing at the same place at the same time may only due to coincidences. Our model can handle these coincidences by weighting compatibility and commitment appropriately in a non-linear fashion (See Fig. 4).

We extracted the information as described above from the IMDB and Wikipedia and ran our experiments on these datasets. Table 1 provides an overview of the datasets used in this section. The first row describes the sizes of celebrity sets, and the second row shows the number of different movies that the corresponding set of celebrities acted in. The last row of the table summarizes the total number of tuples in the format of *<person, movie/episode, time>*, which corresponds to the <who, where, when> (W^3) events.

Table 1. Dataset

# of celebrities	2k	4k	10 k
# of movies and episodes	32k	50k	100k
# of W^3 events	280k	1.1M	4.6M

5.2   Distance Measure and Result Verification

In this section, we ran experiments on each data set and computed social distances using the *GEOSO* model. Next, the distances are normalized and discretized. We divided [0, 1] into 25 of equal-sized buckets and each bucket contains user pairs with distances between a and $a + 1/25$. For example, the first bucket contains user pairs with distances between 0 and 0.04.

The first dataset contains 2,000 celebrities with 280k co-occurrences. Most of the user pairs (96.8% of 280k) have social distances close to 1 (> 0.91), meaning that they are socially far away. Therefore, we drop those user pairs and focus on those who are socially close, which is 8.8k pairs (3.2% of 280k).

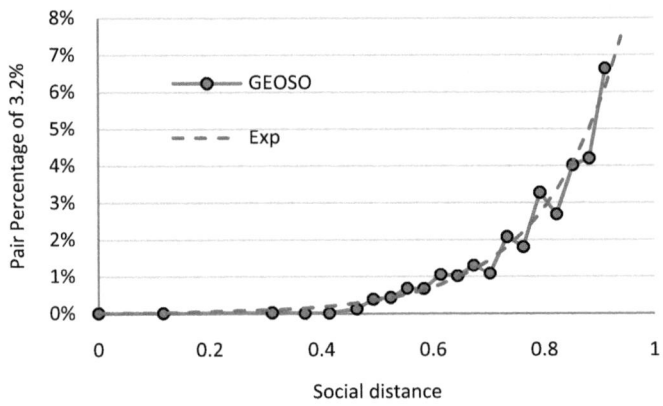

Fig. 5. Percentage of pairs vs. social distances

The relationship between distance values and the user pair percentage, which is calculated out of 8.8k pairs, is shown in Fig. 5. The x-axis shows the social distance calculated by our model and the y-axis shows the percentage of top 3.2% user pairs with smaller distances. Each tipping point in the graph represents a bucket, and as the graph shows, buckets with short social distances have fewer pairs of people (lower percentage) than buckets with long social distances do. Keep in mind that the number of buckets (number of tipping points) does not represent the number of pairs of people, however, the pair percentage corresponding to the bucket (the value on the y-axis) does. Fig. 5 also shows an interesting characteristic that the distribution has the behaviour of an exponential function (the dotted curve) $p = C_1 e^{(C_2 \times d)}$ where C_1 and C_2 are constants and we experimentally found them to be: $C_1 = 1/N$ and $C_2 = 6.92$ where $N = 8,860$. In other words, the *GEOSO* model shows that the percentage of pairs increases *exponentially* as the social distance increases.

Next, we verify the distances using the social information retrieved from IMDB and Wikipedia. The verified results are shown in Fig. 6. The x-axis shows the social distances and the y-axis represents the percentage of successfully verified pairs

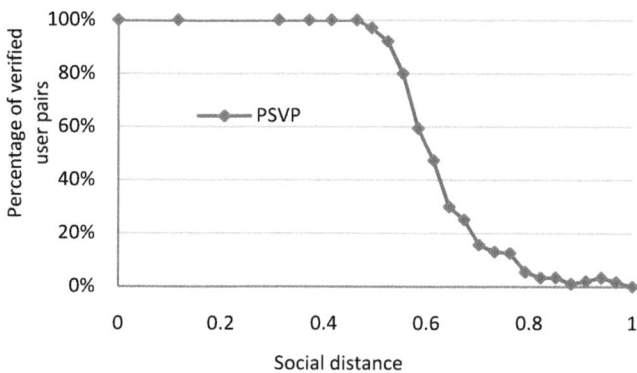

Fig. 6. PSVP vs. social distances – set of 2,000 people

(PSVP) of each individual bucket for all 280k pairs. As Fig. 6 shows, buckets with distances less than 0.55 have PSVP above 80% (150 pairs), and buckets with distance less than 0.6 have PSVP above 59% (301 pairs). As the distance values increase, especially close to the value of 1, the percent of verified user pairs drops dramatically. This is due to the fact that when two persons are far away in social distances, there is no data from IMDB or Wikipedia showing that these two are not friends, family members or in other relationships, which on the other hand proves that our distance measure is consistent with the reality.

We also verify our results by manually checking the first 300 celebrity pairs with the smallest social distances. The user pairs with smallest distances are, for example, twins Close Sprouse and Dylan Sprouse, twins Ashley Olsen and Mary-Kate Olsen, and Ricky Gervais and Steven Merchant. These user pairs acted together in either many TV Series or movies.

In the next set of experiments, we use the dataset of 4,000 people and 1.1M co-occurrence events. The trends of the figures are similar to the previous set of experiments. Fig. 7 shows the relationship between social distances and user pair percentage of 50k pairs corresponding to 4.5% of 1.1M pairs. Again, user pairs with distances greater than 0.9 are dropped as they are considered socially far away. The x-axis shows social distances and the y-axis shows the percentage of pairs in buckets.

As shown in Fig. 7, the graph also exhibits the behaviour of an exponential function $p = C_1 e^{(C_2 \times d)}$. The constants are $C_1 = 1/N$ and $C_2 = 8.76$ where $N = 8,860$. This behaviour holds the best for the buckets with distances less than 0.8. Beyond this point, the higher the distance, the more different the distribution is from its approximated exponential behaviour. This can be explained by the fact that when the size of the set increases, less famous people are added to the set and they acted in less movies/episodes than the more famous ones, hence they have less chance to act together with other people, which results in a sparser social graph and higher numbers of pairs falling into buckets of higher distances.

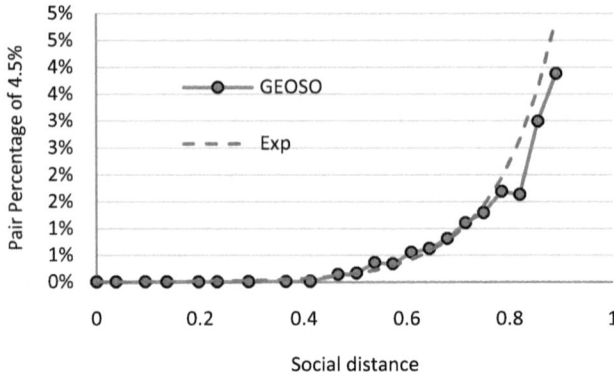

Fig. 7. Percentage of pairs vs. social distances – set of 4,000 people

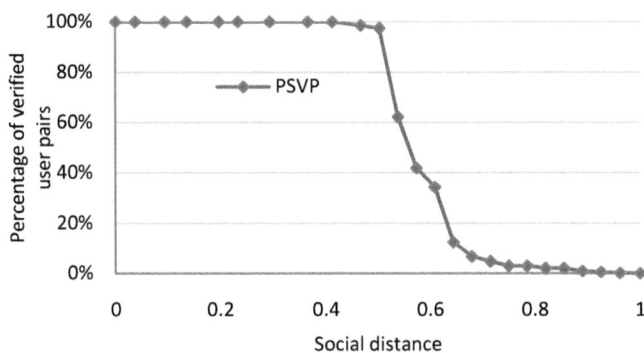

Fig. 8. PSVP vs. social distances – set of 4,000 people

Fig. 8 shows the realtionship between verified user pairs and distances. The x-axis shows the social distances, and the y-axis shows the PSVP values. When the social distance increases, the percentage of PSVP also decreases.

In the last set of experiments, we use a dataset that contains 10,000 people and 4.6M co-occurrence events. Fig. 9 shows the relationship between the percentage of pairs (the y-axes) and the social distance (the x-axis) for top 0.5% user pairs out of 4.6M pairs.

Fig. 9 shows that the majority user pairs do not have close social connection due to the fact that in a large scale social network, most people are not directly socially connected.

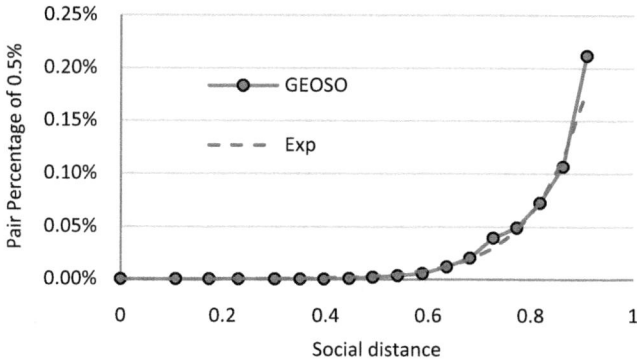

Fig. 9. Percentage of pairs vs. social distances – set of 10,000 people

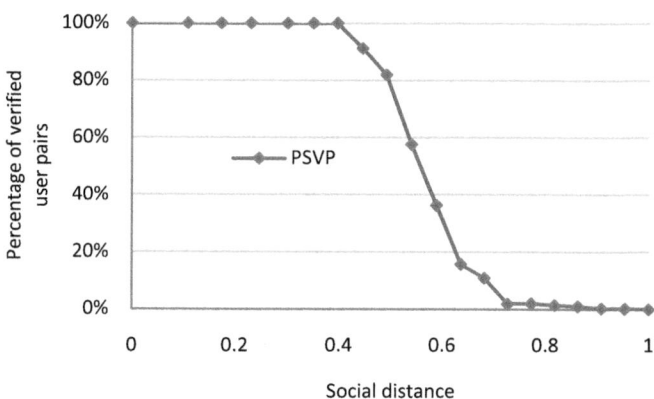

Fig. 10. PSVP vs. social distances – set of 10,000 people

In Fig. 10, we show the relationship between PSVP (y-axis) and social distance (x-axis). Similarly, it shows that user pairs with small distances are verified by the data available. Hence, user pairs that are considered socially close by our model are indeed close in reality.

5.3   Precision and Recall

In this section, we measure our results using the precision and recall model. For each value of the social distance d (the midpoint of each bucket), we calculate the precision and recall for the set of all pairs with social distance less than or equal to d.

$$Precision(d) = \frac{NSVP(d)}{NP(d)}, Recall = \frac{NSVP(d)}{\sum_d NSVP(d)} \tag{5}$$

The term $NSVP(d)$ represents the number of successfully verified pairs with distance no greater than d, and $NP(d)$ is the number of pairs with distance no greater than d.

We present the precision and recall for all three datasets used in the previous sections. In Fig. 11, the x-axis shows the social distance and the y-axis shows the precision and recall measures.

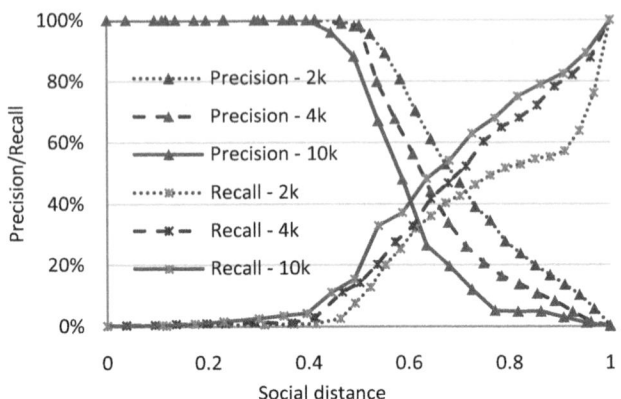

Fig. 11. Precision/Recall vs. Social Distance

As shown in Fig. 11, the precision is high as the distance values are small. However, the recall is low. This is due to two reasons. First, the number of pairs with shorter social distances is only a small fraction (3%-5%) of the total number of user pairs. Although all of them can be verified, they account for only a small percent of all user pairs. Second, user pairs who are close in reality are not reported close in our model. This is because our datasets consist of only co-acting data instead of real spatiotemporal co-occurrence data. Two persons who are father and son might never act together, but they are socially close. This generally is not the case in a real spatiotemporal dataset.

6   Conclusion and Future Work

In this paper, we focused on how to infer social connections among people based on their co-occurrences in space and time. We presented the *GEOSO* model which derives social connections between people based on spatiotemporal events in real world. We also showed that our model captures the intuitive properties of social behaviors. Finally, our experiments demonstrated that the social distances computed by our model are consistent with the real social distances from the datasets.

There are a few future extensions for this work. First, we plan to extract more features from co-occurrence events, for example, the real distances between visits happened in the same cell and the overall time overlaps spent at same locations between two users. Then we can use these features to increase the precision of our social distance measure. Furthermore, once a social closeness is identified, we can also use the geospatial information and time to label the relationship. For example, if two persons go to only work-related places like an office building, a parking garage, and a nearby cafeteria during working hours, they are most likely colleagues. If two persons go to shopping malls, groceries and play sports together, it is more probable that they are friends or life partners.

Acknowledgments. This research has been funded in part by NSF grant CNS-0831505 (CyberTrust) and IS-1115153, the USC Integrated Media Systems center (IMSC), and unrestricted cash and equipment gift from Google, Microsoft and Qualcomm. Any opinions, findings, and conclusions or recommendations expressed in this material are those of the author(s) and do not necessarily reflect the views of the National Science Foundation.

References

1. Crandall, D., Backstrom, L., Cosley, D., Suri, S., Huttenlocher, D., Kleinberg, J.: Inferring social ties from geographic coincidences. Proc. National Academy of Sciences 107(52), 22436–22441 (2010)
2. Shahabi, C., Banaei-Kashani, F.: Efficient and anonymous web usage mining for web personalization. INFORMS Journal on Computing-Special Issue on Data Mining 15(2) (2003)
3. Li, Q., Zheng, Y., Xie, X., Chen, Y., Liu, W., Ma, W.Y.: Mining User Similarity Based on Location History. In: Proc. Of the 16th ACM SIGSPATIAL International Conference on Advances of GIS, New York, NY (2008)
4. Storch, H., Zwiers, F.: Statistical Analysis in Climate Research. Cambridge University Pr. (2001); ISBN 0521012309
5. Diaconis, P., Mosteller, F.: Methods for Studying Coincidences. J. Am. Stat. Assoc. 84, 853–861 (1989)
6. Backstrom, L., Dwok, C., Kleinberg, J.: Wherefore Art Throu R3579X? Anonymized Social Networks, Hidden Patterns, and Structural Steganography. In: Proc. of the 16th International World Wide Web Conference (2007)
7. Schaff, D.P., Waldhauser, F.: Waveform cross-correlation-based differential travel-time measurements at the northern nalifornianeismic network. Bull. Seism. Soc. Am. 96, 38–49 (2006)
8. Rossi, T.M., Warner, I.M.: Pattern Recognition of Two-Dimensional Fluorescence Data Using Cross-Correlation Analysis. Applied Spectroscopy 39(6), 949–959 (1985)
9. Yuan, S.T., Sun, J.: Ontology-based structured cosine similarity in document summarization: with applications to mobile audio-based knowledge management. IEEE Transaction on Systems, Man, and Cybernetics-Part B: Cybernetics 35(5) (2005)
10. Esteva, M., Bi, H.: Inferring Intra-organizational Collaboration from Best-matched Cosine Similarity Distributions in Text. In: Proc. of the 9th ACM/IEEE-CS Joint Conference on Digital Libraries, JCDL (2009)
11. Zhang, D., Du, Y., Hu, L.: On Monitoring the top-k Unsafe Places. In: Proc. of 24th International Conference on Data Engineering (ICDE), Cancun, Mexico (2008)
12. Flicker, http://www.flickr.com/
13. LiveJournal, http://www.livejournal.com
14. IMDB, http://www.imdb.com
15. Kumar, B.V., Savvides, M., Xie, C.: Correlation pattern regconition for face recognition. Proc. of the IEEE (2006)

16. Yuan, S.T., Sun, J.: Ontology-based Structured Cosine Similarity in Document Summarization: with Applications to Mobile Audio-Based Knowledge Management. IEEE Transaction on Systems, Man, and Cybernetics-Part B: Cybernetics 35(5) (2005)
17. Griffiths, T., Tenenbaum, J.: Randomness and Coincidences: Reconciling Intuition and Probability Theory. In: Proc. of the 23rd Annual Conference of the Cognitive Science Society, pp. 370–375 (2001)
18. Wikipedia, http://www.wikipedia.org
19. Pham, H., Hu, L., Shahabi, C.: Towards Integrating Real-World Spatiotemporal Data with Social Networks. In: Proc. of the 19th ACM SIGSPATIAL International Conference on Advances in GIS, Poster Presentation, Chicago, Illinois (2011)
20. Yoon, H., Shahabi, C.: Accurate Discovery of Valid Convoys from Moving Object Trajectories. In: International Workshop on Spatial and Spatiotemporal Data Mining (SSTDM 2009), Miami, Florida, USA (2009)
21. Lee, J.G., Han, J., Whang, K.Y.: Trajectory Clustering: a Partition-and-Group Framework. In: SIGMOD Conference, pp. 593–604 (2007)
22. Lee, J.G., Han, J., Li, X., Gonzalez, H.: TraClass: Trajectory Classification using Hierarchical Region-Based and Trajectory-Based Clustering. Proc. of the VLDB Endowment 1(1) (2008)
23. Vieira, M.R., Bakalov, P., Tsotras, V.J.: On-line Discovery of Flock Patterns in Spatio-Temporal Data. In: GIS, pp. 286–295 (2009)
24. Roh, G.P., Roh, J.W., Hwang, S.W., Yi, B.K.: Supporting Pattern Matching Queries over Trajectories on Road Networks. TKDE (2010)

A Survey on LBS: System Architecture, Trends and Broad Research Areas

Shivendra Tiwari[1], Saroj Kaushik[1], Priti Jagwani[2], and Sunita Tiwari[2]

[1] Dept. of Computer Science and Engg.
[2] Dept. of Information Technology,
IIT Delhi, Hauz Khas, New Delhi, India 110016
{shivendra,saroj}@cse.iitd.ac.in,
{jagwani.priti,sutiwari}@gmail.com

Abstract. The Location Based Services (LBS) seem to be the next revolution on small computing handheld devices in terms of location aware advertising, security alerts, news updates, disaster management, geo-fencing, buddy-findings, gaming, criminal investigations, turn-by-turn navigation and so on. In today's scenario there is an explosion of technologies to communicate with mobile, connected devices and sensors. In this paper we are presenting a literature survey of LBS that includes the architecture of the LBS ecosystem, the key market players, and the latest trends in LBS development. Finally, the broad research areas such as location determination techniques, geo-sensor networks, and location based natural queries, location privacy and authorization, geo-social networks, LBS QoS, and Location Based Recommender Systems (LBRS) have been studied and presented briefly.

Keywords: Location Based Services (LBS), Location Determination, Location Based Service Providers (LSP), Location Determination Technology (LDT), Location Privacy, LBS Research Challenges.

1 Introduction

The Location Based Services (LBS) are information, alerts and entertainment services, accessible with the computers and mobile devices through Over the Air (OTA) network. It facilitates to make use of the geographical position of the mobile device for various services. The LBS refers to the services in which the user location information is used in order to add value to the service as a whole. Terminals can be fixed or mobile; both receive and transmit data. They include wireless phones, laptops, portable navigation devices, and embedded systems. The user location information consists of X-Y coordinates generated by any given Location Determination Technology (LDT), such as Cell-ID, A-GPS, and EOTD etc. These technologies usually require modifications in either the networks or the mobile phones, and in some cases in both. Main service categories for LBS include Emergency and Safety, Communities and Entertainment, Information and Navigation, Tracking and Monitoring, and M-Commerce. LBS have generated a lot of interest in recent years, as a new source for mobile operators to enhance their service offering.

S. Kikuchi et al. (Eds.): DNIS 2011, LNCS 7108, pp. 223–241, 2011.

Predictions of LBS usage have generated a lot of interest and attracted many new players developing and offering numerous applications and services. Operators see it as an integral and inevitable part of their service offering, allowing them to better utilize some of their existing assets in order to be more competitive [6].

The LBS services can be divided into various major categories such as Pull vs Push services; Person vs Device oriented services, and Active vs Passive services. The Push Services keep track of current location of user for services such as security alerts, news updates etc. Such services require real-time location update to the location server. However, the Pull Services are based on demand by the user and thus do not require the continuous update of the user location. The examples of such services are point of interest (POI) Searches, Geocoding, Reverse Geocoding and so on. Person-oriented Services comprise all of those applications where a service is user-based. Thus, the focus of application is to position a person or to use the position to enhance a service. Device-oriented Services are external to the user, where instead of focusing a person's demand, an object (e.g., a car, a bus) or a group of people (e.g., a fleet) could be located. In device-oriented applications, the person or object located is usually not controlling the service e.g., car tracking for theft recovery. In Active Services, the user initiates the service request, whereas in the Passive Services a third party locates one user (locatee) at the request of another user (the locator). Typical Passive location services are friend finder services, location-based gaming, or fleet management [21].

Wireless Networking (WiFi), cellular telephone (GSM), Packet Radio, Radio Frequency Identifiers (RFID), Smart Personal Object Technology (SPOT), global positioning systems (GPS), and sensor networks are various technologies available to communicate with mobile, connected devices and sensors. The navigation systems and LBS informative applications have been useful on Turn-by-Turn navigation, POI Search, location search, Map Display etc. Currently there are several digital data provider companies (i.e. NavTeq, TeleAtlas, KIWI, Map My India) which provide the digitized geographical data. The route calculation between the source and the destination addresses, and proximity searches are some of the applications of the digitized data.

Apart from the brief introduction of LBS in this section, the architecture of an LBS ecosystem is discussed in section-2. The recent trends in LBS and the key players in LBS market are explained in section-3 and 4 respectively. Finally, section-5 talks about the broad research areas in LBS domain and the section-6 concludes the survey.

2   Architecture of an LBS Ecosystem

Due to the variety of positioning technologies, the model shall be independent of the location determination implementation. Also it should be able to work when the user switches from one positioning technology to another [5]. Fig.1 shows a generic architecture of the LBS ecosystem [22]. The components include Positioning, Communication Network, and the Content Providers as the basic infrastructure requirements. The Positioning can be done either by the client device using satellite based GPS (Global Positioning System) or a network positioning service. Afterwards the mobile client sends the service request, which contains the service goals and the position via the communication network. The content/data provider is the actual location engine that provides various LBS services.

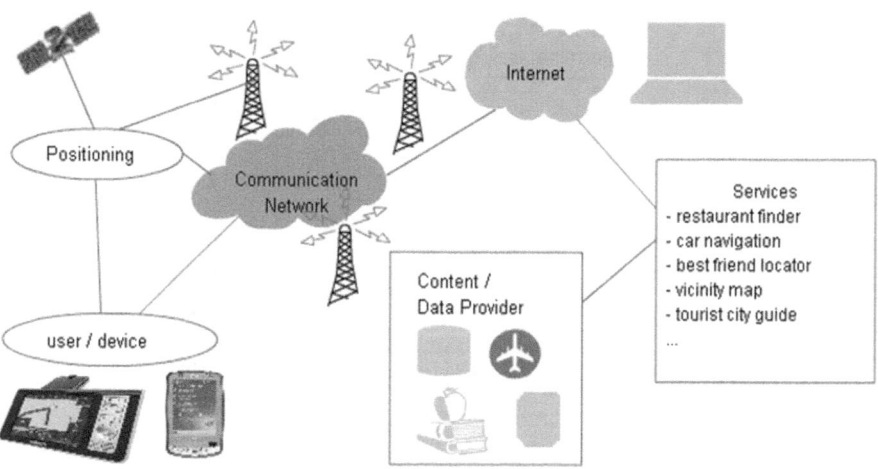

Fig. 1. Location Based System Architecture

Furthermore, the Middleware can be added into the generic architecture to ensure location privacy, subscription management, and transaction accountability. The Middleware based architecture and a popular LBS platform named Kivera Location Platform is discussed in the subsections below.

2.1   Middleware Based Architecture

A Middleware is a set of services that facilitate the development and deployment of distributed applications in heterogeneous environments. Middleware consists of a set of services exposing interfaces, a programming model, and an interaction model to the application developer. For the context of LBS, this refers to the services, abstractions, and models that implement mobile user coordination, information correlation, and information dissemination. A major component of LBS is the integration of location or position information. Various application categories have fundamentally different characteristics and impose a wide spectrum of requirements on the underlying middleware platform. The responsibilities of the middleware systems include managing subscriptions, user profile management, managing a potentially very large number of information providers and so forth. The LBS system needs to support high availability despite node failures. Fig. 2 shows a middleware based architecture where all the location service requests from the clients route through the middleware. Since the middleware has to manage all the subscriptions and work as an application router as well it becomes bottleneck [6]. A Flexible middleware based architecture has been proposed by S. Kaushik et al in 2011 where the middleware works as a certifying authority; however the clients can directly communicate to the actual location based service providers(LSP) [21].

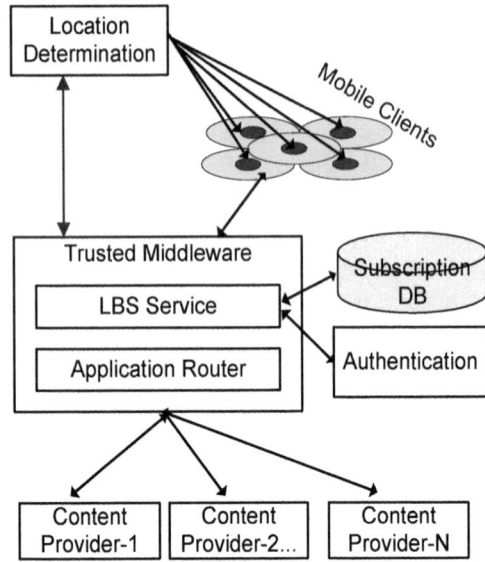

Fig. 2. Middleware Based Architecture of LBS Systems

2.2   Kivera Location Platform

In 2001, Kivera Inc came up with an LBS platform offering different services that was also used by AT&T Wireless for the E-911 services shown in Fig. 3 [6]. The platform exposes a set of services that uses static digitized geographical data along with the dynamic data for traffic flows, and traffic incidents.

LBS Content. The location engine uses both dynamic and static data. The dynamic data includes Live Traffic Flow and Traffic Incidents which get populated by various content providers (i.e. www.inrix.com). The static geospatial data includes the roads, parks, rivers, buildings, and railroads in the digital format. The POI data is a rich database about the user's day-to-day places. The Location Engine uses LBS content to serve the service requests.

Location Engine. The heart of any LBS system is the Location Engine, which contains the software components that add intelligence to digital map data. Though each component is responsible for a separate independent feature; however they might use each other in order to perform their functionalities. For example, the geocoding might be used by routing module as goecoding is necessary to generate a route. The fundamental features of the location engine are geocoding, reverse-geocoding, routing, and map rendering. Geocoding converts a street address to a latitude/ longitude (x, y pair of coordinates) position so it can be accurately placed on a map. The Reverse Geocoding is the process of deriving the location name of the nearest road segment from a given longitude/latitude. Routing is the technique of calculating the optimal path between an origin and destination based on specific criteria. A routing engine evaluates the numerous ways a driver might travel over the streets, while accounting for various attributes of the street networks. Starting at the route origin, the software uses the A* (A-star) algorithm to calculate the optimal route. POI Search, Vector Data generation and Map Rendering are other sub-modules of a Location Engine.

Traffic Server. The traffic server gets the dynamic data from various traffic data vendors and provides the traffic data to Location Engine in compatible format. The traffic server is responsible of parsing the vendor provided traffic information, storing the data in a common format and finally serving to the location engine, and to the other traffic applications. The traffic history is also maintained in the traffic server that can be used for the future predictions and city transport planning. The traffic flows are used by the location engine to render the traffic density on the map and while calculating the routes between two addresses; the routes with the heavy traffic are avoided.

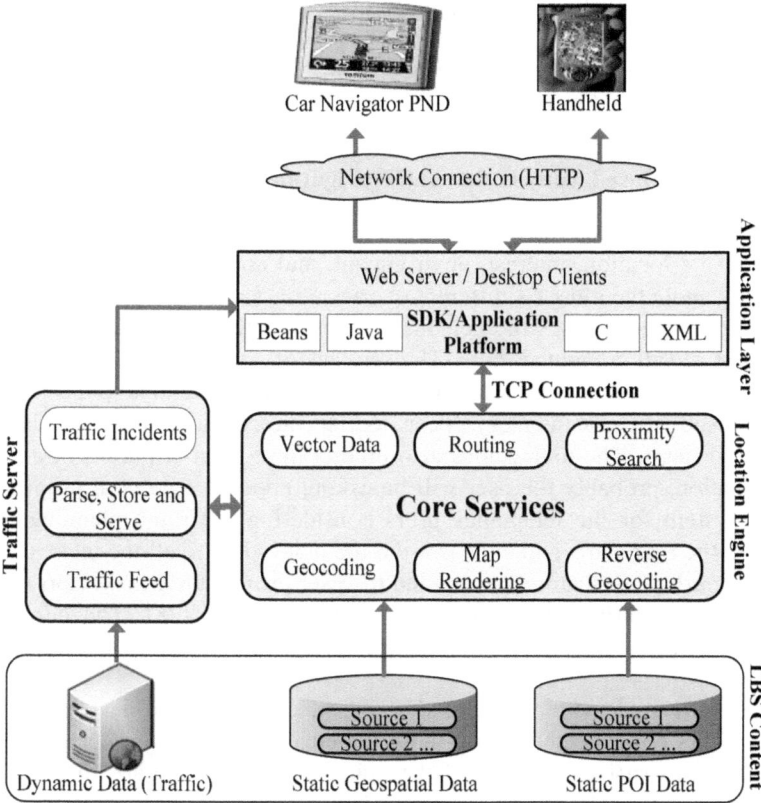

Fig. 3. Architecture of Kivera Location Platform

SDK/Application Platform. The features offered by the location engine can not be directly accessed by the end clients as the location engine is not deployed as a web server. It needs a scalable LBS SDK platform with a set of core services for building applications. The SDK is a set of C, Java, and XML APIs which help application developers to build custom LBS applications, Desktop applications, and Web Services. The APIs communicate to the location engine via TCP socket connection after the successful key verification and handshake procedure. The SDK platform allows the application developers to use the location engine features in their custom applications for different platforms.

3   Recent Trends in LBS

The average consumer now has many choices of navigation and GPS-enabled tools. There are onboard navigation systems for the vehicles and navigation applications available on cell phones or smart phones. The vehicle tracking, fleet management, geo-fencing, location based advertising, and security systems are some of the latest location based applications [23]. Some of the location based applications that are popular these days are discussed below.

3.1   Location Based Tour Guide and Navigation Systems

Location based tour guide is an intelligent system that proactively guides the user on the basis of its location, interest, environment, and context. The tour guide systems are able to handle the tourist's different queries, i.e. "I have 3 hours of time, what can I do?". The tour guide uses the personal interests of the tourists like history, nature and it offers a well computed tours. The services of a tour guide system include tour planning, route finding and navigational assistance, route and plans evaluations, location based site commentary, peer tourist information sharing, adaptive and personalized maps. The tour guides also predict the tourist requirement and it poses the information, probably the user will be asking about. J. Lee et al proposed a tour planning system for the telematics users considering the route planning as a TSP problem as the tour starts and ends from/to the hotel visiting all the interesting tourist POIs. The tourist POI feature vectors and the user profile attribute vectors are used to calculate the similarity and interest based POI filtering [28]. The current digital guidance systems can be classified as follows:

Static Content on Device. Systems that store the audio-video data in the guidance media. Visitors are expected to use these systems by themselves. These systems are limited to some particular aspect of the guidance. Due to the size limitation of the device, only the limited amount of data can be stored.

Static Content on Server. The content is stored in the server. The user can download the multimedia files as per the interest and use them for the desired destination. Examples of such systems are: the Personal Digital Museum Assistant in Japan, the

Wireless Museum PDA Tour Guide System in the Tate Modern Art Gallery in London and the National Palace Museum Tour Guide System in Taipei.

Dynamic Content Based Tour Guide. The client has processing capability and it can compute the location of the user at run time. In such systems most of the data is located at the server. The clients request the computed tours to the server at the runtime along with the current location and get the well computed tours as per the user interest.

3.2   Location Aware Browsing

Location aware browsing is possible through the IP/Network based location determination. IP based location determination is the act of using measurements taken from the access network to calculate or compute the physical location of a device. There are different techniques on network based positing given in [24]. Using the network positioning the web browsers can tell the websites about the user's location. The websites can be more intelligent and hence can find information that is more relevant and more useful. Let us say you are looking for a pizza restaurant in your area. A website will be able to access your location so that simply searching for "pizza" will bring you the answers you need in the appropriate proximity [8]. The web-browsers gathers information about nearby wireless access points and your computer's IP address. Then web-browser sends this information to the default geo-location service provider to get the location in terms of latitudes and longitudes. Accuracy is greatly dependent on the service provider's database accuracy. The location based social networking websites use the network based location determination to locate the users approximately.

3.3   Landmark Based Navigation

The Google Maps directions have been using some new phrases such as "Take the 2nd right" rather than just "Turn right". This is based on natural concepts that relate to the way we think about navigation in real life. Without road names, it's difficult to produce a set of directions that makes sense. The countries like India, the street signs or names tend to be less important than landmarks such as civic buildings and gas stations [9]. The suitable landmarks are selected based on visibility, importance, and closeness to the turns that the user is making. The landmarks are used in two ways: to identify where users need to turn, and to provide confirmation that they are on the right track. Using landmarks in directions helps for two simple reasons: they are easier to see than street signs and they are easier to remember than street names. For example, spotting a pink building on a corner or remembering to turn after a gas station is much easier than trying to recall an unfamiliar street name. Following are the situations in which people resort to landmarks [4].

Assurance to the Location. The landmarks are used when people need to orient themselves, for instance, they just exited a subway station and are not sure which way to go. The older navigation systems would generally say "Head southeast for 0.2 miles". The landmark based navigation system would say "Start walking away from the McDonald's for 02 miles".

Turn Description. This is a situation when people use a landmark to describe a turn. For example, "Turn right after the Starbucks."

Confirmation of the Track. This is the most interesting scenario where the landmarks are used just to confirm that the user is going on the correct path. People simply want to confirm that they are still on the right track and haven't missed their turn.

4   Key Players in LBS Market

The launch of the LBS is driven by both regulation and competition [17]. Other than the mobile operators there are other players like Location Based Service Provider (LSP), Client Application Developers, Trusted Middleware and LBS Regulatory Authorities as explained below:

Network Operators. The network operators play an important role on helping the device determining its location quickly using AGPS method. The operators also help getting the location on the non-GPS mobiles using the cell based location determination techniques. The operators can control the accuracy and the quality of the location services running on the client devices. Sometimes the network operators also play a middleware role for the managing users profile, transaction accounting and the location security.

Location Based Service Providers (LSP). The actual location based service providing entity that take the location as an input and offer the services to the end users. Sometimes the LSPs are integrated with the network operators and the network operators host the location servers.

Client Application Developers, and End Users. The role of application developers include a combination of one time set-up fees, revenue sharing and monthly payments for additional services such as technical support upgrades and customer care. The client applications are developed using various platforms i.e. J2ME, Symbian C++, Android, and iPhone OS. The end users are one of the most important parts of the LBS market. It is important to consider whether subscribers will be willing to pay additional fees to use the offered services. General usage figures based on past experience with other services show that the answer lies in the usability and value services bring to users. The services should be tailored and offered to specific user segments, maximizing their value from such services. Operators are in a key position to define and package such services, and tailor them to the needs of their different subscriber segments [17].

Trusted Middleware Parties and Secure Gateways. The middleware is a trusted party that does authentication, and application request routing. Sometimes the network operators deploy and operate LBS within their own network, leaving less room for others players such as application service providers due to the information sensitivity. In many cases though, operators still lack the expertise and are willing to accept outsourced solutions, using various means to hide the actual user information from the third party. The middleware plays an intermediate role between the users and the actual service providers.

LBS Regulatory Authorities, Standards. The regulatory authorities play an important role on regulating the location sharing agreements, location storage, location privacy laws and service provisions. The regulations help shaping and success path creation for the LBS products. Regulation is likely to have an impact on the accuracy operators will provide, as well as on the use and handling of user information. This will affect both the technology choice and the availability and usability of user location information for the different players. There are separate regulatory bodies for different countries. For example, ETSI for Europe, ANSI T1 for the USA, ARIB and TTC for Japan, TTA for Korea, and CWTS for China [10]. The Open Geospatial Consortium (OGC), an international voluntary consensus standards organization that collaborate in a consensus process encouraging development and implementation of open standards for geospatial content and services, GIS data processing and data sharing [16]. A lot of effort is put in standardizing LBS, both on the network and application side. Main forces are the 3G Partnership Program (3GPP), defining mainly the addition of LBS capabilities to future releases of 3G networks, and Location Interoperability Forum (LIF), formed by vendors and interested parties to develop and promote common and ubiquitous solutions for LBS which are network and LDT (Location Determination Technology) independent [17].

5   Broad Research Areas in LBS Domain

The LBS is not only limited to applications that push promotional offers or other content to cellular subscribers as they move into a particular geographical area. But there is a whole lot more to LBS. The LBS also can be used to help cellular service providers with network management, policy enforcement and billing, and to enable new, productivity-enhancing capabilities within the enterprise. It is a huge domain containing several research areas shown in Fig. 4. Some of the research areas are discussed as below:

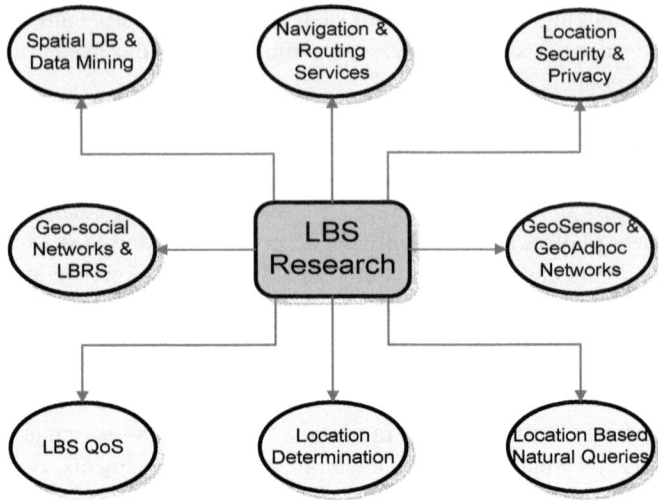

Fig. 4. Broad Research Areas in LBS

5.1   Location Determination Techniques

Mobile positioning has become a popular technology for more than half a decade now. There are various means for doing mobile positioning, but they can generally be divided into four categories i.e. Radiolocation Techniques, Satellite-Based Techniques, Techniques used in Proximity Systems and Dead Reckoning Techniques. Each of these methods has their advantages and disadvantages in their possible application of providing location services in cellular and PCS (Personal Communications Service) networks [12]. Some of the examples of the location determination techniques are – GPS, AGPS, Cell-ID based, and WiFi. A comparison of the various positioning methods is given in Table-1 [13]. Some of challenges in LDT are discussed below [25]:

Accuracy and Precision. The accuracy is a measurement of how close the location has been estimated with respect to the real geographic location. The ability of network-based LDT technologies to achieve desired accuracy levels is a challenge in rural areas, due to the limitations in tower placement and the resulting limits on triangulation capabilities. The satellite based GPS has been able to provide 5 to 20 meters of accuracy in the clear sky. The precision deals with the closeness of a number of position fixes to their mean value.

Yield and Consistency. Yield is the ability to get position fixes in all environments. Consistency is the stability of the accuracy in different environments. Consistency of location data has been an issue across LDT technologies and carrier procedures due the lack of standards early on, and the proliferation of different technologies. It is important for careers and positing entities to test the compliance with the standards and present the location information in the well defined formats.

Overhead. Computational overhead is concerned with the power required for processing the databases and the network while signal overhead occurs in the air and relates to the number of messages that need to be sent. Overhead needs to be taken into account when considering accuracy and precision.

Power Consumption. This is a factor at the terminal device where battery life needs to be taken into account. Usually high overhead leads to high power consumption.

Latency. This is the time delay between each position fix. Time to First Fix (TTFF) depends on the type of system used. A high TTFF is often a factor in the popularity of positioning systems with everyday users.

Roll-out and Operating Costs. Roll-out costs are the costs involved with setting up the infrastructure. Operating costs depend on the complexity of the infrastructure.

Table 1. Comparison of the Positioning Techniques

LDT	Location Accuracy	Time to Fix	Remarks
GPS	- High Precision - Sky Line of Sight - 5 to 20 meters	- 10 to15 mins start time - 1 to 2 second updates	- Device support only (HW) - This is useful for the car navigation, vehicle tracking. - It does not require network operator support.
A-GPS	- Very High - Sky Line of Sight -5 to 50 meters	- 10 to 40 second start time - 5 to10 seconds updates	- Requires GPS hardware. - Needs network operator support for the location determination. - Useful for the mobile devices.
WCDMA/ GSM/ CDMA	- Medium Strength - Depends on cell density 40 to 400 meters	- 6 to10 seconds start and update time.	- Requires Base Station Support (BSS), Mobile Switch Center (MSC) and HLR support and usually always requires - Network operator involvement
Cell-ID	- Quite Weak - Dependent on cell density - 100 to 5500 meters	- 4 to 8 seconds start and update time.	- Needs Mobile Switch Center (MSC) and Home Location Register (HLR) support, or requires device and Cell-ID database.
WiFi	- Quite Strong - Dependent on WiFi AP density < 50 to 250 meters	- 4 to 8 seconds start and update time.	- Device and network support. - Requires WiFi DB.

While GPS has solved most of the outdoor real time positioning problems, it fails to repeat this success indoors. A number of technologies have been used to address the indoor tracking problem and indeed for movement within university campuses. The ability to track the location of people indoors accurately has many applications including medical, military, logistical and social. However, current systems cannot provide continuous real time tracking of a moving target or else they lose capability when coverage is poor. Some of the popular indoor positioning methods are Wi-Fi Positioning, Cellular Positioning, RFID, Infra-RED (IR), and Bluetooth based positioning.

5.2   Spatial Databases and GeoData Mining

Spatial database is optimized to store and query data related to objects in space, including points, lines and polygons i.e. Census Data, terabytes of data satellites imagery, weather and climate data, rivers, farms, ecological impact and medical imaging. It addresses the growing data management and analysis needs of spatial applications such as geographic information systems. It has been an active area of research for couple of decades. Many research problems exist at the logical level of query processing, including query-cost modeling and strategies for nearest neighbor, bulk loading as well as queries related to fields and networks. Query processing in spatial databases containing obstacles, indexing fuzzy data types are some open problems. However, very little work has been done on file clustering and on indices for network spaces such as road maps, telephone networks. Approaches for concurrency-control techniques are needed for spatial indices. The spatial temporal databases are another recent research trend in this area. There a need to apply spatial data management accomplishments to newer applications, such as data warehouses and multimedia information systems. The techniques developed for spatial data management have been driven by the specific applications hence they are mostly not generalized [31].

5.3   LBS QoS (Quality of Services)

With increasing attractiveness of location-based services (LBS), the need for consistent establishment and deployment of the LBS Quality of Service (QoS) hierarchy is strongly demanded [20]. LBS QoS is primarily concerned with position estimation performance, including position estimation errors and response time, achieved by either single position sensor, or a combination of several position estimation sensors and methods. Common LBS QoS establishment approach consists of either "as-is" (i. e. no-guarantee) or "best-effort" (no-guarantee, but with some concern) approach. The LBS QoS has following key points that should be considered:

LBS Quality Assessment. The speed, memory, processing, power consumption, response time, errors on the location estimation and services are some of the LBS quality parameters.

QoS Aware LBS System Modeling. No-Guarantee model, AS-IS model, Best Effort model, guaranteed models are some of the models that are considered depending on the service requirements.

QoS Friendly Navigation Systems. Quality aware location determination, seamless zooming and panning of the maps. The navigation systems are real time applications and need real time system response. For example, there is no use of the instruction "take a right turn" after crossing the intended crossing. It should prompt the turn instruction in well advance so that the user can be prepared. Taking a quick turn in a moving car at high speed could be life critical.

Privacy and Safety Systems. Quality aware privacy protection services, QoS aware traffic safety solutions, for example, predicting if the car coming towards you is in unusual state. The location based incident history data mining can be used to warn the tourists for the dangerous and accident sensitive tourist spots.

5.4   Location Privacy and Authorization

An advertisement where a shopper received a coupon for 10% discount on this mobile device while walking by that coffee shop indicates that the shopper is being tracked in some ways. This is important to share the user's location in order to get the services; however it is also important considering the location privacy and user security. There are various techniques to hide the user's location; however it is still a topic of research for the researchers [14]:

Authorization and Access Control. There are issues to answer the questions: "who and when is allowed to access my location?"; "who is allowed to access what service?".

Location Privacy. The privacy solutions with personalized privacy policies versus performance tradeoffs are on the horizon of LBS research. Location obfuscation techniques, location blurring techniques, and privacy protection strategies (dynamic/static data based) are the key privacy methods.

Identity Privacy. Ubiquitous anonymity within the user device and k-anonymity are the ways to hide the user's identity while revealing the location to the service providers. The anonymity can be achieved by using a trusted middleware or by using pseudonym while communicating to the location based service providers (LSP). The pseudonym generation at the client device and communicating directly with the LSP is still a challenge as hiding the real identity creates issues of authentication and transaction accountability.

5.5   GeoSocial Networks

Many a times, it is important to know the person's physical location to know what their background or interests are. For example, a network of business partners based in

California might be interested in meeting one another face-to-face, or one of the customers in Chicago might like to find a local developer who can meet with them in their offices. The members connected in such community may search, browse, and connect with one another based on their location as well as their expertise. The Fig. 5 shows a screen of GeoSocial network developed by a company known as Leverage Software using Google Maps APIs that allows the member search around a region [30].

Geosocial Networking is a social networking in which geographic services and capabilities such as geocoding and geotagging are used to enable additional social dynamics. User-submitted location data or geolocation techniques can allow social networks to connect and coordinate users with local people or events that match their interests. Geolocation on web-based social network services can be IP-based or use hotspot trilateration positioning. For mobile social networks, mobile phone tracking can enable location-based services to enrich social networking [29]. The Friend Finder application, Ad-hoc networking, food sourcing, location-planning, mood-sourcing, paperless ticketing, location based gaming are some of the key examples of the geo-social networks. The users using mobile based GeoSocial network applications can get an alert – "Your School Friends are in the Same Food Court". Such systems can automatically geocode the address given by the user or it can use the relevant LDT for the mobiles. The location aware browing can be used for the web based applications to get the actual latitudes and longitude coordinates [8, 24]. The research challenges include geo-relation mining, system and framework designing, geo-clusters, co-occurrence analysis, information retrieval and storage techniques, information processing, and performance analysis.

Fig. 5. GeoSocial Network Web Application (Leverage Software Inc)

5.6   GeoSensor and GeoAdhoc Networks

Increasing decentralization is a widespread feature of information system architectures, made possible by the advances in computer networks over the past two decades. Decentralized information systems are acknowledged as offering several advantages over centralized architectures, including improved reliability, scalability, and performance. In a conventional location-based service, each mobile user accesses information services from remote service providers, which perform the task of capturing, managing, and updating any information relevant to their application domain. The centralized remote service provider can act as a weak point in the system. The bottleneck of a single access point decreases system reliability and performance. Advances in sensor technology and the development of inexpensive small-form, general-purpose computing platforms have lead to the study of sensor networks. Sensor networks comprise multiple miniature "PCs", each of which contains a CPU, volatile and stable memory, short-range wireless communication, battery power, and attached sensors. The on-board sensors are used to collect information about the physical world, like temperature, humidity, or the current location of objects. Sensor nodes can be deployed in high density within the physical world and enable the continuous measurement of phenomena in unprecedented detail. A geo-sensor network is defined as a sensor network that monitors phenomena in geographic space [18]. The advent of nanotechnology makes it feasible to deploy low cost, low power devices with on-board sensing and wireless communications capabilities. As a result the fields of GIS and remote sensing face multiple research challenges related to real-time geosensor data collection, data analysis, information management and delivery. Some common geo-sensor applications are: traffic sensors and transportation modeling, ecology observation systems – i.e. assess plant health and growth circumstances, observe and measure geophysical processes and real-time event detection – i.e. volcano sensor network. The geo-sensor networks can be used for various purposes:

Emergency Services. Sensing with active landmarks, low-end devices communicating with GPS enabled devices, resource sharing in the rural and remote areas.

Data Acquisition and Processing. Data selection and queries to geo-sensors, data storage and access model and optimizations, load management and high availability.

Data Analysis and Integration. Visual geo-sensors for 3D sensing, mining geo-sensor data and event predictions, and using geo-sensor data into a variety of applications.

5.7   Location Based Recommender Systems (LBRS)

Web based recommender systems are quite common and are in general using traditional content based, collaborative or hybrid techniques for delivering personalized contents. Since location based systems typically involves "physical entities" (i.e. a shopping center) therefore we cannot directly apply existing web recommendation techniques to

LBRS. The current generation of location-based recommendation does not provide users with personalized recommendations, but mostly suggests nearby POIs based on their distance from the user current location. The new generation of Recommendation Systems (RS) needs to identify user preferences, information needs and aspect related to the context of use, thus suggesting personalized recommendations related to possible POIs in the surroundings. Therefore the location based recommendation techniques should be able to integrate location information, customer needs, and vendor offerings for the success of businesses. Following are some of the challenges for the success of LBRS:

Scalability, Convenience and Latency. High scalability, user convenience, and low latency must be the key requirement while making recommendations in LBRS. These systems have to be scalable to handle to support a rapidly expanding population of mobile users and information. Such RS indicate a very high potential of a users to follow-up on the recommendation – thus, a mobile user requesting a recommendation typically wants to know not about the best match, but rather about the best match that also happens to be conveniently-situated given his current location. Location based recommender system need to provide more appropriate information as the user is not willing to spend much of the time in selecting the information from a small screen device and entering a large amount of inputs through slow input interfaces. Since user carries a more resource-limited device, therefore more specific information should be provided [26].

Dynamic Environment Adaption. LBS pay more emphasis on the dynamics and diversity of the information provided to the user. From the perspective of a mobile user, the environment is ever-changing as user moves from one location to another. Therefore adaptability to the changing environment plays an important role in LBRS.

P2P Architecture. Most of the current recommender systems are based on centralized architecture and the techniques used in such recommender systems are not suitable for P2P environment. P2P architecture is attractive as centralized architecture suffers from shortage in scalability [27]. Even though there has been much work done in the industry and academia on RS research, issues such as sparsity, scalability, cold start problem and accuracy still remain a challenge in LBRS. Therefore P2P architecture can be used as an alternative solution to overcome the problems of traditional recommender systems. People with similar interest are now a day's connected with social networks. The idea of social network can be exploited to provide efficient recommendation in P2P environment.

5.8   Location Based Natural Queries

Another enhancement that may be crucial to the business success of the LBS systems is the use of natural language. Multilingual capabilities in LBS systems will play a major role for tourism industry, location based learning, and navigation systems for the physically challenged people. The interactive LBS queries can be taken in natural languages that will make the system more interactive and user friendly. Most of the current LBS systems take the input through the form based user interface. The free form natural language input in the form of text or speech would be very useful for the technology fledgling users. The natural language queries like – "create me a route from A to B via C"; "where is the nearest ATM?"; "where is my kid this time?" would increase the usability of the system. The phonetic location searches (accent aware location searches), and natural language analysis for geo-spatial relations are some of the research challenges in this area.

6   Conclusion

We have briefly reviewed some of the important technologies, market players, and the research issues in LBS. We discussed the emerging telecommunication platforms and positioning systems along with issues related to contemporary mobile computing. The LBS is surely an area of modern mobile services where considerable growth is observed. The developments in the internet domain, wireless/mobile networking as well as the proliferation of positioning technologies expedited such evolution. The impact on nomadic users is tremendous. The technologies and issues involved in LBS deployment and provision cover a very wide spectrum including operating system capabilities, user interface design, positioning techniques, terminal technologies, and network capabilities. We have also investigated the latest LBS trends and development in this survey. The broad research areas like location determination techniques, geo-sensor and geo-adhoc networks, location based natural queries, location privacy and authorization, geo-social networks, location based recommendation systems (LBRS) and LBS QoS have been studied and presented briefly.

References

1. Global GPS Navigation and Location Based Services Forecast, by IE Market xResearch Corp. ID: IEMR2747104 (2010 – 2014)
2. Weir, C.: Wireless Technology: Location Based Services: A Prototype for Metropolitan Bangkok (2004) A blog at, `http://lbsopinions-asia.blogspot.com` (last accessed on September 27, 2011)
3. The 2011 Ultimate Guide to Location Based Services and Applications. Mind Commerce Publishing. ID: CCJQ6057007
4. Official Google Blog: Go that away: Google Maps India learns to navigate like a local, `http://googleblog.blogspot.com/2009/12/go-thataway-google-maps-india-learns-to.html` (last accessed on August 28, 2011)
5. Di Flora, C., et al.: GenMod: A Generic Architecture for Mobile Location Dependent Services. In: Proceedings of International Conference on Distributed Computing Systems - ICDCS (Workshop), pp. 244–250 (2005)
6. Schiller, J., et al.: Location-Based Services, pp. 29–32. Morgan Kaufmann Publishers, ISBN: 1-55860-929-6
7. Geolocation in Firefox, `http://www.mozilla.com/en-US/firefox/geolocation/` (last accessed on August 24, 2011)

8. IP Based Location Services, QUALCOMM, Incorporated. 3GPP2 S.R0066-0, Version Date (April 17, 2003)

9. Hile, H., et al.: Landmark-Based Pedestrian Navigation with Enhanced Spatial Reasoning. In: Proceedings of the 7th International Conference on Pervasive Computing. Springer, Heidelberg (2009)

10. Adams, P.M., et al.: Location-based services — an overview of the standards. BT Technology Journal 21(1) (January 2003)

11. Rainio, A.: Location-Based Services And Personal Navigation In Mobile Information Society. In: Proceedings of International Conference FIG Working Week, pp. 6–11 (2001)

12. Le, M.H.V.: Indoor Navigation System for Handheld Devices. Worcester Polytechnic Institute, Worcester (October 22, 2009)

13. LBS Technology Overview, http://www.timdavis.com.au/mobile/location-based-services-lbs-technology-overview/ (last accessed on August 25, 2011)

14. Chen, F., et al.: Research on Mobile GIS Based on LBS. In: IEEE International Conference. 0-7803-9050-4/05. IEEE (2005)

15. Location Based Services Market 2008-2013, The Insight Research Corporation. New Jersey, USA, 07005 (2008)

16. Open Geospatial Consortium, http://en.wikipedia.org/wiki/Open_Geospatial_Consortium (last accessed on August 25, 2011)

17. Location Based Services: Considerations and Challenges, Northstream AB (2001), http://www.northstream.se

18. Nittel, S., et al.: Information Dissemination in Mobile Ad-Hoc Geosensor Networks. In: Proc. GIScience, pp. 206–222 (2004)

19. Mokbel, M.F.: Privacy in Location-based Services: State of the art and Research Directions. Department of Computer Science and Engineering, University of Minnesota (2007)

20. Renato, F., et al.: LBS Position Estimation by Adaptive Selection of Positiojning Sensor based on Requested QoS. Springer, Heidelberg (2008)

21. Kaushik, S., et al.: Reducing Dependency on Middleware for Pull Based Active Services in LBS Systems. In: Senac, O., Ott, M., Seneviratne, A. (eds.) ICWCA 2011. LNICST, vol. 72, pp. 90–106 (2011)

22. Location Based System Architecture, http://www.e-cartouche.ch/content_reg/cartouche/LBStech/en/html/unit_LBStechU4.html (last accessed on August 27, 2011)

23. LBS and Field Services: Current Trands – Directions Magazine, http://www.directionsmag.com/articles/lbs-and-field-service-current-trends/122502 (last Accessed on August 27, 2011)

24. NENA Recommended Method(s) for Location Determination to Support IP-Based Emergency Services Technical Information Document NENA 08-505, Issue 1 (December 21, 2006)

25. Curran, K., et al.: Investigations In Location Awareness. JANET Network Access Programme. Intelligent Systems Research Centre, Faculty of Computing and Engineering, University of Ulster (2009)

26. Mekouar, L., et al.: A Recommender Scheme for Peer-to-Peer Systems. In: International Symposium on Applications and the Internet. IEEE (2008)

27. Horozov, T., et al.: Using Location For Personalized POI Recommendations In Mobile Environments. In: Proceedings of the International Symposium on Applications on Internet, January 23-27, pp. 124–129 (2006)

28. Lee, J., et al.: Design and Implementation of a Tour Planning System for Telematics Users. In: Gervasi, O., Gavrilova, M.L. (eds.) ICCSA 2007, Part III. LNCS, vol. 4707, pp. 179–189. Springer, Heidelberg (2007)
29. Geosocial networking, `http://en.wikipedia.org/wiki/Geosocial_networking` (last accessed on August 27, 2011)
30. `http://community.leveragesoftware.com/wiki_entry_view.aspx?topicid=061d9b22c7b34545b0d617db41291e80` (last accessed on September 26, 2011)
31. Shekhar, S., et al.: A Tour of Spatial Databases, pp. 21–30. Prentice Hall Publications (2001)

Using Middleware as a Certifying Authority in LBS Applications

Priti Jagwani[1], Shivendra Tiwari[2], and Saroj Kaushik[2]

[1] School of Information Technology
[2] Dept. of Computer Science and Engg.,
Indian Institute of Technology, Hauz Khas, New Delhi, India 110016
jagwani.priti@gmail.com,
{saroj,shivendra}@cse.iitd.ac.in

Abstract. The trusted middleware is the most commonly used solution to address the location privacy in location based services as generally such service providers are un-trusted entities that can be adversary attack sensitive points. The authors proposed an alternative solution which helps in avoiding a bottleneck in the existing system in terms of performance and availability as the entire client's service transactions are routed through the middleware to the actual Location Based Service Providers (LSP). In the proposed solution, the client and the LSPs can directly communicate with the same level of location security, privacy and anonymity. The trusted middleware is used as certifying authority that generates authentication certificates which contains the Proxy Identity (also called Pseudonyms), and the services subscribed with validity period. The encrypted certificate fulfills the authentication requirements at the LSP servers. In this paper we are reporting the implementation of the proposed system as a proof of concept using Struts Technology of Java. While evaluating the system features such as response time, delay, drop rate etc., the Google Map's location services and the internet browser have been considered as a service provider and client respectively. Performance analysis of our solution and that of prevalent architecture is done using Packmime model for http traffic generation of NS2 (Network Simulator 2) tool. The comparative graphs of the simulation results show that the proposed solution is better in terms of throughput, response time, drop rate and scalability in comparison to the existing middleware architectures in which the request response is every time routed through middleware, thus increasing the overheads.

Keywords: Location Based Services (LBS), Trusted Middleware, Information Security, Authorization, Pseudonyms, Location Based Service Provider (LSP), Location Privacy, NS2, Middleware Performance Analysis.

1 Introduction

Location Based Services (LBS) technologies are used in a wide variety of services such as entertainment, information, alert etc. which are accessible through wireless network on computers and mobile devices. LBS systems comprises of actors such as

S. Kikuchi et al. (Eds.): DNIS 2011, LNCS 7108, pp. 242–255, 2011.

content providers (also called LSP), operators, virtual operators and service administrators etc, all of which can be separate entities. Actual location aware service is provided by LSP that has automatic access to a customer's location. Since the simultaneous observation of the "location, time and identity" of the user creates a threat to user's privacy, LSP should never know the customer's identity or a combination of it along with "location" and/or "time" attributes. Out of three attributes, the "identity" of the user has the highest importance from privacy point of view. The middleware manages a very large number of information providers and high volatility of users' interests. Currently, the middleware architecture is considered to be trusted approach which acts as a three way privacy mediator between the law, the users and the location service providers (LSPs). The use of the middleware as a single window system ensures greater security but at the same time it has to support high availability, service accounting, security and privacy functions etc [15, 16, 18, and 20]. Fig.1 shows the prevalent architecture with Middleware as an entity which interacts with the content providers (LSP) to get various services for client.

Yingying Chen, et al [7] proposed a trusted middleware for facilitating the access control of the location information by ensuing that the mobile devices are only able to access the location information that conforms to their privileges. Pseudonyms are used by Christian Hauser [6] for handling Identity Privacy. Hua Wang et al [12] proposed the ticket based service access scheme for the mobile users which talks about the mobile databases accessed across multiple service domains anonymously. However in their approach, users have to contact the credential center for the ticket clearance all the time.

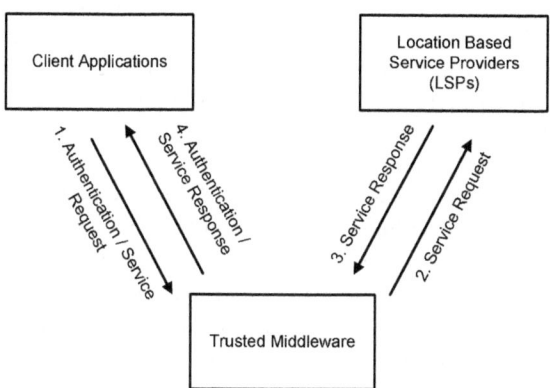

Fig. 1. Transaction Flow in Currently Prevalent Architecture

S. Kaushik et al [20] proposed a new solution as that solves the problem of middleware being bottleneck. The new architecture mainly targets a variety of applications where the availability of the services is probably more important than the location security. The client and the LSPs can communicate directly. Autonomy on the client-server communication increases the possibility of communication even in the scenarios where the middleware is not available due to some unforeseen reasons. It also handles the authentication and security challenges that rise due to independent communication among client and LSP. The trusted middleware is used to generate the authentication certificates containing the Pseudonym to fulfill the authentication requirements at the LSP servers. The rest of transactions among the clients and the LSPs are accomplished independently. Further, the level of anonymity can be tuned by altering pseudonyms generation techniques i.e. "One-to-One", "One-to-Many" and "Many-to-One" depending on the type of the service and security requirements. It also attempts to maintain almost the same level of security for the targeted services.

This paper is the extension of the new flexible middleware architecture proposed by S. Kaushik et al [20]. We have implemented the prototype and analyzed the performance of the new system. The applications of the proposed architecture are mainly pull based applications such as Proximity Search, Turn by Turn Navigation, Geocoding and Reverse Geocoding, Location Based Advertisement, and Near-Me Area Network etc.

The paper consists of various sections. Section 1 gives an introduction of the domain and related research work. Section 2 contains a brief description of the flexible architecture proposed in [20] by the authors. Sections 3 and 4 contain the prototype implementation and Performance Analysis. The limitation and future research possibilities are given in section 5 and finally paper is concluded in section 6.

2   The Flexible Middleware Based System

2.1   Flexible Middleware Architecture

The solution proposed by S. Kaushik et al [20] give rise to flexible middleware based system. The block diagram of the new system is shown in Fig. 2. It mainly consists of three modules i.e. The Client or User Application, the Un-trusted Location Based Service or content Providers, and the Trusted Middleware. The user Authentication and Subscription Management, certificate generation, service request routing, location determination and billing are the key responsibilities of the middleware. The middleware is mainly divided into three parts – Authentication, Service Routing, and the Billing Management module. The Authentication module takes care of the verification of the client's subscription and authenticity. The service request module routes the request to the desired LSP which is as per the old architecture. The Billing management module handles the transaction billing activities. The middleware generates a Pseudonym against a user to hide user's real identity. The applicability of the pseudonyms enables the user to make it anonymous. But on the other hand service provider needs to know if the client is authenticated or client is authorized for the requested service and the period of service availability. This is solved by usage of certificates. The detailed architecture of the proposed system is shown in Fig.2.

Flexibility of the New Architecture. The new architecture is flexible as it can also work as old system where each service request and response is routed through middleware which works as a transaction router. Alternatively, the proposed system can disassociate middleware after generating the certificate(s). Now actual service transactions take place between the client and LSP based on the certificate(s). In this mode middleware works as a certifying authority.

Levels of Anonymity. The new architecture supports different level of anonymity. The AES encryption method has been used to encrypt the user identity to generate a pseudonym. The same user identity is encrypted with the different keys, hence achieves multiple levels of anonymity. Any other symmetric cryptography technique can be used in place of AES/ DES but AES DES algorithms are also safe in our case as the key itself lies with the middleware only, so getting key is not easy.

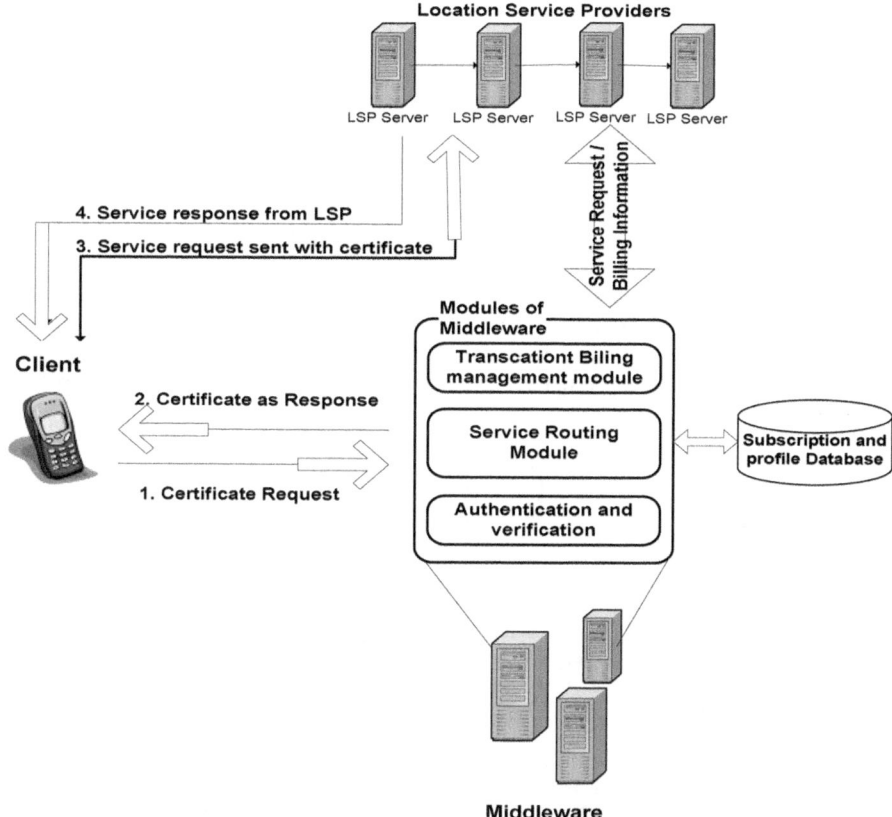

Fig. 2. The Flexible Middleware Architecture with Transaction Flow

Functioning of the proposed system is clear from the above figure. Initially the client sends an authentication request to middleware. In response to the request, the middleware sends a properly encrypted certificate to client containing pseudonym, services subscriptions and service validity. Hence after that the client can directly interact with LSP by sending this certificate along with the service request. This certificate will solve the user authentication problem. Functions of middleware [20] are described briefly as follows:

The Client Authentication. The client initially gets the Authentication Certificate; which will be used for the subsequent request to the location server (LSP).

The middleware generates the pseudonym(s) according to the user's requested level of anonymity. The middleware includes all the required access control information into the certificate like services subscribed and temporal validity of the certificate. The access control information should be stored in the LSP server for the running session with the pseudonym for verifying subsequent requests. The certificate is digitally signed by middleware so as to ensure that the certificate is actually generated by middleware.

Service Billing at Middleware. Middleware keeps the subscription database for each registered user. LSP sends pseudonym and the corresponding transaction records to middleware which decrypts the pseudonym to get the actual username and generates the bills for the specified client.

2.2   Pseudonym Generation

Fig. 3 shows the pseudonym generation and recovering of the real identity from the given pseudonym. The "Key Selector" module of the middleware selects a key randomly from the key-list available with it and encryption module generates pseudonym using the key and user name with Data Encryption Standard (DES)/ Advanced Encryption Standard (AES) method given in [8]. AES/DES algorithms are safe in our case as the key itself lies with the middleware only, so getting key is not easy. However, any other symmetric cryptography technique can be used in place of AES/ DES.

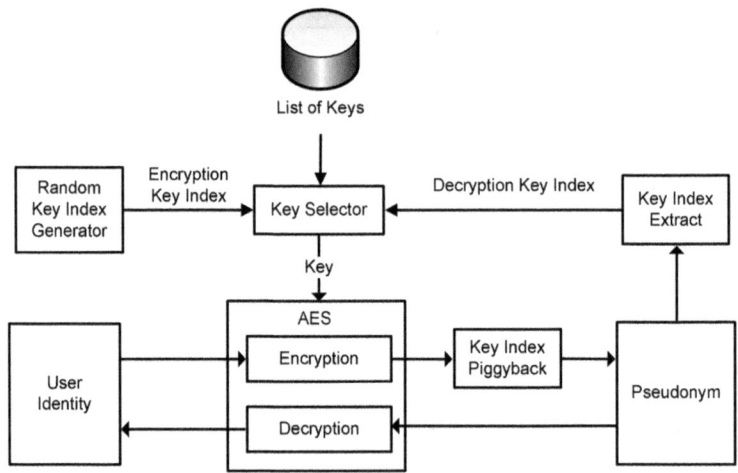

Fig. 3. Pseudonym Generation and Recovering User-id – Flow Diagram

The key index is suffixed with pseudonym for recovering actual identity from a pseudonym by middleware at the time of billing. The new architecture handles the security requirements with multi-level anonymity. For a scenario with rigorous privacy requirements, one can opt for "Many-to-One" or "One-to-Many" pseudonym schemes. Use of these two schemes makes the chances of a user being tracked, very low. One can argue on the reliability of the different anonymity levels. As a drawback, while using the

"One-to-Many" pseudonyms, samples of multiple transactions having the same control information and other attributes may lead to identify the pattern of the requests, in the worst case. Even if the multiple transactions are mapped to one pseudonym, the scenario boils down to a "One-to-One" pseudonym. It still doesn't reveal the user's real identity.

2.3   Certificate Generation at Middleware

The CERT is an XML based certificate that is encrypted by the public key of an LSP (named as LSP-PU) and encrypted certificate LSP-CERT is generated as shown below and is bounded to a particular LSP.

$$\text{LSP-CERT} = E_{\text{LSP-PU}}(\text{CERT}) \tag{1}$$

The LSP-CERT is finally digitally singed by the middleware with its private key (named as MD-PR) and generates the final encrypted certificate CERT_SIGNED as shown below.

$$\text{CERT-SIGNED} = EMD\text{-}PR(\text{LSP-CERT}) \tag{2}$$

Here EK(C) stands for encryption function AES (Advanced Encryption Standard) applied using key K on certificate C.

2.4   Certificate Decryption and Validation at LSP

The certificate is validated and decrypted at the LSP in order to decide whether the client requesting a service is authenticated. The middleware public key MD-PU is used for the decryption of the signed certificate. However the LSP's private key LSP-PR is used to decrypt the final LSP certificate.

Decrypt the certificate with middleware's public key MD-PU:

$$\text{LSP-CERT} = D_{\text{MD-PU}}(\text{CERT-SIGNED}) \tag{3}$$

Decrypt the LSP-CERT with LSP's private key LSP-PR is done as:

$$\text{CERT} = D_{\text{LSP-PR}}(\text{LSP-CERT}) \tag{4}$$

Even though pseudonymization is not a very secure technique but we are introducing another level of security by writing pseudonym in certificate which is coded cryptographically or digitally signed in the proposed architecture.

3   Prototype Implementation

Providing applications with increased levels of service availability and same level of security as that of prevalent architectures has been the holy grail of the proposed system. The Flexible Middleware architecture has been derived from a pragmatic assessment of pull based LBS requirements. There are a large number of pull based application scenarios in which this architecture will work excellent such as geocoding and reverse geocoding, turn by turn navigation, POI search, near me area network etc.

Current section discusses prototype implementation of the above said system. Prototype of the proposed system for the present study was custom built by authors. It is implemented taking Point of Interest (POI) search as an example application. The main objective of prototype implementation and simulation is to evaluate the proposed system in a statistically rigorous manner. The criteria for simulation are response time, security, reliability, overall performance etc.

3.1   Implementation Environment

The advanced Java technology mainly JSP, Servlets and Struts are used as main building blocks of the prototype software system. Three main components namely client, middleware and server of the proposed architecture are implemented. We have considered only one level of anonymity that is one-one anonymity (pseudonym) in implementation for the sake of brevity. The prototype is tested rigorously for a handful of users generated in order to check for any collision or clashes for the generated pseudonyms. Tools used to implement three components mentioned above are described briefly as follows.

Client. Internet Browsers, mobile devices, PDA and Desktop applications can be the potential clients. Here for the prototype implementation simply web browser is taken as a client.

Middleware. It is the core component of the architecture. For middleware functionality JSP, Servlets and Struts are used. Apache Tomcat 6.0 is used as the web-server while Oracle is used as the backend to manage user subscriptions and profile databases.

Server. For the functionality of location Service Provider Google APIs are used.

3.2   Simulation Tool and Topology Setup

After implementation, the prototype is simulated under various real scenarios using Network Simulator 2 (NS2). It is a discrete event simulator targeted at networking research. NS2 provides substantial support for simulation of TCP, routing, and multicast protocols over wired and wireless networks. PackMime is a model of HTTP traffic in NS2 tool, called PackMime-HTTP. The goal of packmime http is to simulate the internet traffic generated between a cloud of clients and a cloud of servers rather than focusing on traffic between a single client and a server. The traffic intensity generated by PackMime-HTTP is controlled by the rate parameter, which is the average number of new HTTP connections started each second. The PackMime-HTTP implementation in NS2 is capable of generating HTTP connections [21]. This model is used along with the delay boxes to introduce delay at different components of network.

For simulation, topologies are setup for both the architectures containing appropriate components like client cloud, server cloud and middleware. These cloud components are generated using packmime model. Further, links with appropriate delay and bandwidth are setup between them. Finally simulation data is collected. All simulations are run for a fixed time interval.

As a result of simulation, different trace files are generated containing various parameters. For trace files, different levels of outputs have been set. On the basis of these output levels, trace files will contain different parameters like delay, packets dropped, response time etc. These trace files have been generated for statistics at various ends like client, server, middleware etc.

By analyzing the two models to be compared, it has been observed that old architecture is similar to a network scenario in which middleware act as a router. Every time the request from client and response from server has to route through middleware only, so it acts as a bottleneck. This model can easily be simulated in NS2 taking middleware as the routing point. At this router, we need to introduce a delay of some amount of time for authentication activity. This authentication activity is performed with every request. Also some fraction of the processing time (at middleware) is also devoted to obfuscation or any other anonymity technique to make the user anonymous.

While in the proposed architecture, a certificate is to be generated at middleware end and sent to the client, hence we need to analyze the certificate generation cost. The certificates are generated for a fixed temporal validity. Hence the certificates are "generate once and use many times" entity. It takes around 3 seconds to send client a request and getting back the encrypted certificate as response, in the real prototype implementation. Since the certificate generation happens in a fixed time interval; the effect of the time taken would be very diminutive when it is spread over real service transactions which are taking place practically within minutes. Also this cost of certificate generation is amortized by the long length of request in old architecture.

4   Performance Analysis and Results

For simulation, the real values measured and taken from real prototype are plugged into various parameters of the topology setup. The scalability of the two models has been tested with the increasing number of requests generated per second from client cloud with variable transaction data size. Every data set in simulation is run and tested at least 5 times, so that error factor (if any) can be taken care of. Graphs for these scenarios are presented below.

4.1   Response Time with Variable Number of Clients

Response time is the time elapsed between the end of an inquiry or demand on a system and the beginning of a response. For the first set of results, both the architectures were simulated for varying number of requests generated (50, 500, 2500, 5000, 25000 and 50000) per second and response time is noted down. The request and response size are kept fixed. On X axis, we have taken increasing no. of requests and on Y axis, response time per http flow in 'ms' is plotted.

It can be clearly seen that with increasing no. of clients (i.e., no. of request generated /sec) response time is increasing with a rapid rate in the old architecture. After 5000 request/ sec, the slope in old architecture is becoming steep indicating sudden increase in response time.

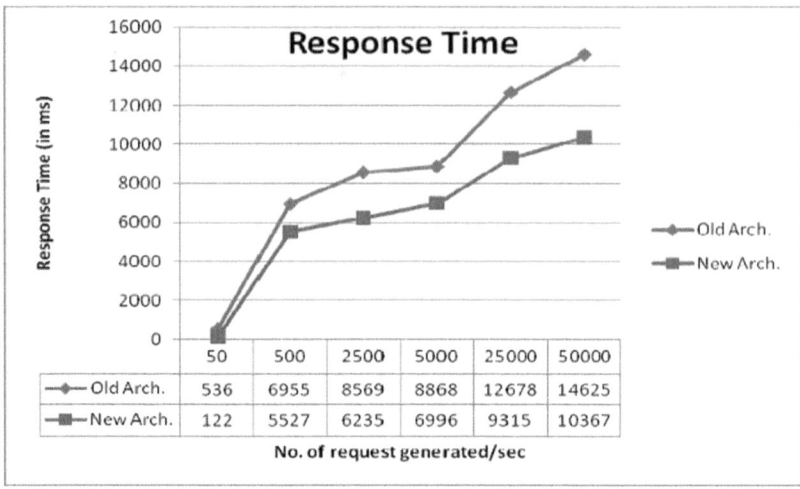

Fig. 4. Response Time vs. varying number of Requests Generated

4.2 Delay with Variable Number of Clients

Using the delay boxes with packmime http model, delays per http flow or connection have been calculated. This delay is actually the network delay; that is total amount of time required by the network to transport a packet from its point of origin to its destination. It is obtained by the use of delay boxes in packmime http model. In the above graph, delay is shown on Y axis vs. number of requests generated on X axis. The request and response sizes are kept fixed and number of request generated / sec are being varied (increased).

It is clear from the graph that delay with number of requests generated per sec in new architecture is marginally increased in contrast to the old system where it increases drastically resulting in poor through put.

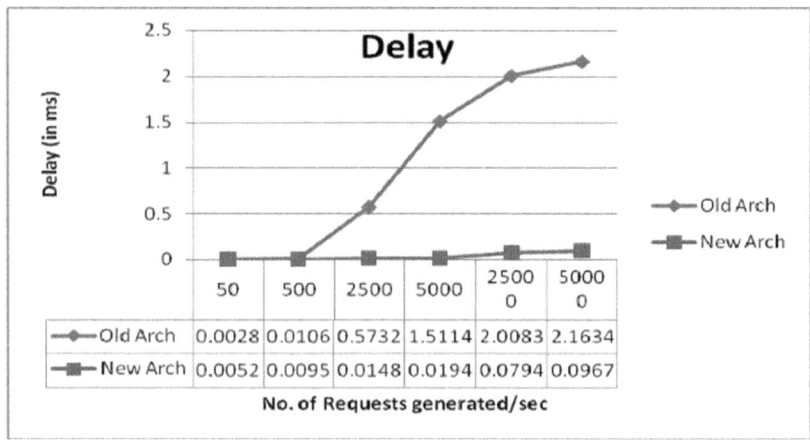

Fig. 5. Delay vs. varying number of Request Generated

4.3   Drop Rate with Variable Number of Clients

We have also analyzed the drop rate at server end with increasing number of requests generated/sec. In the following graph, increasing number of requests are shown on X axis while drop rate (in %) is taken on Y axis.

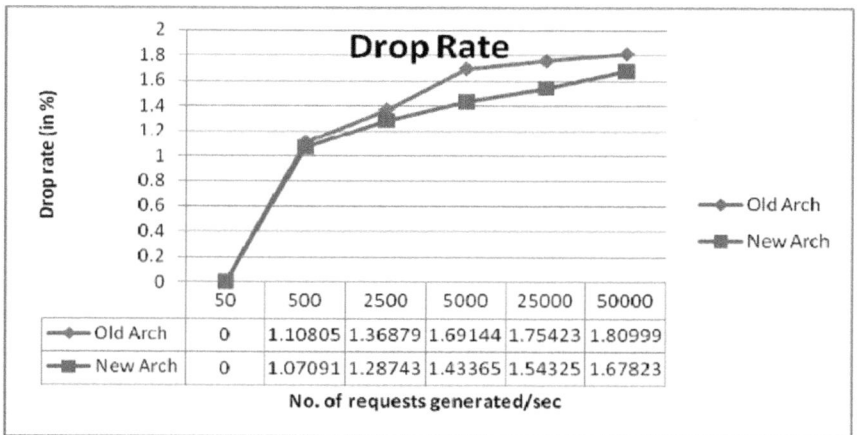

Fig. 6. Drop Rate vs. number of requests

This drop rate is calculated by dividing number of packets dropped by total number of packets transmitted. Total number of packets transmitted is visible in trace files while number of packets dropped can be obtained by setting the appropriate output level of trace files. It is clear from the above graph that initially with less number of requests generated/sec, drop rate is zero but with increasing requests, it starts increasing in both the architectures but rate of increment is more for old architecture.

4.4   Response Time with Variable Request/Response Size

For the graph presented below, the request transaction rate has been kept fixed to 500/sec; however the transaction data size is varying. Response time is taken for request and response sizes of 0.1vs 1k, 0.5 vs 5 k, 1k vs 10k, 5k vs 50 k and 10k vs 100k. Response time is taken on Y axis and increasing sizes of requests and responses on X axis.

Here with increasing request and response sizes, response time is increasing in both the architectures which is an obvious behavior. However, in the old architecture this time is increasing at a rapid rate resulting in slow responses and bad throughputs.

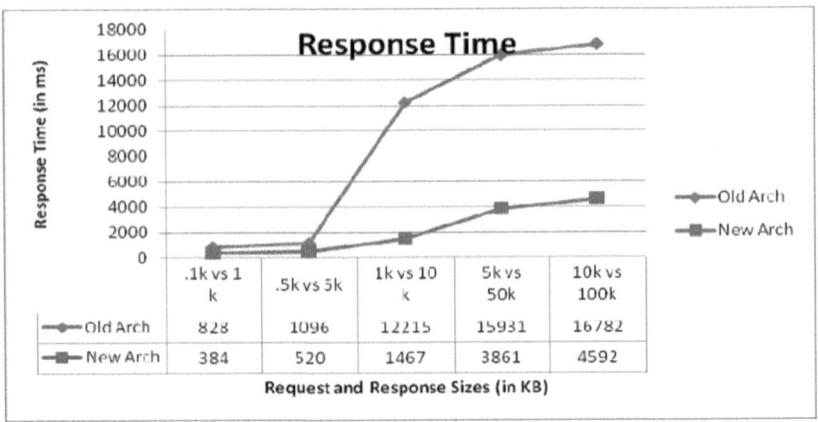

Fig. 7. Response Time vs. Varying Request and Response Sizes

4.5   Delay with Variable Request/Response Size

The graph below shows delay in case of different request and response sizes keeping number of request generated as constant to 500. Delay is plotted on Y axis and increasing size of requests and responses on the X axis. As on the similar lines as that of previous graphs, delay is drastically getting increased in old architecture.

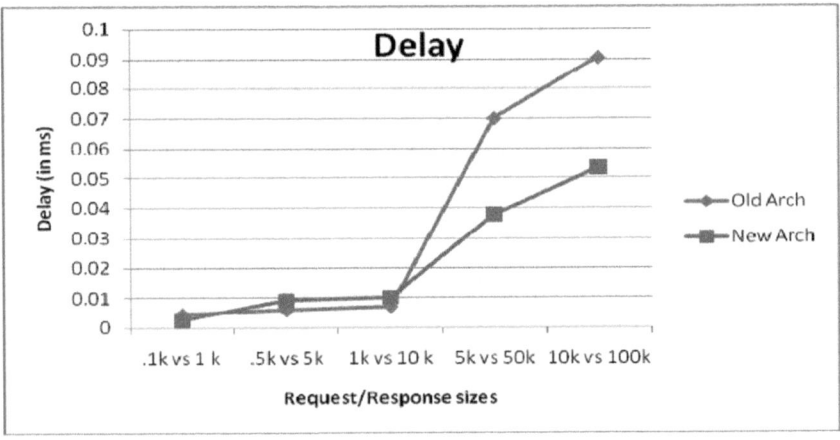

Fig. 8. Delay vs. Varying Request and Response Sizes

4.6   Drop Rate with Variable Request/Response Size

The graph in Fig. 9 depicts drop rate at server end plotted with varying request and response sizes. Here also in new architecture drop rate is shooting up after increasing request/response sizes beyond a limit.

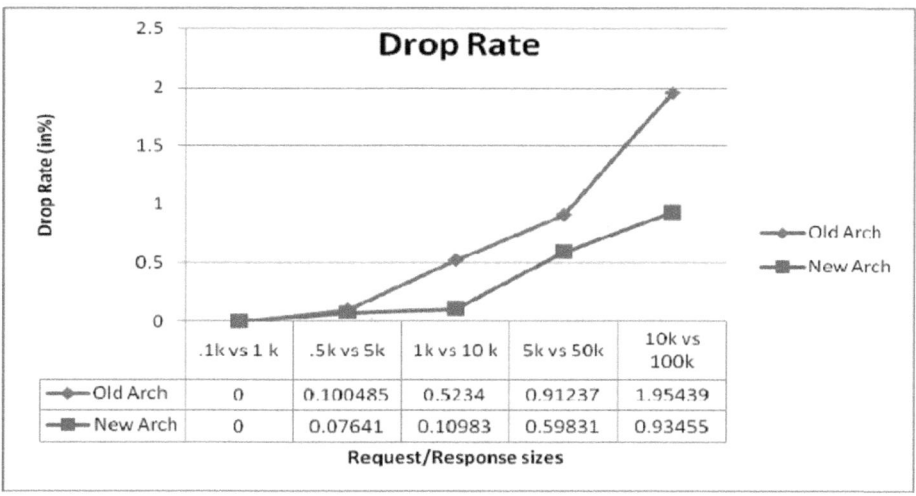

Fig. 9. Drop rate vs. Request/Response sizes

Considering all the graphs and data, it is concluded that new architecture is more acceptable and also it is performing better under heavy loads on a network in terms of response time, delay factor and drop rate also. All these metrics collectively affect overall throughput of the architecture which is greater for the new proposed system. Alternatively we can also say that as the system is supporting heavier loads, scalability is improved. Removing of bottleneck from middleware ensures high availability and reliability of the system. Also in the proposed architecture flexibility of LSP selection is given to user and service transaction autonomy is achieved as middleware is not required for actual transaction between client and LSP.

5   Limitations and Future Work

The proposed architecture is more suitable for the Pull-based Active Services and is less useful for the applications which need continuous tracking of the user such as child fencing. So an open issue is still to minimize the middleware usage for other kinds of location services (including push based services).

Presently, implementation of the prototype is done only for one-one pseudonyms. So group pseudonyms (one-many and many-one) are still to be worked upon. In case of a session loss, certificate has to be sent again to location server and thus creates another computation overhead at LSP while decrypting the certificate.

Further, certificate can be misused by the client itself by sharing it to other users. To prevent the misuse of certificate, we can associate the generated certificate to the device id or the device foot prints which ensures that the authentication certificates are used by the targeted devices only. But again this will raise an issue of only one device being used by a user for all transactions which is another constraint. This is an area of future research.

6   Conclusions

The new architecture has been derived from a pragmatic assessment of pull based LBS requirements and its prototype is implemented taking Point of Interest (POI) search as an example application. The new flexible middleware solution is a methodological way of minimizing the dependency on the middleware and enabling the direct client-LSP communication.

The criteria for building the architecture were response time, security, reliability, overall performance etc. The advanced Java technology mainly JSP, Servlets and Struts are used as main building blocks of the prototype software system. The prototype is implemented and simulated for heavier loads and the proposed system is outperforming for almost all of the measurable metrics. The comparative graphs of the simulation results show that the proposed prototype is better in terms of throughput, response time, drop rate and scalability.

References

1. Lioudakis, G.V., et al.: A Middleware architecture for privacy protection. The International Journal of Computer and Telecommunications Networking 51(16), 4679–4696 (2007)
2. Ardagna, C., Cremonini, M., Damiani, E., De Capitani di Vimercati, S., Samarati, P.: New Approaches for Security, Privacy and Trust in Complex Environments. In: Venter, H., Eloff, M., Lahuschagne, L., Eloff, J., von Solms, R. (eds.). IFIP, vol. 232, pp. 313–324. Springer, Boston (2007)
3. The European Opinion Research Group. European Union citizens' views about privacy: Special Eurobarometer 196 (December 2003)
4. Ardagna, C.A., Cremonini, M., De Capitani di Vimercati, S., Samarati, P.: Access Control in Location-Based Services. In: Bettini, C., Jajodia, S., Samarati, P., Wang, X.S. (eds.) Privacy in Location-Based Applications. LNCS, vol. 5599, pp. 106–126. Springer, Heidelberg (2009)
5. Mohan, A., Blough, D.M.: An attribute-based authorization policy framework with dynamic conflict resolution. In: Proceedings of the 9th Symposium on Identity and Trust on the Internet. ACM International Conference Proceeding Series, pp. 37–50 (2010)
6. Hauser, C., et al.: Privacy and Security in Location-Based Systems With Spatial Models. Institute of Communication Networks and Computer Engineering University of Stuttgart, Germany (2002)
7. Chen, Y., Yang, J., He, F.: A Trusted Infrastructure for Facilitating Access Control. IEEE, Los Alamitos (2008); 978-1-4244-2677-5/08/ 2008
8. Hohenberger, S., Weis, S.A.: Honest-verifier private disjointness testing without random oracles. In: Proceedings of the 6th Workshop on Privacy Enhancing Technologies, pp. 265–284 (June 2006)
9. Hauser, C., Kabatnik, M.: Towards Privacy Support in a Global Location Service. In: Proceedings of the WATM/EUNICE (2001)
10. Schiller, J., et al.: Location-Based Services, vol. 16, pp. 91–96. Morgan Kaufmann Publishers, San Francisco (2005); ISBN: 1-55860-929-6
11. Kin, Y.W.: NAN: Near-me Area Network. In: IEEE Internet Computing. IEEE computer Society Digital Library. IEEE Computer Society, Los Alamitos (2010)

12. Hua, W., et al.: Ticket-based Service Access scheme for Mobile Users. In: ACSC 2002 Proceedings of the Twenty-fifth Australasian Conference on Computer Science, vol. 4 (2002); SBN:0-909925-82-8
13. John, B., et al.: Method for Generating Digital Fingerprint Using Pseudo Random Number Code. International Patent WO 2008/094725 A1
14. Hauser, C., et al.: Privacy and Security in Location-Based Systems With Spatial Models. Institute of Communication Networks and Computer Engineering University of Stuttgart, Germany
15. Duckham, M., Kulik, L.: A Formal Model of Obfuscation and Negotiation for Location Privacy. In: Gellersen, H.-W., Want, R., Schmidt, A. (eds.) PERVASIVE 2005. LNCS, vol. 3468, pp. 152–170. Springer, Heidelberg (2005)
16. Gedik, B., Liu, L.: A Customizable k-Anonymity Model for Protecting Location Privacy. In: ICDCS 2005 (2005)
17. Magkos, E., et al.: A Distributed Privacy-Preserving Scheme for Location-Based Queries. In: Proceedings of the 2010 IEEE International Symposium on A World of Wireless, Mobile and Multimedia Networks, WoWMoM (2010)
18. Hengartner, U.: Hiding Location Information from Location-Based Services. IEEE, Los Alamitos (2007); 1-4244-1241-2/07
19. Quality Attributes, http://www.softwarearchitectures.com/go/ Discipline/DesigningArchitecture/QualityAttributes/tabid/64/ Default.aspx (last visited on April 27, 2011)
20. Kaushik, S., Tiwari, S., Goplani, P.: Reducing Dependency on Middleware for Pull Based Active Services in LBS Systems. In: Senac, O., Ott, M., Seneviratne, A. (eds.) ICWCA 2011. LNICST, vol. 72, pp. 90–106 (2011)
21. The NS manual, http://www.isi.edu/nsnam/ns/ns-documentation.html

Cache Effect for Power Savings of Large Storage Systems with OLTP Applications

Norifumi Nishikawa, Miyuki Nakano, and Masaru Kitsuregawa

Institute of Industrial Science, The University of Tokyo,
4-6-1 Komaba Meguro-ku, Tokyo 153-8505, Japan
{norifumi,miyuki,kitsure}@tkl.iis.u-tokyo.ac.jp
http://www.tkl.iis.u-tokyo.ac.jp/top/

Abstract. The power consumption of modern datacenters is increasing rapidly. Storage in datacenter consumes much power. Today, databases, especially those for OLTP, have become a major storage application in datacenters. Therefore, power-saving management for OLTP applications has become an important task for user budgets and datacenter operations. This paper presents a description of a novel power-saving method for large storage systems based on application I/O behavior of OLTP applications. Features of our approach are (i) measurement of actual RAID storage power consumption, (ii) analysis of I/O behavior characteristics of OLTP applications, and (iii) delayed write operation at a storage cache level based on the I/O behavior of OLTP applications. We present a measured result of power consumption of storages during an OLTP application is running, and simulations results of our power-saving methods with varying cache size of storage, which demonstrate that our method provides substantially lower storage power consumption than that of a conventional OLTP environment.

Keywords: Storage, Energy, Power saving, OLTP, Datacenter.

1 Introduction

Storages and servers aggregation at datacenters have increased datacenters' power consumption. The power consumption of servers and datacenters in the United States is expected to double during 2006 to 2011[1]. Especially, storages consume large quantities of power at large datacenters since the amount of digital data stored and managed at datacenters is increased rapidly as described in [6]. Thus, disk storage power-saving has become a major issue at datacenters[2,3].

Database Management Systems (DBMSs) are reported as major storage applications at datacenters[15]. Storage capacity shipments for DBMS account for more than 60% of all shipments of high-end class storage installations. Shipments for online transaction processing (OLTP) applications such as Enterprise Resource Planning and Customer Relationship Management constitute more than half of the shipments of storage installations for DBMS. Therefore, storages for OLTP applications are expected to be a major power consumption need

S. Kikuchi et al. (Eds.): DNIS 2011, LNCS 7108, pp. 256–269, 2011.

at datacenters. Reducing the power consumption of storage devices for OLTP applications is an important task that must be undertaken to decrease the power consumption of datacenters.

In the past few years, several studies have addressed these problems. The features of these studies are an estimation of I/O-issued timing by analyzing a source code of a transaction[19,17]. If a transaction execution time is enough longer than the time length of turning on/off a storage, we may reduce the storage power consumption easily. But if a transaction execution time is shorter than the time length of turning on/off a storage, it is difficult to decide the timing of turning off the storage. Generally, a transaction execution time of OLTP application is less than a few seconds, that is much shorter than a time length of turning on/off a storage. Therefore, it is difficult to apply these approaches to storages used by OLTP applications. In order to develop a power-saving method for the storages, understanding the detailed characteristics of I/O behavior of the OLTP application at runtime is important. However, no report describes the power consumption of an actual OLTP application running on a large RAID storage. We measure the power consumption characteristics of a storage actually, and analyze I/O behavior of a TPC-C application. Here, the TPC-C application takes as a benchmark program to represent OLTP applications[5]. We propose a novel power-saving method based on the I/O behavior characteristics of TPC-C applications.

The contribution of this paper is that we measured the actual power consumption of OLTP applications on RAID storage in detail using a power meter. The RAID storage we used is an Adaptive Modular Storage 2500 (Hitachi Ltd.). Another contribution of this paper is to propose a new power-saving method offering only slight OLTP performance degradation by considering TPC-C I/O behaviors. A salient feature of our approach is to reduce a storage power consumption by analyzing an I/O behavior of OLTP application and by controlling a storage cache policy based on the I/O behavior. Detailed analysis of I/O behavior while varying the cache size is reported. Modern datacenter's storages have hundreds of GB cache, we, therefore, utilize this cache for power saving of the storages. Finally, we evaluate our power saving approach with consideration of a cache effect. Our power-saving method enables reduction of storage power consumption by approximately 45% in the best case for active TPC-C applications in our simulation results.

2   Related Works

Today, many storage energy saving approaches have been proposed. Approaches described in [12,10,21] tries to enlarge I/O interval by using a cache memory of servers or storages. Other approaches described in [4,13,20,16] concentrate frequently accessed data into a small number of disks and turn off other disks. However, it is difficult to find less frequently accessed OLTP data without application level information because OLTP applications issue very high frequently random I/Os.

Application-aware power saving approaches are also proposed. A salient feature of the application-aware power saving approaches is that they acquire I/O timing and an I/O target disk drive from applications [11,7,9,17,8,14]. Therefore, these approaches show particular effectiveness for long-term applications such as scientific or batch applications. However, no report describes research that has tackled short-term transactions processing such as a TPC-C application.

3   Characteristics of Storage Power Consumption

3.1   Mearement Environment

Figure 1 presents an outline of storage used in power consumption measurements. The storage contains a controller that has two I/O processors (two cores each) and 2GB cache memories, and 10 units, which have 15 disk drives each. The disk drives in each unit constitute a RAID (13D+2P RAID 6). Disk drives in the units are 750 GB SATA 7200 rpm. The storage also has four power distribution units (PDU) which supply power to the controller and units. The controller and units have two power supply cables each. The voltage of each cable is 200 V. We connected two clamp sensors to each cable. The clamp sensor is connected to a power meter (Remote Measurement and Monitoring System 2300 Series; Hioki E.E. Corp.).

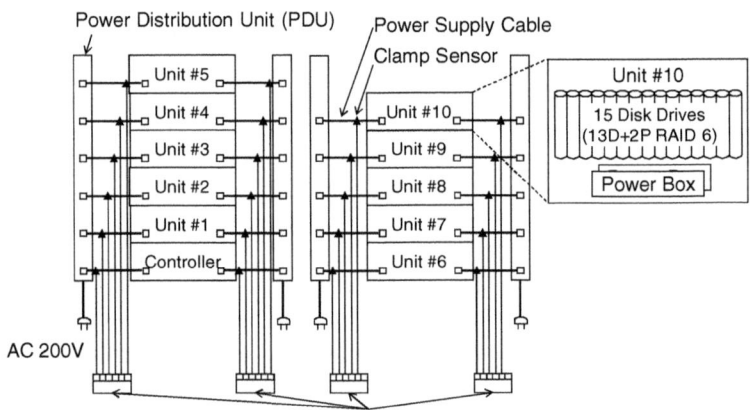

Fig. 1. Measurement Environment of Storage Power Consumption

Figure 2 portrays the system configuration used in our power consumption measurements. A load-generation server and the storage are connected by four 4-Gbit fiber channel cables. The server has 32 processors (2 cores each) and 512 GB memory. The OS of the server is AIX 5.3 64-bit version. The file system is JFS2. A capacity of one unit is 11.25TB and total capacity of the storage is approximately 112.5TB (both before constructing RAID). A capacity of storage cache is 2.0GB.

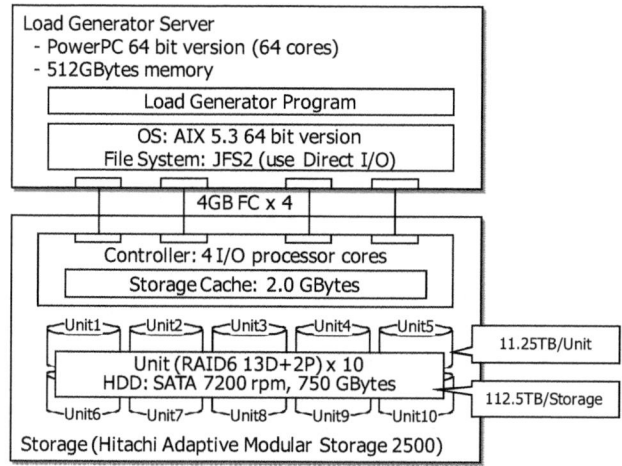

Fig. 2. System Configuration of Power Measurement Environment

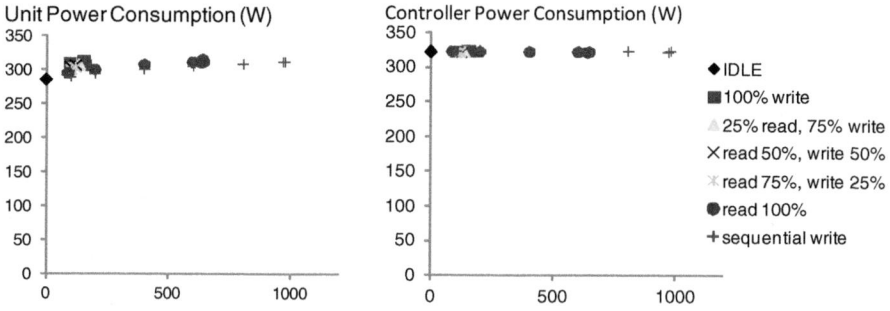

Fig. 3. Power Consumption and I/Os of the Unit (Left) and Controller (Right)

3.2   Power Consumption at an Active/Idle State

Figure 3 (left) depicts the relation between the unit power consumption and I/Os to units per second (IOPS). The I/O size is 8 KB. The figure shows that the power consumption of the unit increases slightly from idle status in accordance with the increase of IOPS. The maximum power consumption is about 315 W (+10.6% from the idle). Figure 3 (right) presents the relation between the controller power consumption and I/Os to the storage controller. As the figure shows, the power consumption of the controller is steady around 320 W.

3.3   Power Consumption of Spin-Down and Power off Modes

Figure 4 depicts the power consumption of the unit in idle, spin-down, and power-off states. The power consumption is decreased by 40.6% when the unit is

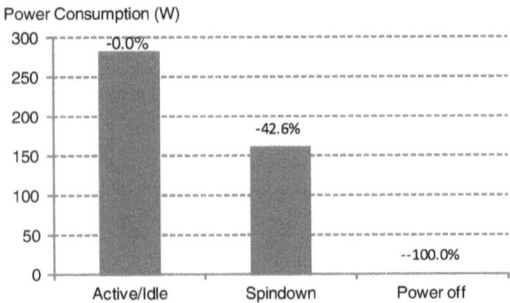

Fig. 4. Power Consumption of the Unit (idle, spin-down, and power off states)

in a spin-down mode. The power consumption is decreased by 100.0% when the unit is in a powered-off mode. The controller, on the other hand, cannot spin down or power off. Therefore, the power consumption of the controller is steady for all power statuses of the units.

4   Power Consumption and I/O Behavior of OLTP Applications

4.1   Experimental Environment

The hardware is the same configuration as that portrayed in Figs. 1 and 2. The software configuration is the following: the OS is a 64-bit version of AIX 5.3; the DBMS is a commercial DBMS for AIX; and the OLTP application is a tpcc-like program [18]. The file system cache is disabled (mounts with the direct I/O option). The DBMS buffer size is 25 GB maximum. The database is approximately 500 GB (the number of Warehouses is 5000), in which the Log data size is not included. With no actual report of power consumption of RAID storage and I/O trace of large OLTP application, we run the tpcc-like program and measured the results. We use 10 units and format them using the JFS2 file system. Log data are placed into Unit #1. All tables and indexes are placed into the other nine units (Units #2 - #10). Data of all tables and indexes are partitioned by hash into these units.

4.2   Power Consumption of TPC-C on RAID

Figure 5 presents the transition of power consumption of RAID storage at Figs. 1 and 2 while the tpcc-like program is running. The tpcc-like program was run for 30 min. The power consumption of the storage controller is steady at 319 W. The power consumption of unit #1 (for Log) is also a small fraction around 278 W. In contrast, the power consumption of units that contain database data was increased more than 10% compared to power consumption of the idle period. For detailed analyses, we used the 7 min of data included in the dashed line box in the figure.

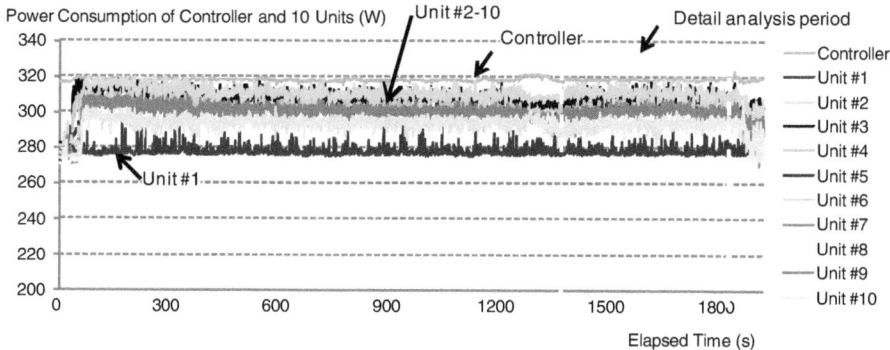

Fig. 5. Power Consumption of RAID Storage

4.3 I/O Behavior Characteristics of TPC-C

Results of Measurements. Figure 6 presents the number of reads and writes per second of each unit issued from the server. As presented there, the number of read I/Os is greater than that of write I/O. The IOPS to Log data (Unit #1) is higher than other units. The IOPS to tables and indexes (Unit #2 to #10) are almost equal among these units except Unit #2 and #10. The IOPS of these units are low because amounts of data in these units are fewer than other units (Unit #3 to Unit #9).

Figure 7 shows the quantities of reads and writes per second of each unit issued from the storage controller to disk drives in the units. As presented there, the quantities of read I/Os of units for tables and indexes are greater than those of write I/Os. The total number, however, is many more I/Os issued from the server. In contrast, the I/Os of unit for Log data are far fewer than I/Os issued from the server. Comparing the number of I/Os to storage controller (in Fig. 6), the number of I/Os issued to disk drives (in Fig. 7) are increased.

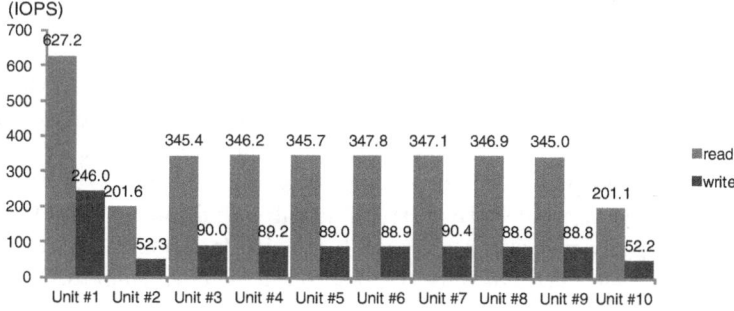

Fig. 6. Reads and Writes per second in a unit for TPC-C (Issued from DBMS to Storage Controller)

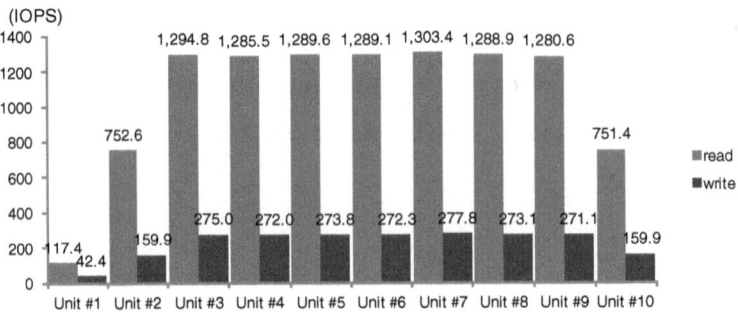

Fig. 7. Reads and Writes per second in a unit for TPC-C (Issued from Controller to Disk Drives of Units)

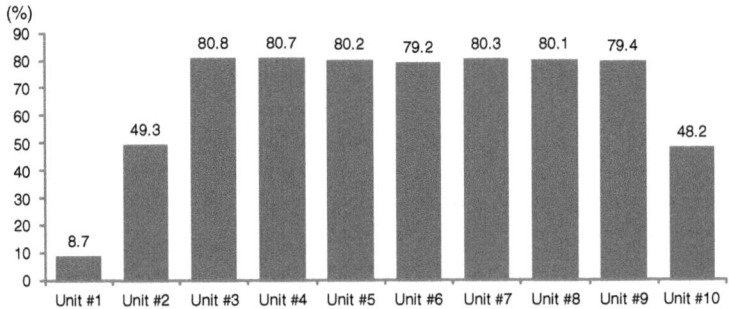

Fig. 8. Average Usage of Disk Drives

Figure 8 shows the average usage of 15 disk drives of each unit. As shown here, the disk drive usage of units for tables and indexes is more than 80% (without Unit #2 and #10). In contrast, the disk drive usage of unit #2 (for Log data) is only 8.7%.

Today's modern storages, on the other hand, have a large storage cache. Therefore we simulated the effect of storage cache in the case that the storage cache size is increased by using TPC-C I/O trace measured at this section. Figure 9 portrays the relation between the percentage of duplicated I/O and the percentage of storage cache size compared with the size of TPC-C database. Here, the duplicated I/O is an I/O which is issued to the same address that I/Os had been issued previously. As presented there, the rates of duplicated I/O are less than 1% when the cache size is less than 1%. The rates of duplicated I/Os, however, are increased rapidly where the storage cache size is larger than 1%. Figure 9 shows that a storage cache of only 5% size reduces more than 20% of I/Os to the disk drives of storage.

I/O Characteristics. I/O characteristics of TPC-C on RAID storage have the following characteristics:

Rate of Duplicated Number of I/O (%)

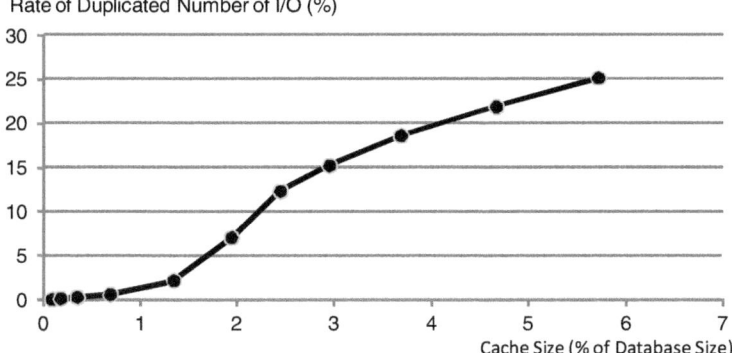

Fig. 9. Rate of Duplicated Number of I/O

1. I/Os are issued almost equally to units containing database tables and indexes (Units #2 to #10 in Fig. 6). This is because the data of all tables and indexes are partitioned into these units by hash.
2. The load of disk drives for Log data is low, and the loads of disk drives for tables and indexes are high (Fig. 8). The usage of disk drives for tables and indexes is greater than 80%, so these disk drives have little space to serve more I/Os.
3. Numbers of I/Os to disk drives containing database data are much higher than those of I/Os issued from the server, which results from calculation of the parity data of RAID 6 (Fig. 7). For one write from the server, the storage controller issues nine I/Os to disk drives (i.e., read old data and two old parity data, write new data and two new parity data. The storage also checks the written data by re-reading them because the SATA drive reliability is low). This overhead is known as a *write penalty*. The number of I/Os of Log data to disk drives are fewer than those of I/Os issued from the server. Most I/O of the Log data is sequential writes. Therefore, the storage controller merges multiple writes to one large write.
4. The writes to the same blocks is very low when the storage cache size is less than 1% of the database size. On the other hand, the writes to the same blocks becomes high for cases in which the capacity of storage cache is a few percent of the database size (see Fig. 9). This result illustrates that a small amount of storage cache reduces the load of disk drives on the storage effectively for TPC-C databases.

5   Power Saving Method for TPC-C Applications

We propose a power-saving method using the characteristics of I/O behaviors of TPC-C applications. To limit the power consumption of the storage, we use the locality of TPC-C application's I/O to disk drives in the storage. The main idea of our proposed method is a reduction of the *write penalty* by absorbing write

I/Os to the same blocks by using a storage cache, consolidation of RAID groups which store database data into a small number of RAID groups, and spin down or power off the remainder of RAID groups. We propose two simple approaches to reduce the number of I/Os to disk drives.

5.1   Allocation of Appropriate Size for Storage Cache

We described that write I/Os to the same blocks of TPC-C application is very low when the storage cache size is smaller than 1% of the TPC-C database size. On the other hand, the storage cache with size of only a few percent of the TPC-C database can reduce the number of I/Os to disk drives (shown in Fig. 9). Our first proposed approach is to allocate the appropriate size for the storage cache and reduce read I/Os to disk drives. The storage cache size of our experimental environment is 2 GB, but the maximum storage cache size of modern storage used at datacenters is hundreds of GB. The main usage of storage cache is to calculate parity data for RAID, to improve read response time by using read locality, and to improve write response time by using write back cache control method. Our proposed method uses the storage cache as an I/O buffer of DBMS with LRU cache replacement policy.

5.2   Write Delay of Storage Cache

The second approach for reducing I/O load of disk drives is a write delay of storage cache. The majority of I/Os to disk drives are a *write penalty*. Therefore, reducing the write penalty of disk drives is useful for the storage consolidation method. We propose a storage cache write delay method that maintains a constant amount of write I/Os into the storage cache and writes to disk drives when the number of dirty blocks reaches a threshold. Here, we select the threshold value as possible as large of storage cache except space required for parity data generation. We expect that this method reduces the number of blocks to be written to the disk drives, while also decreasing the write penalty.

6   Evaluation

To evaluate our proposed methods, we first calculated how many I/Os issued to disk drives would be decreased using our proposed methods. We then estimated the power consumption of the storage using the calculated number of I/Os. We simulated the number of I/Os by varying the storage cache using TPC-C I/O trace data measured in section 4. The experimental environment is the same as Fig 2.

6.1   I/O Rate Reduction

For the simulation of I/O rate reduction, we varied the size of storage cache to 0.4%, 1.0%, 3.0%, 5.0%, 10.0%, and 20.0% of the database size. We also varied the rate of dirty page to 1%, 10%, 25%, 75%, and 95% of the storage cache size. A flush of dirty blocks in the storage cache is delayed until the number of dirty blocks exceeds this dirty block rate (write delay). Multiple updates to the same block are merged to only one write to a disk drive.

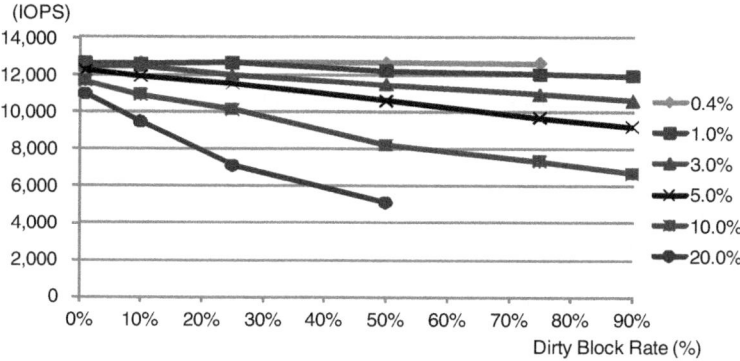

Fig. 10. Number of I/Os to Disk Drives when Changing the Cache Size and Dirty Block Rate

Figure 10 shows that the number of I/Os issued to disk drives is decreased according to the increase of the size of storage cache and the rate of dirty blocks. There is little effect when the storage cache is 0.4% of the TPC-C database size. On the other hand, a storage cache which has only a 3% size of a TPC-C database reduces the number of I/Os to disk drives more than 13% when the rate of dirty blocks is larger than 75% of storage cache size. When the storage cache size is 5% of TPC-C database size, the I/Os are decreased more than 23%. When the storage cache size is 20% of the TPC-C database size, the I/Os are decreased approximately 60%. These results show that a storage cache which has a few percentage size of the TPC-C database with a write delay has the capability of consolidating nine RAID groups to eight or seven RAID groups with little degradation of transaction throughput.

6.2 RAID Group Consolidation and Its Power Saving Effect

RAID Group Consolidation. Based on the preceding discussion, we calculate the necessary number of RAID groups to serve I/Os presented in Fig. 10. To calculate the number of RAID groups, we used a number of I/Os of 75% dirty block rate of each storage cache size (for 20% storage cache size, we used 50% dirty block rate). The number of I/Os that one RAID group can serve is 1,430 IOPS which are measured values shown in section 4. Table 1 shows the relation among storage cache size, number of I/Os to be served by storage, and the number of RAID groups to serve the required number of I/Os.

Table 1. Storage Cache Size and Number of RAID Groups

Storage Cache Size (%)	Number of I/Os to be Served (IOPS)	Number of RAID Groups
0.4	12,657	9
1.0	12,065	9
3.0	10,954	8
5.0	9,690	7
10.0	7,365	6
20.0	5,120	4

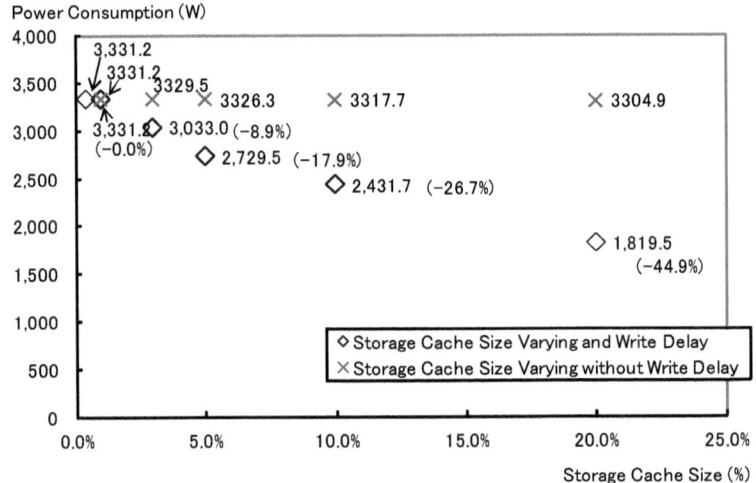

Fig. 11. Power Consumption of Storage when Varying the Storage Cache Size

Storage Power Consumption and Transaction Throughput. We calculated the power consumption of storage applying only the storage cache size varying method, and the RAID group consolidation with storage cache size varying and write delay method. Figure 11 presents the results. Square marks show the power consumption of the RAID Group consolidation method. Cross marks show the power consumption applying only the storage cache size varying method. Values in brackets show the reduction rate of power consumption of RAID Group consolidation method from the power consumption applying only the storage cache size varying method.

Figure 11 shows that the storage cache varying method does not reduce the power consumption of storage irrespective of the increment of storage cache. This is true because the increment of the storage cache size does not reduce the number of I/O to disk drives (1% line of Fig. 9). Therefore, reduction of the number of RAID groups is difficult without degradation of transaction throughput. The storage cache size varying method alone does not decrease the storage power consumption.

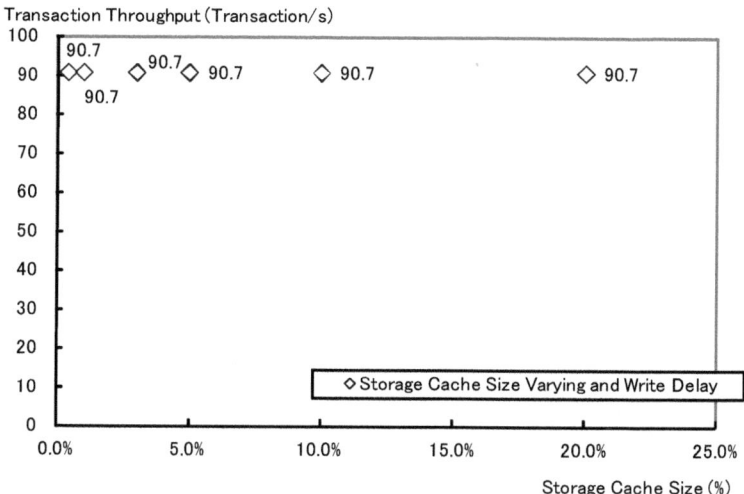

Fig. 12. Transaction Throughput when Varying the Storage Cache Size

However, RAID group consolidation using storage cache size varying and write delay method can reduce power consumption by 8.9% with 3.0% storage cache size, and can reduce power consumption by 17.9% using 5.0% storage cache size. The 5.0% size of the storage cache is approximately 20 GB, for the large TPC-C database with a scale factor such as 5000. The cache size of the high-end storage used at large datacenters can accommodate a storage cache much larger than 20 GB. Therefore, our proposed method is useful for large datacenters. We also calculated the power consumption of storage with cache sizes of 10% and 20%. Fig. 11 shows that the power consumption reduction rates are, respectively, 26.7% and 44.9%. Our proposed method has the capability of reducing the power consumption of storage used by active TPC-C applications drastically when the storage cache size is large.

Figure 12 depicts the calculated transaction throughput for each storage cache size. The transaction throughput is an important indicator. As Fig. 12 shows, the transaction throughput using our proposed method does not degrade the transaction throughput because our RAID group consolidation method using write delays controls the number of I/Os to disk drives to keep it from exceeding the number of I/Os portrayed in Fig. 7.

7   Conclusion

We measured the actual power consumption values of storage and considered the behavior of a TPC-C application in detail. We then proposed a novel power-saving method that reduces the power consumption of storage for TPC-C applications. The salient feature of our approach is the consolidation of the TPC-C database into a few RAID groups using appropriate storage cache size and a write delay method at the storage-cache level based on comprehensive behavior of OLTP DBMS executing multiple transactions. We demonstrated that our method achieves an approximately 45% reduction of the storage power consumption for a TPC-C application with little throughput degradation.

References

1. U.s. environmental protection agency energy star program, report to congress on server and data center energy efficiency public law, 109–431 (2007)
2. Bauer, R.: Building the green data center: Towards best practices and technical considerations (2008)
3. Chu, P.B., Reinsel, E.: Green storage ii: Metrics and measurement (2008)
4. Colarelli, D., Grunwald, D.: Massive arrays of idle disks for storage archives. In: ACM /IEEE 2002 Conference on Supercomputing, pp. 47–57 (2002)
5. Transaction Processing Performance Council. Tpc-c, an online transaction processing benchmark
6. Gens, F.: Idc predictions 2011: Welcome to the new mainstream. IDC White Paper #225878 (2010)
7. Gniady, C., Hu, Y.C., Lu, Y.H.: Program counter based techniques for dynamic power management. In: Proc. of 10th International Symposium on High Performance Computer Architecutre, pp. 24–35. IEEE (2004)
8. Harizopoulos, S., Shah, M.A., Meza, J., Ranganathan, P.: Energy efficiency: The new holy grail of data management systems research. In: 4th Biennial Conf. on Innovative Data Systems, pp. 112–123 (2009)
9. Heath, T., Pinheiro, E., Hom, J., Kremer, U., Bianchini, R.: Application transformations for power and performance-aware device management. In: 11th International Conference on Parallel Architectures and Compilation Techniques, pp. 121–130 (2002)
10. Li, D., Wang, J.: Eeraid: Power efficient redundant and inexpensive disk arrays. Proc. 11th Workshop on ACM SIGOPS European Workshop, 174–180 (2004)
11. Mandagere, N., Diehl, J., Du, D.H.-C.: Greenstor: Application-aided energy-efficient storage. In: MSST, pp. 16–29. IEEE Computer Society (2007)
12. Papathanasiou, A.E., Scott, M.L.: Energy efficient prefetching and caching. In: Proc. of USENIX 2004 Annual Technical Conference, pp. 255–268. USENIX Association Berkeley (2004)
13. Pinheiro, E., Bianchini, R.: Energy conservation techniques for disk array based servers. In: Proc. 18th Annual International Conference on Supercomputing, pp. 68–78. ACM (2004)
14. Poess, M., Nambiar, R.O.: Tuning servers, storage and database for power efficient data warehouse. In: 26th IEEE International Conf. on Data Engineering, pp. 1006–1017. IEEE Computer Society (2010)
15. Reinsel, D.: White paper datacenter ssds: Solid footing for growth. IDC White Paper # 210290 (2008)
16. Son, S.W., Chen, G., Kandemir, M.T.: Disk layout optimization for reducing energy consumption. In: ICS, pp. 274–283. ACM (2005)
17. Son, S.W., Kandemir, M., Choudhary, A.: Software-directed disk power management for scientific applications. In: Proc. of 19th IEEE International Parallel and Distributed Proceesing Symposium. IEEE Computer Society (2005)
18. Tkachenko, V.: tpcc-mysql

19. Ueno, Y., Goda, K., Kitsuregawa, M.: A study on disk array power reduction using query plan for database systems (2007)
20. Oldham Weddle, C., Qian, M.J., Wang, A.A.: Paraid: A gear-shifting power-aware raid. In: 5th USENIX Conference on File and Storage, pp. 245–267. USENIX Association (2007)
21. Yao, X., Wang, J.: Rimac: A novel redundancy based hierarchical cache architecture for power efficient. In: Proc. 2006 EuroSys Conference on High Performance Storage System, pp. 249–262 (2006)

Live BI: A Framework for Real Time Operations Management

Chetan Gupta, Umeshwar Dayal, Song Wang, and Abhay Mehta

Hewlett Packard Laboratories,
Palo Alto, CA, USA
{chetan.gupta,umeshwar.dayal,songw,abhay.mehta}@hp.com

Abstract. The increasing instrumentation of real world physical systems provides an opportunity for real time operations management for the purpose of efficient management of large complex systems. Real time operations management solutions for such large, complex systems such as a transportation network, massive data centers, etc., share many common characteristics and requirements. In this paper, we identify these common challenges in terms of data characteristics and system requirements. We then point out the insufficiencies in current solutions in addressing these requirements and present some results that help meet the challenges.

Keywords: Real time operations management, Outlier detection, Complex event processing, Event Mining.

1 Introduction

With the ever increasing instrumentation of real world physical systems, real time operations management and control applications are becoming increasingly relevant. Real time operations management has applications in domains such as managing transportation networks, managing large computer systems and massive data centers, managing electric grids, etc.

In a typical operations management (OM) scenario, be it traffic management or IT operations, systems are fitted with sensors and other measuring devices which produce a constant stream of data. Since the data streams in from many sources, including raw data, and triggered events, the data is heterogeneous in nature. Human operators often man *operations centers* (or networked operations centers (NOCs)) to monitor this streaming data. However, due to the sheer complexity and volume of the incoming data, operators often react to incidents *after* they have occurred. This leads to downtime and loss of efficiency. Moreover, due to the complexity of the systems being managed, human operators are unable to optimize the normal running of the system causing a suboptimal use of resources.

Such large complex system will continue to grow and place an increasing burden on our resources. For example, the US EPA estimates that the energy usage at data centers is expected to double every five years. Given this, it has become imperative that we come up with techniques for efficient management of these systems. In such a

S. Kikuchi et al. (Eds.): DNIS 2011, LNCS 7108, pp. 270–285, 2011.

scenario, systems that employ data management and analysis/mining techniques have a significant role to play. There is a need for systems that can detect events for automated action, filter and correlate events for better management and reduce costs, provide the operators with aggregated view and visualizations for better insights, and provide access to historical data for root cause analysis, etc.

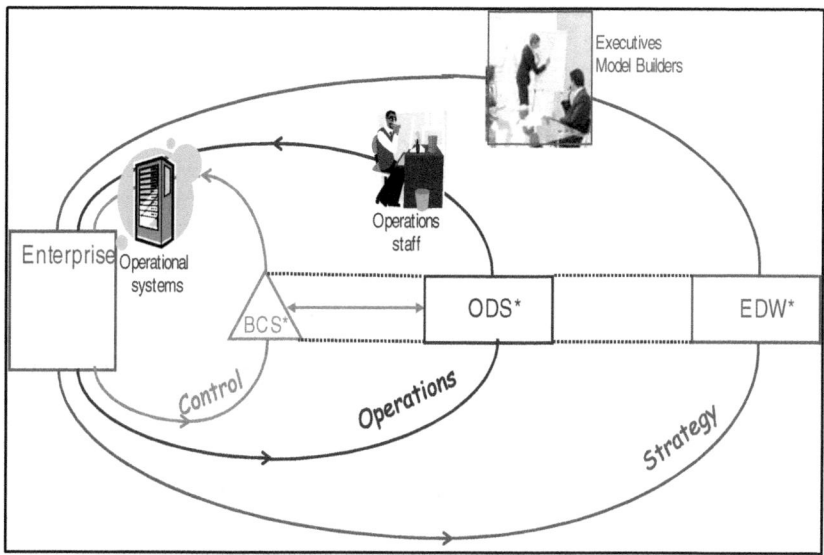

Fig. 1. Control, Operations and Strategy Data Life Cycles

This class of applications can also be understood in terms of the life cycle of data. In Figure 1, we have depicted the typical life cycle of data. The outside cycle is the *strategy cycle*, where the senior executives use historical data stored in a data warehouse (EDW) to take long term decisions, the middle cycle is *daily operations cycle* where the operations staff takes day to day decisions such as inventory management, and of our interest, there is the innermost cycle - the *control or the operations management (OM) cycle*, which is aimed at responding in real time to changes in the state of the enterprise for efficient management of resources. The requirements of all the three cycles are different, and in this work we are focused on the innermost or the OM cycle.

In a typical OM scenario, data streams in from a large number of components that comprise the system. These components are of course related but their interaction is often not well understood, and hence is difficult to model. Measurements or messages from these components are themselves treated as *event instance tuples* or transformed into event instances. Sometimes, these events need to be correlated to form *complex events*. These events (complex or otherwise) can be composed across the various dimensions and resolutions in data. From these inputs of raw sensor and event data, the challenge then is to *rapidly and appropriately respond in real time*. These events also also represent the state of the system, and are stored for *what-next* and *root-cause* analysis. "What-next" is typically an on-demand analysis, whereas the "root-cause" is an offline analysis.

In this paper, we attempt a systematic study of Operations Management by: (i) Discussing two use cases (ii) Teasing out some general requirements for effective operations management (iii) Presenting a conceptual and a system framework for addressing the OM problem (iv) Briefly presenting some algorithms, that we developed to address specific problems in the OM domain.

The two domains, we study in this paper are Traffic Management and IT-Operations Management. For traffic management, we get sensor data from vehicles, and the challenge then is to help in efficient management of traffic. Effective traffic management will lead not only to reduction in fuel consumption but also to a reduction in green house emissions. The increasing amount of power needed to maintain our digital life is well known. To reduce this energy consumption we need to reduce downtimes and run our data centers at optimal consumption. To achieve this, for IT-OM we not only consider traditional hardware/software event data but also temperature sensor, utilization data [14] from data centers.

Overall, the paper is organized as follows: In Section 2, we discuss two OM use cases and use them to present the characteristics and requirements of a general OM problem. In Section 3, we discuss existing relevant technologies and their shortcomings. In Section 4, we present the system design and a conceptual architecture for OM applications. In Section 5, we discuss some of the algorithmic approaches we have been working on to address the challenges of a real time OM applications. Finally, we conclude in Section 6.

2   Requirements of an OM System

To elucidate the requirements of a typical OM system, we present discussion of two OM scenarios: Traffic Management and Operations Management for IT. We choose these two applications, since they emphasize different aspects of the challenges we need to address when solving for an OM problem.

2.1   Smart Traffic Management

In the future, it can be assumed that each vehicle is fitted with a sensor that relays a position report to a central server (such simulated data is already available [4]) at fixed time intervals. The road network is thought to be divided into segments, where a segment could be any abstraction. In our study we assume one segment to be one mile of road in one direction (essentially ten blocks) and that every vehicle sends a position report every 30 seconds. Many cities such as London are implementing rudimentary versions of these for the purpose of congestion pricing. This data would be useful to both the driver and the traffic planner and can be used for computing dynamic tolls. The driver can use it to find the route that is least congested, is safest (least number of large vehicles) or both.

DBSPI10-82: Data logging failed for DBSPI_MSS_GRAPH . Make sure Performance Agent is installed and running.
BlackBerry Dispatcher   WBCXOE B021 {0x2710} 8304: (#50099) BlackBer ry Dispatcher Shutdown complete

Fig. 2. Sample IT-OM Events

However, we are more interested in the OM application of this data. For this purpose, the position reports emitted by the vehicles allow us to compute the following quantities [4]: (i) Average velocity of a vehicle, (ii) Average velocity on a segment and, (iii) The number of vehicles on any segment. Many highway systems have embedded sensors that directly report some of these quantities[1], but for the purpose of this paper (and for a more general solution) we compute the segment statistics from vehicle data.

For the purpose of traffic management, we detect a number of types of events over the computed quantities mentioned above:(i) To compute *"outlier segment events"*, we identify the segments that have deviated from their averaged behavior (taking into account seasonality) in a "significant" way (ii) To compute *"accident events"*, we identify two vehicles with nearly identical position reports within a very short span of time (ii) To compute *"erratic behavior"* events, we find outliers over vehicle velocity and the number of other vehicles in the segment. These types of events are meant for real time response, where either through automated rules or manual intervention some action is performed. Many of these events need to be computed at various levels of abstractions, for example: We need to be able to answer if instead of just segments, if there are regions (localities, neighborhoods, zip code regions) that are congested.

Besides automatic response the traffic manager is interested in "what-next" analysis. For this purpose we store the state of the road network at discreet intervals as the results of a skyline query [6] over all the segments average velocity and the average number of vehicles. The idea behind what-next analysis is that, if at any point of time the operator wants to predict what might happens next, then from history all those instances can be recovered that are "similar" to the current state and then from these set of instances, what might happen next can be inferred using conditional probabilities.

2.2   IT Operations Management (IT-OM)

Unlike the previous use case of traffic management where data is primarily in the form of sensor data, most IT systems today report problem and issues through events and hence this use case helps illustrate a different set of problems.

The events in an IT-OM system emanate from hundreds of networked systems, running thousands of heterogeneous software components and applications, which together provide the business services required to support the enterprise. Each individual hardware, middleware, and software component reports exceptional conditions

---

[1] www.pems.dot.ca.gov

(and also routine updates) as they are detected. These conditions are reported as human readable events. A few example events are shown in Figure 2.

Typically, these detected events are streamed to a Network Operations Center (NOC), where operators process these events with the aim of keeping the enterprise systems running smoothly. A problem in one component can ripple through the enterprise and result in many events being reported for the same problem. For example, a disk read error might get reported by the disk subsystem, the database system, the application querying the database, all the way up to the business service that needs that piece of data. The large number of events can easily overwhelm the NOC operators. Furthermore, each of these events might get assigned to different teams of operators, resulting in many uncoordinated actions across multiple systems. The processing then of these IT-OM events is mostly manual and expensive. Hence, a key goal is to reduce the number of events that a NOC operator has to manage.

Current commercial IT-OM systems use event-correlation technology to filter and process incoming events and assist in the identification of relevant events. Most of these systems are rule-based (like expert systems). Currently, these systems require domain experts to recognize correlations, express them in terms of rules and then maintain the rules. This requirement leads to significant costs for maintaining an up-to-date rule set and consequently results in little or poorly managed rules. Hence, to reduce the overall cost of processing these events and to help the operator run IT systems efficiently, *a key goal is to find an automatically discover rules for the purpose of event correlation.*

The idea behind automated rule discovery to find correlations is simple: From historical data find "statistically significant" correlations between events and use these correlations to automatically construct rules to suppress current events and replace them with an event at a higher abstraction level. For instance say we discover that every time Event A occurs it is accompanied by Event B and Event C. This discovery allows us to automatically construct a rule encoding the above. Then, an occurrence of *{A, B, C}* can be replaced by an occurrence of some group label. This would reduce the volume of events that the operator has to process in real time.

We now use these two OM use cases to first discuss the data characteristics for such a system then discuss the system requirements.

2.3   Data Characteristics

Different OM scenarios share different data characteristics, we point out some of the important ones in light of the discussion of the two use cases discussed in the previous section:

a. *Input Complexity*: By input complexity we mean that the system under study has hundreds if not thousands of real time inputs whose inter-relationships are not well understood and hence difficult to model. Furthermore, several inputs are transient and erratic. In the IT-OM context, an example of such an input is a human user who chooses to test a new program and in the process causing several types of events to be published, such as memory overflow, cpu maximization, etc. In the traffic management case, there are tens of thousands of drivers who come in and out of network and some of whom might not drive in a predictable way.

b. *Volume*: Another important characteristic of an OM system is the large volume of data. In the case of IT-OM, components issue events, not only when there are errors and faults but also to indicate status. Even in a medium sized IT system with thousands of components, these can add up to a large number of events. In the case of traffic management, if each vehicle emits a position report say every minute, then even for a moderate sized city, the number of positions reports coming in would be very large.

c. *Heterogeneity*: In a real world OM scenario, since the incoming data is derived from various sources it is heterogeneous in nature. Moreover, many such incoming streams themselves are multidimensional and composed of heterogeneous data types. For example, in IT-OM the data streaming in from an integration server is composed of 25 attributes comprising categorical, integer, character, and string data types. In the traffic OM case, the data we study in this paper is relatively homogenous. However, in the next step we are working on a solution that integrates sensor data with incidents reports from highway patrol, and with weather data, making the data extremely heterogenous.

d. *Various Abstraction Levels*: Streaming data, like other data exists at various abstraction levels. This is evident in both the traffic management and the IT-OM use cases.

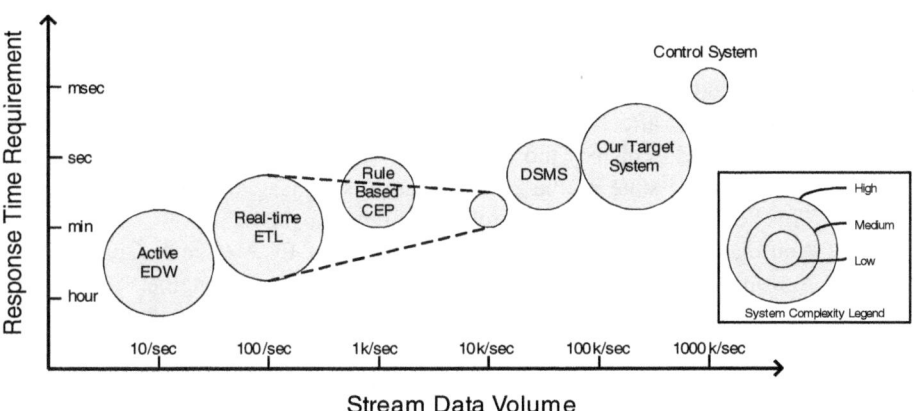

Fig. 3. Existing Solution Comparison

2.4 System and Methods Requirements

The two use cases help us bring out some common requirements for an OM system. From our perspective, the primary difference in these two use cases is that for IT-OM, the events are predefined by the various components and in the case of traffic management we have to discover these events.

1) Firstly we need to be able to discover events in real time. For this:
   a) We need to an ability to query streaming data with SQL like queries at various abstraction levels. For example an event might be defined over different abstractions such as street, a neighborhood, a zip, a city, etc.
   b) Perform higher order analysis such as outlier detection, and skylines over various dimensions and abstraction levels. Outliers can be detected not only over raw sensor data but also over event data to obtain higher order events. For example, in IT operations management, where various hardware and software components are issuing events, some events would be defined as outlier alerts from hardware components, whereas some other events might be defined over software components. These could obviously, share dimensions such as severity, creation time, etc, while having different dimensions that relate to components. In such a case, we need to be able to use the knowledge that some dimensions are shared between different events.
2) When the events are predefined as in the IT-OM scenario (or have been discovered), we need to reduce the number of events that need to be processed by an operator:
   a) We need a method for automatic discovery of correlation over historical event data. These correlations are typically expressed as correlation rules. For example, an event indicating missing distribution template file leads to an event indicating pending distribution configuration, which leads to an event indicating distribution problems. These three events are correlated and the method should discover the correlation.
3) Once we have the set of desirable events, in both use cases we need on-demand analysis and automated action.
   a) For on-demand analysis we need to be able to run *hybrid* queries, i.e., queries that take as input both stored and streaming data. For example, in traffic management, after a "outlier segment" event is detected, we run a hybrid query to find in history those instances which share similar "outlier segment" and a similar state as the current state (as indicated by the skyline query). This helps give us an idea as to what might happen next.
   b) Automated actions typically take the form of ECA (Event, Condition, and Action) rules which are implemented through a rules engine. The matching can happen at various abstraction levels and different patterns can share computation. For example, a pattern "disk failure, database failure" can be hierarchically matched to the pattern "hardware failure, database failure".

These challenges dictate our solutions for addressing operations management. We call our systems platform Live BI. Problem 1a dictates a need for a system that can handles queries over streaming data [10]. In terms of addressing Problem 1b, a number of solutions exist for outlier detection. In addition to the current technologies for outlier detection ([9] , [2]), specifically for OM we need a method for outlier detection over large volumes streaming data, such that outliers over any combination of dimension, abstraction level for each of these dimensions, and arbitrary time window can be obtained. We give a brief outline for a solution to this problem in Section 5.1. In Section 5.2 we present a solution based on frequent itemset mining [3] for Problem 2.

For Problem 3, we discuss the system requirements in Section 4 and we have developed an approach called ECube [12] to address some of the challenges. This list of problems and solutions is obviously not complete. We discuss some more of the challenges in the section on future works and conclusions.

Before going into our solutions, we discuss existing technologies.

3   Existing Technologies

In this section, we discuss some existing technology with reference to the data characteristics and system requirements discussed previously. It places our work in the context of current approaches and underscores the inadequacies of the current approaches in their basic forms for OM applications. Many of these technologies are a precursor to an OM solution hence, instead of reinventing these technologies, we aim to address the OM application space by extending and integrating some of these existing technologies.

We will discuss three broad areas in existing technologies: (i) Control Systems (ii) ETL (Extract, Transform, Load) Engines and EDWs (Enterprise Data Warehouse) (iii) DSMS (Data Stream Management Systems) and CEP (Complex Event Processing) Engines. In Figure 3, we have plotted these different system approaches on the axis of response time and stream data volume. Here the bubble size indicates the complexity of analysis possible with the technology, the x-axis indicates the stream speeds these systems are traditionally able to handle, and y-axis indicates the real time response requirements that these systems are designed to achieve.

3.1   Control Systems

Control systems typically model a few well understood variables such as temperature, pressure under some distributional assumptions. In OM systems such as traffic management and IT-OM, these single variable control models are insufficient since: (i) Firstly, because of many interacting variables, the behavior of a single variable is difficult to model and (ii) Secondly, as shown in traffic management scenario, higher order analysis such as outlier detection over multivariate data is required, which the control systems are not designed to do. So, as depicted in Figure 3, these control systems are able to process large volume of streaming data and provide a quick response time, but the operations they traditionally perform are not very complex.

3.2   EDW and ETL

Database centric technologies such as EDW and ETL have had great success in arriving at generalized solutions across industries. These engines are designed to handle large volumes of heterogeneous data and can perform fairly complex tasks. However, as shown in Figure 3, EDWs are designed for static data and are not meant for a real time response. For a more real time response, active EDW systems have triggers, but these would be unsuitable for large volumes of fast moving data as is the case in OM scenarios.

ETL engines are capable of handling tasks of varying complexity and response requirements. However, these engines are not specifically designed for real time response. Many researchers have started working on real time ETL engines [7]. However, with real time ETL the set of standard operations consists primarily of traditional database operators. These standard operations are a subset of the operators is required for an OM application. For instance, traditional ETL operators do not include data mining operators such as outlier detection. Furthermore, traditionally none of these technologies handle hybrid queries (which are needed for on-demand analysis) and are not designed for executing rules. In Figure 3, we have depicted ETL engines to possess a varying set of capabilities, none of which in their basic forms are suitable for OM applications.

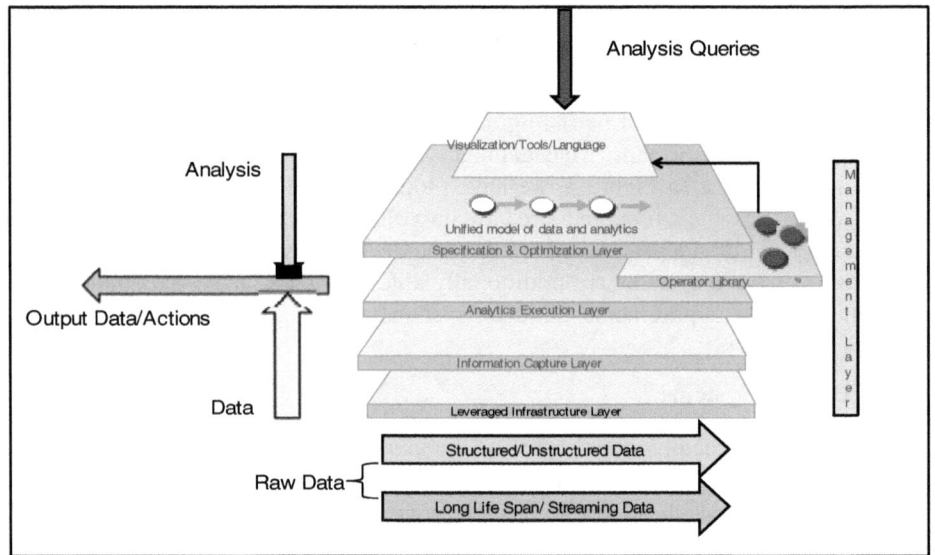

Fig. 4. Live BI Platform Architecture

3.3   CEP and DSMS

Both CEP and Data Stream Management Systems (DSMS) are designed to work with streaming data. Complex Event Processing (CEP) [8] engines arose from expert systems and systems research. They are well designed for real time response. Rule-based CEP engines are primarily meant for matching pre-defined "complex patterns" with streaming event data and enabling real time action. However, as depicted in Figure 3, these CEP engines provide a narrow class of functionalities, and hence are unsuitable for OM applications.

DSMS engines [1], [5] can handle complex operations and are designed for fast streams (but are still slower than a control system). DSMS are primarily designed for continuous SQL query processing but they do not provide the rich analysis functionality needed for OM applications. Furthermore, like EDWs and ETL engines there is no direct mechanism for real time action.

As depicted in Figure 3, DSMSs are closest to what we desire in an OM system since these systems are meant to handle large volumes of streaming heterogeneous data. For designing OM systems, our best is in enhancing DSMS with additional functionality and combining this with a CEP engine to enable real time action (and a DBMS for quick access stored historical data). With this we introduce our target system.

4   Live BI for OM

By Live BI (Business Intelligence), we mean a platform and a set of attendant operators such that we can execute SQL and higher order analysis operators (such as outlier detection), over streaming and stored data, and for structured and unstructured data. For the OM case, we do not need all the capabilities of a Live BI platform but many are needed. In Figure 4, we show the conceptual architecture of a Live BI platform.

Among the features we need from a Live BI platform for addressing the OM problem, one is an ability to execute hybrid queries for on-demand analysis, meaning a query that is executed over both stored and streaming data. We also need a rich library of operators, especially event detection operators such as those for outlier detection. Outlier detection does not require one but many different operators to cover for the variety of cases involved in an OM scenario. For example, outlier detection over time series data for threshold violation is a distinct operator as compared to the outlier detection method for outlier detection over heterogeneous data (as discussed in the next section). Since our data in a general OM case is heterogeneous and can be both unstructured and structured data, we need to be able to process both data types. Finally, such a system needs to be massively parallel to process large volume of data while meeting the real time constraints.

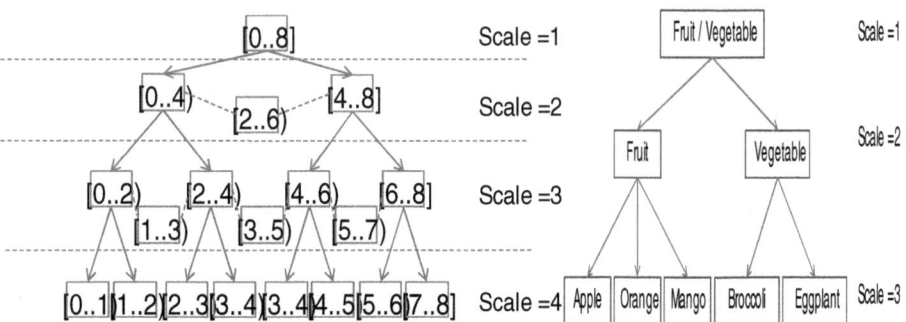

Fig. 5. Sample HNT for Numerical Data (Left) and for Categorical Data (Right)

Besides these, we need a visualization layer for end user control over the OM system and to allow the user to ask visual intelligent queries [11]. This would allow an operator to study a scenario and make judgments. There is a need for new techniques in visual analytics, such as correlation analysis over streaming data but in this paper we skip that discussion.

5   Methods for OM

We now briefly discuss two solutions that arise out of various domains we have been studying, which are important as analysis tools for an OM application (i) Outlier Detection and (ii) Frequent Itemset Mining.

5.1   Outlier Detection

As discussed previously, in OM finding outliers is critical. These outliers need to be detected efficiently over streaming heterogeneous data. Furthermore, the outliers may exist at an arbitrary set of dimensions over different abstraction levels. For example, in IT-OM, where various hardware and software components are issuing events, some user might be interested in events primarily concerned with outlier alerts from hardware components, whereas some other user might be primarily interested in events from software components. These could obviously, share dimensions such as severity, creation time, etc.

The challenge then is to build a framework that can detect these outliers over streaming window, over arbitrary window sizes [5], over heterogeneous data. Furthermore to cope with large volumes, it is preferable that computation can be shared for outlier detection over different sets of dimensions. We call this framework *Outlier Cube*. In outlier cube, each outlier (hence an event) is defined by a continuous query specifying the dimensions of interest, and the sliding window size over which the outliers need to be computed. The results of each query are a continuously updated list of outliers along with some measure of each outlier's "*outlierliness*".

In outlier cube, for each dimension, the data is stored in a hierarchical tree such that, given a set of dimensions, the trees corresponding to the specified dimensions can be combined over streaming data for outlier detection. The tree, which we call HNT (Hierarchical Neighborhood Tree), represents a scale based division of space and each level of the tree corresponds to a scale at which the data is being studied. The overall solution can be conceptually understood as a multidimensional cube in some space, where by recursively dividing this space we arrive at smaller scale based cubes. The cardinality in this cube determines if a point is an outlier or not. Example tree for numerical data and for categorical data are shown in Figure 5.

For the purpose of outlier detection, we define an outlier to be a point that has less than some threshold points in its "*scale based neighborhood*". By scale based neighborhood of a point, we mean those points are within a scale-based distance of the point in each dimension. (This is preferable to considering all the dimensions together since this allows us to share computations). For numerical data, we take distance to be $(max\text{-}min)/2^{scale}$ (where *max-min* represents the span in the dimension).

With an increase in scale this neighborhood becomes tighter. (For example in the Figure 5, we can observe that within each node of the tree, the span is getting smaller.)

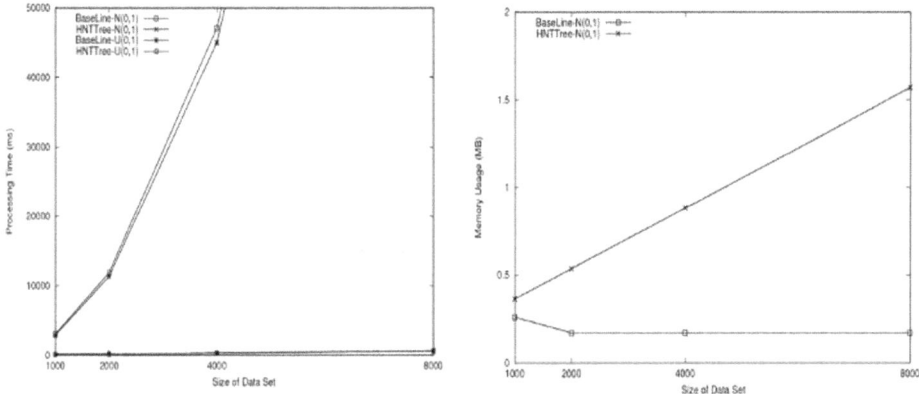

Fig. 6. Memory and CPU Consumption Comparison

As the neighborhood becomes smaller, the number of neighbors a point has also goes down, till at some scale a point is declared to be an outlier, or we reach max scale. The scale then essentially is an indicator of "outlierliness".

Algorithmically, as a multidimensional point streams in, it is inserted into the HNTs of each of the dimensions, which means insertion from the root node to the leaf node of the HNT. Inserting into a node essentially informs us of all the neighbors the point has at the scale which the node represents. For example, a point with a value of 2.5 in a dimension will be in the node *[2...4)* and *[1...3)* at *Scale =3* in the example HNT above. We can show that for an l_∞ distance, all points that are within *(max-min)/* 2^{scale}, (where *max-min* represents the span in the dimension), distance of a point are its neighbors at that scale. The HNT for numerical data gives us approximate neighborhoods and hence speeds up the computation of neighbors. The approximation is that some points that are not the neighbors are also included in the neighborhood relationship.

Then to find if a point is an outlier at a scale, we do an intersection on its neighbors from each dimension. If the cardinality of intersection is less than a threshold, the point is an outlier at that scale. This method allows us to say a couple of things: (i) At a scale *s*, assuming that we consider only real and categorical variables, where the real variable are scaled as descried before and the user specifies a HNT for categorical data, our approach finds outliers such that at scale *s*, there are no false positives (ii) If we specify the maximum scale s_{max}, our method will identify all outliers as defined by up to $s_{max} - 1$, but will have some false negatives at scale s_{max}.

The tradeoff we get the loss of some accuracy is that we gain on efficiency. Because of use of a tree per dimension, where such a tree is encoded and accessed using bitwise operations our approach in practice is linear in complexity. We have evaluated our approach both in terms of accuracy of outlier detection and the efficiency of our method. In Figure 6 (left), we show that whereas for a Naïve approach the CPU increases exponentially with the data size, in an HNT based approach, it increases linearly. This is done at the cost of linear increase in memory consumption, as shown in Figure 6 (right).

5.2   Event Correlation with Frequent Itemsets Mining

As mentioned earlier, we are interested in finding correlation over events that have occurred in the past to reduce the number of events in the present, i.e., from historical data find correlations between events and use them to automatically construct rules to suppress current events.

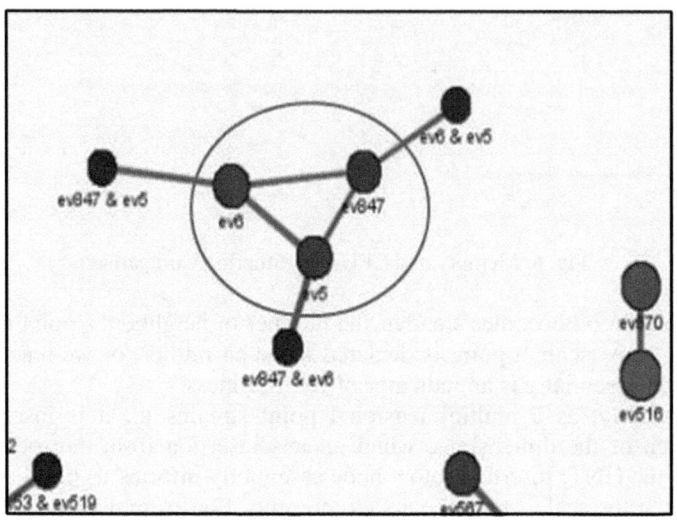

Fig. 7. Example of Correlation Analysis

In Figure 7, we give an example of a correlation with high support and confidence that was obtained using correlation analysis on a customer data set. The three events found are *ev6, ev5, ev847*, where *ev6* indicates a *distribution file problem*, *ev5* indicates an *inability to read a file*, and *ev847* indicates a *problem with distribution*. Our domain expert's interpretation is that the group of event essentially says that for an application an inability to find a file that specifies how distribution needs to be done lead to a distribution failure. To reduce the operator's workload, we can create rule which says that when these three events occur together they can be replaced by single event type, say *evDistribution,* which reflects the distribution problem. By doing this, we have reduced the number of events that an operator has to process from three to one for every occurrence of the three events together and by ensuring that discovered correlations have a high support, we ensure that the volume of events that an operator has to process in real time is reduced. Furthermore, we have provided the operator with a higher order insight.

We use frequent set mining to find these correlations. The reason to use sets instead of sequences is that very often the events arrive in an out of order fashion. We present our approach in brief. We first perform *event typing*. The events that flow into the Networked Operation Center (NOC) are verbose and we need to cast them into an event type for ease of analysis. This is done by decomposing and comparing the event descriptions from historical event logs, where "similar" event descriptions results in the same event type. We mine for correlation rules as frequent itemsets over these event types; hence for the purpose of discovering these rules, we use association rule mining over the event types obtained after event typing.

Although, association rule mining is a well understood KDD process, as a first step we need a mapping in the OM context to a market basket. We call such a mapping an *episode*. We divide the overall time range into two series of overlapping windows: *[0...T), [T...2T), ...,* and *[0.5T...1.5T), [1.5T...2.5T], ...,* . This way of creating episodes ensures that every event that occurs within $\pm T/2$ of an occurrence event e is in the same episode as e. (It also adds some events that are occur more than $\pm T/2$ of an occurrence of e.)

Once the episodes have been created, we treat the episodes as a market basket and perform traditional association rule mining to obtain correlation rules. The challenge when working with real data is that the number of such rules obtained is very large, whereas we want a fewer number of rules that can be easily and quickly verified by a domain expert. Furthermore, many of these are cross-supported itemsets [16], which are not very useful as correlation rules.

We then need a mechanism for finding rules that have high support, are not cross-supported and can lead to a significant reduction in the number of events that are processed by an operator. To do this we use *h-confidence* [16]. The overall steps are the following:

1) We start with a frequent itemset S_1 obtained from regular association rule mining.
2) We use h-confidence (begin with a low initial value) and find all itemsets above this threshold to obtain S_2 from S_1.
3) We then obtain *maximal itemsets* [16] S_3 from S_2.
4) We slowly raise the h-confidence till an independence set S_4 is obtained. (By *independence* we mean that intersection of any two itemsets is empty).
5) We then compute the reduction achieved. (*Reduction* is computed as a percentage change in the space needed with the correlations.)
6) Raise the value of h-confidence and go to Step 2. This process terminates since beyond some value of h-confidence no itemsets are obtained.

From the above steps we choose that itemset S_4 that gives us the largest reduction (obtained in Step 5) in the number of events.

Table 1. Results Obtained over Operations Management Data

Data Set	Number of Itemsets	Reduction
1	15	12.4%
2	16	19.9%
3	15	11.2%
4	17	15.3%
5	4	7.5%

In Table 1, we give results for event reduction obtained on five different real life IT-OM data sets. The results show that with a small number of correlations we are able to obtain good reduction in the number of events that would require an operator to process.

6   Conclusions and Future Work

In this paper, we have discussed the problem of real time operations management. This means analyzing large amount of heterogeneous streaming data to provide real time insights. We have identified the general characteristics and requirements of such applications and discussed the state of the art and its shortcomings. Finally, we present, in brief, new solutions that can help overcome these shortcomings.

This problem is by no means solved. There are many architectural challenges before us: lack of standards and naming conventions, lack of common integration framework, etc. Besides these, there will always be a need for better algorithms for outlier detection and event correlation and need to handle uncertainty in data (This can be particularly the case with sensor data). Solving for hybrid queries is also an emerging area in the database community. As we introduce new operators, an important consideration is that the operators need to be designed keeping in mind the requirements and characteristics of OM system described before.

Finally, in large scale deployment of such a system, as we design our execution flows, we will need to optimize for various competing objectives such as response time and degree of approximation, latency and recoverability, etc. We have started investigating this problem [15], but many challenges remain.

References

[1]   Abadi, D., et al.: Aurora:A New Model and Architecture for Data Stream Management. VLDB Journal 12(2), 120–139 (2003)
[2]   Aggarwal, C.: Data Streams: Models and Algorithms. Springer, Heidelberg (2007)
[3]   Agrawal, R., Srikant, R.: Fast Algorithms for Mining Association Rules in Large Databases. Proceedings of VLDB, 487–499 (1994)
[4]   Arasuet, A., et al.: Linear Road: A Stream DataManagement Benchmark. Proceedings of VLDB (2004)
[5]   Babcock, B., et al.: Models and issues in data stream systems. In: ACM PODS, pp. 1–16 (2002)
[6]   Börzsönyi, S., Kossmann, D., Stocker, K.: The Skyline Operator. In: Proceedings of the 17th International Conference on Data Engineering, pp. 421–430 (2001)
[7]   Bruckner, R.M., List, B., Schiefer, J.: Striving Towards Near Real-Time Data Integration for Data Warehouses. In: Kambayashi, Y., Winiwarter, W., Arikawa, M. (eds.) DaWaK 2002. LNCS, vol. 2454, pp. 317–326. Springer, Heidelberg (2002)
[8]   Barga, R.S., Goldstein, J., Ali, M.H., Hong, M.: Consistent Streaming Through Time: A Vision for Event Stream Processing. In: CIDR, pp. 363–374 (2007)
[9]   Chandola, V., Banerjee, A., Kumar, V.: Anomaly detection: A survey. ACM Compute Survey 41(3) (2009)

[10] Gupta, C., et al.: CHAOS.A Data Stream Analysis Architecture for Enterprise Applications. In: IEEE CEC, pp. 33–40 (2009)

[11] Hao, M., Dayal, U., Keim, D.: Morent.Intelligent visualanalytics queries. In: IEEE Symposium on Visual AnalyticsScience and Technology, pp. 91–98 (2007)

[12] Liu, M., et al.: E-Cube: multi-dimensional event sequence analysis using hierarchical pattern query sharing. In: SIGMOD, pp. 889–900 (2011)

[13] Madden, S., Shah, M., Hellerstein, J.M., Raman, V.: Continuouslyadaptive continuous queries over streams. In: SIGMOD, pp. 49–60 (2002)

[14] Marwah, M., et al.: Data analysis,visualization and knowledge discovery in sustainabledata centers. In: COMPUTE 2009: Proceedings of the 2nd Bangalore Annual Compute Conference, pp. 1–8. ACM (2009)

[15] Simitsis, A., Wilkinson, K., Castellanos, M., Dayal, U.: QoX-driven ETL design: Reducing the cost of ETL consulting engagements. In: SIGMOD Conference, pp. 953–960 (2009)

[16] Tan, P.-N., Steinbach, M., Kumar, V.: Introduction to Data Mining. Addison Wesley (2006)

A Position Correction Method for RSSI Based Indoor-Localization

Taishi Yoshida[1], Junbo Wang[2], and Zixue Cheng[2]

[1] Graduate School of Computer Science and Engineering
[2] School of Computer Science and Engineering,
University of Aizu, Aizuwakamatsu, Japan
`{m5141136,j-wang,z-cheng}@u-aizu.ac.jp`

Abstract. Thanks to the development of wireless communication and sensor technology, a smart object that is embedded sensors and/or communication equipment in objects that we use in daily lives is researched. Also the Internet of Things (IoT) is a networking technology by using the smart objects and attracts high attention. Furthermore, a smart home which consists of these technologies is expected to be spread widely. In the smart home, it is important to get the information of location/position accurately in order to provide services based on the information of person or object. One of the most popular methods for estimating the position of person or object, the Receive Signal Strength Indicator (RSSI) method is used for many systems. RSSI method uses a behavior that strength of a signal from beacon node is inversely proportional to distance. However, the location of the wireless nodes which receive a signal has to fix and be discovered in advance. Therefore if the nodes are moved from an original position, the person or object cannot be detected accurately. Accordingly, we propose a method that estimating the positions of moved nodes and updating the position information by adding node for the RSSI positioning method. Currently, we have performed preliminary implementation of the system. In the future we will finish the implementation of the methods designed in the paper and evaluate the methods in details.

Keywords: Localization, positioning, RSSI.

1   Introduction

Recently, thanks to the development of wireless communication and sensor technology, a smart object that is embedded sensors and/or communication equipment in objects that we use in daily lives such as glasses, wallets and pens is going to be realized. Also the Internet of Things (IoT), the networks which are formed by using the smart objects, attracts more attention and is researched all over the world. Furthermore, a smart home which consists of the smart object is expected to be spread widely and it will contribute to care elderly peoples from remote places with networks. In addition, the smart home is able to manage energies that are consumed in the house such as electricity, and is expected to save energies. These systems provide services based on the information of person or object. Therefore it is important to get the information of location/position accurately.

S. Kikuchi et al. (Eds.): DNIS 2011, LNCS 7108, pp. 286–295, 2011.

We develop a detecting system for person or object using wireless communication technology embedded in smart objects. Although the existing systems for localization need some dedicated devices, we aim to eliminate the need of the dedicated devices by using the wireless communication devices of smart objects.

We consider the use of the Receive Signal Strength Indicator (RSSI) as the detecting method. The RSSI method uses a behavior that strength of a signal from beacon node is inversely proportional to distance. The benefit of using RSSI is easy to install and relatively inexpensive, since RSSI method uses commonly-used wireless applications. In this method, the wireless tag transmits a signal, and some wireless nodes receive the signal and measure the strength of the signal. After that, the position of the tag is estimated by comparing the signal strength with other signal strengths which are measured in advance at arbitrary reference points. To estimate accurate position of tags by the method, the location of the wireless nodes has to fix and be discovered. Accordingly, the tags cannot be detected accurately if the positions of the nodes are changed. The information of position of the nodes has to update in order to detect accurately.

To update the position information of moved wireless nodes, we use the remaining nodes that are not moved. The remaining nodes communicate with the moved node and get the RSSI from the signal of moved node. By calculating the distance between the moved node and some remaining nodes based on the RSSI values, the position information of the moved node is estimated and updated.

2   Related Researches

Some Localization methods are proposed and can be mainly classified into two general groups. One is Range-based localization and the other is Range-free localization. Firstly, we introduce some typical methods based on Range-free localization. The Range-free localization uses beacon nodes, i.e. their position is known in advance and then estimates the location of unknown node based on the relation of nodes or hops.

Bulush et al. [1] proposed the localization method by calculating centroid of several nodes. This method uses the nodes called reference points. Each reference point broadcasts beacons which includes their position information periodically to their neighbor nodes. Each unknown node hears the beacons from neighbor reference points, and calculates centroid of the reference points. Finally the node determines the calculated centroid as their position. To estimate position accurately, unknown node needs a lot of position information of reference point.

DV-Hop [2] estimates the position based on the number of hops from the landmark node and the average distance per one hop. Each landmark floods packets including their position information and hop count. The hop count is incremented when the packet is relayed. Each landmark calculates an average distance per one hop based on the distance and the number of hops to other landmarks. The node calculates a distance from the landmark based on the average distance per one hop and the hop counts from the landmark. Finally the position of node is estimated by using triangulation.

APIT [3][4] estimates the position of the node by conducting Approximate Point-in-Triangulation (APIT) test repeatedly. The test evaluates which the target node resides inside or outside of the triangle area that is made of three arbitrary anchor nodes. The target node exchanges the RSSI data with their neighbors and judges which node is closer to the anchor. Then if the neighbor that is further from three anchors than the target node exists, the target node resides outsides of the triangle area. If the target node is near the side of the triangle, some errors may be observed.

Range-based localization estimates the position based on signal propagation time, direction of arrival and the signal strength.

Time of Arrival (TOA) uses the propagation time that takes during the radio wave or sound wave which is transmitted from sender node arrives at the receiver node. The method is used in Global Positioning System (GPS). TOA needs the time synchronization between sender node and receiver node and expensive devices.

Relative to the usage of the signal propagation time for TOA, Time Difference of Arrival (TDOA) uses the difference of a signal arrival time at some receiver nodes. This method does not need to synchronize the time between sender node and receiver node. n the other hand, the method depends on the expensive devices. TDOA method is adopted in Active Bat[5] and Cricket[6].

Angle of Arrival (AOA) is the extended method of TOA and TDOA. AOA estimates direction of the arrival signals. While this method uses at least two nodes, also requires particular kind of devices such as an antenna array or a directional microphone. AOA is adopted in [7].

Receive Signal Strength (RSS) and Receive Signal Strength Indicator (RSSI) which is a quantification of RSS, use the principle that a strength of a signal which is transmitted from a node attenuates inversely proportional to the distance. As compared to other range-based method, RSS and RSSI do not have to use the special devices and is able to use existing wireless communication devices. Therefore RSS and RSSI reduce costs. However, the methods are more sensitive to interference, diffraction and attenuation. On the other hand, some signal propagation model are proposed for this problem. RADAR [8] is an indoor location and tracking system based on RSS. In RADAR system, the beacon signal which is transmitted a mobile host is received by some base stations. Based on the signal strength, RADAR estimates the location of the mobile host by using triangulation. For correcting variation of the signal strength by environment, the Wall Attenuation Factor (WAF) radio propagation model is used.

3   Model and Problem

3.1   Model

Our proposed system has two behaviors. One is a normal behavior and the other is a behavior when smart object is moved. In the normal behavior, the system estimates position of person or object using smart objects which have wireless communication equipment in the house. For accurate positioning, the system needs at least three smart objects. Fig. 1 shows the model of the normal behavior. First of all, the smart objects which are located around a person or object that a user wants to get the position information receive signals and transmit the RSSI data to a computer. Based on the RSSI of each smart object, the system estimates position/location on the computer. At the end, the system provides some sort of service appropriate to the position/location information. We assume the using smart object such as a wristwatch and an accessory for estimating the position/location of person. Fig. 2 shows the model when the position of some objects changed. In this model, we assume scissors that one of the smart objects is moved. When the scissors moved, other objects which reside it receive signals from scissors and calculate RSSI. Then, send it to the computer as well as the normal behavior. The computer gets a correct position of the scissors from the RSSIs and positions of the objects which is neighbor of scissors. After that, the system behaves same as normal behavior.

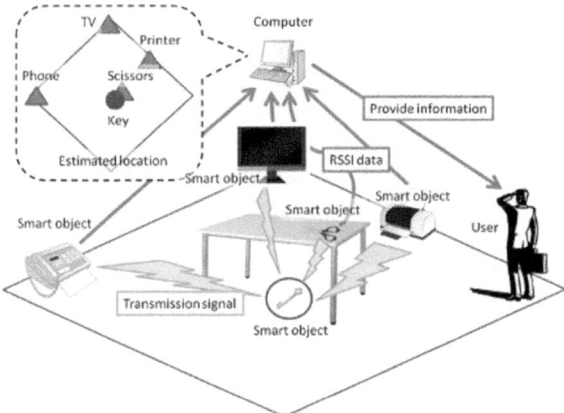

Fig. 1. A Use Case of Normal Behavior

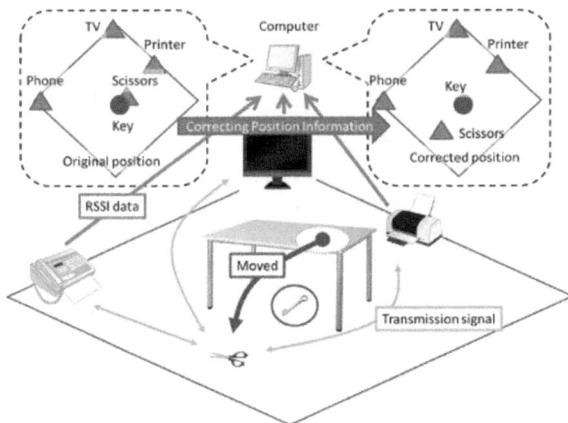

Fig. 2. A Behavior in the Case that Object is Moved

3.2   Definition of Problems

We have to solve the following problems to realize our proposed system. First is that the system needs to detect that a node was moved for correcting position of the node. The second is the correction of position in which case the number of the nodes is three. When the number of the nodes is four or more, the system can correct the position of moved node by using at least three nodes. However, if one of the nodes is moved, the system have to correct the position of the node using remaining nodes in which case there are no more than three nodes.

4   Position Correction Method

4.1   RSSI Based Localization

In this part, we describe a system and method that we propose. We will explain about the system flow and a localization algorithm that we used for base of our system at first, and then explain about the method of position correction.

   Firstly we explain the system flow. We defined the node which estimates the position of the unknown node as the *estimation node*. The proposed system consists of estimation nodes, a sink node and a computer. At the beginning the estimation

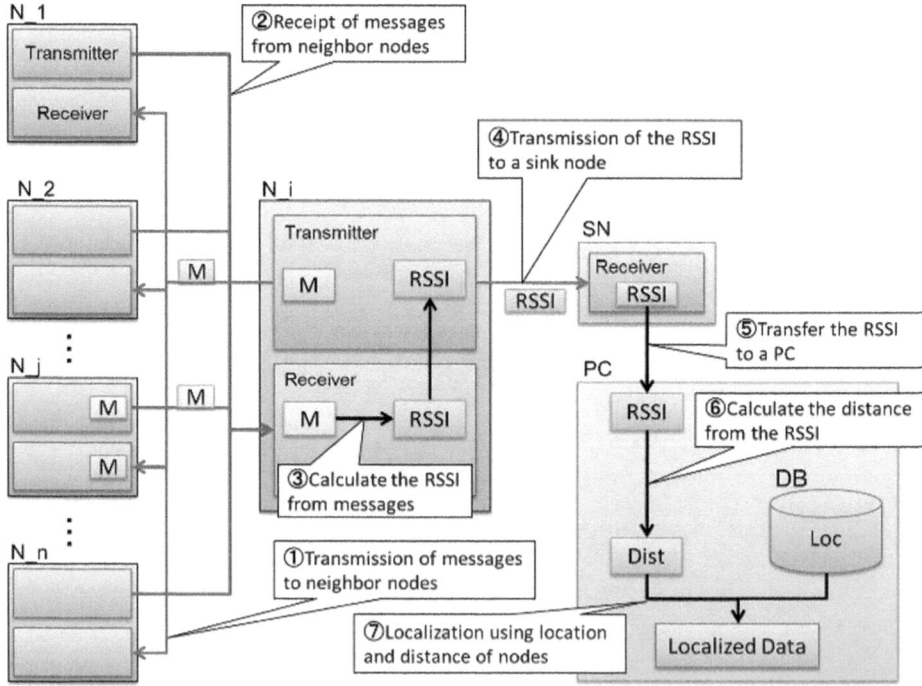

Fig. 3. System Model

nodes transmit messages to neighbor nodes and receive messages from the neighbor nodes. After that, the estimation nodes calculate RSSI value from the messages and transmit the RSSI to the sink node. The estimation nodes repeat this procedure. Sink node receives RSSI data from each estimation nodes and transfers the data to computer. The computer has two kinds of database, one is to store distance information between two nodes and other one is to store position coordinate information of estimation nodes. When the computer receives RSSI data from sink node, then it calculates distance based on the RSSI and stores the distance into the distance database. Finally, the computer estimates and corrects node position using the distance and position data. Figure 3 shows the system flow. In Fig. 3, N_1 to N_n represent estimation nodes. Also SN and PC are a sink node and a computer respectively.

We explain the system adopts multilateration based on the RSSI value as basic localization algorithm. As the method for calculating a distance from RSSI value, the log normal shadowing model is generally used. This method is used in many localization using signal strength [8][9]. The log normal shadowing model is expressed by the formula as follows.

$$RSSI(d) = P_T - P_L(d_0) - 10n \log_{10}\left(\frac{d}{d_0}\right) + X_\sigma \qquad (1)$$

Where, P_T is transmission power and $P_L(d_0)$ is attenuation at the place where distant d_0 from the transmitter. Also n is path loss exponent and X_σ is measurement error. To derive the distance from RSSI value, the following formula is used.

$$d = d_0 \cdot 10^{\left(\frac{P_T - P_L(d_0) + X_\sigma - RSSI(d)}{10n}\right)} \qquad (2)$$

On the other hand, the multilateration algorithm [10] is the method that estimates the position of the unknown node by calculating simultaneous equation the distance between the beacon nodes and the unknown node and position coordinates of more than three beacon nodes. We suppose the position coordinate of unknown node and estimation node and the distance between two nodes as (x_u, y_u), (x_i, y_i), d_{iu} respectively, the position of unknown node (x_u, y_u) can be derived using a formula as follows:

$$f(x_u, y_u) = d_{iu} - \sqrt{(x_u - x_i)^2 + (y_u - y_i)^2} \qquad (3)$$

4.2   Position Correction

In this section, we describe position correction method of moved estimation node. If estimation node is moved, the position of unknown node cannot be estimated accurately. Therefore the position of moved estimation node must be corrected. The position correction has two phases. First phase is the detection of moved estimation node. Second phase is the position correction of the node. Firstly we explain the detection phase.

4.2.1   Detection of Moved Node

To correct the position of estimation node, the system has to detect the movement of estimation node. The system judges whether the estimation node is moved or not based on the RSSI value of the signal from the moved node to its neighbor nodes. Here, we assume that only one estimation node moves at one time and N_i is the moved node. N_j, is the neighbor nodes of N_i, receives messages from N_i and calculate RSSI value $RSSI_{ij}$. The system sums the RSSI and averages the sum by increments. After that, the system gets $RSSI\_DIFF_{ij}$ by subtracting the previous average of RSSI $RSSI_{ij}(t\text{-}1)$ from the current average of RSSI $RSSI_{ij}(t)$ and compares it with the predefined threshold Th. When the $RSSI\_DIFF_{ij}$ between N_i and all its neighbors N_j are higher than Th, the system judges node N_i moved. We show the algorithm of detection phase below.

```
// Detection of moved node
foreach(all neighbors of N_i){
    // Average RSSI between N_i and N_j
    RSSI_ij(t)=averageRSSI(RSSI_ij, WINDOW_SIZE);
    // Subtraction previous RSSI
    RSSI_DIFF_ij=|RSSI_ij(t)-RSSI_ij(t-1)|;
}
// Comparison with threshold
// If all RSSI_DIFF are higher than the threshold, N_i is
// assumed a moved node
if(all neighbors' RSSI_DIFF_ij>Th){N_i.moved=TRUE;}
```

4.2.2   Correction of Node Position

When the move of the node is detected, the system transitions from the detection phase to the position correction phase. Update of the position is performed based on the RSSI value of the moved node derived at neighbor nodes. Same as previous section, we assume the node N_i is moved. The neighbor nodes N_j derive RSSI value of N_i from received message and calculate average $RSSI_{ij}(t)$. The system calculates the distance between N_i and N_j from $RSSI_{ij}(t)$ which is derived from each its neighbor N_j. After that, the system calculates multilateration based on d_{ij} and $loc(N_j)$ which is the position coordinate of N_j, and updates $loc(N_i)$ which is the position of node N_i by the result of multilateration.

```
if(N_i.moved = TRUE){
    // Receipt messages from neighbor nodes
    // Calculation of RSSIs from the messages
    for(j=1; j<n; j++){
        if(message from N_j exists){
            RSSI_ij(t)=averageRSSI(RSSI_ij, WINDOW_SIZE);
            // Calculate distance from RSSI
```

```
      d_{ij}=getDist(RSSI_{ij}(t));
    }
  }
  // Update by new location data which is derived by
  // multilateration
  loc(N_i)=multilaterate(loc(N_j), d_{ij});
}
```

4.2.3   Case of Only Three Estimation Nodes

The number of estimation nodes which is needed for localization is at least three nodes. In the case of the number of estimation nodes is four, the system can correct the position of one moved node. On the other hand, in case of the number of nodes is three, the system has to correct the position of one node using remaining two nodes. So we use the original position data of the moved node and the derived current distance between two nodes. When a moved node detected, the system calculates the distance between the moved node and remaining estimation nodes using the remaining estimation nodes. Then, two candidates of the new position of the moved node are possible. The system sets closer one to the original position of the moved node as the new position.

```
if(Num of Nodes==3){
  // two candidates of new position
  (loc(N_i'), loc(N_i''))=multilaterate(loc(N_j), d_{ij});
  // select position coordinate which is closer to
  // original position of moved node
  if(|loc(N_i')- loc(N_i)|>=| loc(N_i'')- loc(N_i)|){
    loc(N_i)=loc(N_i');
  }
  else if(|loc(N_i')- loc(N_i)|<| loc(N_i'')- loc(N_i)|){
    loc(N_i)=loc(N_i'');
  }
}
```

5   Preliminary Implementation

Currently, we have performed preliminary implementation of the system based on TEXAS INSTRUMENTS CC2530 ZigBee Development Kit. We used four SmartRF05 Battery Boards and one Smart RF05EB for estimation nodes and a sink node. We used DELL INSPIRON 6400 which is installed Microsoft Windows XP SP3 for storing data and calculating position of node. Fig.4 shows an implementation model. Where we defined the unknown node, estimation nodes sink node as UN, EN, and SN respectively. Fig.5 shows a photo of implementation testbed.

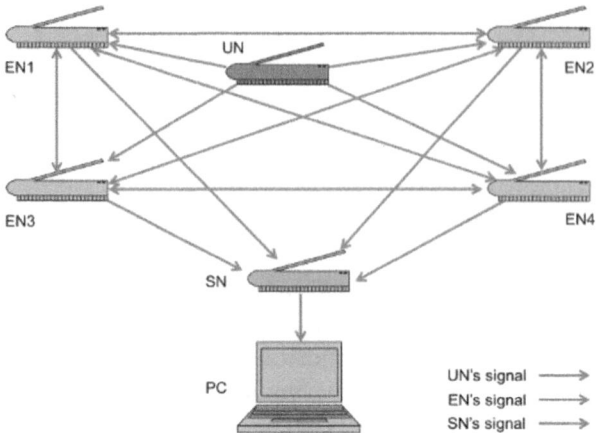

Fig. 4. Implementation Model

Fig. 5. Implementation Testbed

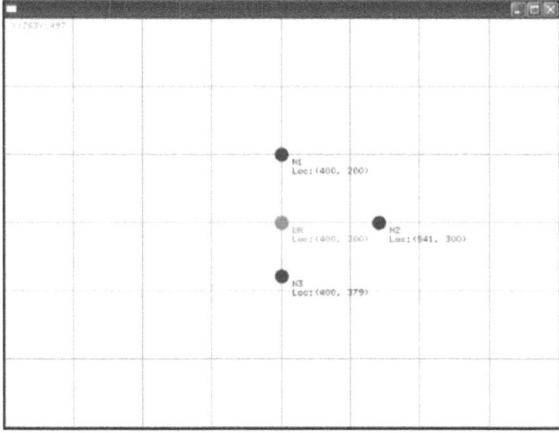

Fig. 6. Experimentation Procedure

Also we used Code:Blocks and C++ as the development environment and language for a localization program. Fig.6 shows a screen image of the localization program.

6   Conclusion

We proposed novel method to correct position of a moved node for indoor-localization system. Currently, we have performed preliminary implementation of the system. In the future we will finish the implementation of the methods designed in the paper and evaluate the methods in details.

References

1. Bulush, N., Heidemann, J., Estrin, D.: GPS-less Low Cost Outdoor Localization For Very Small Devices. IEEE Personal Communications Magazine, Special Issue on Smart Spaces and Environments (2000)
2. Niculescu, D., Nath, B.: DV Based Positioning in Ad Hoc Networks. Telecommunication Systems 22(1-4), 267–280 (2003)
3. He, T., Huang, C., Blum, B.M., Stankovic, J.A., Abdelzaher, T.: Range-Free Localization Schemes for Large Scale Sensor Networks. In: Proc. ACM MOBICOM, pp. 81–95 (2003)
4. He, T., Huang, C., Blum, B.M., Stankovic, J.A., Abdelzaher, T.F.: Range-Free Localization and Its Impact on Large Scale Sensor Networks. ACM Transactions on Embedded Computing Systems 4(4), 877–906 (2005)
5. Ward, A., Jones, A., Hopper, A.: A New Location Technique for the Active Office. IEEE Personal Communications 4(5), 42–47 (1997)
6. Priyantha, N.B., Chakraborty, A., Balakrishnan, H.: The Cricket Location-Support System. In: Proc. ACM MOBICOM, pp. 32–43 (2000)
7. Niculescu, D., Nath, B.: Ad Hoc Positioning System (APS) Using AOA. In: Proc. IEEE INFOCOM, pp. 1734–1743 (2003)
8. Bahl, P., Padmanabhan, V.N.: RADAR: An In-Building RF-based User Location and Tracking System. In: Proc. IEEE INFOCOM, pp. 775–784 (2002)
9. Guo, Z., Guo, Y., Hong, F., Jin, Z., He, Y., Feng, Y., Liu, Y.: Perpendicular Intersection: Locating Wireless Sensors With Mobile Beacon. IEEE Transactions on Vehicular Technology 59(7), 3501–3509 (2010)
10. Savvides, A., Han, C.C., Strivastava, M.B.: Dynamic Fine-Grained Localization in Ad-Hoc Networks of Sensors. In: Proc. ACM MOBICOM, pp. 166–179 (April 2001)

A Novel Network Coding Scheme for Data Collection in WSNs with a Mobile BS

Jie Li[1], Xiucai Ye[1], and Yusheng Ji[2]

[1] Department of Computer Science
University of Tsukuba, Japan
[2] Information Systems Architecture Science Research Division
National Institute of Informatics, Japan

Abstract. In this paper, we present a novel network coding scheme called separate network coding (SNC) for data collection in WSNs with a mobile Base Station (mBS). SNC not only provides efficient storage method for continuous data to collect all the data segments generated in one time interval, but also maintains a high success ratio of data collection. The performance evaluation has been conducted through comprehensive computer simulation. It further demonstrates the feasibility and superiority of our scheme.

Keywords: separate network coding, wireless sensor networks, data collection, mobile base stations.

1 Introduction

Wireless sensor networks (WSNs) consist of hundreds or thousands of sensor nodes which do not rely on any pre-deployed network architecture. The sensor nodes are capable of sensing, processing, and transmitting environmental information, which are deployed to monitor certain physical phenomena or to detect and track certain objects in an area of interests [1]. A single sensor node may only be equipped with limited resources, such as low CPU power, limited communication capability, limited battery and memory storage [1]. One sensor node can store only a small amount of data collected from its surroundings. To collect the information from sensor networks, a Base Stations (BS) function as intermediate gateway between the sensor network and the application end user.

WSNs have enabled new classes of applications that benefit a large number of fields, including environmental monitoring, battlefield surveillance, biological detection, smart spaces, industrial diagnostics, etc. [2,3]. A very interesting problem that arises in application of WSNs is how to collect data from harsh and extreme environments [4,5]. In these environments, the data are continuously sensed by the sensor nodes, while the communication between the sensor nodes and a BS is expensive and scarce. Thus, Data collection by the BS is only performed occasionally. Sensor nodes shall temporarily store the data and provide the desired data when the BS approaches. Typical examples include the Great Duck Island habitat monitoring system [7], seabird colonies are extremely

S. Kikuchi et al. (Eds.): DNIS 2011, LNCS 7108, pp. 296–311, 2011.

sensitive to human interaction. A fast data retrieval is usually desired in each data collection. This paper addresses the data collection issue in WSNs with a mobile BS.

Network Coding is an emerging technique that has several interesting applications in practical networking systems [8]. Network Coding was first introduced for improving the performance of multicast routing [9]. Our study is different from the original applications in routing. We extend the idea of network coding for data collection in WSNs with a mBS. Similar idea of network coding extent for the applications of data storage and distribution can be found in [10,11], in which the code is created over the connecting of data and storage nodes. The further theoretically study about network coding for data distribution and the practical system for random file distribution are presented in [12] and [13]. Using network coding for ubiquitous data collection was introduced in [14,15] for wireless sensor networks.

An interesting network coding based data collection scheme was proposed by Dimakis et al. [14], which encodes all data segments in each node. The distinct benefit is the improvement of success ratio of data collection. However, the data segments to be collected are static and fixed. This scheme cannot support data collection in which the number of data segments is not predetermined. Wang et al. [6] proposed another interesting network coding base data collection scheme, known as Partial Network Coding (PNC). By encoding only part of the original data segments and removing the older data segments, PNC allows efficient storage for data collection to collect the part of newer data segments. Since the number of original data segments encoded in each combined data segment is a variable respect to time, the combined data segments cannot be always decoded by the BS. Thus, the the success ratio of data collection in PNC is no so high.

In this paper, we focus on the data collection issue in WSNs with a mobile BS, which is similar to that considered in [6]. Consider that the data are continuously sensed while data collection by a BS is only performed occasionally. *Note that PNC [6] can only collect a part of m latest data segments.* Here m is the number of latest data segments in a time interval in which $n(t)$ ($n(t) > m$) data segments are generated. In some practical applications, collect the amount of latest data segments is not enough. They need to collect as much detailed data as possible, then can try various physical models and test various hypotheses over the data. Our proposed Separate Network Coding (SNC) scheme can collect all the $n(t)$ data segments. SNC bases on the the mobile BSs randomly accessing. By separately encoding a certain number of data segments in a combined data segment, and storing it in the corresponding buffer, SNC not only provide efficient storage method for continuous data, but also maintains a high success ratio of data collection. We address a set of practical concerns toward SNC-based data collection in WSNs. It further demonstrates the feasibility and superiority of our scheme.

The remainder of this paper is organized as follows. In Section 2, we describe the system model and problem formulation. We present the proposed

SNC scheme for data collection in Section 3. In Section 4, we evaluate the performance of SNC by simulations. Finally, we conclude the paper in Section 5.

2 System Description and Problem Formulation

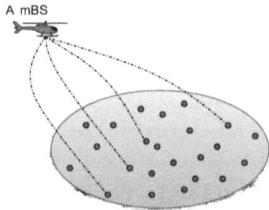

Fig. 1. Data collection by a mBS

Consider that there are N sensor nodes in a WSN with a mobile Base Station (mBS). The sensor nodes are with limited storage space. Each sensor node has B buffers, i.e., the buffer size of each sensor node is B. Each buffer can store only one data segment. In our scheme, by network coding each buffer stores one encoded data segment which encodes a number of data segments. We denote the B buffers as $b_i, i = 1, ..., B$. Consider to collect the information of event (e.g., the temperature goes above 20 °C) of environment by using a WSN. The events are generated continuously. Without loss of generality, we consider there is one mBS which performs data collection occasionally. For example, a helicopter acts as the mBS. The helicopter is with data collection equipment, which is capable of transmitting and receiving radio signals, as illustrated in Fig 1. In each data collection, the mBS will randomly contact some sensor nodes to collect data. Let W ($\leq N$) denote the number of sensor nodes contacted by the mBS in one time interval of data collection. As the bad weather may prohibit the mBS from performing data collection for a long period of time, the sensor nodes in the WSN have no information about when the BS will perform data collection.

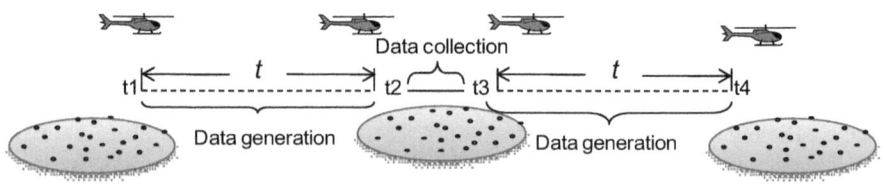

Fig. 2. Data collection by a mBS. At time t_1 and t_3, data collection is finished. At time t_2 and t_4, data collection is started to perform again.

An event is represented by one data segment, denoted by c_j, and generated at a fixed time slot. For convenience, we assume c_q is newer than c_p if $q > p$, i.e., c_q is generated after c_p if $q > p$. The total number of data segments generated in one time interval of data collection is $n(t)$, where the variable t is a data collection time interval. Note that $n(t)$ may increase as t increase. The value of time interval t depends on the time interval that the mBS performs data collection. As an example shown in Fig 2, data collection is finished at time t_1. At time t_2, data collection is started to perform again and then stop at time t_3. At time t_4, data collection is started to perform again. The data collection by the mBS is performed between time t_2 and t_3. The time interval between t_1 and t_2 and the time interval between t_3 and t_4 are the data collection time interval t. During this time interval t, the environment data are continuously generated. So t is also seen as the data generation time. Consider that the data collection time is much less than the data generation time. The data segments generated during data collection time can be negligible for the sake of convenience.

In this paper, we consider to collect *all the data segments* generated in one time interval of data collection. The total number of data segments to be collected is $n(t)$, as shown in Fig 3.

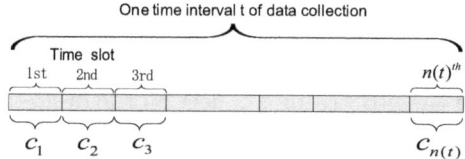

Fig. 3. Data generation in one time interval of data collection. c_i is generated in the ith time slot.

We assume that each data segment is recorded by all the sensor nodes whenever generated. More specifically, some data nodes sense the data and transmit to all the storage nodes, then data coding is done in the storage nodes [6]. As our main work focus on the encoding and data storage in the storage nodes, we omit the data nodes for ease exposition. And the sensor nodes mentioned in this paper function as the storage nodes.

For the network coding, we define a linear function

$$f_i = \sum_{j=1}^{r} \beta_{ij} c_j. \tag{1}$$

It is used to combine an amount of data segments (r data segments, $1 \leq r < n(t)$) as a coded data segment f_i. Here, $\boldsymbol{\beta} = (\beta_{i1}, \beta_{i2}, \cdots, \beta_{ir})$ is a coefficient vector. Each item β_{ij} is randomly generated from a finite field F_q, $\beta_{ij} \neq 0$, $j = 1, ...r$. Since the coding can be viewed as a combination process, f_i is also referred to as a combined data segment, and c_j as an original data segment. Notice that by network coding one buffer can store one combined data segment which encodes a number of original data segments. We use $C(f_i)$ to denote the number of original

Table 1. List of Notation

Notation	Definition
m	Number of latest data segments to be collected
B	Buffer size of each sensor node
b_i	Buffer of each sensor node with index i
W	Number of sensor nodes contacted by the BS for each access
t	Time interval of data collection
$n(t)$	Number of data segments generated in one time interval of data collection
c_j	Original data segment with index j
f_i	Combined data segment by sensor node i
β_{ij}	Coding coefficient for c_j in f_i
$C(f_i)$	Number of data segments combined in f_i
q	Size of finite field for coefficients

data segments combined in f_i. For the sake of convenience, a summary of the notations are given in Table 1.

When the mBS performs data collection, the sensor nodes communicated with it will upload the stored combined data segments and the related coefficient vectors. We further assume that there are packet acknowledgements. Therefore, no packets are lost. If the mBS cannot collect all the desired data, it will perform data collection again and again until succeed. As a result, the WSN will consume more energy and the mBS will spend more time. Thus, the success ratio of data collection serves as a major evaluation criterion in our study, and is defined as follows.

Definition 1 (Success ratio of data collection). *The success ratio of data collection is the probability that the mBS successfully collects all the desired original data segments.*

3   Separate Network Coding Based Scheme for Data Collection

In this section, we introduce a novel network coding scheme called SNC. SNC provides efficient storage method to store all the continuous data segments generated in one time interval, and also maintains a high success ratio of data collection.

3.1   Overview of SNC

In the scheme, each sensor node separately encodes a certain number of original data segments in a combined data segments and stores it in the corresponding buffer. $f^i = (f_{i_1}, f_{i_2}, ..., f_{i_B})$ are the combined data segments stored in sensor

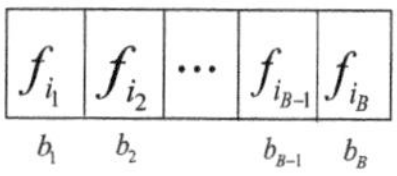

Fig. 4. Data storage in the buffers of sensor node i to collect all data segments

node i, where f_{i_k} is stored in buffer b_k, as shown in Fig 4. The total number of original data segments encoded in the combined data segments in node i is $C(f^i)$, $C(f^i) = \sum_{j=1}^{k} C(f_{i_k})$.

We consider the following two cases: 1) right arrival case that the mBS arrives on time, 2) late arrival case that the mBS arrives lately. In general condition, the mBS performs data collection at regular time interval t_0, $t_0 = minimum\{t\}$. This case is called right arrival case. The total number of original data segments generated in time interval t_0 is $n(t_0)$, $n(t_0) \leq n(t)$. Let W_0 $(\leq N)$ to denote the number of sensor nodes that the BS contacts in the regular time interval t_0. If the mBS arrives when the time interval $t \geq t_0$, we call this case late arrival case.

The encoding and decoding processes in the two cases are with some differences. The encoding and decoding processes in right arrival case is easier, as the total number of original data segments generated in time interval t_0 is a fixed value $n(t_0)$. While in late arrival case, the total number of original data segments generated in time interval $t \geq t_0$ may increase as the time interval increases. A challenge issue is how to let the fixed buffers in each sensor node to store all the data segments whether the mBS arrives on time or lately. We first present the encoding and decoding processes for right arrival case, the enhancement to late arrival case will be presented later.

3.2 Encoding and Decoding Processes in the Right Arrival Case

Data Encoding and Storage. The sensor nodes separately encode a certain number of original data segments in a combined data segment. We first use x $(x \leq W_0)$ to denote this certain number. Once a sensor node receives one or more (until x) data segments, it will select coefficients to multiply the received data segments and subsequently add them to construct one encoded data segment. The coefficients are randomly generated from a finite field F_q. The next received data segments (until the number reaches x) will be encoded in another combined data segment and stored in the corresponding buffer. The sensor nodes also store the coefficient vector of each combined data segment. The storage of coefficient vector introduces an overhead storage that can be made arbitrarily small by coding over larger data segment [16].

The encoding process is incremental. It is performed by each sensor node. Every time an original data segment c_j is encoded with the combined data segment f^i in sensor node i $(i = 1, ..., N)$. The data encoding algorithm (Algorithm 1) is locally executed at each sensor node.

```
Algorithm 1: Data Encoding (f^i, c_j)
Input: original data segment c_j
Output: combined data segment f^i
For k=1 to B
    f_k = 0
end
for j=1 to n(t_0)
    Let k = ⌈j/x⌉
    Randomly generate β_{i_k.j} from F_q;
    f_{i_k} = f_{i_k} + β_{i_1.j}c_j;
end
```

As we assume that the number of original data segments encoded in each combined data segment f_{i_k} is x, $k = 1, ...B$, $x \leq n_0$. Then the total number of data segments encoded in the combined segments in each sensor node $C(f^i)$ is at most Bx. To guarantee each sensor can encode all the data segments, Bx should satisfy

$$Bx \geq n(t_0). \tag{2}$$

Then,

$$B \geq n(t_0)/x. \tag{3}$$

From formula (3), and since B is an integer, we let

$$B = \lceil n(t_0)/x \rceil. \tag{4}$$

Then we have

Lemma 1. *In right arrival case, each sensor node with buffer size $B = \lceil n(t_0)/x \rceil$ is enough to store the combined data segments which encode all the original data segments.*

Data Decoding. The decoding process is performed by the mBS. Note that in $f^i = (f_{i_1}, f_{i_2}, ..., f_{i_B})$, for the forward $B-1$ combined data segments $C(f_{i_k}) = x$, $k = 1, ..., B-1$. As the value of $n(t_0)/x$ is not always an integer, for the last combined data segment $C(f_{i_B}) \leq x$ and $C(f_{i_B}) = n(t_0) - (B-1)x$.

When the mBS arrives, it randomly contacts W_0 sensor nodes to collect BW_0 combined data segments $\mathbf{f} = [f^1, f^2, ..., f^{W_0}]$, where $f^i = (f_{i_1}, f_{i_2}, ..., f_{i_B})$ is the combined data segments collected from sensor node i, $i = 1, ..., W_0$. The mBS also collects the related coefficient vectors $(\overrightarrow{\beta_{i_1}}, \overrightarrow{\beta_{i_2}}, ..., \overrightarrow{\beta_{i_B}})$ about the combined data segments. The decoding process of $\mathbf{f}$ includes B stages, decoding about $\mathbf{f}_1$, $\mathbf{f}_2,...,\mathbf{f}_B$, where $\mathbf{f}_k = [f_{1_k}, f_{2_k}, ..., f_{W_{0k}}]$ is the combined data segments collected from buffer k of W_0 sensor nodes, $k = 1, ..., B$. Decoding about $\mathbf{f}_k$ is to decode the original data segments encoded in the combined data segments which are stored in buffer k of the contacted sensor nodes.

In $\mathbf{f}_1, \mathbf{f}_2,...,\mathbf{f}_{B-1}$, the combined data segments encode the same number of original data segments, which all equal to x. For the sake of convenience, we describe the decoding process of them together. Denote them as $\mathbf{f}_k = [f_{1_k}, f_{2_k}, ..., f_{W_{0k}}]$,

$k = 1, ..., B - 1$. For $\mathbf{f}_k = [f_{1_k}, f_{2_k}, ..., f_{W_{0_k}}]$ and the corresponding coefficient vectors $[\overrightarrow{\beta_{1_k}}, \overrightarrow{\beta_{2_k}}, ..., \overrightarrow{\beta_{W_{0_k}}}]$, $k = 1, ..., B - 1$. The coefficient vectors of $\mathbf{f}_k$ form a $W_0 \times x$ coefficient matrix $\mathbf{A}_k$.

$$\mathbf{A_k} = \begin{pmatrix} \beta_{1_k.(k-1)x+1} & \beta_{2_k.(k-1)x+1} & \cdots & \beta_{W_{0_k}.(k-1)x+1} \\ \beta_{1_k.(k-1)x+2} & \beta_{2_k.(k-1)x+2} & \cdots & \beta_{W_{0_k}.(k-1)x+2} \\ \vdots & \vdots & \ddots & \vdots \\ \beta_{1_k.(k-1)x+x} & \beta_{2_k.(k-1)x+x} & \cdots & \beta_{W_{0_k}.(k-1)x+x} \end{pmatrix} \tag{5}$$

The set of linear equations about $\mathbf{f}_k$, $k = 1, ..., B - 1$, with the x original data segments $\mathbf{c}_k = [c_{(k-1)x+1}, c_{(k-1)x+2}, ..., c_{(k-1)x+x}]$ to be the variables are as follows.

$$\begin{cases} f_{1_k} = \sum_{j=(k-1)x+1}^{(k-1)x+x} \beta_{1_k.j} c_j \\ f_{2_k} = \sum_{j=(k-1)x+1}^{(k-1)x+x} \beta_{2_k.j} c_j \\ \vdots \\ f_{W_{0_k}} = \sum_{j=(k-1)x+1}^{(k-1)x+x} \beta_{W_{0_k}.j} c_j \end{cases} \tag{6}$$

In $\mathbf{f}_B$, the combined data segments encode $n(t_0) - (B-1)x$ original data segments. The coefficient vectors of $\mathbf{f}_B$ form a $W_0 \times (n(t_0) - (B-1)x)$ coefficient matrix $\mathbf{A}_B$.

The set of linear equations about $\mathbf{f}_B$, with the $n(t_0) - (B-1)x$ original data segments $\mathbf{c}_B = [c_{(B-1)x+1}, c_{(B-1)x+2}, ..., c_{n(t_0)}]$ to be the variables.

We apply Gaussian Elimination [17]. If the rank of $\mathbf{A}_k$ is not less than x (except $\mathbf{A}_B$ is not less than $n(t_0) - (B-1)x$), the set of linear equations about $\mathbf{f}_k = [f_{1_k}, f_{2_k}, ..., f_{W_{0_k}}]$ is decodable , $k = 1, ...B$. Otherwise the rank of $\mathbf{A}_k$ is less than x (except $\mathbf{A}_B$ is less than $n(t_0) - (B-1)x$) and the set of equations is insoluble.

For the above linear equations of $\mathbf{f}_k$, there are at most x variables. The value of x should satisfy $x \leq W_0$ to guarantee the decoding. Thus the probability of solve the linear equations is very close to 100% for a large enough field size q. After solving all the linear equations, the mBS can obtain all the original data segments $\mathbf{c} = \bigcup_{k=1}^{B} \mathbf{c}_k$.

From formula (4), we know that B is inversely proportional to x. The value of x is better to set bigger then each sensor node can encode all the data segments in the combined fashions with a smaller buffer size B. Let x_0 denote the optimal value of x, then

$$x_0 = maximum\{x\}. \tag{7}$$

As the value of x should also satisfy

$$x \leq W_0. \tag{8}$$

From formula (7) and (8), we obtain

$$x_0 = W_0. \tag{9}$$

Then we have the following Lemma.

Lemma 2. *The optimal value of the number of original data segments encoded in each combined data segment equals to W_0.*

From Lemma 2 and formula (4), we can obtain the following Theorem.

Theorem 1. *In right arrival case, the optimal value of the buffer size B in each sensor node to encode all data segments generated in on time interval equals to $B = \lceil n(t_0)/W_0 \rceil$.*

It is also important to note that the value of W_0 can be adjusted to make the buffer size B not too big. The BS can contact more sensor nodes to make the buffer size be available at a tiny sensor node. The value of x will be set to the optimal value $x = W_0$ in the rest of this paper.

3.3   Encoding and Decoding Processes in the Late Arrival Case

From Lemma 1 and Theorem 1, in right arrival case, the combined data segments stored in each sensor node with buffer size $B = \lceil n(t_0)/W_0 \rceil$ can encode all original data segments. But there is still one problem. If the mBS arrives lately, the sensor nodes do not know in which time and how long the mBS will delay, they just separately combine W_0 (the optimal value of x) original data segments in a combined data segment and store it in the corresponding buffer. If the total number of original data segments $n(t) \leq BW_0$, by continuing to encode the rest original data segments in the last combined data segment f_{i_B}, the buffers are till enough. But if $n(t) > BW_0$, the data segments will exceed the total storage space of the sensor nodes if they still combine W_0 original data segments in a combined fashion. Then we will give a formal description of the encoding and storage process for the late arrival case.

Data Encoding and Storage. The encoding and storage process when $n(t) \leq BW_0$ are the same as right arrival case, as shown in Fig 5 (a), (b). For the sake of convenience, here we define

$$[c_1, ..., c_r] = \sum_{j=1}^{r} \beta_{i_k.j} c_j \tag{10}$$

to denote the combined data segments in node N_i, omiting the the coefficients $\beta_{i_k.j}$ ($j = 1, ..., r, k = 1, 2.$). When $n(t) > BW_0$, each sensor node will continue to encode the excess original data segments one by one in the existing combined segments from f_{i_1} to f_{i_B}. As shown in Fig 5 (c), when c_{13} is generated, it is continued to encode in f_{i_1}. When c_{14} is generated, it is continue to be encoded in f_{i_2}. As shown in Fig 5 (d), when c_{17} is generated, it is continue to be encoded

$$N_i: \left\{ f_{i_1} = \left[c_1, c_2, c_3\right], f_{i_2} = \left[c_4, c_5, c_6\right], f_{i_3} = \left[c_7, c_8, c_9\right], f_{i_4} = \left[c_{10}\right] \right\}$$

(a) $n(t_0) = 10$

$$N_i: \left\{ f_{i_1} = \left[c_1, c_2, c_3\right], f_{i_2} = \left[c_4, c_5, c_6\right], f_{i_3} = \left[c_7, c_8, c_9\right], f_{i_4} = \left[c_{10}, c_{11}, c_{12}\right] \right\}$$

(b) $n(t) = 12$

$$N_i: \left\{ f_{i_1} = \left[c_1, c_2, c_3, c_{13}\right], f_{i_2} = \left[c_4, c_5, c_6, c_{14}\right], f_{i_3} = \left[c_7, c_8, c_9\right], f_{i_4} = \left[c_{10}, c_{11}, c_{12}\right] \right\}$$

(c) $n(t) = 14$

$$N_i: \left\{ f_{i_1} = \left[c_1, c_2, c_3, c_{13}, c_{17}\right], f_{i_2} = \left[c_4, c_5, c_6, c_{14}\right], f_{i_3} = \left[c_7, c_8, c_9, c_{15}\right], f_{i_4} = \left[c_{10}, c_{11}, c_{12}, c_{16}\right] \right\}$$

(d) $n(t) = 17$

Fig. 5. Data encoding and storage in sensor node i by SNC-ADC. $W_0 = 3, n(t_0) = 10, B = 4$. (a) $n(t) = 10$, (b) $n(t) = 12$, (c) $n(t) = 14$, (d) $n(t) = 17$. We omit the coefficients for the combined data segments.

in f_{i_1}. And the c_{15} and c_{16} which are generated before c_{17} have been encoded in f_{i_3} and f_{i_4}.

The encoding process is incremental. It is performed by each sensor node. Every time a original data segment c_j is encoded with the combined data segment f^i in node i ($i = 1, ..., N$). The data encoding algorithm (Algorithm 2) is locally executed at each sensor node.

```
Algorithm 2: Data Encoding (f^i, c_j)
Input: original data segment c_j
Output: combined data segment f^i
For k=1 to B
    f_k = 0
end
For j=1 to n(t)
   If j ≤ W_0
      Let k = ⌈j/W_0⌉;
      Randomly generate β_{i_k.j} from F_q;
      f_{i_k} = f_{i_k} + β_{i_k.j}c_j;
   Else
      Let k = j mod B;
      Randomly generate β_{i_k.j} from F_q;
      If k ≠ 0 then
         f_{i_k} = f_{i_k} + β_{i_k.j}c_j;
      else
         f_{i_B} = f_{i_B} + β_{i_B.j}c_j;
      end
   end
end
```

Notice that when $n(t) \leq BW_0$, for the forward B-1 combined data segments $C(f_{i_k}) = W_0$, $k = 1, ..., B - 1$ and for the last combined data segment $C(f_{i_B}) \leq W_0$. When $n(t) > BW_0$, for each combined data segment $C(f_{i_k}) \geq W_0$, as they may encode more than W_0 original data segments. From the encoding process, we know that $C(f_{i_p}) \geq C(f_{i_q})$ if $p < q$. Thus,

$$C(f_{i_1}) = maximum\{C(f_{i_k})\}. \tag{11}$$

The original data segments encoded in f_{i_1} include two parts. One part are generated before the mBS delays, the number is W_0. The other part are generated after the mBS delays, we denote the number of original data segments in this part as v, $v = \lceil (n(t) - BW_0)/B \rceil$. Then

$$C(f_{i_1}) = W_0 + v. \tag{12}$$

From formula (11) and (12), we can obtain

$$maximum\{C(f_{i_k})\} = W_0 + v. \tag{13}$$

When the mBS decodes the linear equations about the combined data segments, the number of sensor nodes it contacts (equals to the number of equations) should not less than $maximum\{C(f_{i_k})\}$ (equals to the number of variables). Thus, we have the following Lemma.

Lemma 3. *When $n(t) > BW_0$, the number of sensor nodes that the mBS need to contact is at least $W_0 + v$ ($\leq N$), $v = \lceil (n(t) - BW_0)/B \rceil$.*

Notice that the value of $W_0 + v$ should not be bigger than the total number of sensor nodes N. Since $v = \lceil (n(t) - BW_0)/B \rceil$ and $B = \lceil n(t_0)/W_0 \rceil$. By adjusting the value of B, the value of $W_0 + v$ can be adjusted to not too big, and the value of v can be adjusted to not increase too quickly. Thus, $W_0 + v \leq N$ is achievable.

Before describing the decoding process, we first to have a more specific expression about $C(f_{i_k})$: the number of original data segments encoded in each combined data segments f^k, $k = 1, ..., B$. Assume that the last original data segment $c_{n(t)}$ is encoded in f_{i_u}, $u = (n(t) - BW_0) \bmod B$. From the encoding process, we have

$$C(f_{i_1}) = C(f_{i_2}) = ... = C(f_{i_u}), \tag{14}$$

and

$$C(f_{i_u+1}) = ... = C(f_{i_B}) = C(f_{i_1}) - 1. \tag{15}$$

From formula (14), (15) and (12), we can obtain

$$C(f_{i_k}) = \begin{cases} W_0 + v & 1 \leq k \leq u \\ W_0 + v - 1 & u < k \leq B \end{cases}, \tag{16}$$

where $v = \lceil (n(t) - BW_0)/B \rceil$, $u = (n(t) - BW_0) \bmod B$.

Data Decoding. When $n(t) \leq BW_0$, the decoding process is the same as the case of the mBS arrives on time. We then give the decoding process when $n(t) > BW_0$. Assume that the mBS has randomly contacted $W_0 + v$ sensor nodes to collect the combined data segments $\mathbf{f} = [f^1, f^2, ..., f^{W_0+v}]$, where $f^i = (f_{i_1}, f_{i_2}, ..., f_{i_B})$ is the combined data segments collected from sensor node i, $i = 1, 2, ..., W_0 + v$. $C(f_{i_k}) = \begin{cases} W_0 + v & 1 \leq k \leq u \\ W_0 + v - 1 & u < k \leq B \end{cases}$, $v = \lceil (n(t) - BW_0)/B \rceil$, $u = (n(t) - BW_0) \bmod B$.

The decoding process of $\mathbf{f}$ includes B stages, decoding about $\mathbf{f}_1, \mathbf{f}_2,...,\mathbf{f}_B$, where $\mathbf{f}_k = [f_{1_k}, f_{2_k}, ..., f_{(W_0+v)_k}]$ is the combined data segments collected from buffer k of $W_0 + v$ sensor nodes, $k = 1, ..., B$. Decoding about $\mathbf{f}_k$ is to decode the original data segments encoded in the combined data segments which are stored in buffer k of the contacted sensor nodes.

In the forward combined data segments $\mathbf{f}_k$ ($k \in \{1, 2, ..., u\}$), they all encode the same number of original data segments, which all equal to $(W_0 + v)$. We describe the decoding process of them together for the sake of convenience. Assume that the mBS randomly contacts $(W_0 + v)$ sensor nodes. The coefficient vectors of $\mathbf{f}_k$ ($k \in \{1, 2, ..., u\}$) are $[\overrightarrow{\beta_{1_k}}, \overrightarrow{\beta_{2_k}}, ..., \overrightarrow{\beta_{(W_0+v)_k}}]$, which form a $(W_0 + v) \times (W_0 + v)$ coefficient matrix $\mathbf{A}_k$.

$$\mathbf{A_k} = \begin{pmatrix} \beta_{1_k.(k-1)W_0+1} & \beta_{2_k.(k-1)W_0+1} & \cdots & \beta_{(W_0+v)_k.(k-1)W_0+1} \\ \beta_{1_k.(k-1)W_0+2} & \beta_{2_k.(k-1)W_0+2} & \cdots & \beta_{(W_0+v)_k.(k-1)W_0+2} \\ \vdots & \vdots & \ddots & \vdots \\ \beta_{1_k.(k-1)W_0+W_0} & \beta_{2_k.(k-1)W_0+W_0} & \cdots & \beta_{(W_0+v)_k.(k-1)W_0+W_0} \\ \beta_{1_k.BW_0+k} & \beta_{2_k.BW_0+k} & \cdots & \beta_{(W_0+v)_k.BW_0+k} \\ \beta_{1_k.BW_0+B+k} & \beta_{2_k.BW_0+B+k} & \cdots & \beta_{(W_0+v)_k.BW_0+B+k} \\ \vdots & \vdots & \ddots & \vdots \\ \beta_{1_k.BW_0+(v-1)B+k} & \beta_{2_k.BW_0+(v-1)B+k} & \cdots & \beta_{(W_0+v)_k.BW_0+(v-1)B+k} \end{pmatrix} \tag{17}$$

The set of linear equations about $\mathbf{f}_k$ ($k \in \{1, 2, ..., u\}$), with the original data segments $\mathbf{c}_k = [c_{(k-1)W_0+1}, c_{(k-1)W_0+2}, ..., c_{(k-1)W_0+W_0}, c_{BW_0+k}, c_{BW_0+B+k}, ..., c_{BW_0+(v-1)B+k}]$ to be the variables are as follows.

$$\begin{cases} f_{1_k} = \sum_{j=(k-1)W_0+1}^{(k-1)W_0+W_0} \beta_{1_k.j} c_j + \sum_{j=0}^{v-1} \beta_{1_k.BW_0+jB+k} c_{BW_0+jB+k} \\ f_{2_k} = \sum_{j=(k-1)W_0+1}^{(k-1)W_0+W_0} \beta_{2_k.j} c_j + \sum_{j=0}^{v-1} \beta_{2_k.BW_0+jB+k} c_{M_0(jB+1)} \\ \vdots \\ f_{(W_0+v)_k} = \sum_{j=(k-1)W_0+1}^{(k-1)W_0+W_0} \beta_{(W_0+v)_k.j} c_j + \sum_{j=0}^{v-1} \beta_{(W_0+v)_k.BW_0+jB+k} c_{BW_0+jB+k} \end{cases} \tag{18}$$

Perform Gaussian Elimination. If $\mathbf{A}_k \neq 0$, $\mathbf{c}_k = \mathbf{A}_k^{-1} \mathbf{f}_k$, ($k \in \{1, 2, ..., u\}$). Otherwise the rank of $\mathbf{A}_k$ is less than $W_0 + v$ and the set of equations is insoluble.

In the latter combined data segments $\mathbf{f}_k$ ($k \in \{u+1, u+2, ..., B\}$), they all encode ($W_0 + v - 1$) original data segments. We describe the decoding process of them together for the sake of convenience. The coefficient vectors of $\mathbf{f}_k$ ($k \in \{u+1, u+2, ..., B\}$) are $[\overrightarrow{\beta_{1_k}}, \overrightarrow{\beta_{2_k}}, ..., \overrightarrow{\beta_{(W_0+v)_k}}]$, which form a $(W_0+v) \times (W_0+v-1)$ coefficient matrix $\mathbf{A}_k$. The set of linear equations about $\mathbf{f}_k$ ($k \in \{u+1, u+2, ..., B\}$), with the original data segments $\mathbf{c}_k = [c_{(k-1)W_0+1}, c_{(k-1)W_0+2}, ..., c_{(k-1)W_0+W_0},$ $c_{BW_0+k}, c_{BW_0+B+k}, ..., c_{BW_0+(v-2)B+k}]$ to be the variables.

Perform Gaussian Elimination. If the rank of $\mathbf{A}_k$ is not less than $W_0 + v - 1$, the set of linear equations about $\mathbf{f}_k$ ($k \in \{u+1, u+2, ..., B\}$) is decodable. Otherwise the rank of $\mathbf{A}_k$ is less than $W_0 + v - 1$ and the set of equations is insoluble.

For every $\mathbf{f}_k$ ($k \in \{1, 2, ..., B\}$), there are no more than $W_0 + v$ variables with $W_0 + v$ linear equations, they are decodable. The probability of solving the linear equations is very close to 100% for a large enough field size q. After solving all the linear equations, the BS can obtain all the original data segments $\mathbf{c} = \bigcup_{k=1}^{B} \mathbf{c}_k$, and then it will arrange the order of the original data segments.

Theorem 2. *The success ratio of data collection by SNC with buffer size $B = \lceil n(t_0)/W_0 \rceil$ to collect all the data segments is 100% (neglecting linear dependency of the coefficients).*

Proof. When the mBS arrives on time, from Lemma 1, each sensor node with buffer size $B = \lceil n(t_0)/W_0 \rceil$ is enough to encode all original data segments. When the BS delays, the sensor nodes continue to encode the original data segments in the exist combined segments, so each sensor node can encode all the original data segments in the combined segments. If delays, the mBS will contact $W_0 + v$ ($v = \lceil (n(t) - BW_0)/B \rceil$) sensor nodes to guarantee the decodable of the linear equations. The probability of decoding the combined segments are very close to 100% for a large enough field size q.

It is also worth noting that, the value of W_0 will affect the energy consumption of the network, and the value of W_0 has to satisfy $B = \lceil n(t_0)/W_0 \rceil$. We will give a further discussion about it in the simulation.

4   Performance Evaluation

In this section, we evaluate the performance of proposed scheme by simulation. we deploy 1000 sensor nodes randomly into a field of 300m × 300m. The distance between the sensor nodes and the mBS is much longer than the distance between the sensor nodes, as suggested in Lindsey and Raghavendra [18]. Without necessarily entering deep into the sensor field, the mBS can perform data collection, which is useful for collecting data from a dangerous area. The solution of linear equations in network coding are using the Gaussian Elimination [17]. The coefficient field is $q = 2^8$, which can be efficiently implemented in a 8-bit or more advanced microprocessor [15]. Table 2 demonstrates part of the important parameters and settings in the simulation.

Table 2. System Parameters and Settings

System Parameters	Settings
Length × Width	300 m ×300 m
Number of sensor nodes	1000
Transmit range between sensors	20 m
Transmit range between sensors and BS	150 m $\sim$ 250 m
Data generate time interval	30 sec
Energy consumption for sending a message	20nAh
The coefficient field q	2^8
Confidence interval	95%

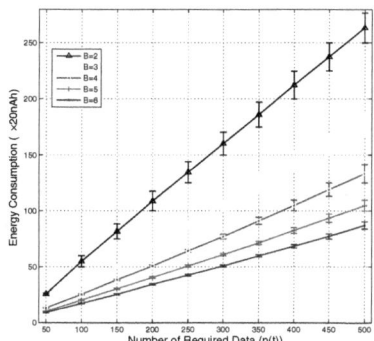

Fig. 6. Transmission energy consumption vs. $n(t)$ with different B for all data segment collection

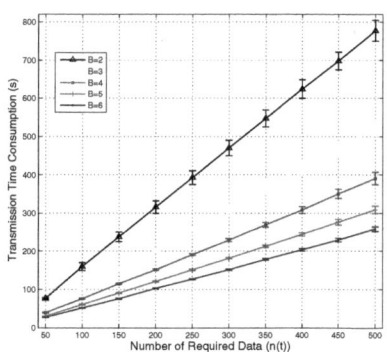

Fig. 7. Transmission time consumption vs. $n(t)$ with different B for all data segment collection

We first evaluate success ratio of data collection about SNC as a function of the buffer size B. Since PNC can not apply in all data segment collection, we do not compare with it in the simulation. In the simulation, we vary the total number of data segments $n(t)$ from 200 to 500, and vary the buffer size from 2 to 20. Our simulation result shows that the success ratio of data collection for SNC maintains at 100% for different buffer sizes. This fact is also proved in Theorem 2.

We have proved that the success ratio of of all data segment collection is 100% by setting the buffer size of sensor nodes to $B = \lceil n(t_0)/W_0 \rceil$. Notice that B is inversely proportional to W_0. So if the buffer size of the sensor nodes is smaller, the mobile BS has to contact more sensor nodes to guarantee the decoding of the data. As a result, the sensor network will consume more energy and take more time to perform the data collection. Since the case of all data segment collection cannot be achieved by PNC, in this experiment we just consider SNC with different buffer size B. We use the energy model by Mainwaring et al [7]. The energy consumption for transmitting one packet is 20 nAh (10.9 Ampere hour). We assume that the time cost for the mBS to send the query to a node is 1 second, the time cost to transmit one packet is 2 second. For simplicity, we neglect other affecting factors which is much less than the transmission time. As shown in Fig 6 and Fig 7, the buffer size B varies from 2 to 6, and the energy consumption and transmission time consumption decrease as B increases with different $n(t)$. For bigger B, the energy and time consumption increase trends are more smooth as $n(t)$ increases. Not surprisingly, SNC performs better with bigger B, but too big buffer size may not be available at a tiny sensor node and the price of sensor nodes with bigger buffer size are higher, so it has to trade off in the practical applications.

5   Conclusion

In this paper, we present a novel network coding scheme, called Separate Network Coding (SNC), which effectively collect all the data segment in WSNs with a mBS. In SNC, each sensor node is able to provide efficient storage method for continuous data, and also maintains a high success ratio of data collection. We introduce the data encoding, storage and decoding processes of the proposed schemes. We prove that the success ratio of SNC scheme is 100% (neglecting linear dependency of the coefficients). Furthermore, we address several practical concerns toward implementing SNC for data collection in WSNs, and demonstrate the feasibility and superiority of the proposed scheme.

References

1. Akyildiz, I.F., Su, W., Sankarasubramaniam, Y., Cayirci, E.: Wireless sensor networks: A survey. Comm. ACM 38(4), 393–422 (2002)
2. Culler, D., Estrin, D., Srivastava, M.: Overview of sensor networks. IEEE Comput. Special Issue on Sensor Networks 37(8), 41–49 (2004)
3. Bahl, P., Chancre, R., Dungeon, J.: SSCH: Slotted seeded channel hopping for capacity improvement in IEEE 802.11 ad-hoc wireless networks. In: Proceeding of the 10th International Conference on Mobile Computing and Networking (MobiCom 2004), pp. 112–117. ACM, New York (2004)

4. Cerpa, A., Elson, J., Estrin, D., Girod, L., Hamilton, M., Zhao, J.: Habitat monitoring: Application driver for wireless communications technology. In: Proceeding of SIGCOMM LA 2001 Workshop on Data Communication in Latin America and the Caribbean, pp. 20–41. ACM, San Jose (2001)
5. Wang, F., Liu, J., Sun, L.: Ambient data collection withwireless sensor networks. EURASIP Journal onWireless Communications and Networking 2010(10) (2010)
6. Wang, D., Zhang, Q., Liu, J.: Partial network coding: Concept, performance, and application for continuous data collection in sensor networks. ACM Transactions on Sensor Networks 4(3), 1–22 (2008)
7. Mainwaring, A., Polaster, J., Szewczyk, R., Culler, D., Anderson, J.: Wireless sensor networks for habitat monitoring. In: Proceeding of the 1st ACM International Workshop on Wireless Sensor Networks and Applications, pp. 88–97. ACM, Atlanta (2002)
8. Fragouli, C., LeBoudec, J.Y., Widmer, J.: Network coding: an instant primer. SIGCOMM Comput. Commun. Rev. 36(1), 63–68 (2006)
9. Ahlswede, R., Cai, N., LI, S., Yeung, R.: Network information flow. IEEE Trans. on Information Theory 46(4), 1204–1216 (2000)
10. Dimakis, A.G., Godfrey, P.B., Wu, Y., Wainwright, M.J., Ramchandran, K.: Network coding for distributed storage systems. IEEE Trans. Info. Theory 56(9), 4539–4551 (2010)
11. Kon, Z., Aly, S., Soljanin, E.: Decentralized coding algorithms for distributed storage in wireless sensor networks. IEEE Journal on Selected Areas in Communications 28(2), 261–267 (2010)
12. Acedanski, S., Deb, S., Medard, M., Koetter, R.: How good is random linear coding based distributed networked storage. In: Proceedings of First Workshop Network Coding, Theory, and Applications (NetCod 2005), Riva del Garda, Italy (2005)
13. Gkantsidis, C., Rodriguez, P.: Network coding for large scale content distribution. In: Proceedings of INFOCOM 2005, pp. 2235–2245. IEEE, Miami (2005)
14. Dimakis, A., Prabhakarna, V., Ramchandran, K.: Ubiquitous access to distributed data in large-scale sensor networks through decentralized erasure codes. In: Proceeding of of the International Conference on Information Processing in Sensor Networks (IPSN 2005), pp. 111–117. ACM (2005)
15. Widmer, J., Andboudec, J.: Network coding for efficient communication in extreme networks. In: Proceedings of the 2005 ACM SIGCOMM Workshop on Delay-tolerant Networking, pp. 284–291. ACM, Philadelphia (2005)
16. Dimakis, A.G., Prabhakaran, V., Ramchandran, K.: Decentralized erasure codes for distributed networked storage. IEEE Trans. Info. Theory 52(6), 2809–2816 (2006)
17. Gentle, J.: Numerical Linear Algebra for Applications in Statistics. Springer, Heidelberg (1998)
18. Lindsey, S., Raghavendra, C.: Pegasis: Power-efficient gathering in sensor information systems. In: IEEE in Aerospace Conference Proceedings, pp. 1125–1130. IEEE (2002)

Deferred Maintenance of Indexes
and of Materialized Views

Harumi Kuno and Goetz Graefe

Hewlett-Packard Laboratories
Palo Alto, CA

Abstract. Maintenance of secondary indexes and materialized views can cause the latency and bandwidth of concurrent information capture to degrade by orders of magnitude. In order to preserve performance during temporary bursts of update activity, e.g., during load operations, many systems therefore support deferred maintenance, at least for materialized views. However, deferring maintenance means that index or view contents may become out-of-date. In such cases, a seemingly benign choice among alternative query execution plans affects whether query results represent the latest database contents. We propose here a system that distinguishes between the maintenance of of logical contents and physical structure. This distinction lets us compensate for deferred logical maintenance operations while minimizing the impact of deferred physical maintenance operations, and results in support for concurrent high update rates and immediate, index-based query processing with correct transaction semantics.

1 Introduction

Consider a database user looking for a small list of query results, perhaps people sorted by name. Seeing too many names starting with 'A' and thus fearing a large query result when a small list is desired, the user adds another predicate to the query. Now imagine that the second query produces a smaller result set as desired, yet includes a name beginning with 'A' that wasn't included in the first query result. Clearly, this user has good reason to doubt the trustworthiness and the correctness of the database contents and of the query processing software. Note that this situation can occur in most database products even without any concurrent updates, i.e., without any effects due to non-serializable snapshot isolation or other weak transaction isolation levels.

Most likely, the problem is unsafe usage of materialized views. Conventional wisdom says that the transactional storage manager is responsible for index maintenance while the query processor is responsible for materialized view maintenance, and thus different mechanisms and standards apply to index vs. view maintenance. Due to the performance overhead of traditional maintenance techniques, often materialized views are not updated as part of user transactions. Instead, their maintenance is deferred such that they are updated periodically, e.g., nightly.

In the example case, the first query execution plan might employ a materialized view, whereas the second query execution plan might search the base tables and their indexes using the additional predicate. Thus, the second query is answered using up-to-date information, whereas the first query produces stale results. Again, note that this is not

S. Kikuchi et al. (Eds.): DNIS 2011, LNCS 7108, pp. 312–323, 2011.

an issue of weak transaction isolation levels; it is due to deferred updates not being considered and compensated for during query processing, which in turn is due to slow traditional techniques for incremental maintenance of materialized views. The problem is exacerbated by automatic query optimization, including automatic re-optimization, which prevents users from knowing whether a query result is current or stale.

In contrast, we advocate here that materialized views and indexes should be treated similarly, and distinguish instead between updates to logical contents and the refinement of the physical structures. In this paper, we focus on the deferred maintenance of indexes and of materialized views with minimal overhead and correct transactional semantics.

1.1 Motivation for Deferred Maintenance

As sketched in Figure 1 (left side, below), index maintenance is notorious for contending for resources with concurrent queries, causing spikes in system load. The risk of incurring spikes due to maintenance discourages the use of indexes and materialized views, and leads to the repeated dropping and rebuilding of indexes to accommodate system maintenance tasks.

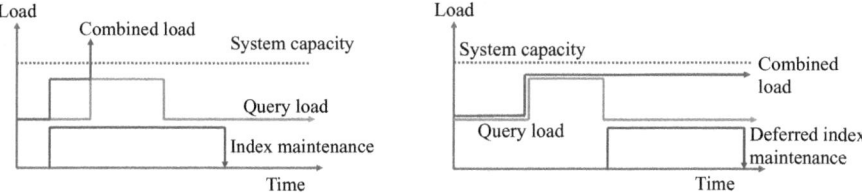

Fig. 1. Deferring index maintenance avoids spikes in combined system load

In order to protect against such spikes, service providers overprovision, and as a result, servers lie idle on average 70% of the time [1,3]. Since an unloaded server consumes 50% of the energy of a fully-loaded server, there are energy savings available in reducing the intensity of these spikes.

James Hamilton wrote of provisioning in cloud data centers [10]: "...sufficient hardware must be provisioned to support the peak capacity requirement for that workload. Cost is driven by peak requirements but monetization is driven by the average. Looking at an extreme, a tax preparation service has to provision enough capacity to support their busiest day and yet, in mid-summer, most of this hardware is largely unused."

Deferred maintenance of secondary indexes and of materialized views, as sketched in the right side of Figure 1, helps prevent spikes in system load by shifting work from periods of peak load to other periods. Avoiding such spikes enables databases to save energy and capital costs. Moreover, efficient maintenance techniques permit databases with more indexes and materialized views. Shifting some effort for searching and matching database entries from query execution to index maintenance creates even more opportunity for reducing the peak load and thus hosting a workload efficiently.

Finally, deferring maintenance enables the optimization of update plans. For example, during insertion or deletion of N rows in a table, a traditional row-by-row update reads, modifies, logs, and writes N leaf pages in each secondary index. An index-by-index update touches the same number of pages but in an optimized sequence and with full benefit of read-ahead and write-behind. If each index leaf contains K entries and the insertion or deletion affects more than 1 in K rows of the table, index-by-index update touches each leaf only once, even those with multiple changes. Deferred maintenance can thus reduce the initial update cost to N/K pages newly formatted and written but neither read nor logged, i.e., orders of magnitude less than even index-by-index updates.

1.2   Contributions

Our research focuses on a uniform mechanism that enables the deferred maintenance of indexes and of materialized views with minimal overhead and without compromising correctness. It includes techniques for data structures and algorithms (in particular B-trees and bulk updates), for concurrency control and recovery (in particular key range locking and "increment" locks), and for workload management (in particular "load shedding" by performing or completing updates during period of low system load). These mechanisms require only moderate changes to the data structure and its core algorithms. The data structures and algorithms described here enable:

1. burst insertion latency and bandwidth close to the hardware write speed (e.g., disk writes),
2. sustained insertion bandwidth less by only a small factor (e.g., 3-5×),
3. support for multiple concurrent load operations,
4. support for insertions, deletions, and updates of all sizes (row counts),
5. immediate support for range queries (e.g.,"≤" and "between"), for exact-match queries (e.g., "=" and "in"), and for joins (in particular index nested loops join),
6. transactional correctness of all updates and query results,
7. logging and recovery using traditional techniques plus some moderate optimizations,
8. online index creation for tables and for materialized views,
9. efficient updates on storage with a "small write penalty" (e.g., flash storage, RAID-4/5/6 arrays), and
10. a uniform design for primary indexes, secondary indexes, and materialized views.

1.3   Outline

Section 2 introduces the components of our approach. We focus on B-tree indexes as a ubiquitous data structure in databases, information retrieval, file systems, and other data-intensive systems with need for large data, incremental updates, and sorting or searching. The essential technique exploits partitioned B-trees in the manner of differential files. The essential benefit is the combination of high update rates and immediate, index-based query processing with correct transaction semantics.

Section 3 focuses on the deferred maintenance and optimization of secondary index structures, whereupon Section 4 focuses on the deferred maintenance of materialized views and their indexes. Finally, in Section 5, we offer a summary and our conclusions from this research effort.

2 Components of Approach

The key to our approach is to distinguish the maintenance of logical contents from the maintenance of physical structure. This distinction lets us compensate for deferred logical maintenance operations while minimizing the impact of deferred physical maintenance operations.

We achieve this goal by leveraging a number of techniques for performing logical update operations with a minimal of changes to physical structures. Our core technique is that we use partitioned B-trees to capture and index both master data and change set in a single data structure that permits efficient queries and updates. In addition, we also use ghost records and anti-matter records to effect logical deletions and insertions. Sections 2.3 and 2.4 largely abstract a more complete discussion found in [7].

2.1 Deferred Operations: Logical and Physical

Deferred physical maintenance refers to delayed optimization of index structures. That is, the initial update of an index captures the changes in the index, so results will be correct, but the data structure is not yet fully optimized, so queries may incur some performance overhead. For example, in a partitioned B-tree, capturing new index entries in new partitions defers optimizing the B-tree for the fastest possible query performance, i.e., merging partitions. Merge operations can then be scheduled actively, e.g., during periods of low load, or on demand, i.e., as side effect of query execution [4].

Deferred logical maintenance refers to the logical contents of tables, materialized views, and indexes. When a materialized view falls behind, i.e., fails to reflect the latest database updates, the contents of materialized view and base table is out of synchrony. When an index falls behind, it (typically) turns into a partial index, even if only temporarily. A table may fall behind if foreign key constraints, in particular those with cascading, are applied separately from the original database update.

2.2 Partitioned B-Trees vs. Differential Files

Differential files enable the deferred maintenance of secondary indexes or materialized views by confining modifications to a specific area of physical storage [13]. However, database queries must then either suffer the overhead of searching the differential file or else possibly return out-of-date results.

We find partitioned B-trees an ideal mechanism for capturing and indexing both master data and change set in a single data structure that permits efficient queries and updates. Storing differential results in partitioned B-tree partitions, enables fast loads, low-overhead search that enables fast queries, and efficient merging with base data when applying updates.

The original purpose and design of partitioned B-trees [4] focused on sorting (with the artificial leading key field as run identifier), index creation (with index search enabled as soon as all future index entries are searchable albeit not yet merged), and loading (with new data in new partitions).

The proposed techniques for deferred maintenance of partitioned B-trees is most similar to loading: new data items form new partitions. The Figure 2(left) shows how

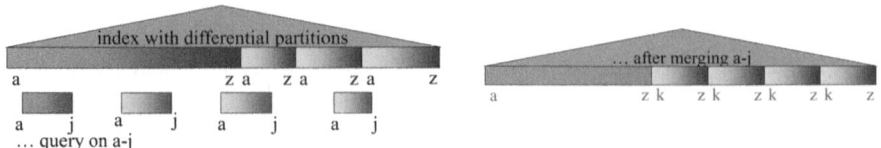

Fig. 2. Instead of differential files, we use a partitioned B-tree to manage differential partitions

we use a partitioned B-tree to store differential partitions (colored grey) that capture log-ical updates to database contents (colored green). Until these partitions are merged into the main or master partition Figure 2(right), the new partitions capture recent changes in a densely packed representation yet in sorted order suitable for efficient search as well as efficient propagation to other data structures. In other words, partitions in parti-tioned B-trees serve the purpose of differential files [13] without the need for new data structures. In fact, just as traditional B-trees must support efficient search operations, so do the partitions that serve as differential files. Moreover, differently from traditional differential files, the partitions are sorted and enable efficient query execution plans that require sorted scan results.

2.3 Anti-matter Records

In order to perform logical updates such as insertions or deletions while the physi-cal structures are still being created, updates may be captured elsewhere and applied after the main index creation activity is complete. This approach is known as "side file" [7,11]. The "no side file" approach, on the other hand, captures updates in the recovery log or in the target index.

Anti-matter records address the situation in the "no side file" approach where an up-date transaction deletes a key in a key range that has not yet inserted by a concurrent index creation process. For example, index creation may be sorting records to be in-serted into the new index and another transaction may delete one of those records. Such deletions can be represented by a negative or anti-matter record. When the index cre-ation process encounters an anti-matter record, the corresponding record is suppressed and not inserted into the new index. At that time, the anti-matter record has served its function and can be removed. When the index creation process has inserted all its records, all anti-matter records must have been removed from the B-tree index.

2.4 Ghost Records

Ghost records provide a lightweight mechanism for logically deleting a record with minimal impact on physical structures. Ghost records are a technique that help trans-actions ensure that neither space allocation and unique key constraints will fail when rolling back record deletion operations [7]. The basic technique marks a deleted record invalid (e.g., but flipping a single status bit in the record header), but retains the physical record and its key in the B-tree. The record and its key remain locked until the deleting transaction commits. Such a pseudo-deleted record is called a ghost record.

Where an anti-matter record represents an incomplete deletion, a ghost record represents a completed deletion. From the perspective of deferred maintenance, the benefit is to delay or even avoid some effort for space management as a logical deletion turns into a modification of the ghost bit in the physical storage.

3   Deferred Maintenance of Indexes

Deferred maintenance of any sort relies on separate storage locations for the master data and the change. A partitioned B-tree typically has one large partition with the long-existing data and one or more smaller partitions with recent changes. Pure insertions are the simplest case. Deletions require some means of "anti-matter" marker. Updates can be captured as a deletion followed by an insertion. Thus, change partitions in partitioned B-trees can serve all the traditional functions of differential files.

3.1   Primary Indexes

In primary indexes (also known as clustered indexes), adding partitions captures changes with high bandwidth and defers maintenance of the index structure. More specifically, the data structure remains a correct B-tree at all times but optimization is deferred. The index is optimized by merging one or multiple change partitions with the master partition. The required algorithm is well-known from external merge sort. If the change set includes deletions, the merge must include aggregation, where a valid record ("matter") and a deletion marker ("anti-matter") cancel each other out.

The changes may come from a single transaction, e.g., a load operation, or from many individual transactions. If the changes are not sorted by key value, random insertions are required. Ideally, random insertions are limited to a small, in-memory partition, which will be called the destination partition here. It may even be required to limit the size of the destination partition to the size of the CPU cache.

When the destination partition fills up, i.e., exceeds the size of the available buffer pool or workspace, the destination partition is saved, e.g., on disk, and a new, empty partition is created to serve as destination partition for the next set of changes. Each destination partition is saved when its size reaches that of the buffer pool or the workspace.

In some applications, some data records may have life spans shorter than the time an destination partition remains in the buffer pool or workspace. In those case, the deletion may be applied directly within the destination partition. Similarly, frequent updates or an update immediately after the initial insertion may be applied within the buffer pool or workspace. In most cases, however, a deletion requires insertion of anti-matter to be resolved during a subsequent merge step.

The above process is similar to an external merge sort with a strict read-sort-write cycle. While run generation in such sort algorithms is typically implemented using quicksort, an in-memory in-sertion sort also works well, in particular if free space creates some flexibility. If the destination partition is retained as a B-tree in memory, the standard B-tree logic manages appropriate free space. If the destination partition were maintained as a sorted array, the appropriate variant of insertion sort is library sort [2]. In either B-trees or library sort, both the search for the correct insertion location and the actual insertion have complexity of $O(log N)$.

In external merge sort, replacement selection is an alternative technique for run generation that can easily be adapted to partitioned B-trees. It requires two concurrent destination partitions as well as a moving threshold key value that determines whether a new change goes into one or the other destination partition.

When the buffer pool or workspace is full, the threshold is increased and some part of the older destination partition can be saved on disk. Future changes in that key range will be saved in the newer destination partition. Eventually, the threshold reaches the domain maximum ($+\infty$), whereupon the older destination partition is retired from this role, newer destination partition becomes the older destination partition, and an empty partition is created to serve as the newer destination partition.

Note that movement of the threshold key is independent of the rate of change. Moving the threshold key particularly fast reduces the size of the required buffer pool or workspace; moving slower increases the size. Thus, using two destination partitions creates additional flexibility for resource management in addition to absorbing data changes as fast as they can be written from the buffer pool or workspace to an appropriate storage location.

Another adaptive mechanism pertains to the input's incidental sort order. If the input sequence has a positive correlation with the desired key sequence in the index, the initial partitions can be more than twice the size of the buffer pool or the workspace. If, on the other hand, the input sequence has a negative correlation with the desired key sequence, reversing the direction of movement of the threshold key (from $+\infty$ towards $-\infty$) also produces initial partitions larger than twice the size of the buffer pool or the workspace.

3.2 Secondary Indexes

In primary indexes, the same data structure serves as differential file and enables deferred maintenance of the data structure. For secondary indexes (also known as non-clustered indexes), these functions can be separated or they can be used in multiple stages.

In the first case, partitions in the primary index may capture the change set. When the change set is merged with the master partition of the primary index, the same changes are applied to each secondary index. The secondary indexes are traditional B-trees without partitions and without a artificial leading key field to serve as partition identifier.

In the second case, each secondary index is a partitioned B-tree in its own right. Thus, each secondary index can absorb changes more efficiently than a traditional B-tree. During a merge step in the primary index, index entries are formed for each secondary index, partially sorted in a workspace or in the buffer pool, and appended to each secondary index as new partitions. For each secondary index, there may be one or two destination partitions as discussed above for the primary index.

Deferred maintenance of secondary indexes illustrates the different aspects that render partitioned B-trees ideal for the purpose: change partitions enable breaking index maintenance into separate steps for initial capture of index contents and final optimization of index structure, i.e., appending new entries versus merging them into a single sorted sequence; the change partitions in the secondary index permit deferment of physical maintenance, i.e., they precisely capture the work deferred during initial capture of index records; and the change partitions in the primary index permit deferment of logical maintenance, i.e., they precisely capture the information not yet propagated to a redundant structure.

Note that the partition identifiers in the primary and secondary indexes are independent of each other. Consider, for example, a logical row recently inserted into a table with a primary and three secondary indexes. In the primary index, the appropriate record might have been merged into the master partition (with partition identifier 0 or NULL). In one secondary index, the appropriate record might have ended up in partition 5. In another secondary index, the appropriate record might have landed in partition 9, perhaps due to larger index entries or less workspace used to form initial partitions in this index. In the last index, the appropriate record might already have been merged into the local master partition.

If each secondary index is a partitioned B-tree, it can absorb index entries very efficiently. Thus, it seems reasonable to create index entries for all secondary indexes while merging partitions in the primary index. It is possible to devise more sophisticated propagation schemes, in particular if the column set in one secondary index is the subset of that in another, but the value of such optimizations seems incremental.

3.3   Multiple Update Streams

If there are many small transactions, all updates may be captured in a single destination partition in memory or in a pair of destination partitions with a threshold value.

If two load operations add data to the same table concurrently, it probably is best to separate them. In other words, each of them uses its own in-memory workspace and its own set of destination partitions. When both load operations are complete, merging begins. If a load operation creates very many new partitions, some merge steps may proceed concurrently.

If many small update transactions and one or more load operations run concurrently, each load operation should have its own workspace and destination partitions.

In all those cases, separation of destination partitions is driven by the data source, e.g., two big loads or a big load and many small transactions. Alternatively, in particular during a log operation, destination partitions may be defined by key values. For example, imagine a set of orders and order details loaded from a stream sorted by order date into an index sorted by ship date. For items on hand, the ship date immediately follows the order date; for back-ordered items, the ship date is 2–4 week later than the ship date. The load process might employ two separate destination partitions. In case of a moving threshold, two pairs of destination partitions are needed, one pair for order details with an immediate ship dates and one pair for back-ordered items. For the items on-hand, even a very small priority queue will produce very large partitions. If all back-ordered items are assigned ship dates uniformly 3 weeks after the order date, they, too, can be sorted into very large partitions with a very small priority queue.

While this example is a special case in which two small priority queues might be better than one large one, other such cases exist. The crucial aspect is that the input sequence contains two separate distributions that can be optimized more effectively using two half-sized priority queues than one full-sized priority queue.

3.4   Query Execution Plans

In addition to efficient updates, partitioned B-trees and their function as differential files permit efficient query execution plans that produce correct transactional results. Specifically, a query might search all partitions in a primary index and merge the results. When using a secondary index, a query execution plan might search all partitions in the secondary index, fetch records from the master partition in the primary index as appropriate, scan the change partitions in the primary index, and merge all results. The same technique — merging results found in a secondary index with scans of the recent changes in the primary index — also applies to more complex query execution plans that employ multiple secondary index for a single table, including even sophisticated star joins.

For example, Figure 3, taken along with the following explanation from [5], shows a part of a query execution plan relevant to nonclustered index maintenance in an update statement. Not shown below the spool operation is the query plan that computes the delta to be applied to a table and its indices. In the left branch, no columns in the index's search key are modified. Thus, it is sufficient to optimize the order in which changes are applied to existing index entries. In the center branch, one or more columns in the search key are modified. Thus, index entries may move within the index, or alternatively, updates are split into deletion and insertion actions. In the right branch, search key columns in a unique index are updated. Thus, there can be at most one deletion and one insertion per search key in the index, and matching deletion and insertion items can be collapsed into a single update item. In spite of the differences among the indices and how they are affected by the update statement, their maintenance benefits from sorting, ideally data-driven sort operations.

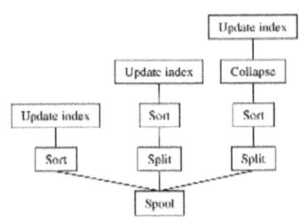

Fig. 3. Optimized index maintenance plan

3.5   Adaptive Content Refresh

Partitioned B-trees functioning as differential files also enable the merging of found sets from multiple partitions in a single secondary index (sorted on the key of that index), merging found sets from multiple secondary indexes (sorted on the search key of the primary index), interleaved probing into the master partition with probes into all change partitions in the primary index in order to produce a single sorted result set. Additional considerations for merging including adaptive merging, e.g., index optimization in the primary index while probing (rather than scanning) [9,8].

3.6   Summary

In summary, all indexes permit deferred maintenance of their structure, in particular if partitioned B-trees are employed. In addition, secondary indexes permit deferred maintenance of their contents. Both forms of deferred maintenance permit transactional and correct query results, but require different query execution plans. Deferred maintenance of structure requires searching the index in multiple places, e.g., in multiple partitions. Deferred maintenance of contents requires a union of two search results, namely those in the secondary index and those obtained from those change partitions in the primary index that still await propagation to the secondary indexes.

4   Deferred Maintenance of Materialized Views

Maintenance of materialized views is similar to maintenance of secondary indexes. It differs by the complexity of the required transformation, by the optimal methods for concurrency control and recovery, and by the number of data structures. For example, a materialized view might require a join or aggregation operation. In the former case, the materialized view contains multiple foreign keys, each of which might be served by an index, only one of which can be the primary index. In the latter case, also known as a summary view, "increment" locks might be more appropriate than standard "read" (shared) or "write" (exclusive) locks.

Deferred maintenance applies both to logical contents and to physical structures for secondary indexes. If a materialized view is stored in multiple indexes, each of them may be a partitioned B-tree and employ deferred maintenance of the physical structure.

Although index maintenance is traditionally the responsibility of the transactional storage manager and materialized view maintenance is traditionally the responsibility of the query processor, materialized views are very similar to secondary indexes in that we can distinguish between updates to logical contents, which in the case of a view are defined using a query, and refinement of the physical structures, for which we use a partitioned B-tree. The deferred maintenance of materialized views is then similar to the deferred maintenance of secondary indexes and similar techniques can be used as described above. For example, views defined upon multiple source tables can treat updates to the different sources similar to multiple update streams, directing each source's updates into separate destination partitions that can then be adaptively merged. In another example, the deferred maintenance of the logical contents of a materialized view is similar to the deferred maintenance of indexes, specifically partial indexes, such that might be supported for both for tables and for views.

That said, because views are defined by queries, more complex queries complicates the maintenance of materialized views. Correct query results may require combining results from a (possibly-out-of-date) materialized view and the re-calculation of materialized view information from the base tables, in particular the partitions not yet propagated to the materialized view. In the remainder of this section we discuss the maintenance of summary tables, i.e., materialized views defined by a query with a "group by" clause.

With respect to concurrency control, immediate maintenance of summary rows and their index entries leads to high concurrency contention or requires "increment" locks [12,6]. Deferred maintenance, on the other hand, exploits an economy of scale more than for other materialized views. If a materialized view is only occasionally updated, and if there is only single actual update operation, and in particular if this update operation employs an optimized update plan, concurrency conflicts are vastly reduced.

With respect to efficient derivation and maintenance of the change set, aggregation can begin in the destination partition in memory. Counts and sums can be added up just as during query execution. Deletions are represented by negative counts and sums; for a group with multiple insertions and deletions, the counts and sums can toggle from positive to negative and vice versa. In a permanent record, a count of zero indicates a ghost record that can be removed; in a change set, a record can be removed only if the count as well as all sums are zero.

The in-memory sort is akin to an insertion sort; this enables easy recognition if a group already exists in the change set in memory and a new change can be added into that record rather than creating a new record. If a pair of destination partitions and a threshold key are used, an in-memory insertion sort is more appropriate than replacement selection using a priority queue because replacement selection with early aggregation requires an additional data structure, e.g., a hash table, in order to match up change records update the same group.

5 Summary

In summary, explicitly considering deferred maintenance of logical contents (e.g., in materialized views or in partial indexes) and of physical data structures (e.g., merging partitions in a B-tree) enables deferred maintenance both of redundant information (secondary indexes, materialized views) and also of primary information (primary indexes). Of course, non-redundant information permits deferred maintenance only of physical structures, not of logical information con-tents.

The proposed design assumes that each index is a B-tree (both primary and secondary indexes), implemented as a partitioned B-tree, and that each B-tree has its own partitioning (and partition identifiers). Partitioned B-trees not only make good differential files, they also permit separate steps for information capture and incremental structure optimization. These steps are quite similar to run generation and merging in external merge sort.

Deferred maintenance offers many advantages when combined with appropriate workload management. These advantages include the ability to shift work to periods of peak load to other periods. The obvious advantage is that update effort can be moved. Since efficient index maintenance permits creation and maintenance of more indexes, it also permit query execution effort to be moved. While update effort is shifted forward (delayed), query execution effort is shifted backward. In other words, full exploitation of this ability requires proactive index creation.

Deferred maintenance applies separately to logical contents and physical structure. In a database table with several dependent redundant structures such as materialized views and secondary indexes, deferred maintenance of those can increase burst update performance by a commensurate factor. For a table with no redundant structures or with deferred maintenance of those, differential file techniques can improve update performance by orders of magnitude. Appropriate implementation techniques and indexing structures permit combining differential file techniques with efficient query processing, i.e., immediate indexing of new database contents.

The advantages of deferred maintenance can be realized with relatively little implementation effort. Rather than requiring a new index structure, traditional B-tree indexes merely require adding an artificial leading key field to be used as partition identifier. Thus, a single unifying data structure and appropriate algorithms can increase sustained bandwidth in information capture as well as burst bandwidth, and can apply to deferred maintenance of physical structures (e.g., secondary indexes) and logical contents (e.g., materialized views).

When both old data records and recent updates are indexed, query results can correctly reflect the most recent database changes without excessive scanning and searching. Thus, deferred maintenance and appropriate, high-performance implementation techniques contribute not only to performance and efficiency of data management but also to transactional correctness and responsiveness of data analytics solutions.

References

1. Barroso, L.A., Hölzle, U.: The case for energy-proportional computing. IEEE Computer 40(12), 33–37 (2007)
2. Bender, M.A., Farach-Colton, M., Mosteiro, M.: Insertion sort is $O(nlogn)$. In: Fun with Algorithms, pp. 16–23 (2004)
3. Gandhi, A., Gupta, V., Harchol-Balter, M., Kozuch, M.A.: Optimality analysis of energy-performance trade-off for server farm management. Perform. Eval. 67(11), 1155–1171 (2010)
4. Graefe, G.: Sorting and indexing with partitioned B-trees. In: CIDR (2003)
5. Graefe, G.: Implementing sorting in database systems. ACM Comput. Surv. 38 (September 2006)
6. Graefe, G.: A survey of b-tree locking techniques. ACM Trans. Database Syst. 35, 16:1–16:26 (2010)
7. Graefe, G.: Modern B-tree techniques. Foundations and Trends in Databases 3(4), 203–402 (2011)
8. Graefe, G., Kuno, H.: Self-selecting, self-tuning, incrementally optimized indexes. In: Proceedings of the 13th International Conference on Extending Database Technology, EDBT 2010, pp. 371–381. ACM, New York (2010)
9. Graefe, G., Kuno, H.: Fast Loads and Queries. In: Hameurlain, A., Küng, J., Wagner, R., Bach Pedersen, T., Tjoa, A.M. (eds.) Transactions on Large-Scale Data. LNCS, vol. 6380, pp. 31–72. Springer, Heidelberg (2010)
10. Hamilton, J.: Spot instances, big clusters, & the cloud at work. Amazon Cloud Blog Post (September 2011)
11. Mohan, C., Narang, I.: Algorithms for creating indexes for very large tables without quiescing updates. In: Stonebraker, M. (ed.) Proceedings of the 1992 ACM SIGMOD International Conference on Management of Data, June 2-5, pp. 361–370. ACM Press, San Diego (1992)
12. O'Neil, P.E.: The escrow transactional method. ACM Trans. Database Syst. 11, 405–430 (1986)
13. Severance, D.G., Lohman, G.M.: Differential files: their application to the maintenance of large databases. ACM Trans. Database Syst. 1, 256–267 (1976)

Adaptive Spatial Query Processing
Based on Uncertain Location Information*

Yoshiharu Ishikawa[1,2,3]

[1] Graduate School of Information Science, Nagoya University
[2] Information Technology Center, Nagoya University
Furo-cho, Chikusa-ku, Nagoya 464-8601, Japan
[3] National Institute of Informatics, Tokyo 101-0003, Japan
ishikawa@itc.nagoya-u.ac.jp

Abstract. In recent years, representation and management of *uncertain data* have gained much interests in the research field of database technologies. In this talk, we especially focus on spatio-temporal databases and consider the problems due to uncertain location information. Uncertainty of location information in spatio-temporal databases usually occur because of measurement errors, incorrect sensor readings, lack of signals, and movement of the objects, and results in non-accurate and non-reliable query results.

In this talk, we provide an overview of the current database technologies for managing uncertain location information. First, the background and the motivations are introduced. Some examples are taken from the fields of sensor databases and mobile applications. Second, a survey of interesting ideas in this field is provided. It covers not only uncertain location issues but also some related problems such as uncertain data streams and probabilistic frameworks for supporting uncertain queries.

Then we describe our past and current works for supporting adaptive spatial query processing considering uncertain location information. It includes a framework for probabilistic spatial queries, an indexing technique for uncertain spatial objects, and so on. We also show the application of the technologies to the decision support of mobile robots. Finally, the future research directions in uncertain location management are provided.

* This research was partly supported by the Funding Program for World-Leading Innovative R&D on Science and Technology (First Program) and the Grant-in-Aid for Scientific Research (23650047) from JSPS.

Author Index